"The only goal of my life was to write."

Jean-Paul Sartre

sartre

Writer: Mathilde Ramadier
Art: Anais Depommier
Colors: Anais Depommier & Nawelle Saidi

nbm GRAPHIC
NOVELS
Nantier · Beall · Minoustchine
N E W   Y O R K

A Philosopher's Life

"If I relegate impossible Salvation to the proproom, what remains? A whole man, composed of all men and as good as all of them and no better than any." Recounting the life of a philosopher is always a challenge, so great is the risk of missing the essentials including particularly the influence of his books and the power of his inquisitive mind, as dry and difficult as it was. This difficulty is all the more pronounced when drawing the road, from one bubble to the next. Nevertheless, if Sartre taught us anything it is that his thought cannot be summarized by his writing alone. It is a stakeholder in his existential project, in choosing, he chooses to enlist all men in the exercise of his freedom. It is each one of these relationships that makes up the fabric of this exemplary existence: those who are in conversation with his family and his multiple heritages, whether he accepts them or frees himself from them, with the books read, whether moved aside or held onto, the friends made, Nizan, Merleau-Ponty, the men and women loved, the engagements upheld. He always returns to one responsibility: his own, which shares itself willingly. When we read Sartre today and we follow him in this thought adventure that was his existence, it is of the whole ensemble of his relationships for which we are forever grateful. For the author of *Nausea* and *Being and Nothingness*, these works are inseparable from his meetings with Simone de Beauvoir and the bond that united them throughout their long lives. These encounters serve as the common thread, chosen by Mathilde Ramadier and Anaïs Depommier to guide us through the life of one of them, which is also the life of the other, from their first meeting at l'École Normale Supérieure to the public renown for existentialism in the days following the Second World War. They follow Sartre step by step through his moments of doubt, his disappointments, but also his epiphanies, the origins of his thought, whose influence in every corner of the globe, thirty years after his death, continues to surprise us. In the space of a moment, their comic book brings to life before our eyes the author of *Words*; around him, the bodies enliven; we can almost hear once again, not without some nostalgia, the sound of conversation, the explosion of an argument, the common desire to understand, to analyze, to teach. We will discover, in the disarray of our time, that Sartre never faded in importance, which is both a great endorsement and an aide. Here we are ready to read.

Marc Crépon

Marc Crépon is a *normalien* (graduate of the Ecole Normale Superieure), philosopher and director of research at the prestigious National Center for Scientific Research (CNRS-Archives Husserl) and, since 2001, Chair of the Department of Philosophy at the École Normale Supérieure. He is the author of over a dozen works.

Pastor Schweitzer
Born in Alsace around 1820

A catholic lawyer
Somewhere in a town in Alsace.

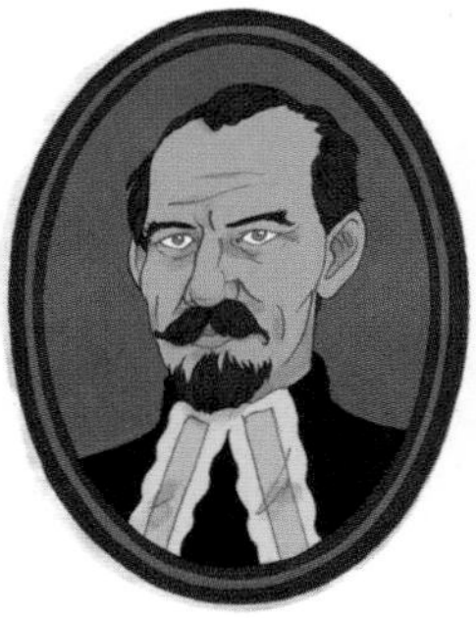

Louis Schweitzer
Obedient Pastor

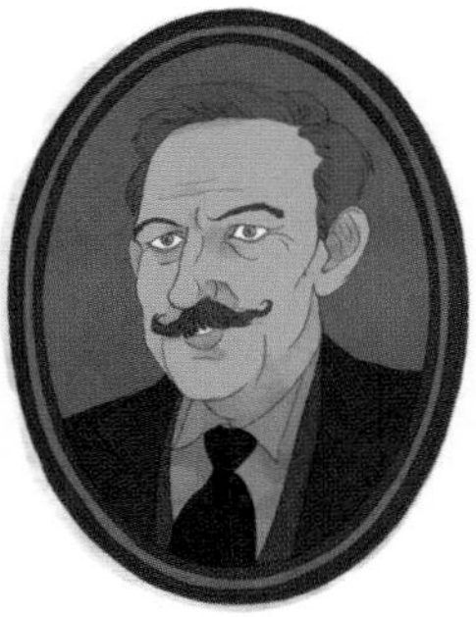

August Schweitzer
Mediator.
Lives a peaceful life.

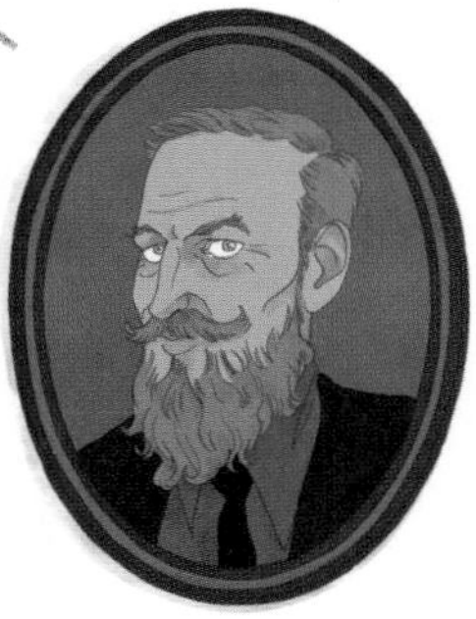

Charles Schweitzer
German Teacher.
Role model to Jean-Paul.
He takes up a lot of space, his beard is too long, he is a little bit arrogant, but all is forgiven because he looks like God.

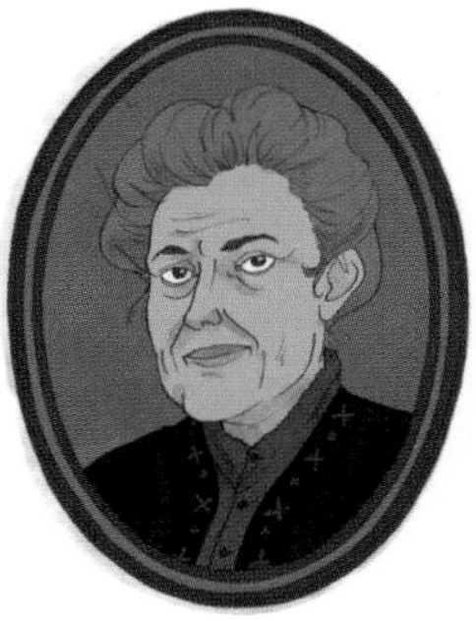

Louise Guillemin
Plump Alsatian, often in a bad mood. Always claims she only ate leek greens until he brought her to the train station restaurant for their honeymoon. Otherwise, she loves telling stories of their wedding night.

They have their first child who died young. Followed by Georges Schweitzer, polythechnicien*, and Emile Schweizter**, a German teacher. Then finally Anne-Marie.

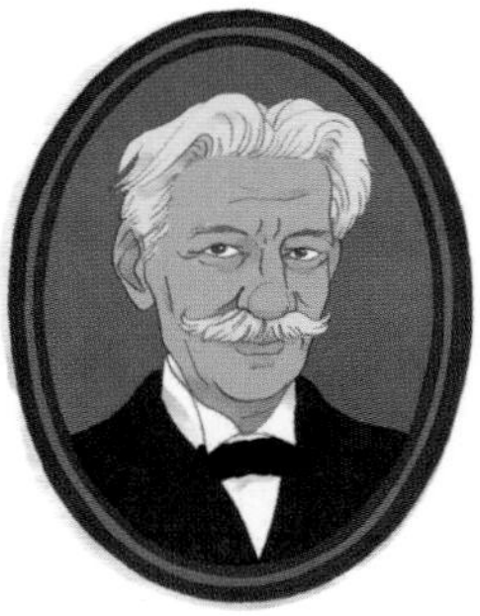

Albert Schweitzer
Theologian, doctor.
Star of the family.
Nobel Peace Prize in 1952.
(Sartre is his first cousin once removed.)

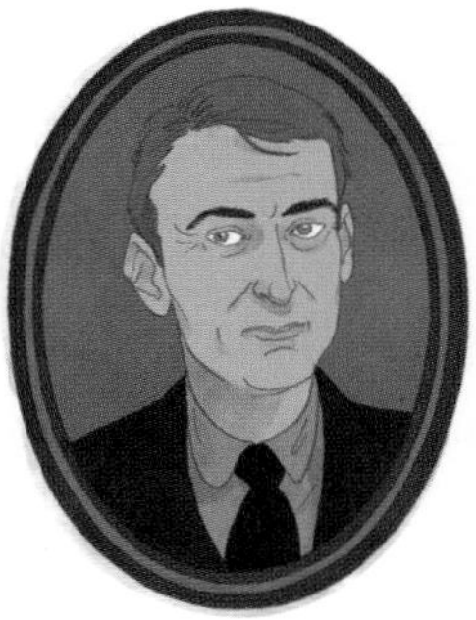

Joseph Mancy
Polytechnicien and engineer in the navy. Anne-Marie remarries to him in 1917. He is no fun at all.

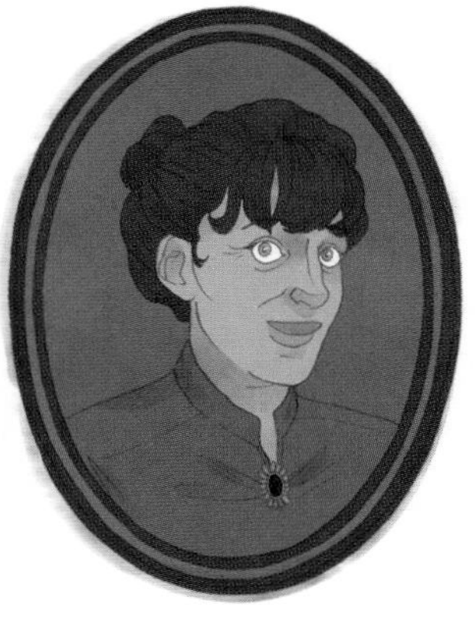

Anne-Marie Schweitzer
Reserved, gentle girl.
Prefers duty to pleasure.

*A polytechnicien studied at the prestigious École Polytechnique, the French engineering school.
**Émile would lose his mind and die in 1927.
They found one hundred pairs of socks full of holes under his pillow.

Family of peasants
"Lou Sartrou" comes from *sartor* which means "in-home tailor" in Perigordian patois.

Chavoix and Theulier Families
Pharmacists from father to son, local politicians and rich proprietors in Thiviers, in the Périgord.

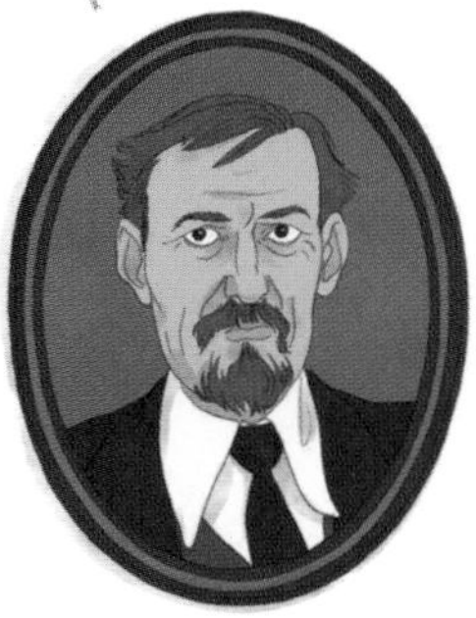

The good doctor Eymard Sartre
It is said that he did not speak to his wife for 40 years because she lied to him about the amount of her dowry.

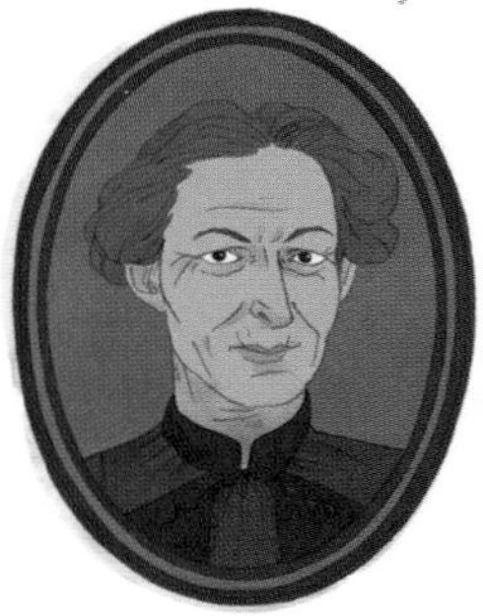

Elodie Chavoix
The Queen of goose foie gras with truffles. After becoming Elodie Sartre, she will go through 46 years of indifferent and silent marriage.

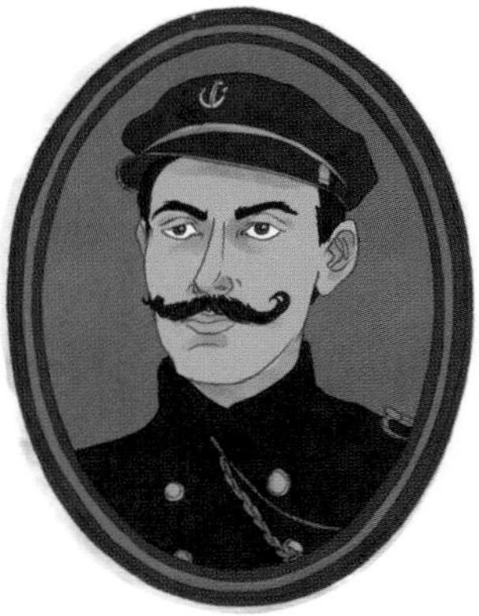

Jean-Baptiste Sartre
Young polytechnicien, naval officer. Meets Anne-Marie in 1904 before dying in Paris in 1906.

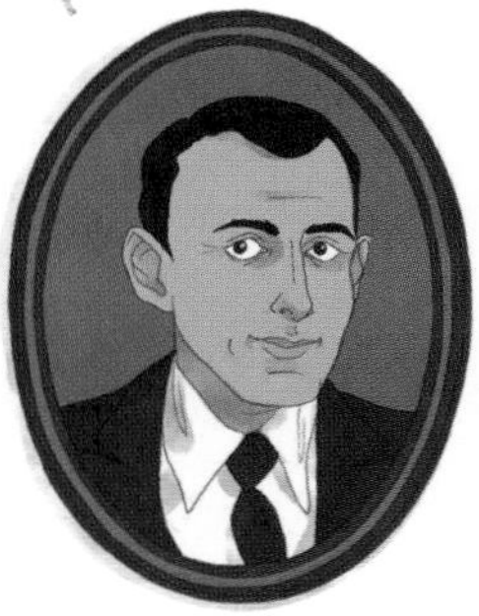

Joseph Sartre
The "happy idiot" as he was known in Thiviers.

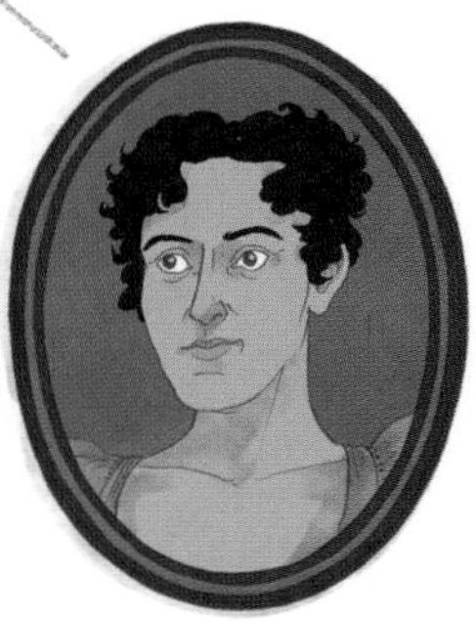

Hélène Lannes,
Known as "Madame de Rentre-en-Ville." Married an insane military officer. She and Jean-Baptiste were close.

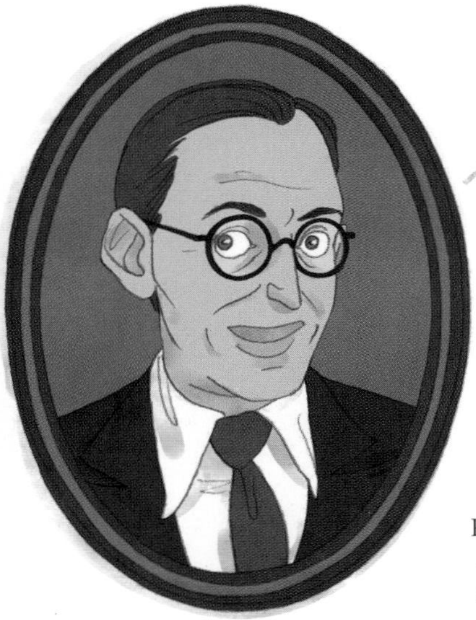

Jean-Paul-Charles-Eymard Sartre
Paris, June 21, 1905 – Paris, April 15, 1980
A whole man, composed of all men and as good as all of them and no better than any.

I dedicate this book to all those who are not free.

Thank you to my friends and my family, who believed in it from the beginning.
Thank you to Phil, who gifted me Letters to Sartre and Letters to Beaver (and others)
in beautiful giftwrap with two genuine homemade bookmarks.

"I love you, you other my life."

Mathilde

To Geneviève, my sweet grandmother.

Thank you to Ben for his unerring support, his insane patience, and for absolutely everything else...
Thank you to my parents, to my sister, to my brother and to my whole family, to my friends in Lyon, in Paris,
and elsewhere for their constant encouragement. I want to thank most particularly Nawëlle Saïdi, Florence
Chatellain, Benjamin Dupouy, Cédric Mayen, Florent Garcia et Thomas Brissot for their invaluable help on
the colors. Finally, thank you to Mathilde for her confidence, her friendship and for welcoming me into the vast
world of Sartre.

Anaïs

Thank you to François Le Bescond for his benevolence, his support and for having believed in us from the
beginning. A big thank you also to Pauline Mermet, Renaud de Châteaubourg, Ève Bardin, Adrien Samson,
Philippe Ravon and to the whole Dargaud team for their care and their astounding welcome.

Mathilde & Anaïs

Notice to readers:

Narrative texts are against a white backdrop
Narrative texts by J.-P. Sartre are against a yellow-green backdrop
Narrative texts by S. de Beauvoir are on a green backdrop

ISBN: 978-1-68112-101-7
Library of Congress Control Number: 2017942220
© Dargaud 2015
Originally published as *Sartre, Une existence, des libertés*.
© NBM for the English translation 2017
Translation by Peter Russella
Lettering by Ortho
Printed in China
1st printing August 2017
ALSO AVAILABLE WHEREVER EBOOKS ARE SOLD

PART ONE:

"I WAS NEVER TAUGHT TO BE OBEDIENT"

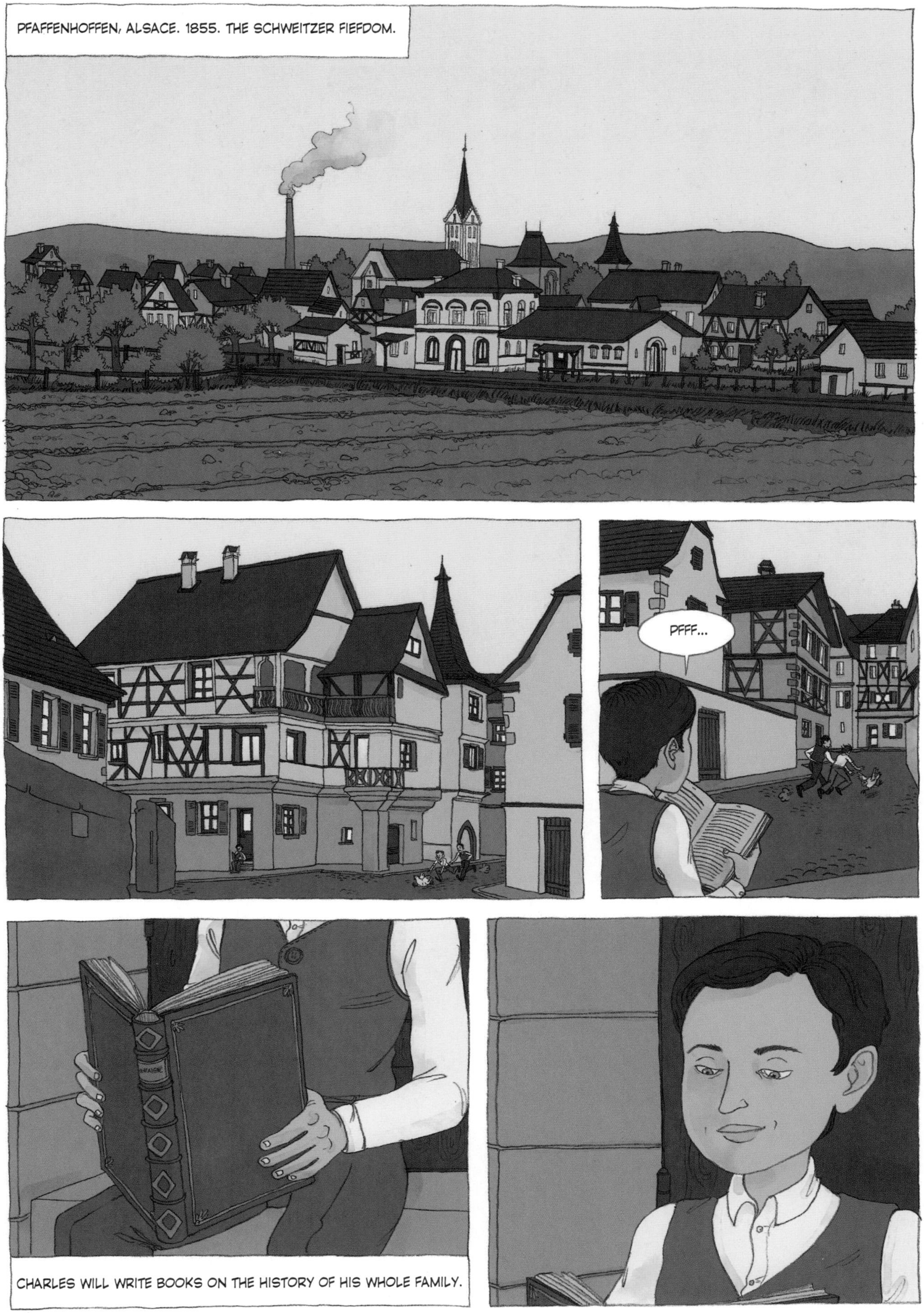
PFAFFENHOFFEN, ALSACE. 1855. THE SCHWEITZER FIEFDOM.
PFFF...
CHARLES WILL WRITE BOOKS ON THE HISTORY OF HIS WHOLE FAMILY.

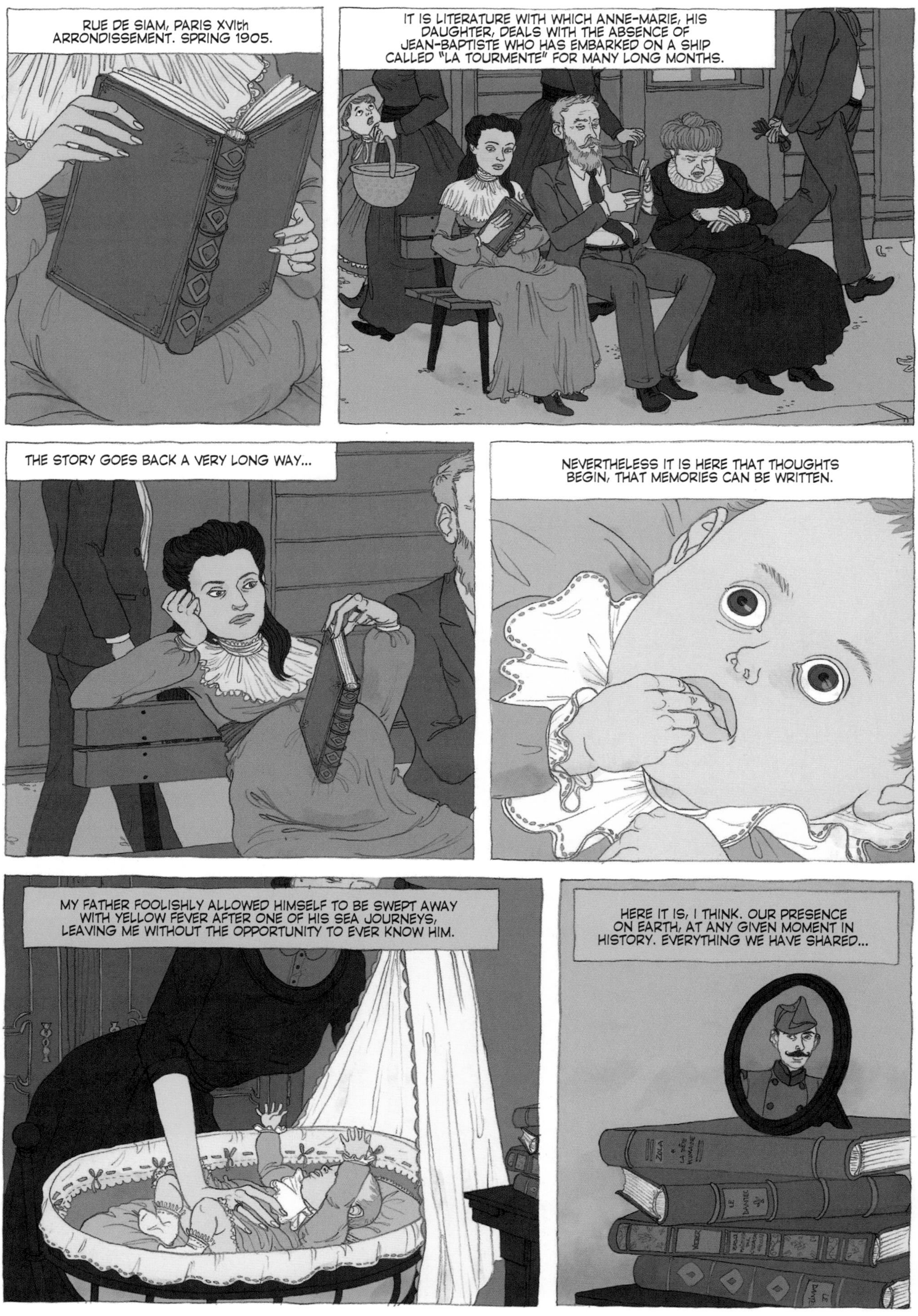
RUE DE SIAM, PARIS XVIth ARRONDISSEMENT. SPRING 1905.
IT IS LITERATURE WITH WHICH ANNE-MARIE, HIS DAUGHTER, DEALS WITH THE ABSENCE OF JEAN-BAPTISTE WHO HAS EMBARKED ON A SHIP CALLED "LA TOURMENTE" FOR MANY LONG MONTHS.
THE STORY GOES BACK A VERY LONG WAY...
NEVERTHELESS IT IS HERE THAT THOUGHTS BEGIN, THAT MEMORIES CAN BE WRITTEN.
MY FATHER FOOLISHLY ALLOWED HIMSELF TO BE SWEPT AWAY WITH YELLOW FEVER AFTER ONE OF HIS SEA JOURNEYS, LEAVING ME WITHOUT THE OPPORTUNITY TO EVER KNOW HIM.
HERE IT IS, I THINK. OUR PRESENCE ON EARTH, AT ANY GIVEN MOMENT IN HISTORY. EVERYTHING WE HAVE SHARED...

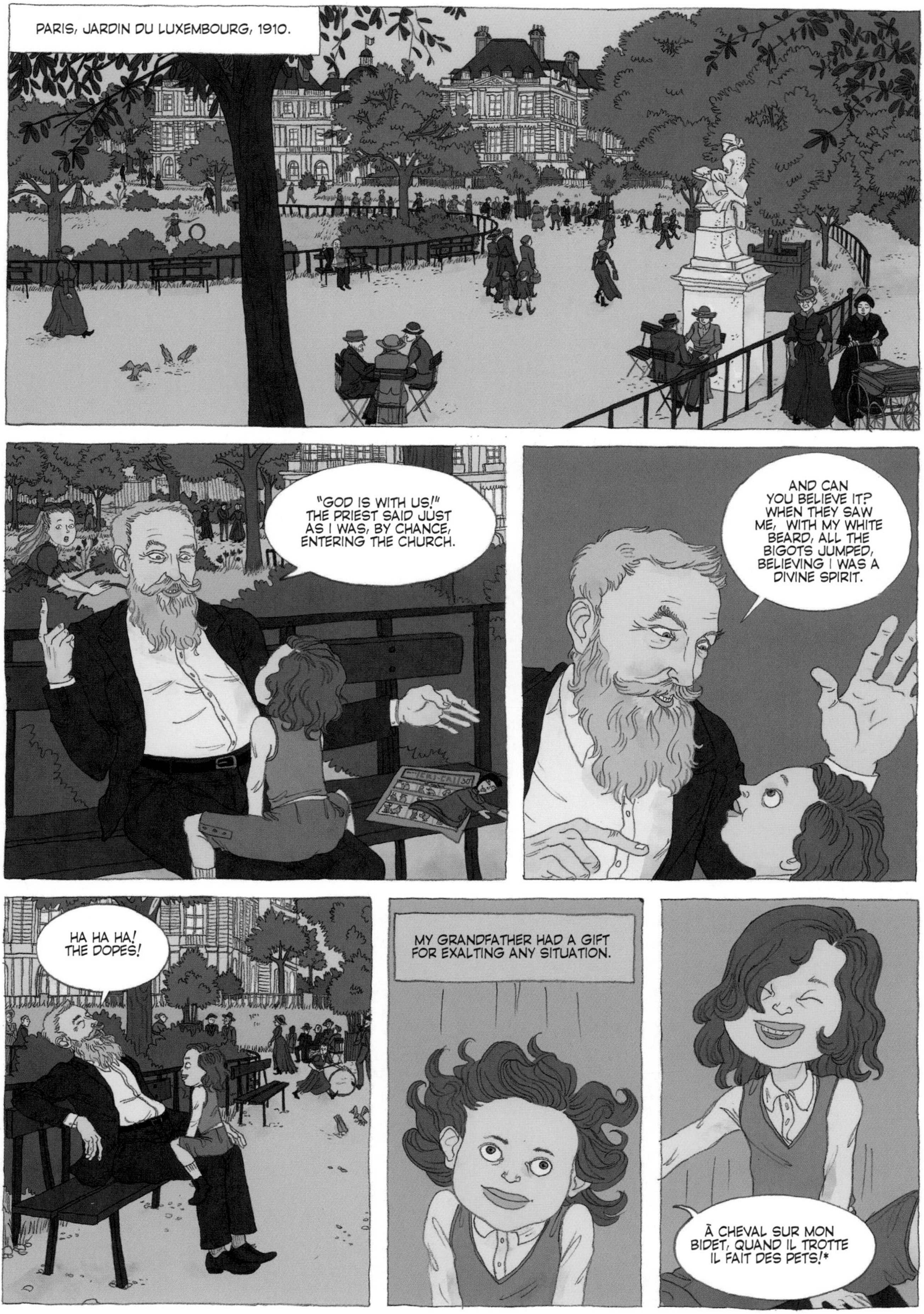
PARIS, JARDIN DU LUXEMBOURG, 1910.
"GOD IS WITH US!" THE PRIEST SAID JUST AS I WAS, BY CHANCE, ENTERING THE CHURCH.
AND CAN YOU BELIEVE IT? WHEN THEY SAW ME, WITH MY WHITE BEARD, ALL THE BIGOTS JUMPED, BELIEVING I WAS A DIVINE SPIRIT.
HA HA HA! THE DOPES!
MY GRANDFATHER HAD A GIFT FOR EXALTING ANY SITUATION.
À CHEVAL SUR MON BIDET, QUAND IL TROTTE IL FAIT DES PETS!*

*ON HORSEY ON MY BIDET, WHEN HE TROTS HE LETS OUT FARTS.

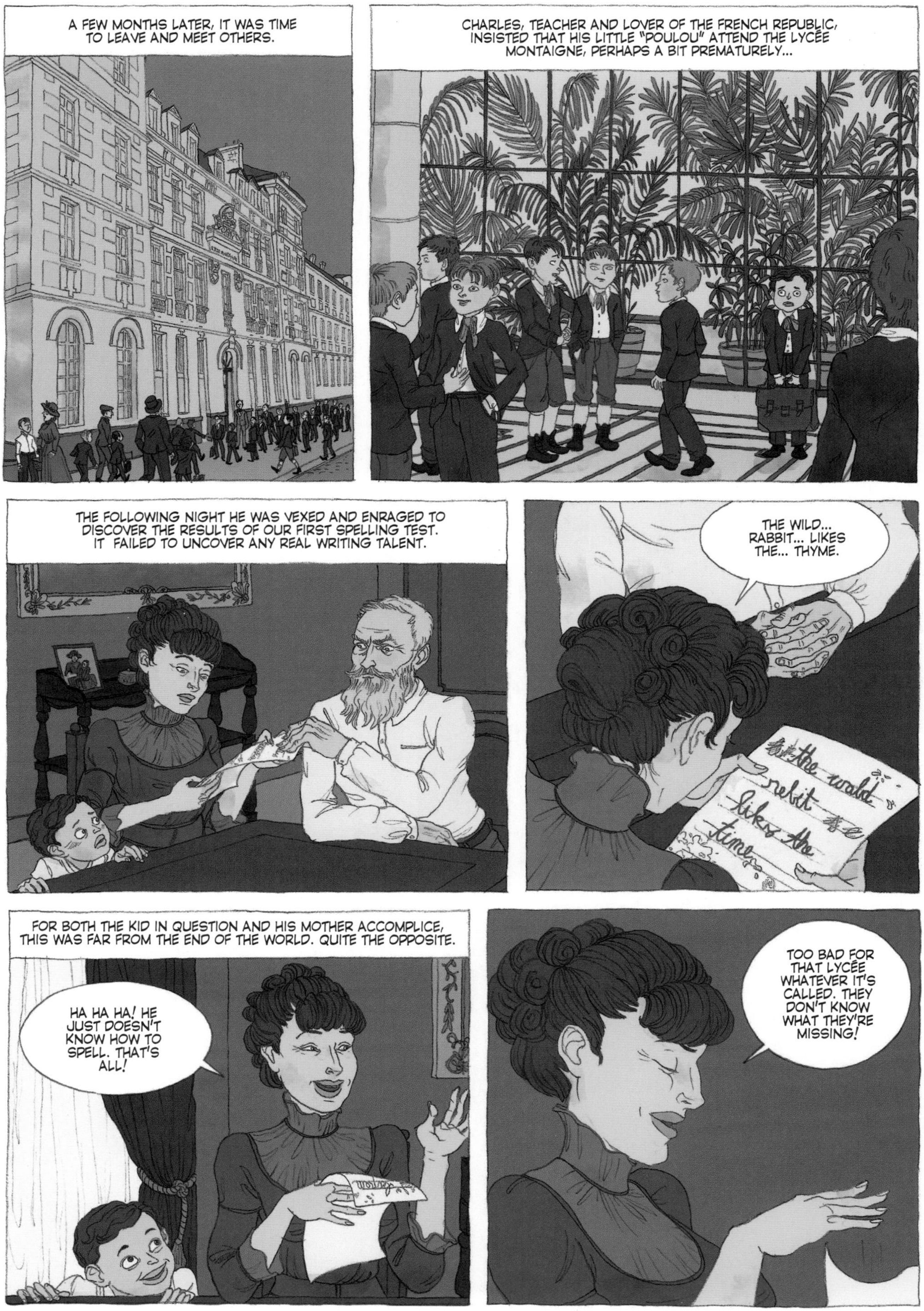
A FEW MONTHS LATER, IT WAS TIME TO LEAVE AND MEET OTHERS.
CHARLES, TEACHER AND LOVER OF THE FRENCH REPUBLIC, INSISTED THAT HIS LITTLE "POULOU" ATTEND THE LYCÉE MONTAIGNE, PERHAPS A BIT PREMATURELY...
THE FOLLOWING NIGHT HE WAS VEXED AND ENRAGED TO DISCOVER THE RESULTS OF OUR FIRST SPELLING TEST. IT FAILED TO UNCOVER ANY REAL WRITING TALENT.
THE WILD... RABBIT... LIKES THE... THYME.
the wald
rebit
liks the
time
FOR BOTH THE KID IN QUESTION AND HIS MOTHER ACCOMPLICE, THIS WAS FAR FROM THE END OF THE WORLD. QUITE THE OPPOSITE.
HA HA HA! HE JUST DOESN'T KNOW HOW TO SPELL. THAT'S ALL!
TOO BAD FOR THAT LYCÉE WHATEVER IT'S CALLED. THEY DON'T KNOW WHAT THEY'RE MISSING!

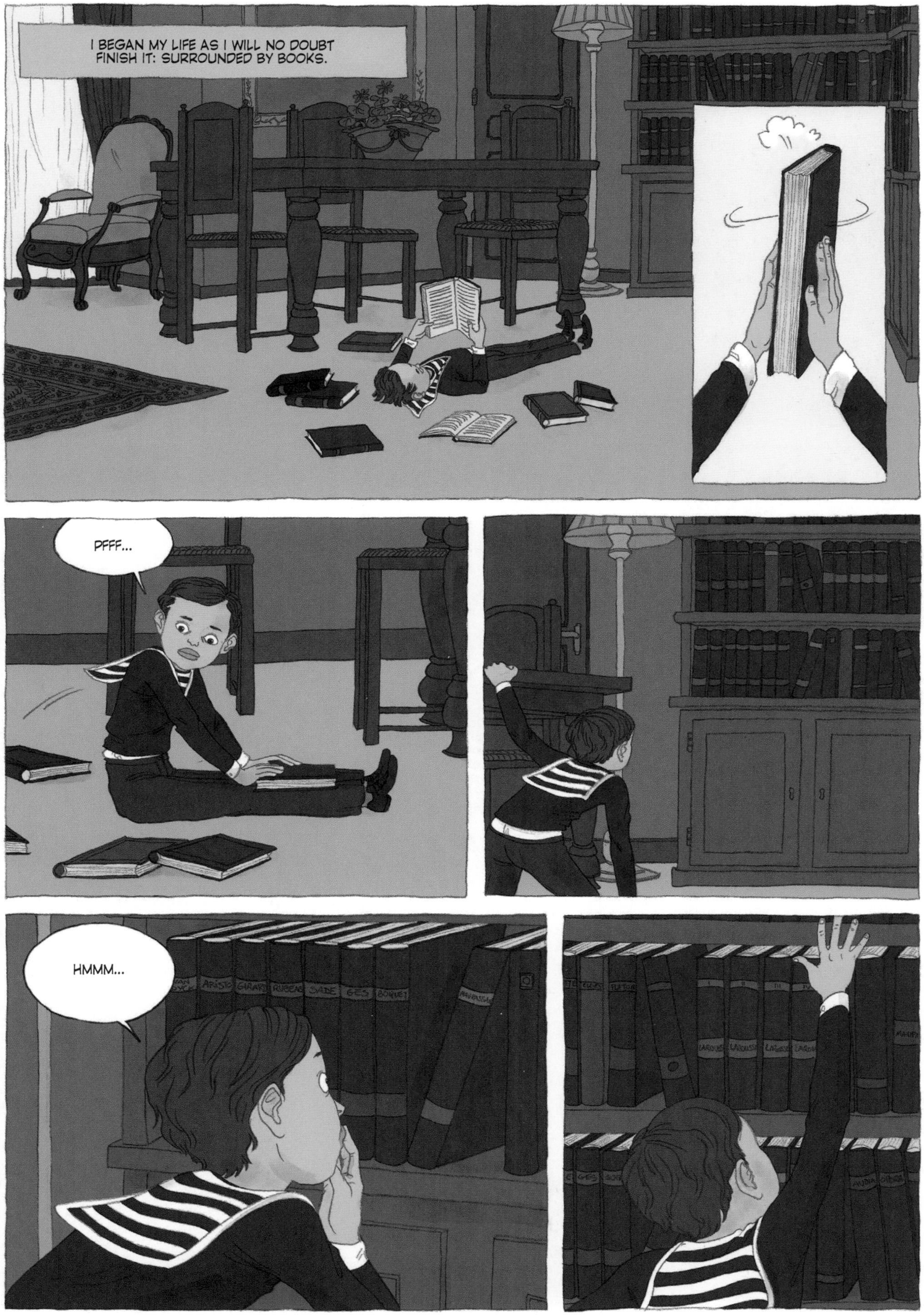
I BEGAN MY LIFE AS I WILL NO DOUBT FINISH IT: SURROUNDED BY BOOKS.
PFFF...
HMMM...

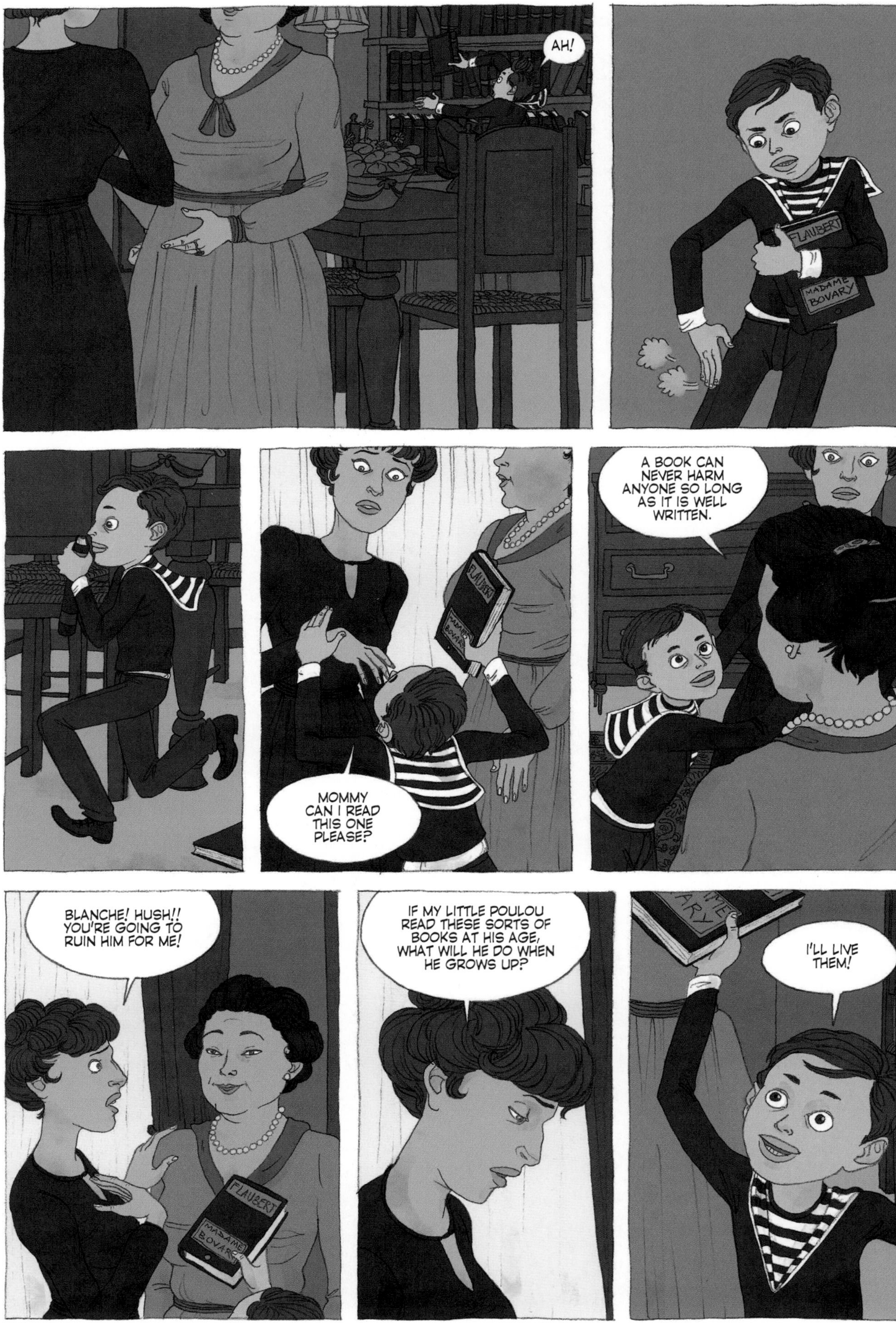
AH!
FLAUBERT
MADAME BOVARY
MOMMY CAN I READ THIS ONE PLEASE?
A BOOK CAN NEVER HARM ANYONE SO LONG AS IT IS WELL WRITTEN.
BLANCHE! HUSH!! YOU'RE GOING TO RUIN HIM FOR ME!
IF MY LITTLE POULOU READ THESE SORTS OF BOOKS AT HIS AGE, WHAT WILL HE DO WHEN HE GROWS UP?
I'LL LIVE THEM!

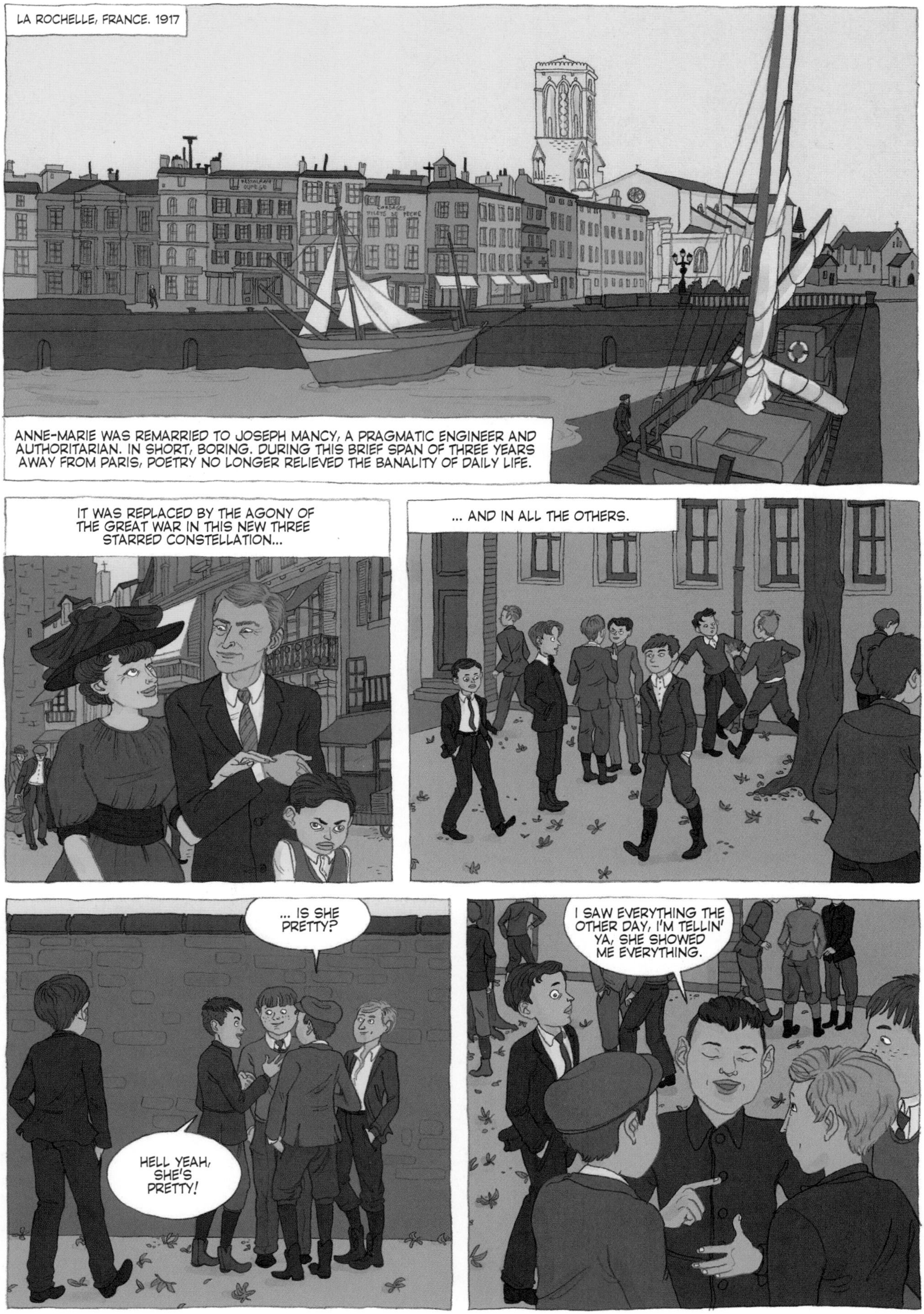
LA ROCHELLE, FRANCE. 1917
ANNE-MARIE WAS REMARRIED TO JOSEPH MANCY, A PRAGMATIC ENGINEER AND AUTHORITARIAN. IN SHORT, BORING. DURING THIS BRIEF SPAN OF THREE YEARS AWAY FROM PARIS, POETRY NO LONGER RELIEVED THE BANALITY OF DAILY LIFE.
IT WAS REPLACED BY THE AGONY OF THE GREAT WAR IN THIS NEW THREE STARRED CONSTELLATION...
... AND IN ALL THE OTHERS.
... IS SHE PRETTY?
HELL YEAH, SHE'S PRETTY!
I SAW EVERYTHING THE OTHER DAY, I'M TELLIN' YA, SHE SHOWED ME EVERYTHING.

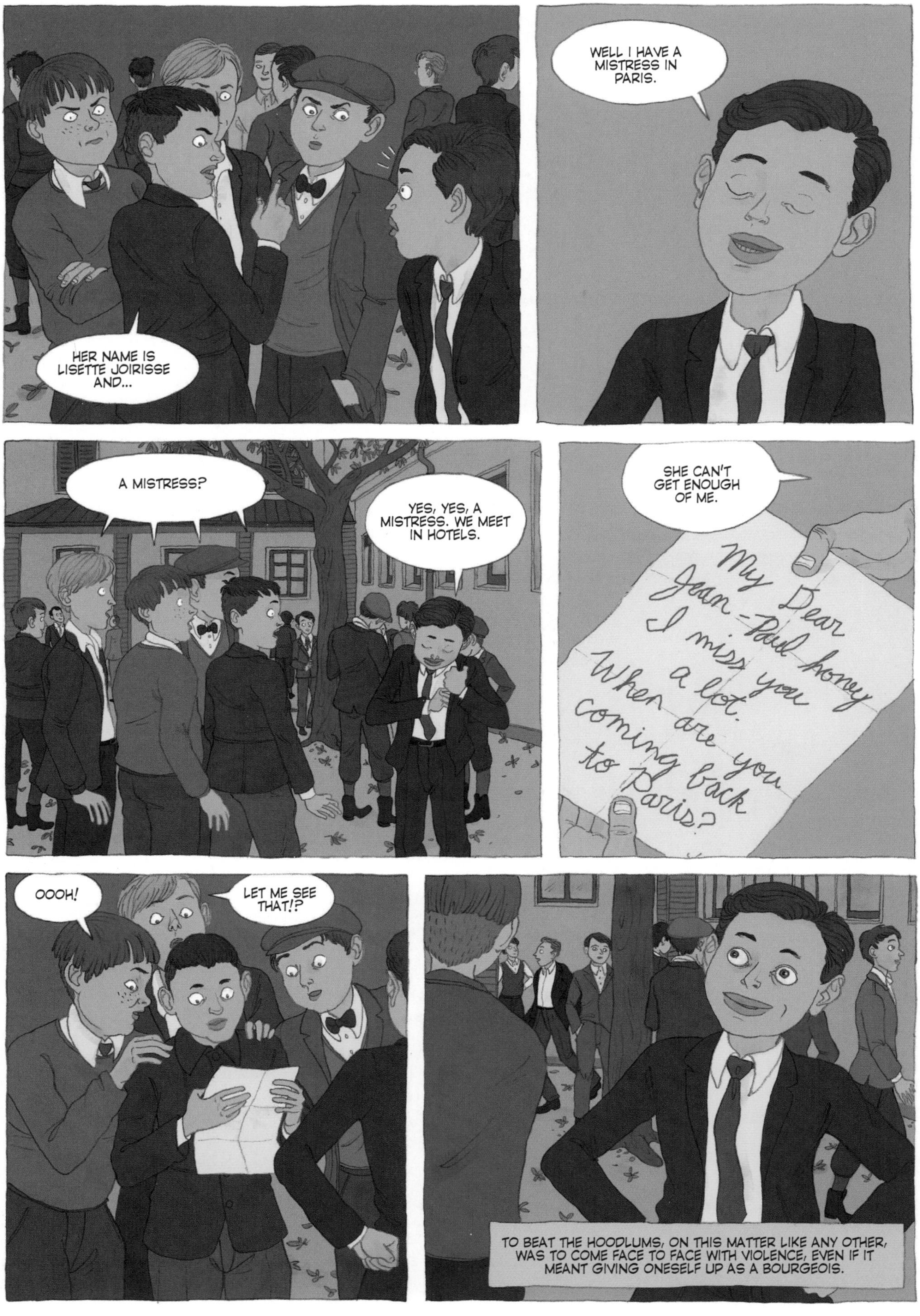
HER NAME IS LISETTE JOIRISSE AND...
WELL I HAVE A MISTRESS IN PARIS.
A MISTRESS?
YES, YES, A MISTRESS. WE MEET IN HOTELS.
SHE CAN'T GET ENOUGH OF ME.
My Dear Jean-Paul honey I miss you a lot. When are you coming back to Paris?
OOOH!
LET ME SEE THAT!?
TO BEAT THE HOODLUMS, ON THIS MATTER LIKE ANY OTHER, WAS TO COME FACE TO FACE WITH VIOLENCE, EVEN IF IT MEANT GIVING ONESELF UP AS A BOURGEOIS.

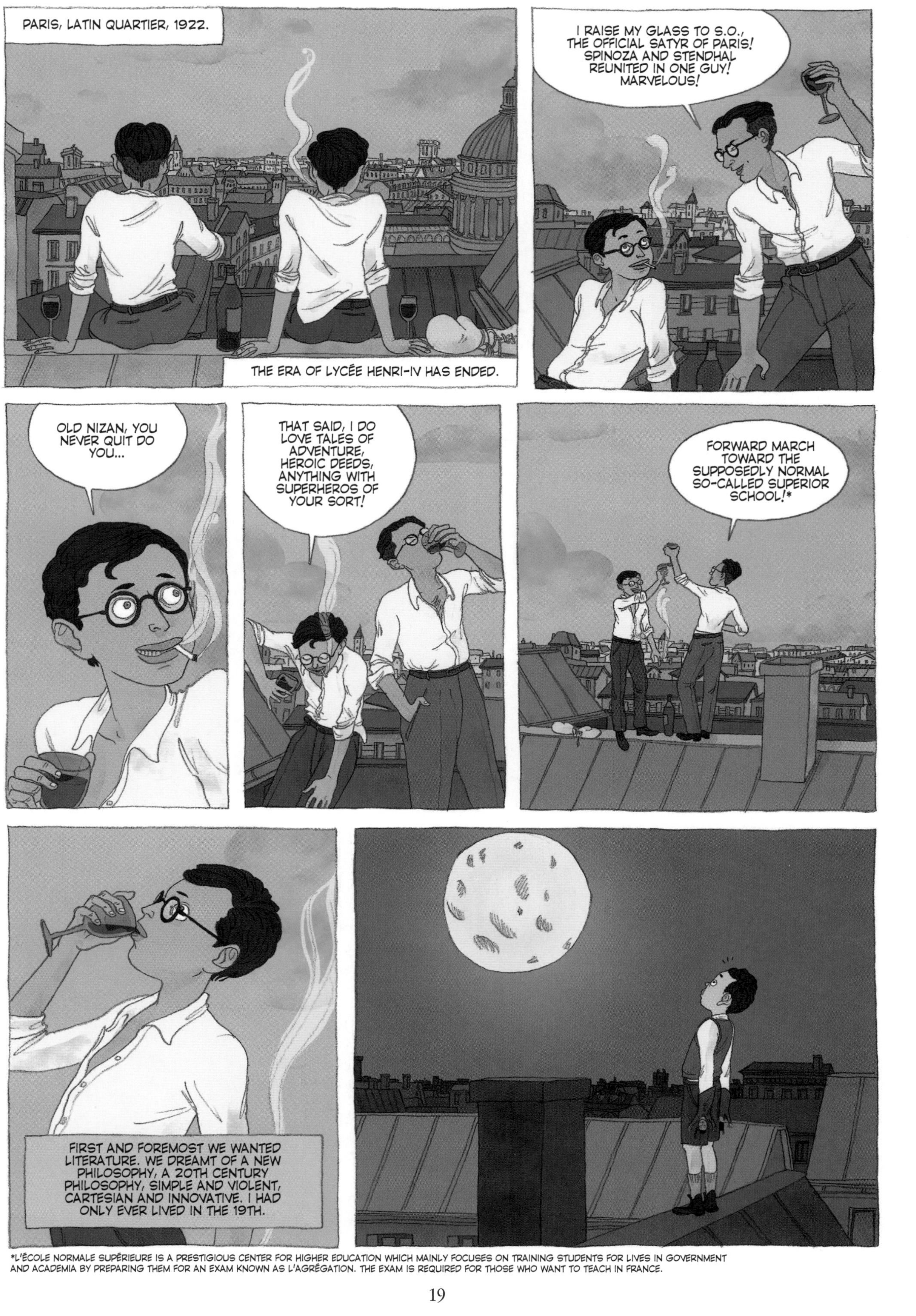
PARIS, LATIN QUARTIER, 1922.
THE ERA OF LYCÉE HENRI-IV HAS ENDED.
I RAISE MY GLASS TO S.O., THE OFFICIAL SATYR OF PARIS! SPINOZA AND STENDHAL REUNITED IN ONE GUY! MARVELOUS!
OLD NIZAN, YOU NEVER QUIT DO YOU...
THAT SAID, I DO LOVE TALES OF ADVENTURE, HEROIC DEEDS, ANYTHING WITH SUPERHEROS OF YOUR SORT!
FORWARD MARCH TOWARD THE SUPPOSEDLY NORMAL SO-CALLED SUPERIOR SCHOOL!*
FIRST AND FOREMOST WE WANTED LITERATURE. WE DREAMT OF A NEW PHILOSOPHY, A 20TH CENTURY PHILOSOPHY, SIMPLE AND VIOLENT, CARTESIAN AND INNOVATIVE. I HAD ONLY EVER LIVED IN THE 19TH.

*L'ÉCOLE NORMALE SUPÉRIEURE IS A PRESTIGIOUS CENTER FOR HIGHER EDUCATION WHICH MAINLY FOCUSES ON TRAINING STUDENTS FOR LIVES IN GOVERNMENT AND ACADEMIA BY PREPARING THEM FOR AN EXAM KNOWN AS L'AGRÉGATION. THE EXAM IS REQUIRED FOR THOSE WHO WANT TO TEACH IN FRANCE.

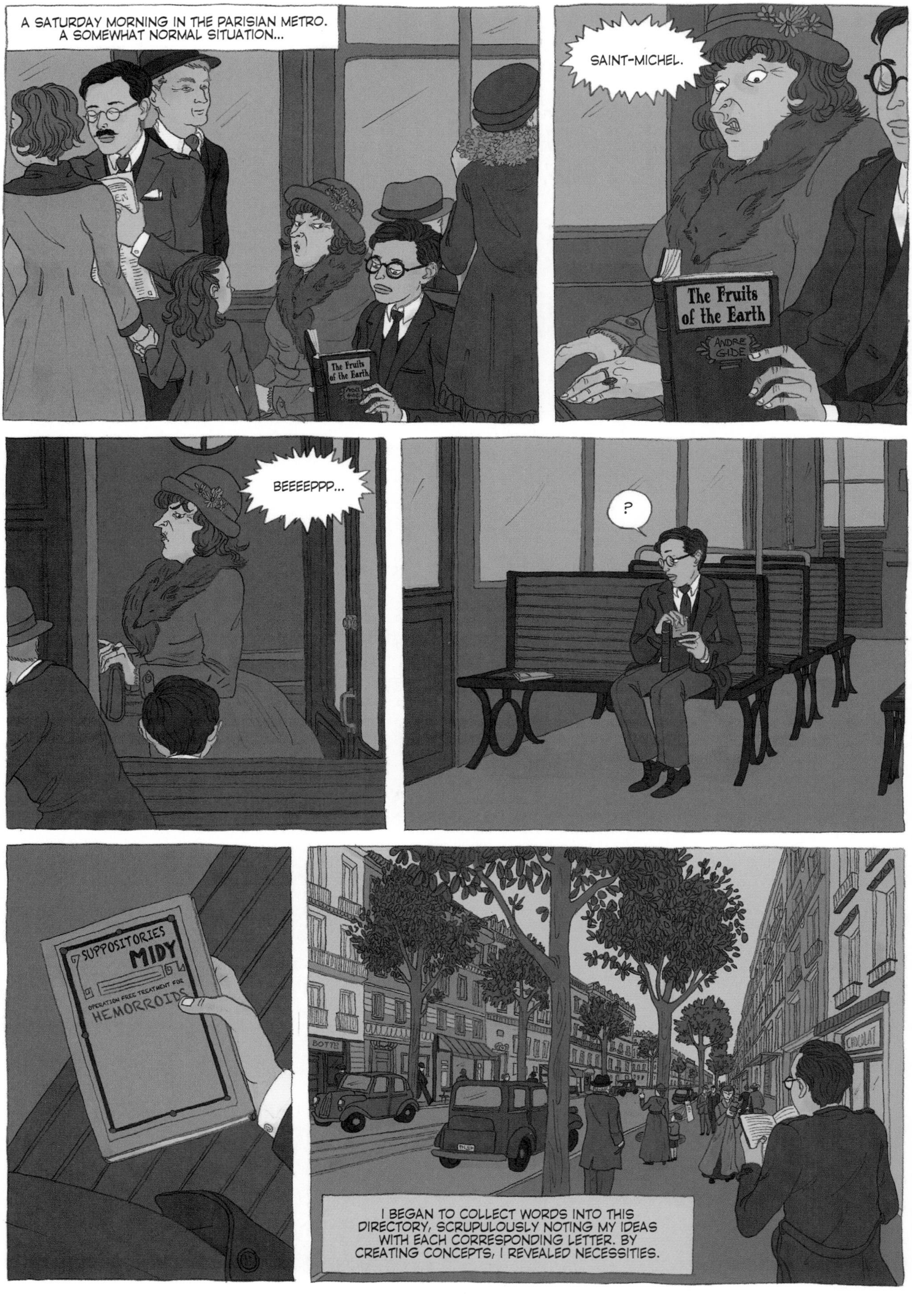
A SATURDAY MORNING IN THE PARISIAN METRO. A SOMEWHAT NORMAL SITUATION...
The Fruits of the Earth
SAINT-MICHEL.
The Fruits of the Earth
ANDRÉ GIDE
BEEEEPPP...
?
SUPPOSITORIES
MIDY
OPERATION FREE TREATMENT FOR
HEMORROIDS
CHOCOLAT
I BEGAN TO COLLECT WORDS INTO THIS DIRECTORY, SCRUPULOUSLY NOTING MY IDEAS WITH EACH CORRESPONDING LETTER. BY CREATING CONCEPTS, I REVEALED NECESSITIES.

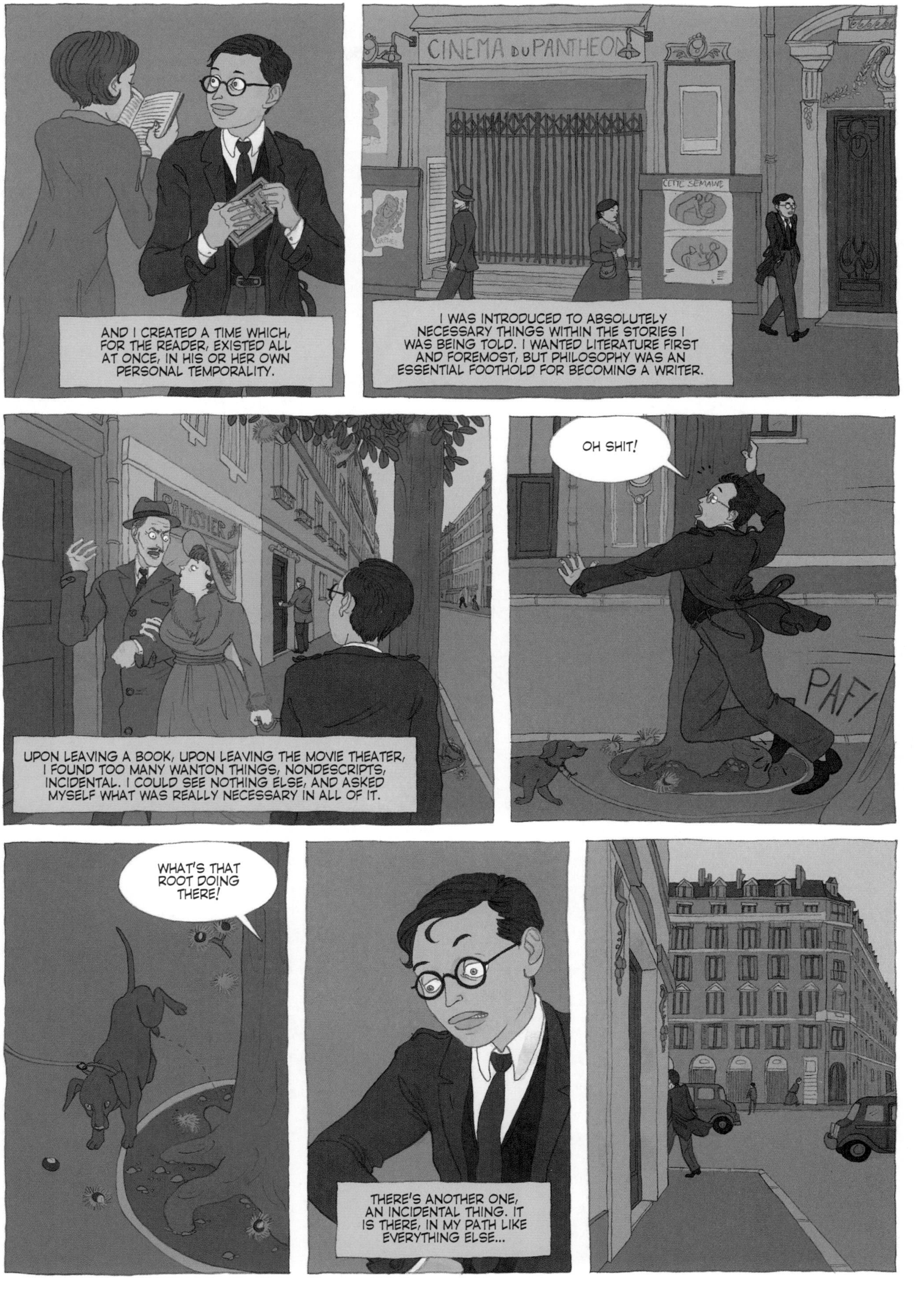
AND I CREATED A TIME WHICH, FOR THE READER, EXISTED ALL AT ONCE, IN HIS OR HER OWN PERSONAL TEMPORALITY.
CINEMA DU PANTHEON
CETTE SEMAINE
I WAS INTRODUCED TO ABSOLUTELY NECESSARY THINGS WITHIN THE STORIES I WAS BEING TOLD. I WANTED LITERATURE FIRST AND FOREMOST, BUT PHILOSOPHY WAS AN ESSENTIAL FOOTHOLD FOR BECOMING A WRITER.
PATISSIER
UPON LEAVING A BOOK, UPON LEAVING THE MOVIE THEATER, I FOUND TOO MANY WANTON THINGS, NONDESCRIPTS, INCIDENTAL. I COULD SEE NOTHING ELSE, AND ASKED MYSELF WHAT WAS REALLY NECESSARY IN ALL OF IT.
OH SHIT!
PAF!
WHAT'S THAT ROOT DOING THERE!
THERE'S ANOTHER ONE, AN INCIDENTAL THING. IT IS THERE, IN MY PATH LIKE EVERYTHING ELSE...

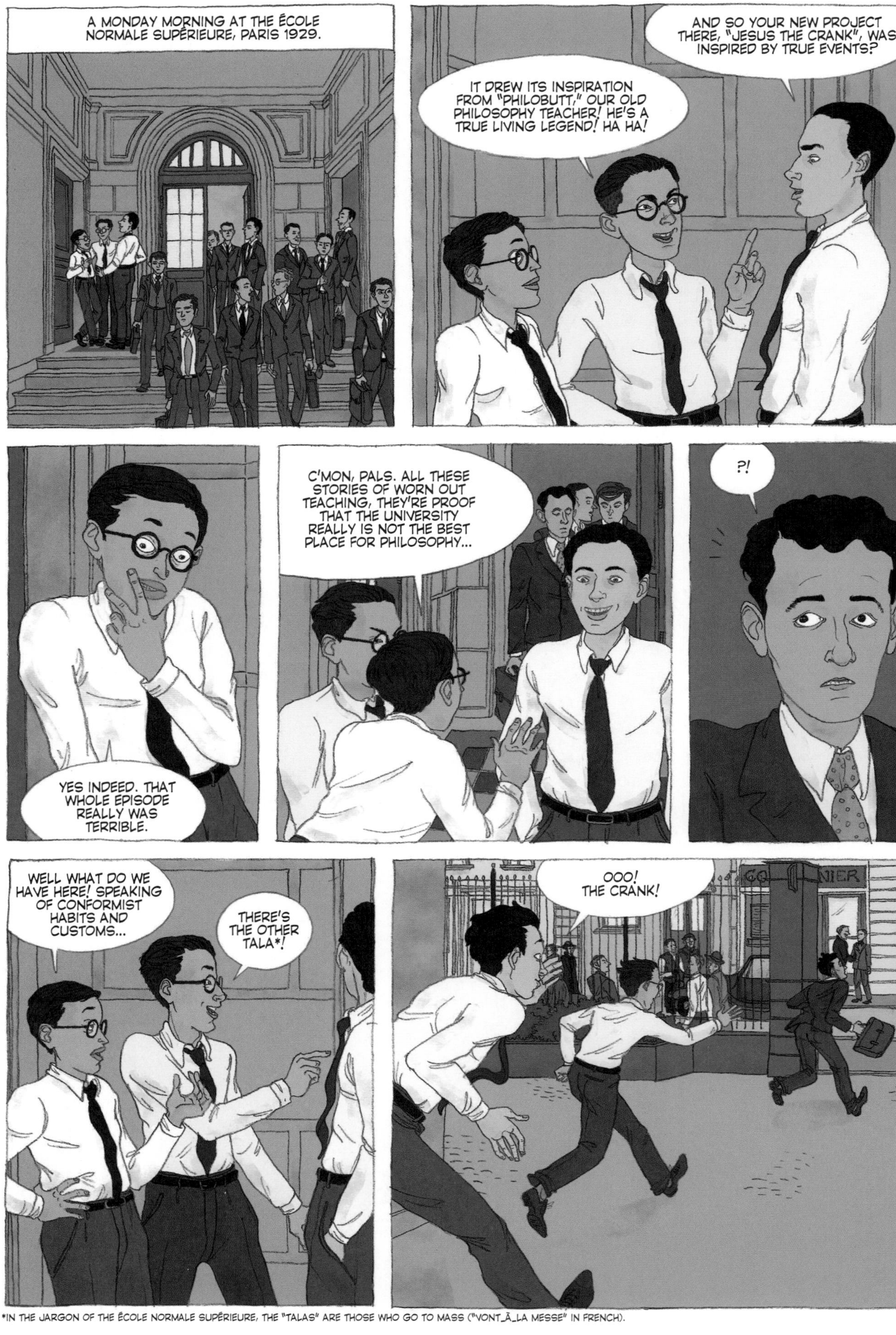
A MONDAY MORNING AT THE ÉCOLE NORMALE SUPÉRIEURE, PARIS 1929.
AND SO YOUR NEW PROJECT THERE, "JESUS THE CRANK", WAS INSPIRED BY TRUE EVENTS?
IT DREW ITS INSPIRATION FROM "PHILOBUTT," OUR OLD PHILOSOPHY TEACHER! HE'S A TRUE LIVING LEGEND! HA HA!
YES INDEED. THAT WHOLE EPISODE REALLY WAS TERRIBLE.
C'MON, PALS. ALL THESE STORIES OF WORN OUT TEACHING, THEY'RE PROOF THAT THE UNIVERSITY REALLY IS NOT THE BEST PLACE FOR PHILOSOPHY...
?!
WELL WHAT DO WE HAVE HERE! SPEAKING OF CONFORMIST HABITS AND CUSTOMS...
THERE'S THE OTHER TALA*!
OOO! THE CRANK!

*IN THE JARGON OF THE ÉCOLE NORMALE SUPÉRIEURE, THE "TALAS" ARE THOSE WHO GO TO MASS ("VONT_À_LA MESSE" IN FRENCH).

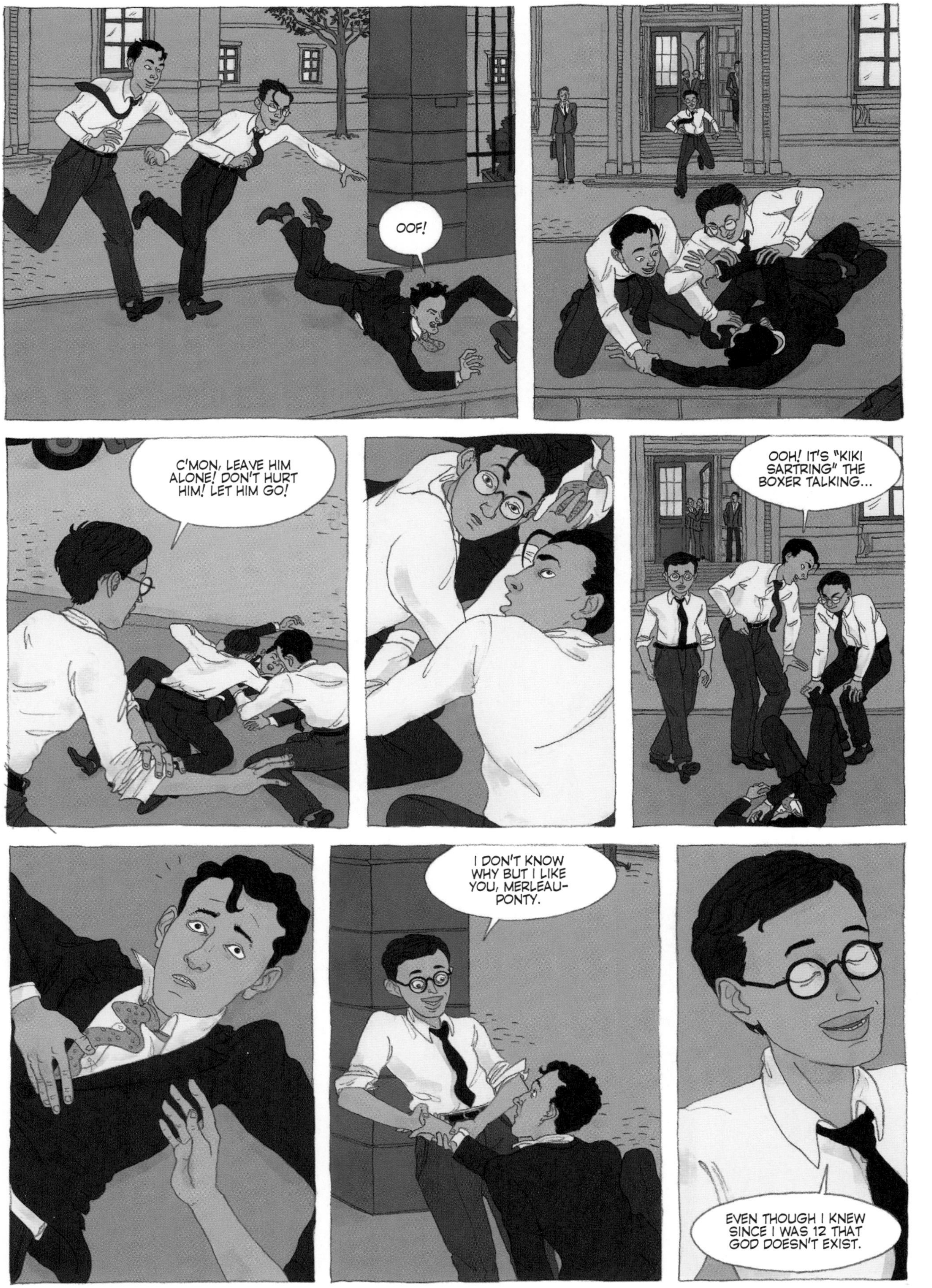
OOF!
C'MON, LEAVE HIM ALONE! DON'T HURT HIM! LET HIM GO!
OOH! IT'S "KIKI SARTRING" THE BOXER TALKING...
I DON'T KNOW WHY BUT I LIKE YOU, MERLEAU-PONTY.
EVEN THOUGH I KNEW SINCE I WAS 12 THAT GOD DOESN'T EXIST.

A FEW MONTHS LATER, IN THE 'COUR AUX ERNESTS.' STUDYING HARD FOR THE "AGRÉGATION" IN PHILOSOPHY...

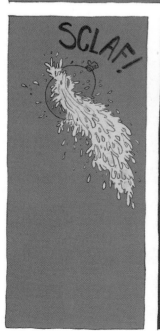

SCLAF!

THUS PISSED ZARATUSTRA!

OH, THE ENERGY WE HAVE TO EXERT TO GET THESE PSEUDO-NIETZSCHEAN, PETIT-BOURGEOIS TO LOOSEN UP.

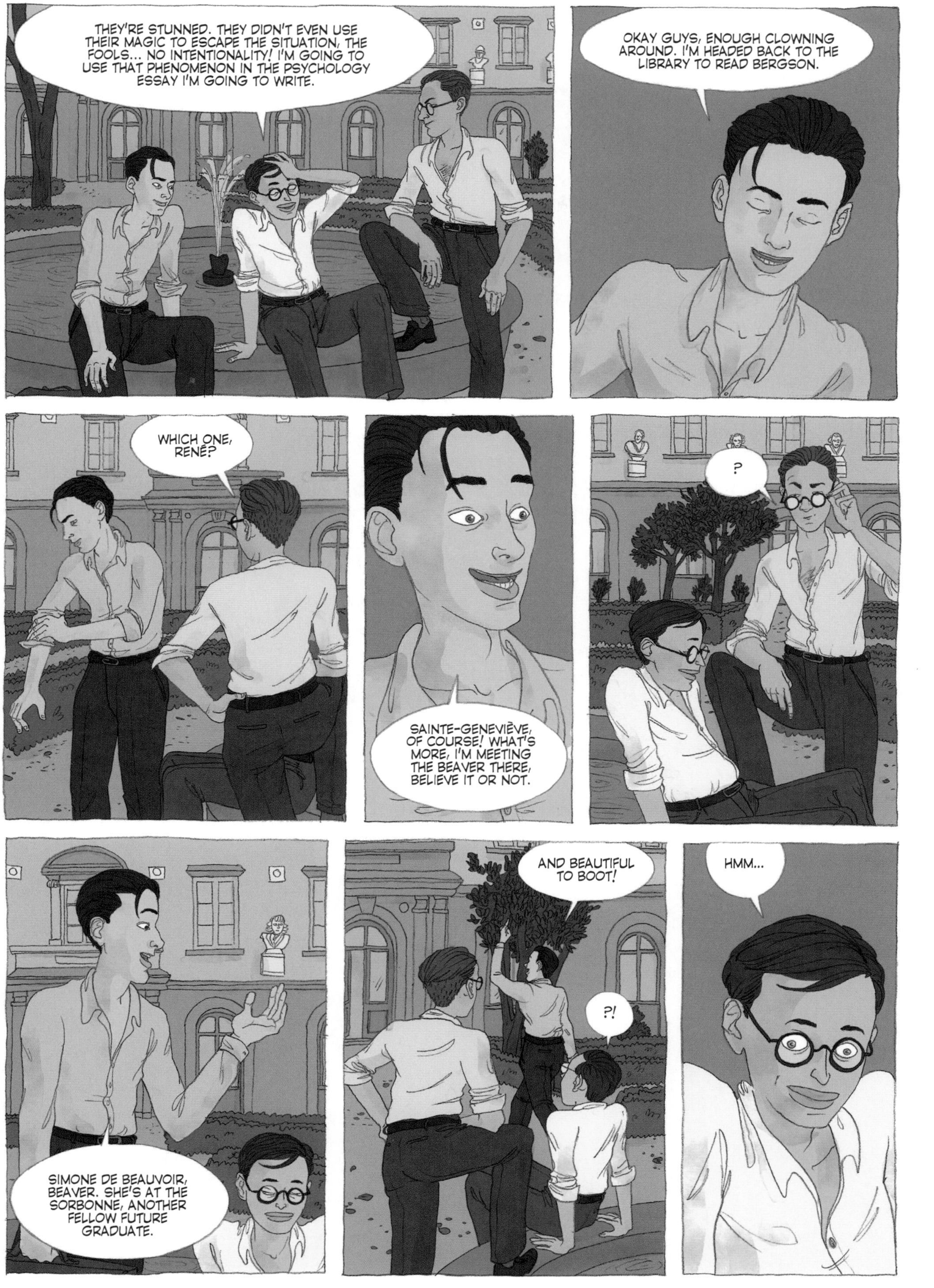
THEY'RE STUNNED. THEY DIDN'T EVEN USE THEIR MAGIC TO ESCAPE THE SITUATION, THE FOOLS... NO INTENTIONALITY! I'M GOING TO USE THAT PHENOMENON IN THE PSYCHOLOGY ESSAY I'M GOING TO WRITE.
OKAY GUYS, ENOUGH CLOWNING AROUND. I'M HEADED BACK TO THE LIBRARY TO READ BERGSON.
WHICH ONE, RENÉ?
SAINTE-GENEVIÈVE, OF COURSE! WHAT'S MORE, I'M MEETING THE BEAVER THERE, BELIEVE IT OR NOT.
?
SIMONE DE BEAUVOIR, BEAVER. SHE'S AT THE SORBONNE, ANOTHER FELLOW FUTURE GRADUATE.
AND BEAUTIFUL TO BOOT!
?!
HMM...

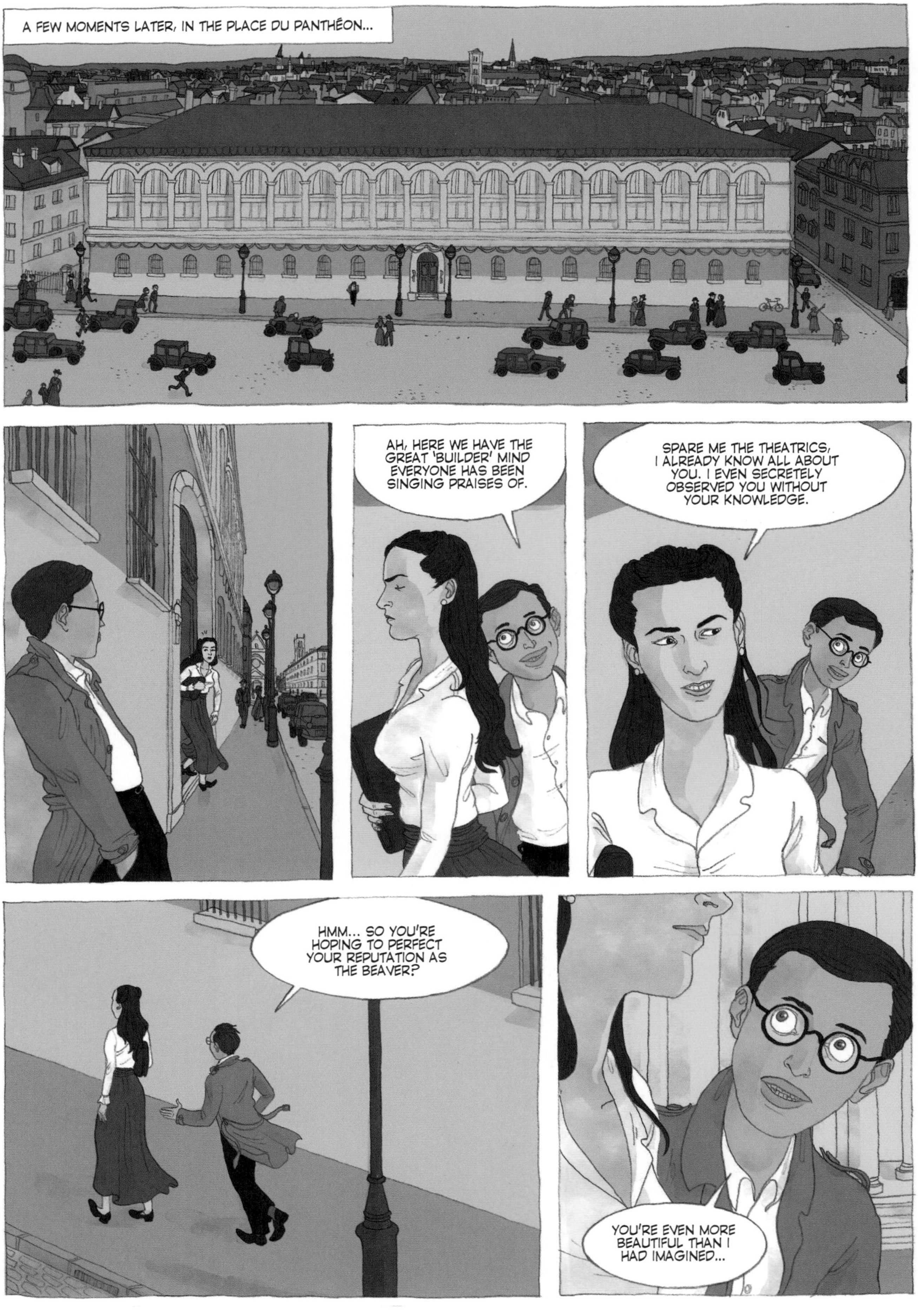
A FEW MOMENTS LATER, IN THE PLACE DU PANTHÉON...
AH, HERE WE HAVE THE GREAT 'BUILDER' MIND EVERYONE HAS BEEN SINGING PRAISES OF.
SPARE ME THE THEATRICS, I ALREADY KNOW ALL ABOUT YOU. I EVEN SECRETELY OBSERVED YOU WITHOUT YOUR KNOWLEDGE.
HMM... SO YOU'RE HOPING TO PERFECT YOUR REPUTATION AS THE BEAVER?
YOU'RE EVEN MORE BEAUTIFUL THAN I HAD IMAGINED...

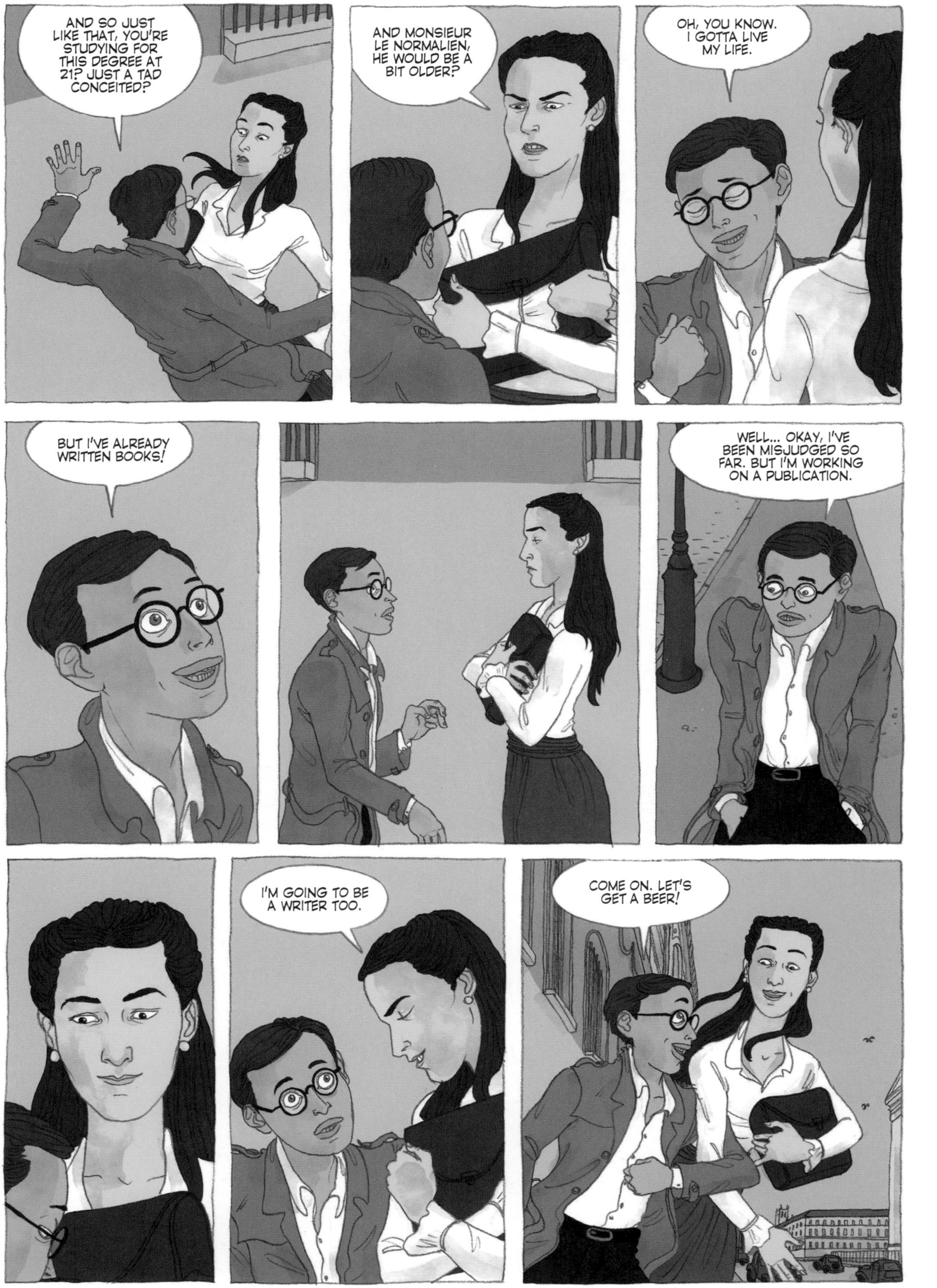
AND SO JUST LIKE THAT, YOU'RE STUDYING FOR THIS DEGREE AT 21? JUST A TAD CONCEITED?
AND MONSIEUR LE NORMALIEN, HE WOULD BE A BIT OLDER?
OH, YOU KNOW. I GOTTA LIVE MY LIFE.
BUT I'VE ALREADY WRITTEN BOOKS!
WELL... OKAY, I'VE BEEN MISJUDGED SO FAR. BUT I'M WORKING ON A PUBLICATION.
I'M GOING TO BE A WRITER TOO.
COME ON. LET'S GET A BEER!

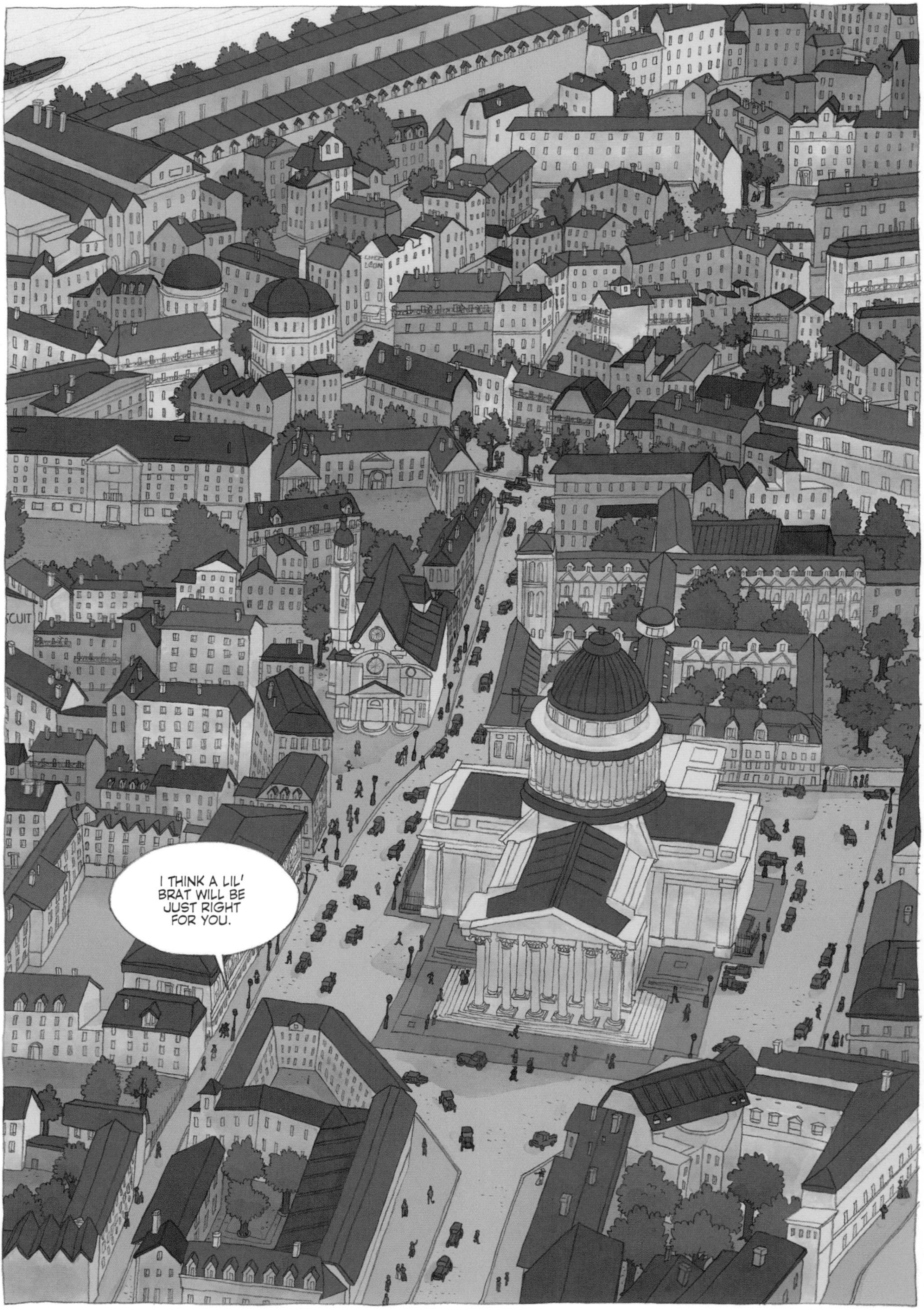
I THINK A LIL' BRAT WILL BE JUST RIGHT FOR YOU.

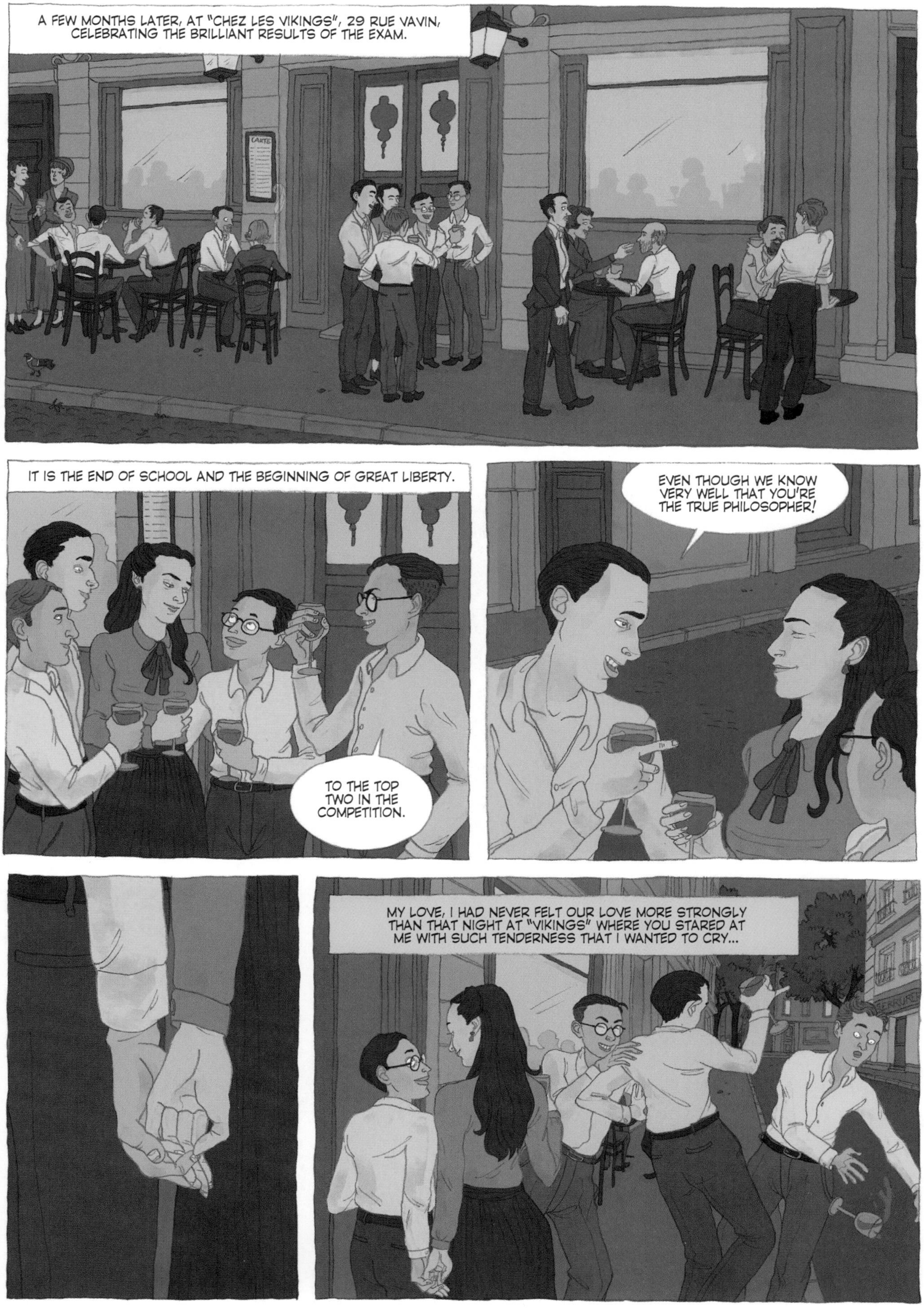
A FEW MONTHS LATER, AT "CHEZ LES VIKINGS", 29 RUE VAVIN, CELEBRATING THE BRILLIANT RESULTS OF THE EXAM.
CARTE
IT IS THE END OF SCHOOL AND THE BEGINNING OF GREAT LIBERTY.
TO THE TOP TWO IN THE COMPETITION.
EVEN THOUGH WE KNOW VERY WELL THAT YOU'RE THE TRUE PHILOSOPHER!
MY LOVE, I HAD NEVER FELT OUR LOVE MORE STRONGLY THAN THAT NIGHT AT "VIKINGS" WHERE YOU STARED AT ME WITH SUCH TENDERNESS THAT I WANTED TO CRY...

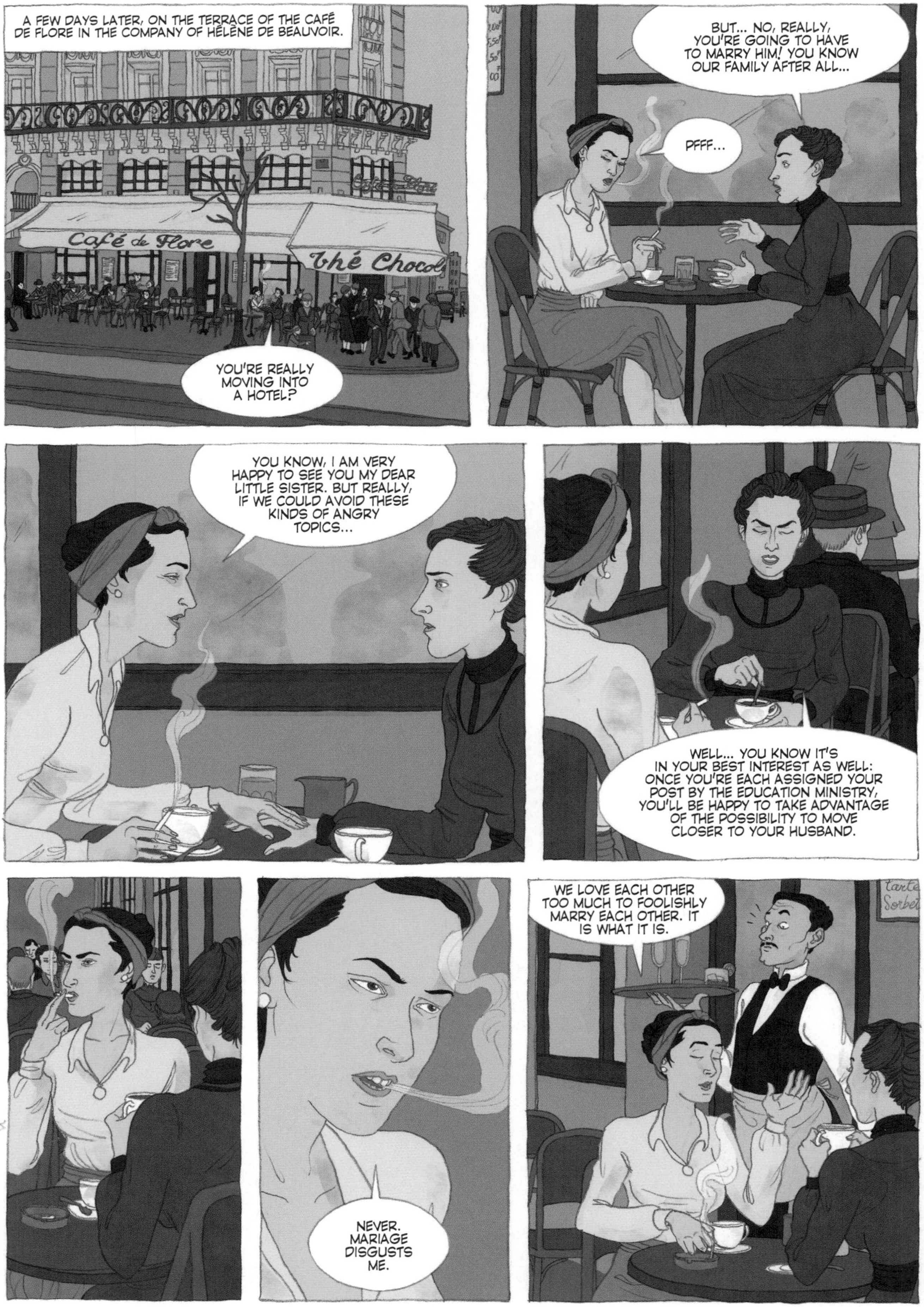
A FEW DAYS LATER, ON THE TERRACE OF THE CAFÉ DE FLORE IN THE COMPANY OF HÉLÈNE DE BEAUVOIR.
Café de Flore
YOU'RE REALLY MOVING INTO A HOTEL?
BUT... NO, REALLY, YOU'RE GOING TO HAVE TO MARRY HIM! YOU KNOW OUR FAMILY AFTER ALL...
PFFF...
YOU KNOW, I AM VERY HAPPY TO SEE YOU MY DEAR LITTLE SISTER. BUT REALLY, IF WE COULD AVOID THESE KINDS OF ANGRY TOPICS...
WELL... YOU KNOW IT'S IN YOUR BEST INTEREST AS WELL: ONCE YOU'RE EACH ASSIGNED YOUR POST BY THE EDUCATION MINISTRY, YOU'LL BE HAPPY TO TAKE ADVANTAGE OF THE POSSIBILITY TO MOVE CLOSER TO YOUR HUSBAND.
NEVER. MARIAGE DISGUSTS ME.
WE LOVE EACH OTHER TOO MUCH TO FOOLISHLY MARRY EACH OTHER. IT IS WHAT IT IS.

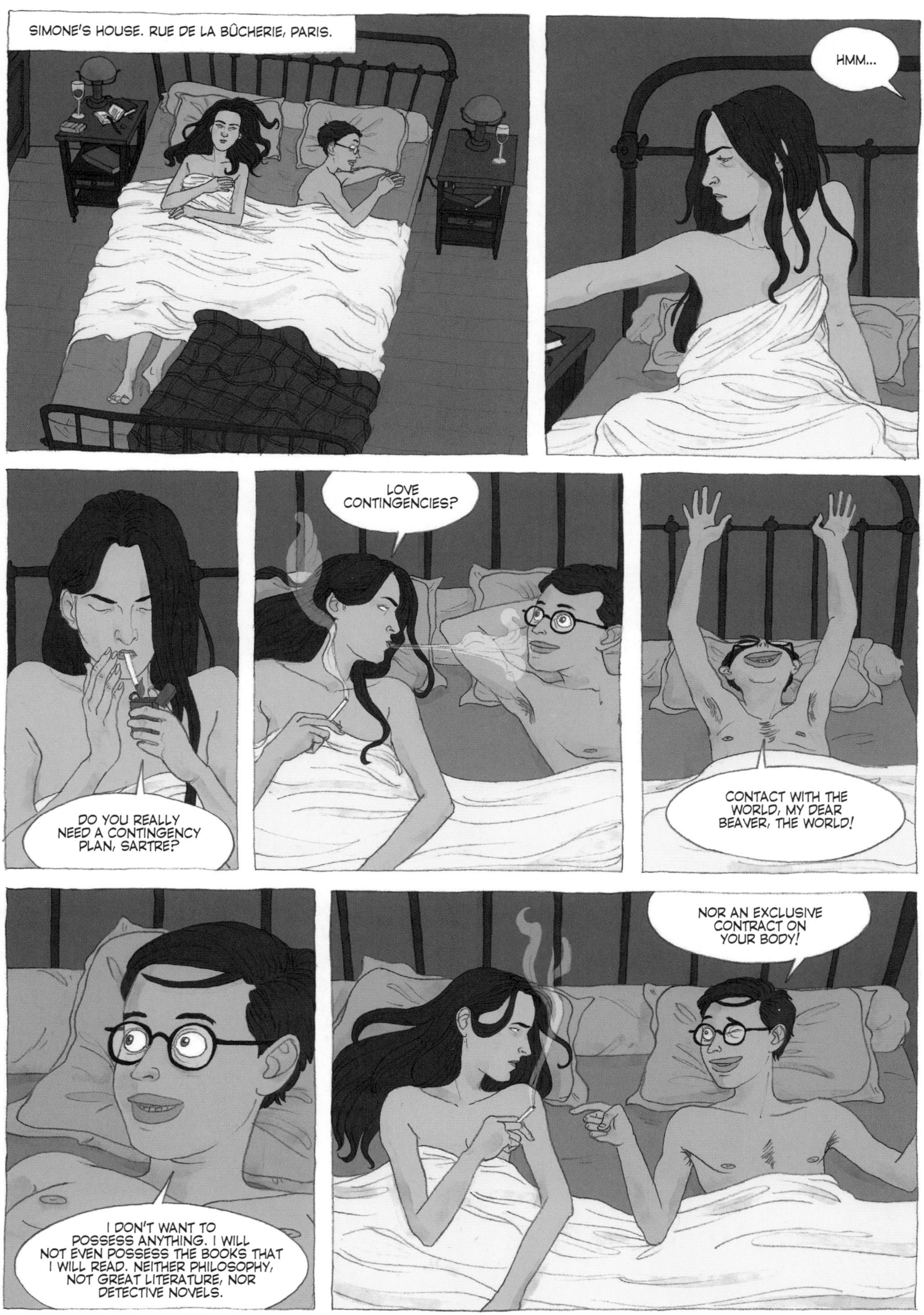
SIMONE'S HOUSE. RUE DE LA BÛCHERIE, PARIS.
HMM...
DO YOU REALLY NEED A CONTINGENCY PLAN, SARTRE?
LOVE CONTINGENCIES?
CONTACT WITH THE WORLD, MY DEAR BEAVER, THE WORLD!
I DON'T WANT TO POSSESS ANYTHING. I WILL NOT EVEN POSSESS THE BOOKS THAT I WILL READ. NEITHER PHILOSOPHY, NOT GREAT LITERATURE, NOR DETECTIVE NOVELS.
NOR AN EXCLUSIVE CONTRACT ON YOUR BODY!

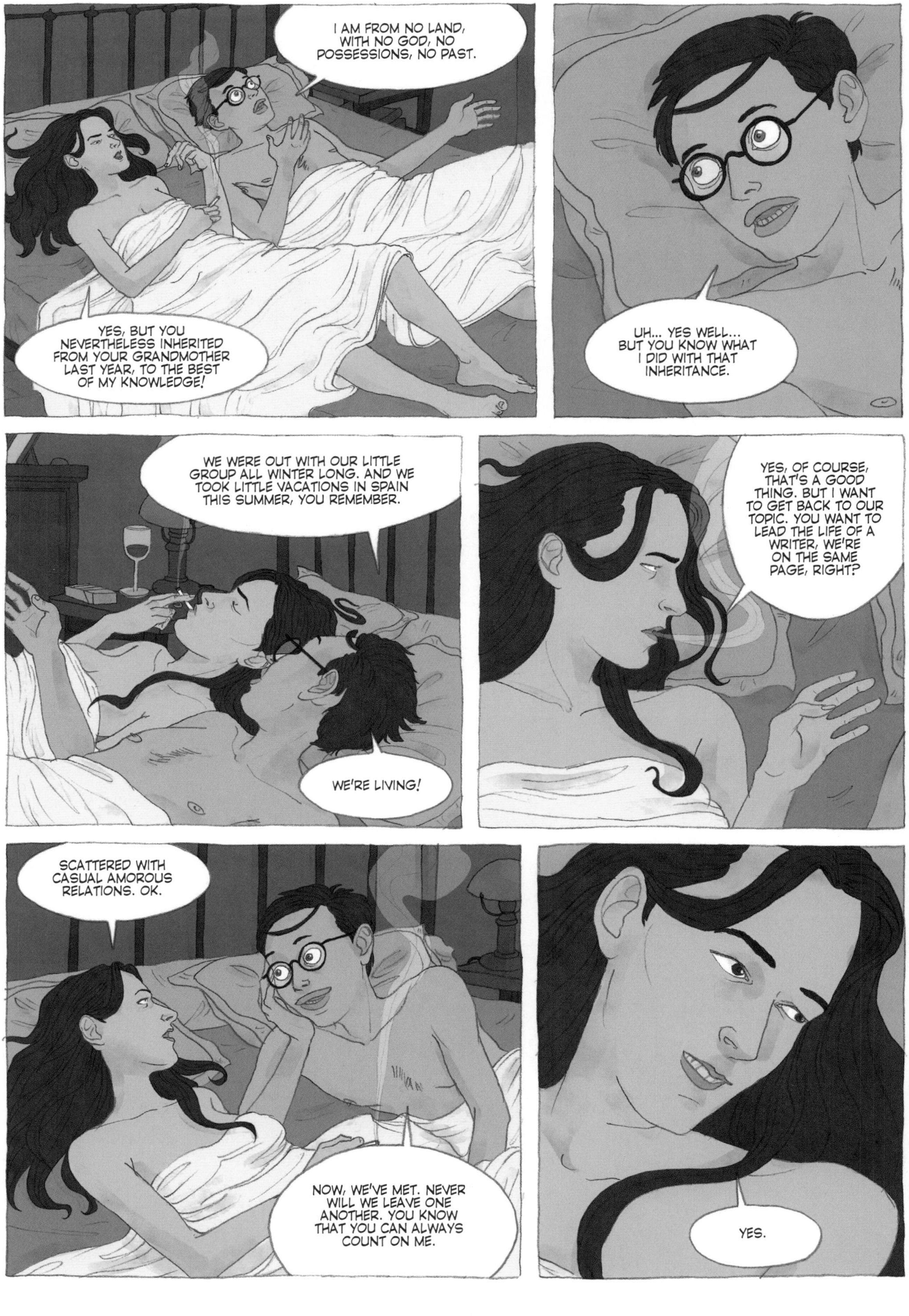
I AM FROM NO LAND, WITH NO GOD, NO POSSESSIONS, NO PAST.
YES, BUT YOU NEVERTHELESS INHERITED FROM YOUR GRANDMOTHER LAST YEAR, TO THE BEST OF MY KNOWLEDGE!
UH... YES WELL... BUT YOU KNOW WHAT I DID WITH THAT INHERITANCE.
WE WERE OUT WITH OUR LITTLE GROUP ALL WINTER LONG. AND WE TOOK LITTLE VACATIONS IN SPAIN THIS SUMMER, YOU REMEMBER.
WE'RE LIVING!
YES, OF COURSE, THAT'S A GOOD THING. BUT I WANT TO GET BACK TO OUR TOPIC. YOU WANT TO LEAD THE LIFE OF A WRITER, WE'RE ON THE SAME PAGE, RIGHT?
SCATTERED WITH CASUAL AMOROUS RELATIONS. OK.
NOW, WE'VE MET. NEVER WILL WE LEAVE ONE ANOTHER. YOU KNOW THAT YOU CAN ALWAYS COUNT ON ME.
YES.

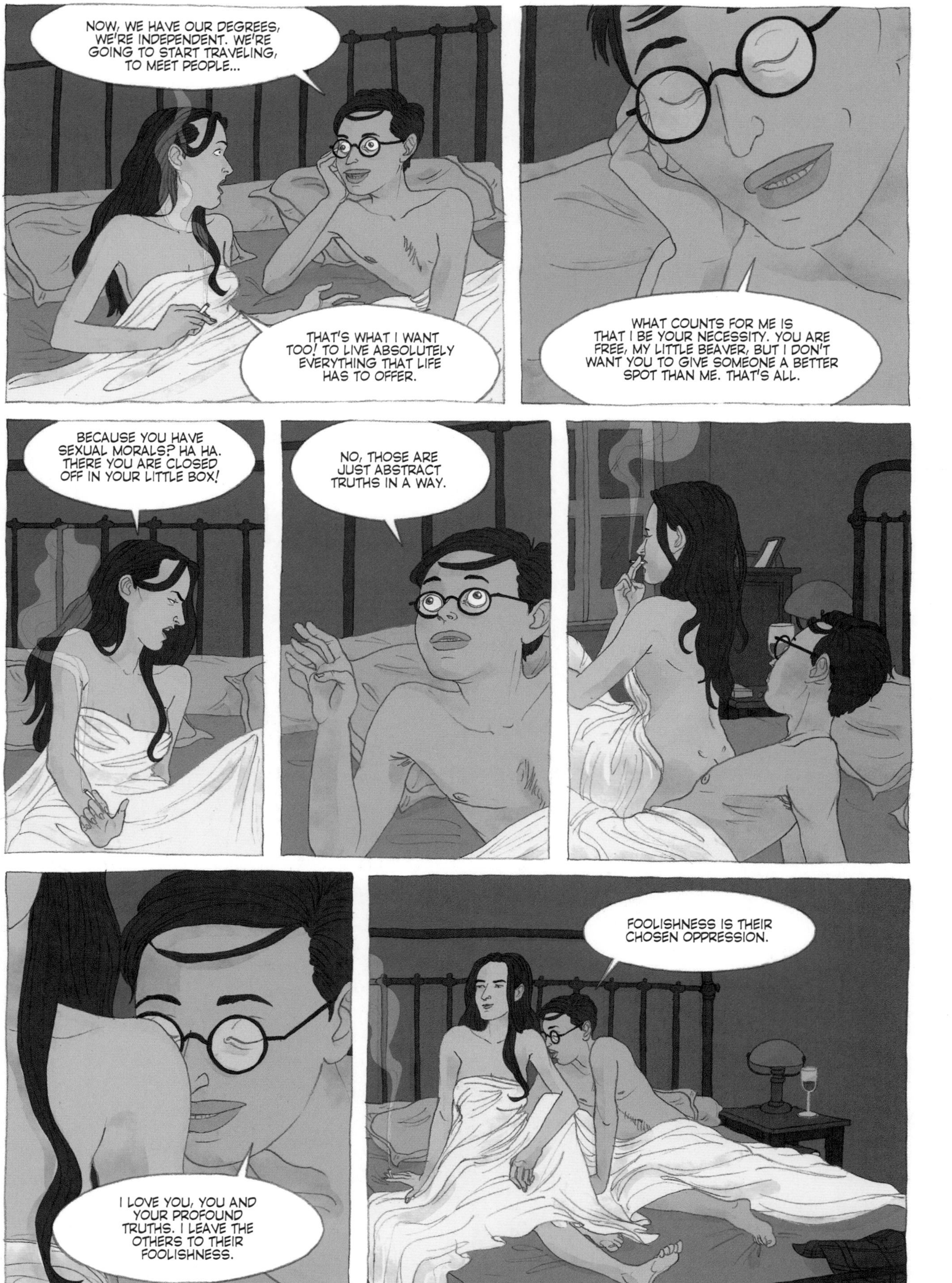
NOW, WE HAVE OUR DEGREES, WE'RE INDEPENDENT. WE'RE GOING TO START TRAVELING, TO MEET PEOPLE...
THAT'S WHAT I WANT TOO! TO LIVE ABSOLUTELY EVERYTHING THAT LIFE HAS TO OFFER.
WHAT COUNTS FOR ME IS THAT I BE YOUR NECESSITY. YOU ARE FREE, MY LITTLE BEAVER, BUT I DON'T WANT YOU TO GIVE SOMEONE A BETTER SPOT THAN ME. THAT'S ALL.
BECAUSE YOU HAVE SEXUAL MORALS? HA HA. THERE YOU ARE CLOSED OFF IN YOUR LITTLE BOX!
NO, THOSE ARE JUST ABSTRACT TRUTHS IN A WAY.
I LOVE YOU, YOU AND YOUR PROFOUND TRUTHS. I LEAVE THE OTHERS TO THEIR FOOLISHNESS.
FOOLISHNESS IS THEIR CHOSEN OPPRESSION.

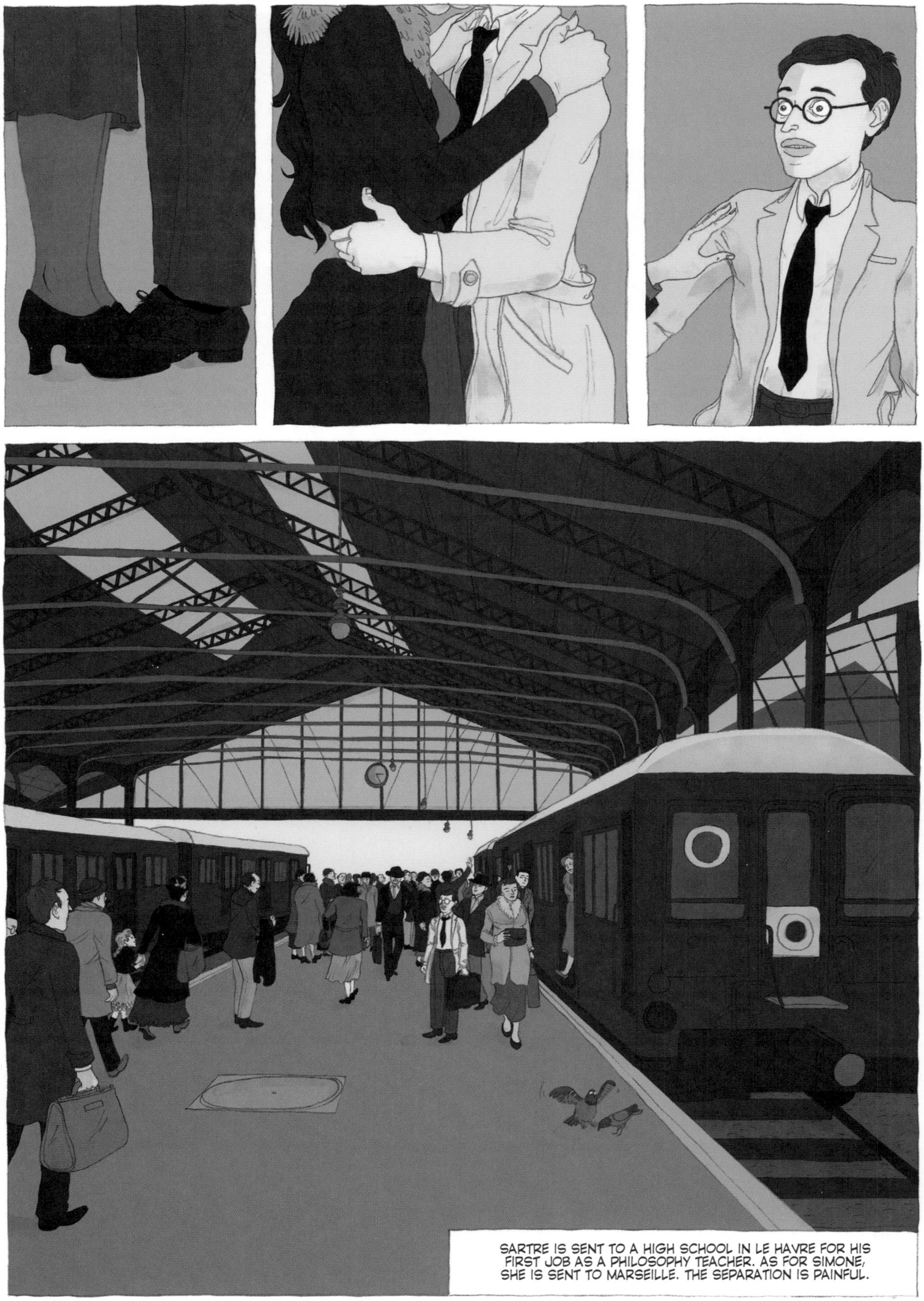
SARTRE IS SENT TO A HIGH SCHOOL IN LE HAVRE FOR HIS FIRST JOB AS A PHILOSOPHY TEACHER. AS FOR SIMONE, SHE IS SENT TO MARSEILLE. THE SEPARATION IS PAINFUL.

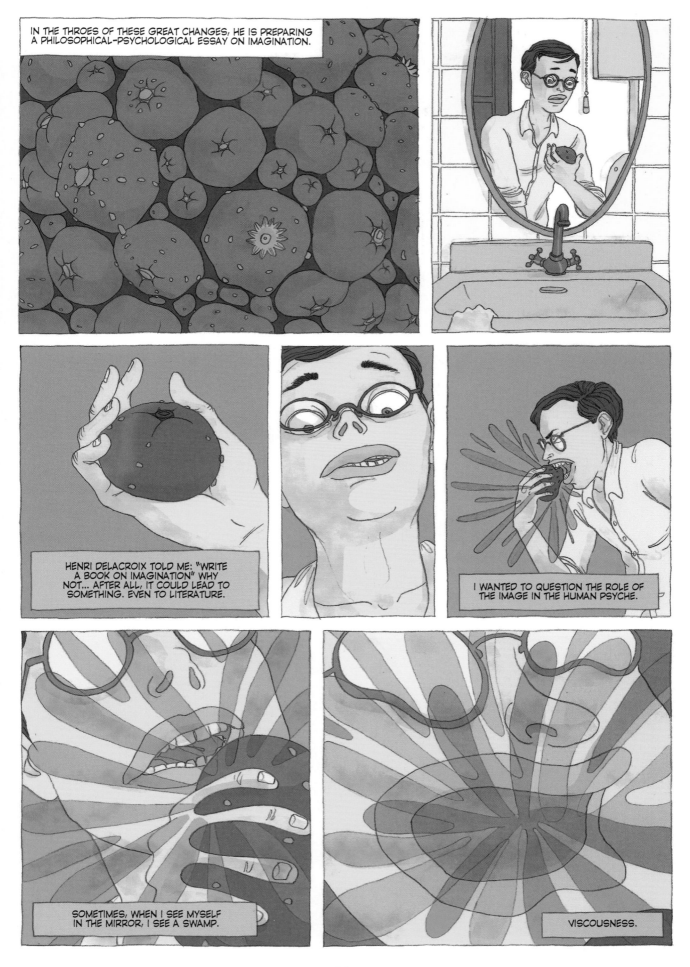

IN THE THROES OF THESE GREAT CHANGES, HE IS PREPARING A PHILOSOPHICAL-PSYCHOLOGICAL ESSAY ON IMAGINATION.

HENRI DELACROIX TOLD ME: "WRITE A BOOK ON IMAGINATION" WHY NOT... AFTER ALL, IT COULD LEAD TO SOMETHING. EVEN TO LITERATURE.

I WANTED TO QUESTION THE ROLE OF THE IMAGE IN THE HUMAN PSYCHE.

SOMETIMES, WHEN I SEE MYSELF IN THE MIRROR, I SEE A SWAMP.

VISCOUSNESS.

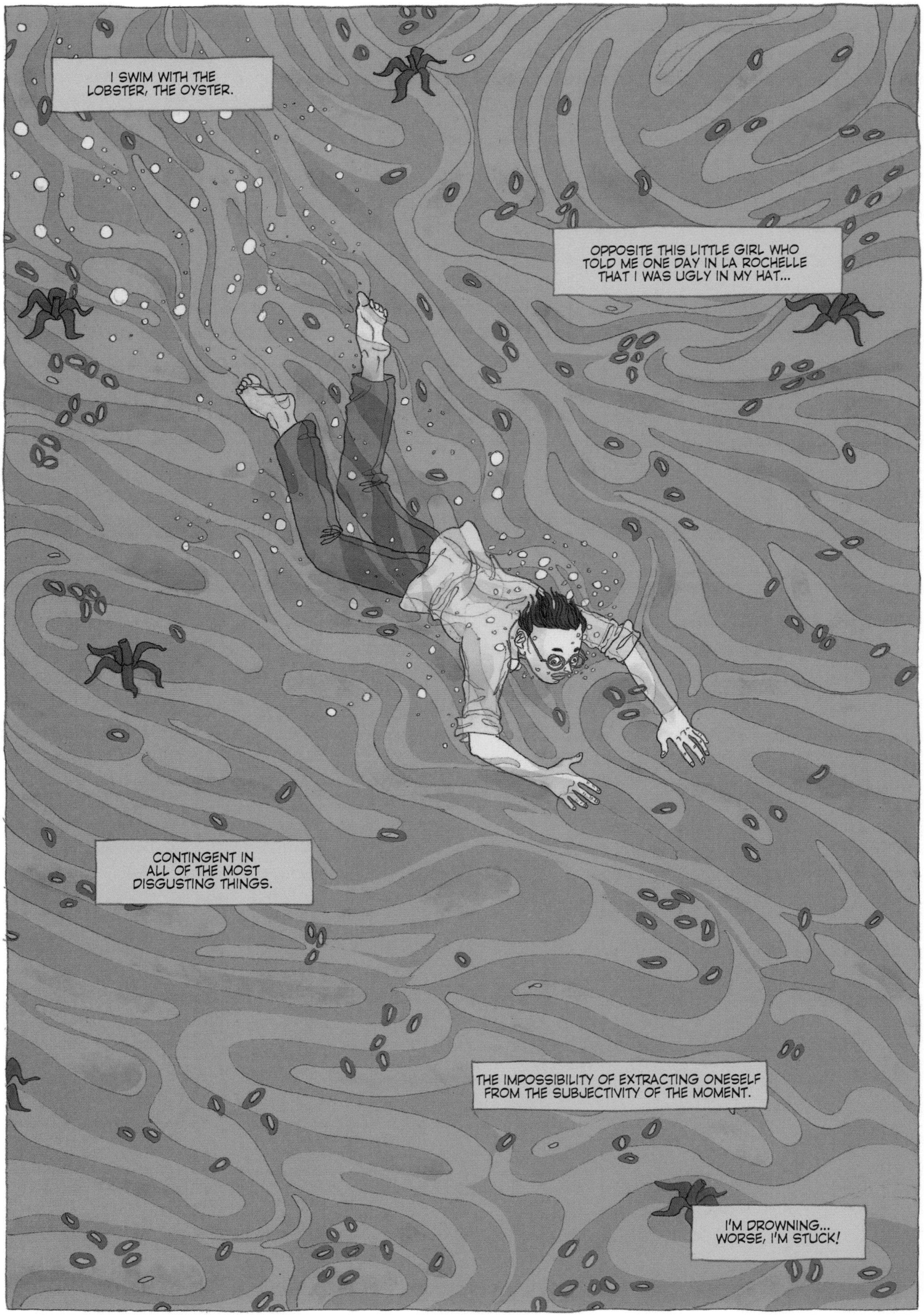
I SWIM WITH THE LOBSTER, THE OYSTER.
OPPOSITE THIS LITTLE GIRL WHO TOLD ME ONE DAY IN LA ROCHELLE THAT I WAS UGLY IN MY HAT...
CONTINGENT IN ALL OF THE MOST DISGUSTING THINGS.
THE IMPOSSIBILITY OF EXTRACTING ONESELF FROM THE SUBJECTIVITY OF THE MOMENT.
I'M DROWNING... WORSE, I'M STUCK!

PART TWO:

"THE CONSTELLATION OF THE BEAVER"

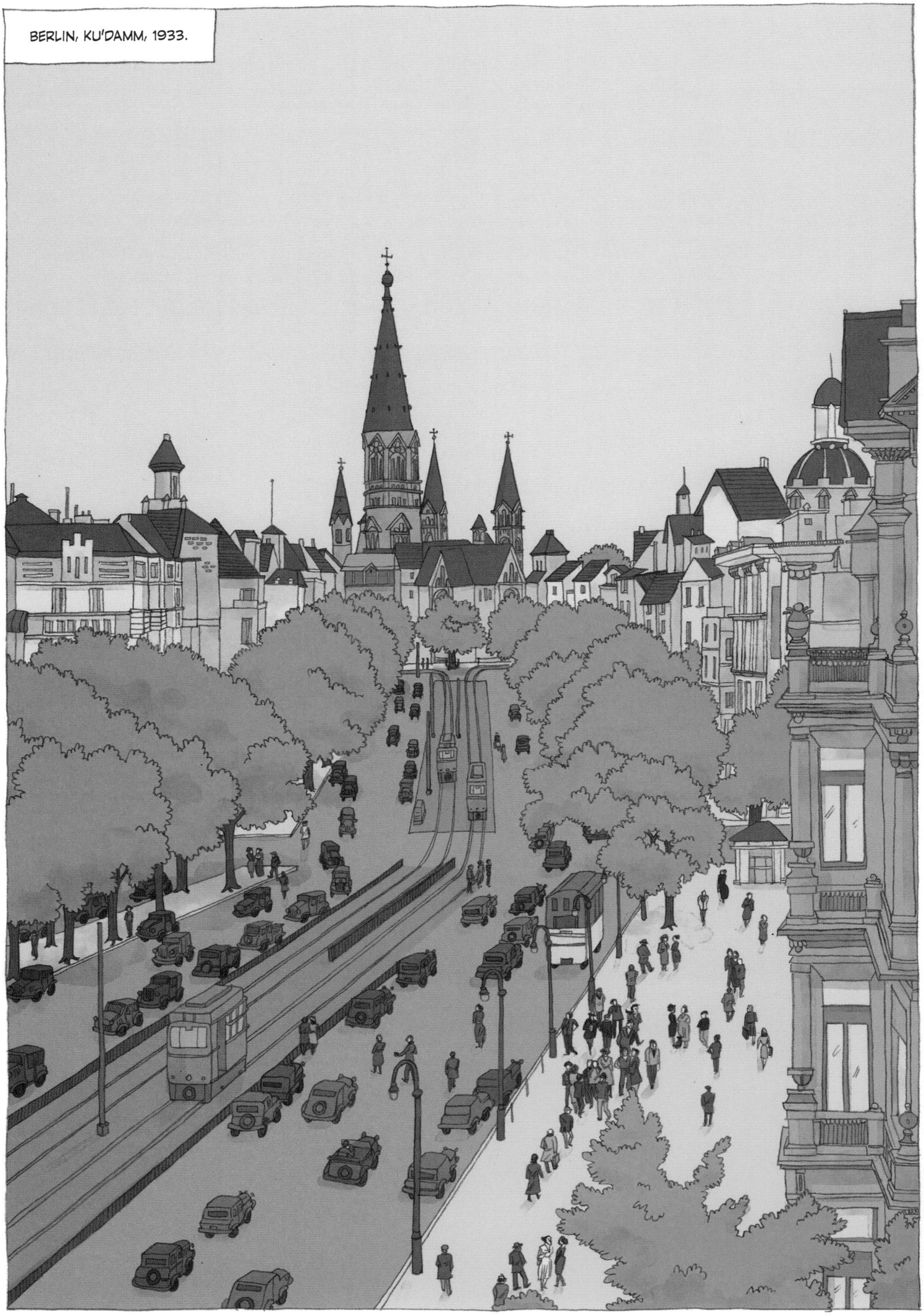
BERLIN, KU'DAMM, 1933.

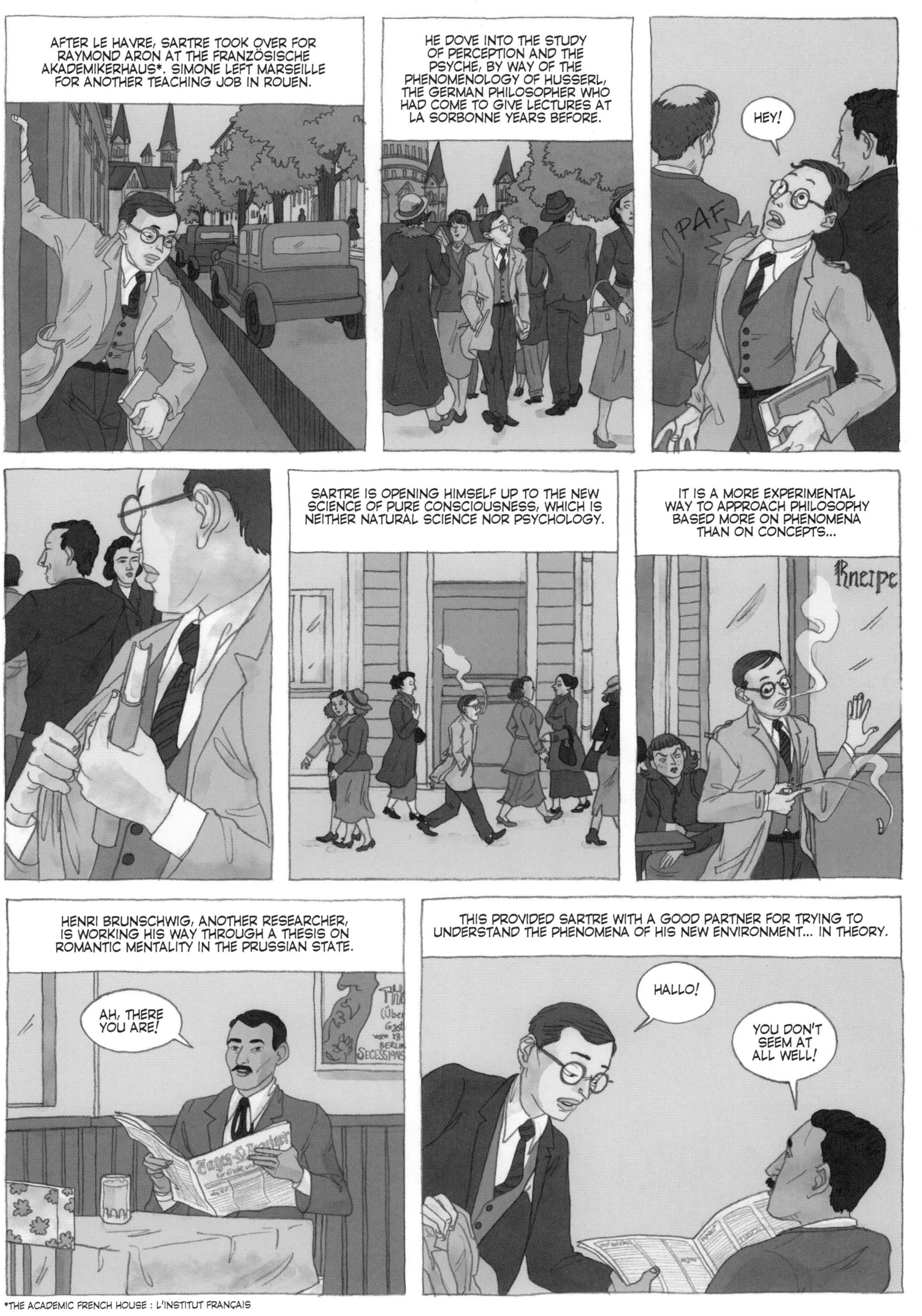
AFTER LE HAVRE, SARTRE TOOK OVER FOR RAYMOND ARON AT THE FRANZÖSISCHE AKADEMIKERHAUS*. SIMONE LEFT MARSEILLE FOR ANOTHER TEACHING JOB IN ROUEN.
HE DOVE INTO THE STUDY OF PERCEPTION AND THE PSYCHE, BY WAY OF THE PHENOMENOLOGY OF HUSSERL, THE GERMAN PHILOSOPHER WHO HAD COME TO GIVE LECTURES AT LA SORBONNE YEARS BEFORE.
HEY!
PAF
SARTRE IS OPENING HIMSELF UP TO THE NEW SCIENCE OF PURE CONSCIOUSNESS, WHICH IS NEITHER NATURAL SCIENCE NOR PSYCHOLOGY.
IT IS A MORE EXPERIMENTAL WAY TO APPROACH PHILOSOPHY BASED MORE ON PHENOMENA THAN ON CONCEPTS...
Kneipe
HENRI BRUNSCHWIG, ANOTHER RESEARCHER, IS WORKING HIS WAY THROUGH A THESIS ON ROMANTIC MENTALITY IN THE PRUSSIAN STATE.
AH, THERE YOU ARE!
THIS PROVIDED SARTRE WITH A GOOD PARTNER FOR TRYING TO UNDERSTAND THE PHENOMENA OF HIS NEW ENVIRONMENT... IN THEORY.
HALLO!
YOU DON'T SEEM AT ALL WELL!

*THE ACADEMIC FRENCH HOUSE : L'INSTITUT FRANÇAIS

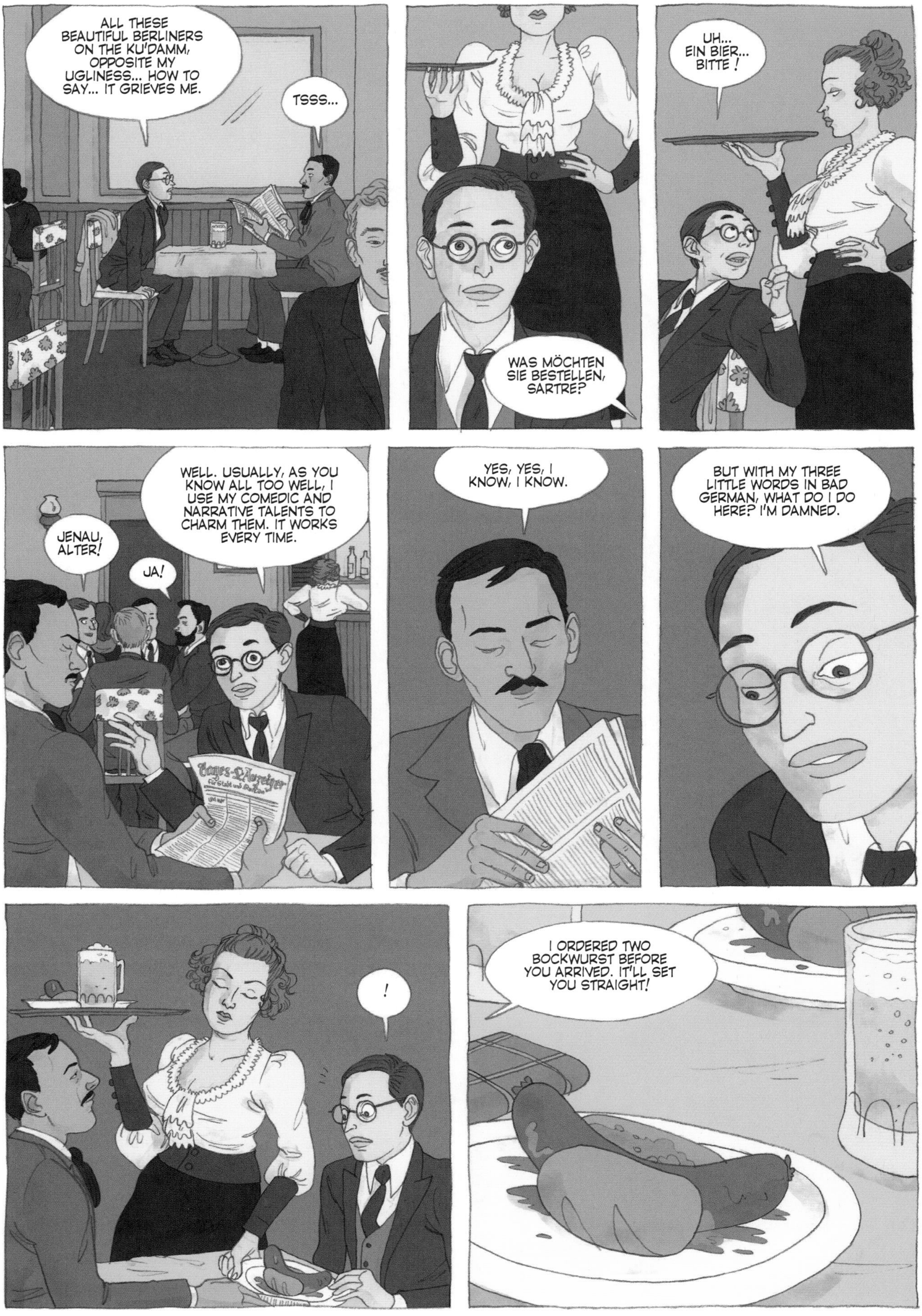
ALL THESE BEAUTIFUL BERLINERS ON THE KU'DAMM, OPPOSITE MY UGLINESS... HOW TO SAY... IT GRIEVES ME.
TSSS...
WAS MÖCHTEN SIE BESTELLEN, SARTRE?
UH... EIN BIER... BITTE !
WELL. USUALLY, AS YOU KNOW ALL TOO WELL, I USE MY COMEDIC AND NARRATIVE TALENTS TO CHARM THEM. IT WORKS EVERY TIME.
JENAU, ALTER!
JA!
YES, YES, I KNOW, I KNOW.
BUT WITH MY THREE LITTLE WORDS IN BAD GERMAN, WHAT DO I DO HERE? I'M DAMNED.
!
I ORDERED TWO BOCKWURST BEFORE YOU ARRIVED. IT'LL SET YOU STRAIGHT!

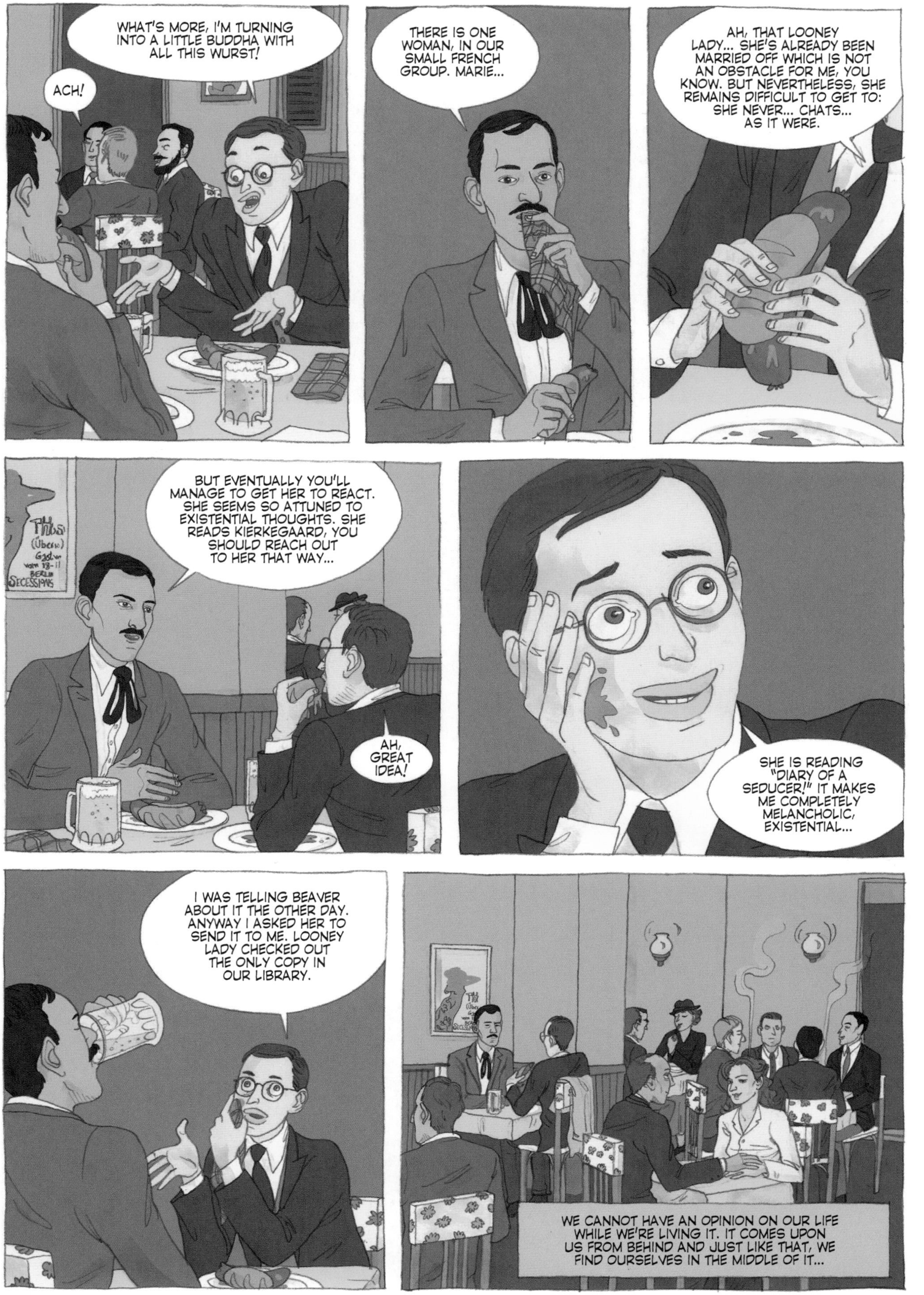
WHAT'S MORE, I'M TURNING INTO A LITTLE BUDDHA WITH ALL THIS WURST!
ACH!
THERE IS ONE WOMAN, IN OUR SMALL FRENCH GROUP. MARIE...
AH, THAT LOONEY LADY... SHE'S ALREADY BEEN MARRIED OFF WHICH IS NOT AN OBSTACLE FOR ME, YOU KNOW. BUT NEVERTHELESS, SHE REMAINS DIFFICULT TO GET TO: SHE NEVER... CHATS... AS IT WERE.
BUT EVENTUALLY YOU'LL MANAGE TO GET HER TO REACT. SHE SEEMS SO ATTUNED TO EXISTENTIAL THOUGHTS. SHE READS KIERKEGAARD, YOU SHOULD REACH OUT TO HER THAT WAY...
AH, GREAT IDEA!
SHE IS READING "DIARY OF A SEDUCER!" IT MAKES ME COMPLETELY MELANCHOLIC, EXISTENTIAL...
I WAS TELLING BEAVER ABOUT IT THE OTHER DAY. ANYWAY I ASKED HER TO SEND IT TO ME. LOONEY LADY CHECKED OUT THE ONLY COPY IN OUR LIBRARY.
WE CANNOT HAVE AN OPINION ON OUR LIFE WHILE WE'RE LIVING IT. IT COMES UPON US FROM BEHIND AND JUST LIKE THAT, WE FIND OURSELVES IN THE MIDDLE OF IT...

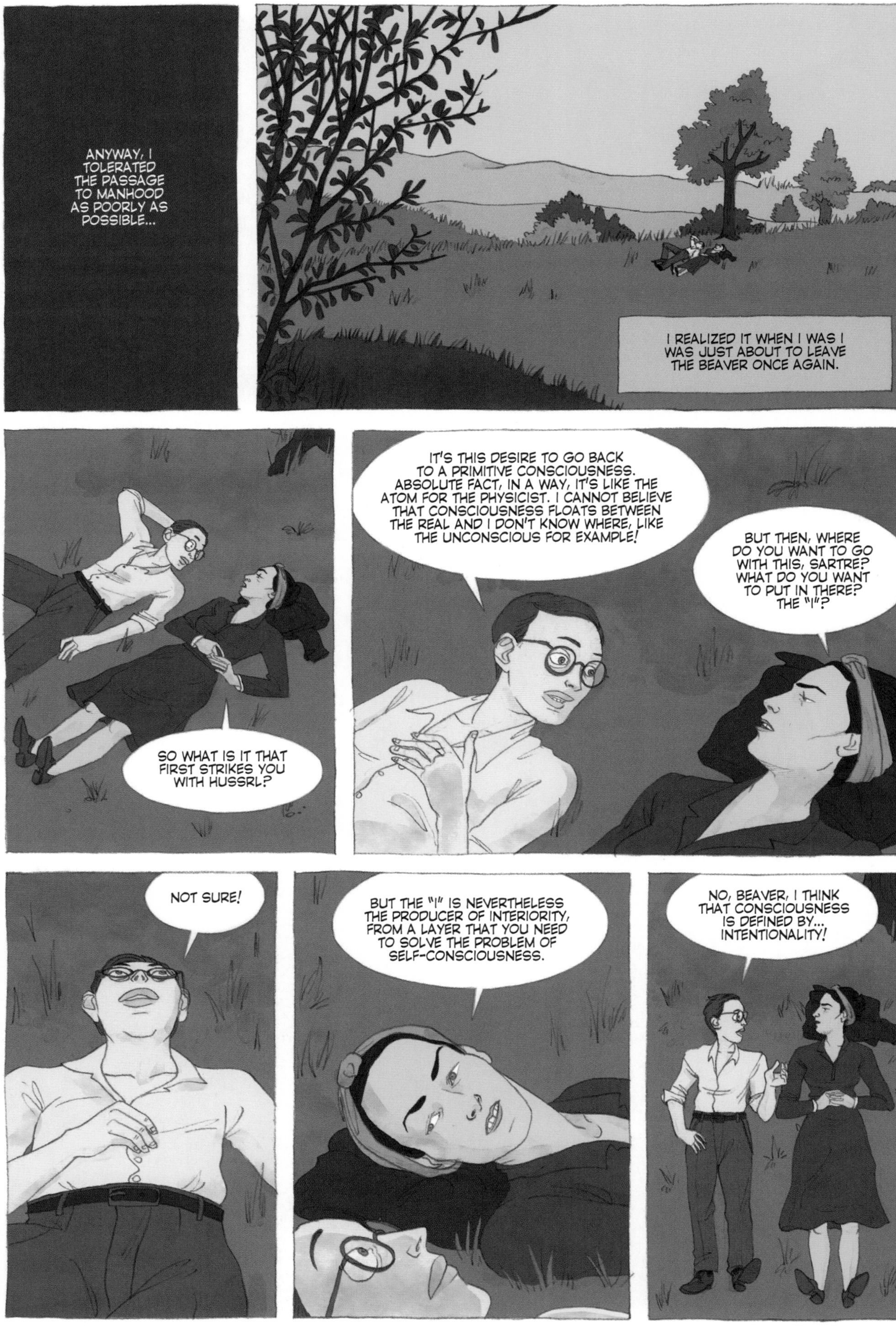
ANYWAY, I TOLERATED THE PASSAGE TO MANHOOD AS POORLY AS POSSIBLE...
I REALIZED IT WHEN I WAS I WAS JUST ABOUT TO LEAVE THE BEAVER ONCE AGAIN.
SO WHAT IS IT THAT FIRST STRIKES YOU WITH HUSSRL?
IT'S THIS DESIRE TO GO BACK TO A PRIMITIVE CONSCIOUSNESS. ABSOLUTE FACT, IN A WAY, IT'S LIKE THE ATOM FOR THE PHYSICIST. I CANNOT BELIEVE THAT CONSCIOUSNESS FLOATS BETWEEN THE REAL AND I DON'T KNOW WHERE, LIKE THE UNCONSCIOUS FOR EXAMPLE!
BUT THEN, WHERE DO YOU WANT TO GO WITH THIS, SARTRE? WHAT DO YOU WANT TO PUT IN THERE? THE "I"?
NOT SURE!
BUT THE "I" IS NEVERTHELESS THE PRODUCER OF INTERIORITY, FROM A LAYER THAT YOU NEED TO SOLVE THE PROBLEM OF SELF-CONSCIOUSNESS.
NO, BEAVER, I THINK THAT CONSCIOUSNESS IS DEFINED BY... INTENTIONALITY!

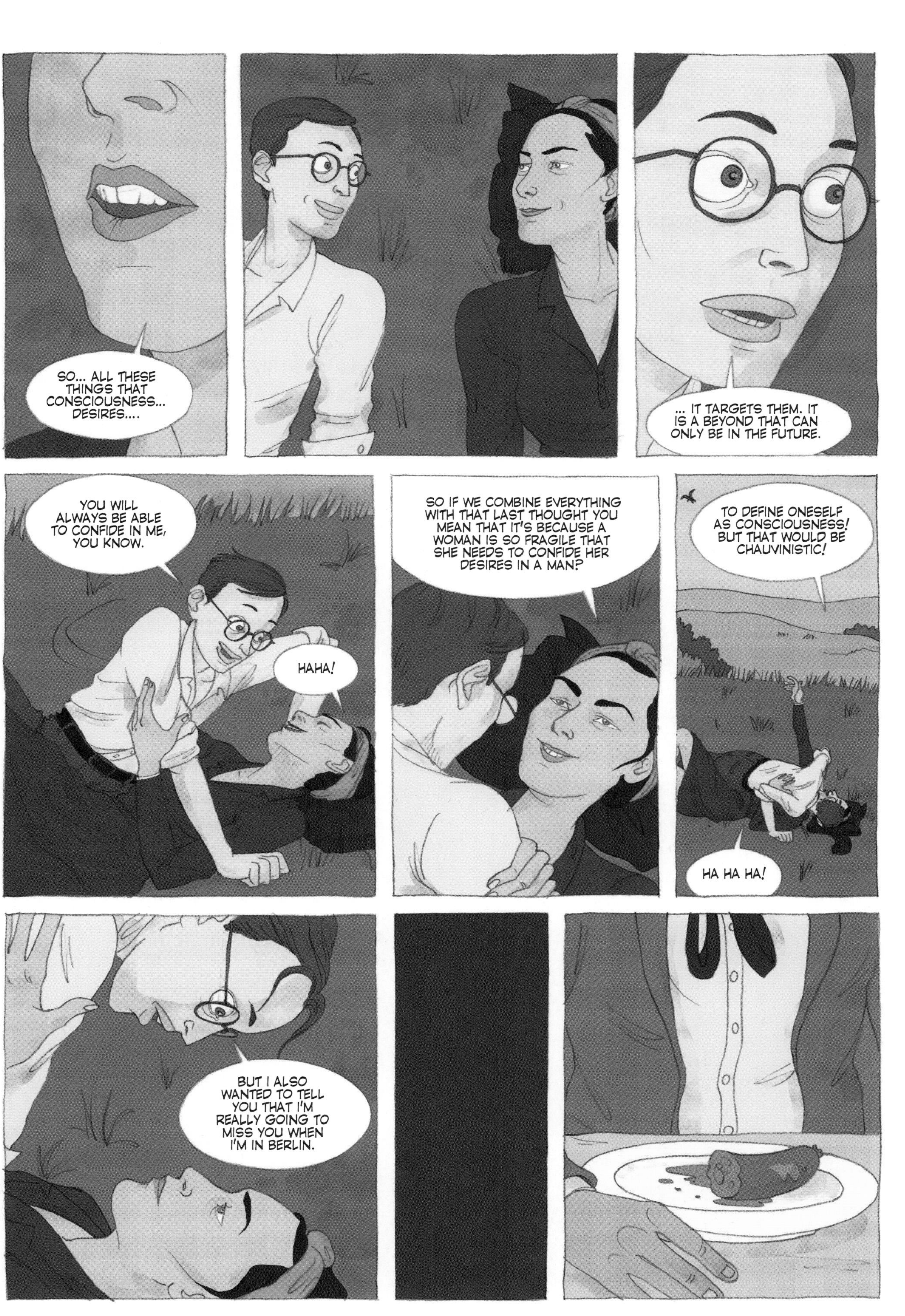
SO... ALL THESE THINGS THAT CONSCIOUSNESS... DESIRES....
... IT TARGETS THEM. IT IS A BEYOND THAT CAN ONLY BE IN THE FUTURE.
YOU WILL ALWAYS BE ABLE TO CONFIDE IN ME, YOU KNOW.
HAHA!
SO IF WE COMBINE EVERYTHING WITH THAT LAST THOUGHT YOU MEAN THAT IT'S BECAUSE A WOMAN IS SO FRAGILE THAT SHE NEEDS TO CONFIDE HER DESIRES IN A MAN?
TO DEFINE ONESELF AS CONSCIOUSNESS! BUT THAT WOULD BE CHAUVINISTIC!
HA HA HA!
BUT I ALSO WANTED TO TELL YOU THAT I'M REALLY GOING TO MISS YOU WHEN I'M IN BERLIN.

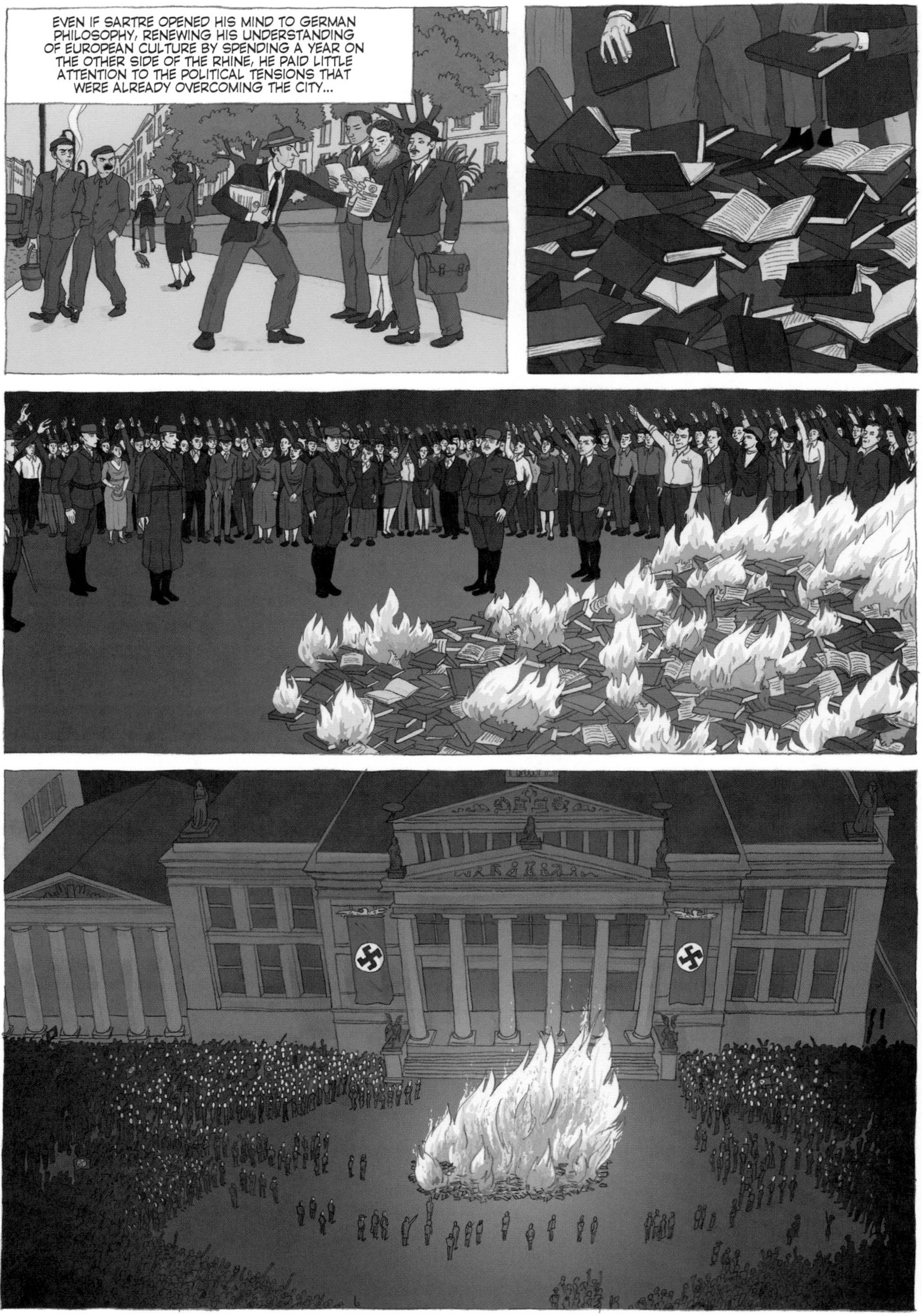
EVEN IF SARTRE OPENED HIS MIND TO GERMAN PHILOSOPHY, RENEWING HIS UNDERSTANDING OF EUROPEAN CULTURE BY SPENDING A YEAR ON THE OTHER SIDE OF THE RHINE, HE PAID LITTLE ATTENTION TO THE POLITICAL TENSIONS THAT WERE ALREADY OVERCOMING THE CITY...

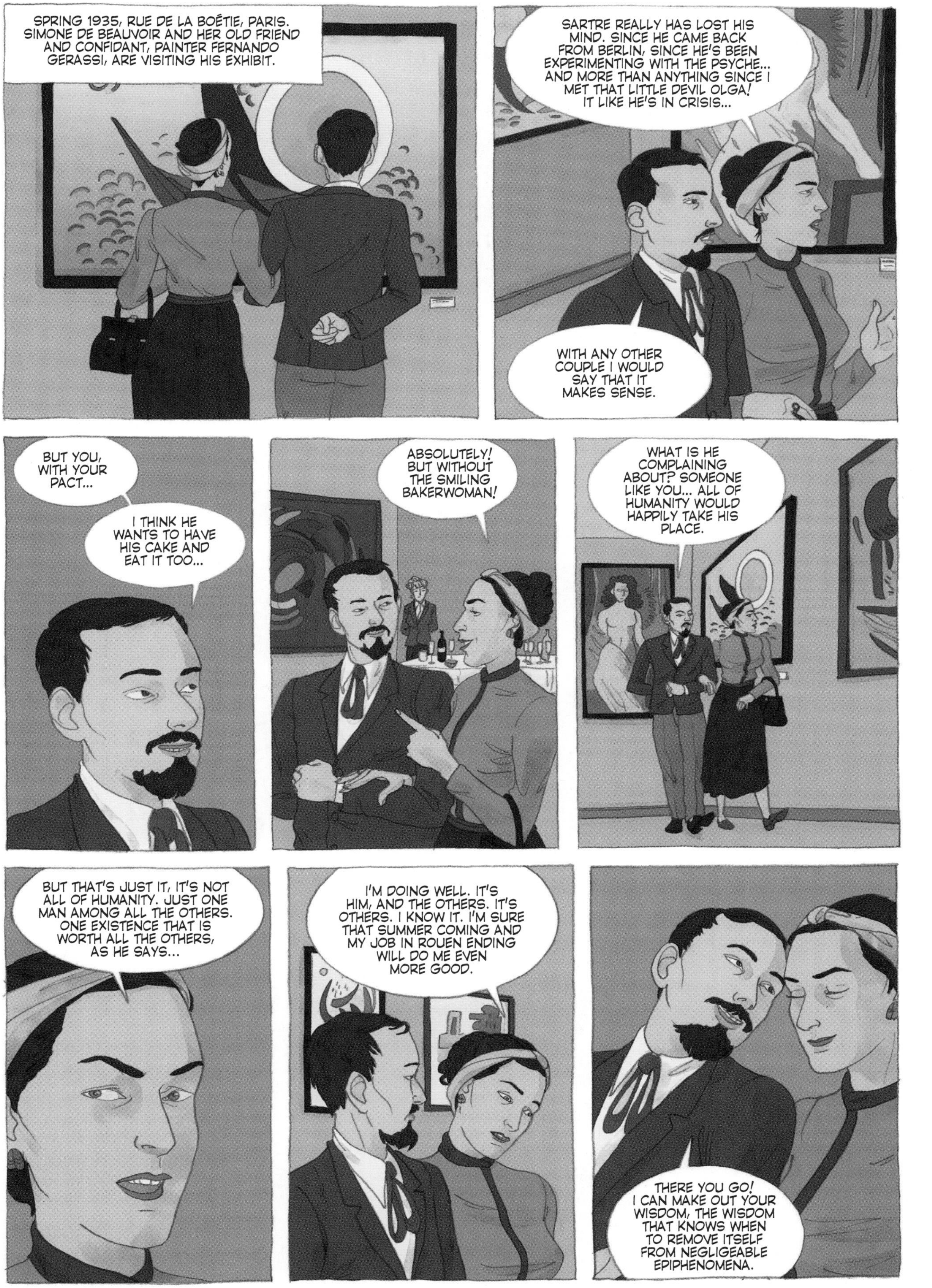

SPRING 1935, RUE DE LA BOÉTIE, PARIS. SIMONE DE BEAUVOIR AND HER OLD FRIEND AND CONFIDANT, PAINTER FERNANDO GERASSI, ARE VISITING HIS EXHIBIT.
SARTRE REALLY HAS LOST HIS MIND. SINCE HE CAME BACK FROM BERLIN, SINCE HE'S BEEN EXPERIMENTING WITH THE PSYCHE... AND MORE THAN ANYTHING SINCE I MET THAT LITTLE DEVIL OLGA! IT LIKE HE'S IN CRISIS...
WITH ANY OTHER COUPLE I WOULD SAY THAT IT MAKES SENSE.
BUT YOU, WITH YOUR PACT...
I THINK HE WANTS TO HAVE HIS CAKE AND EAT IT TOO...
ABSOLUTELY! BUT WITHOUT THE SMILING BAKERWOMAN!
WHAT IS HE COMPLAINING ABOUT? SOMEONE LIKE YOU... ALL OF HUMANITY WOULD HAPPILY TAKE HIS PLACE.
BUT THAT'S JUST IT, IT'S NOT ALL OF HUMANITY. JUST ONE MAN AMONG ALL THE OTHERS. ONE EXISTENCE THAT IS WORTH ALL THE OTHERS, AS HE SAYS...
I'M DOING WELL. IT'S HIM, AND THE OTHERS. IT'S OTHERS. I KNOW IT. I'M SURE THAT SUMMER COMING AND MY JOB IN ROUEN ENDING WILL DO ME EVEN MORE GOOD.
THERE YOU GO! I CAN MAKE OUT YOUR WISDOM, THE WISDOM THAT KNOWS WHEN TO REMOVE ITSELF FROM NEGLIGEABLE EPIPHENOMENA.

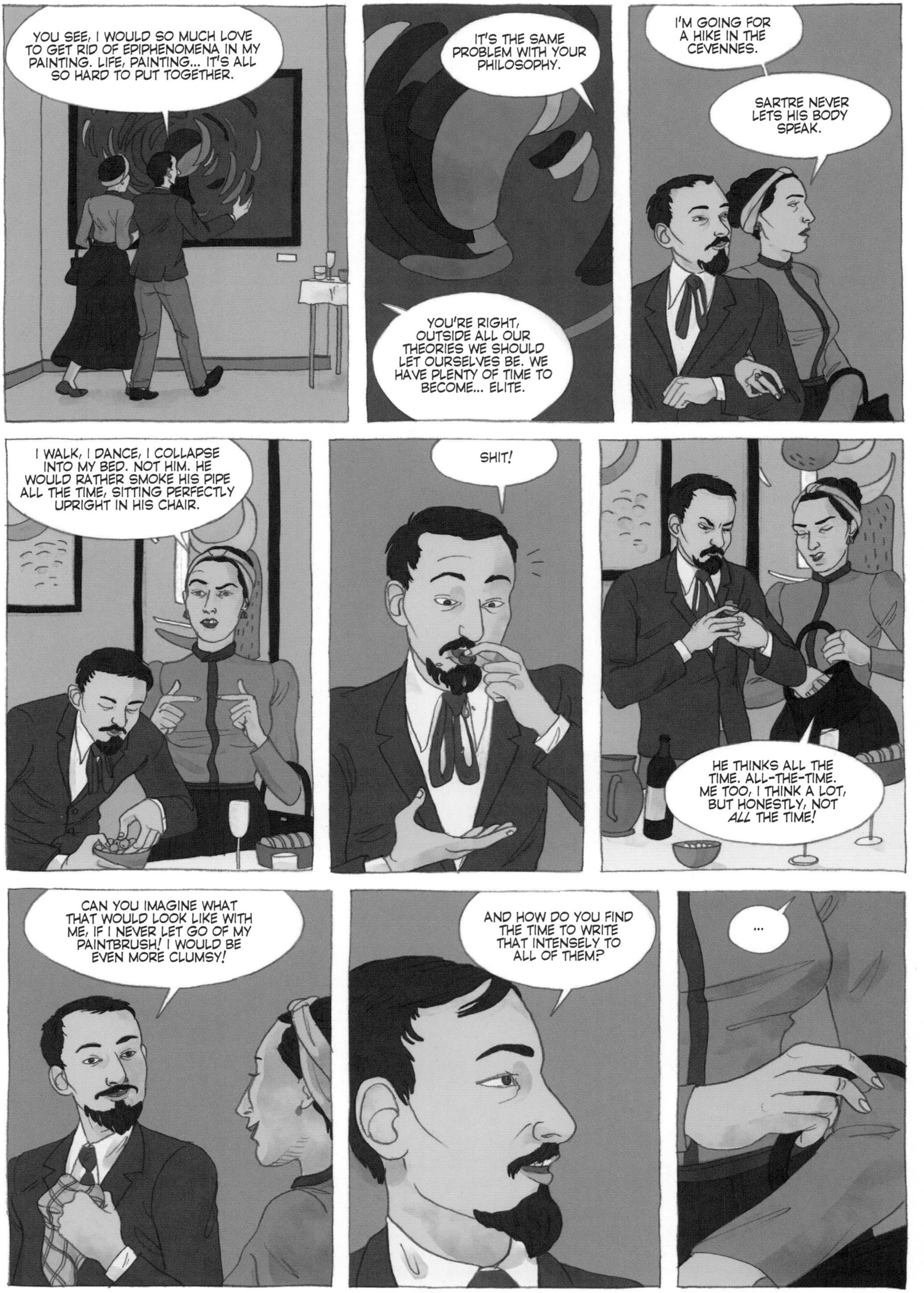
YOU SEE, I WOULD SO MUCH LOVE TO GET RID OF EPIPHENOMENA IN MY PAINTING. LIFE, PAINTING... IT'S ALL SO HARD TO PUT TOGETHER.
IT'S THE SAME PROBLEM WITH YOUR PHILOSOPHY.
YOU'RE RIGHT, OUTSIDE ALL OUR THEORIES WE SHOULD LET OURSELVES BE. WE HAVE PLENTY OF TIME TO BECOME... ELITE.
I'M GOING FOR A HIKE IN THE CEVENNES.
SARTRE NEVER LETS HIS BODY SPEAK.
I WALK, I DANCE, I COLLAPSE INTO MY BED. NOT HIM. HE WOULD RATHER SMOKE HIS PIPE ALL THE TIME, SITTING PERFECTLY UPRIGHT IN HIS CHAIR.
SHIT!
HE THINKS ALL THE TIME. ALL-THE-TIME. ME TOO, I THINK A LOT, BUT HONESTLY, NOT *ALL* THE TIME!
CAN YOU IMAGINE WHAT THAT WOULD LOOK LIKE WITH ME, IF I NEVER LET GO OF MY PAINTBRUSH! I WOULD BE EVEN MORE CLUMSY!
AND HOW DO YOU FIND THE TIME TO WRITE THAT INTENSELY TO ALL OF THEM?
...

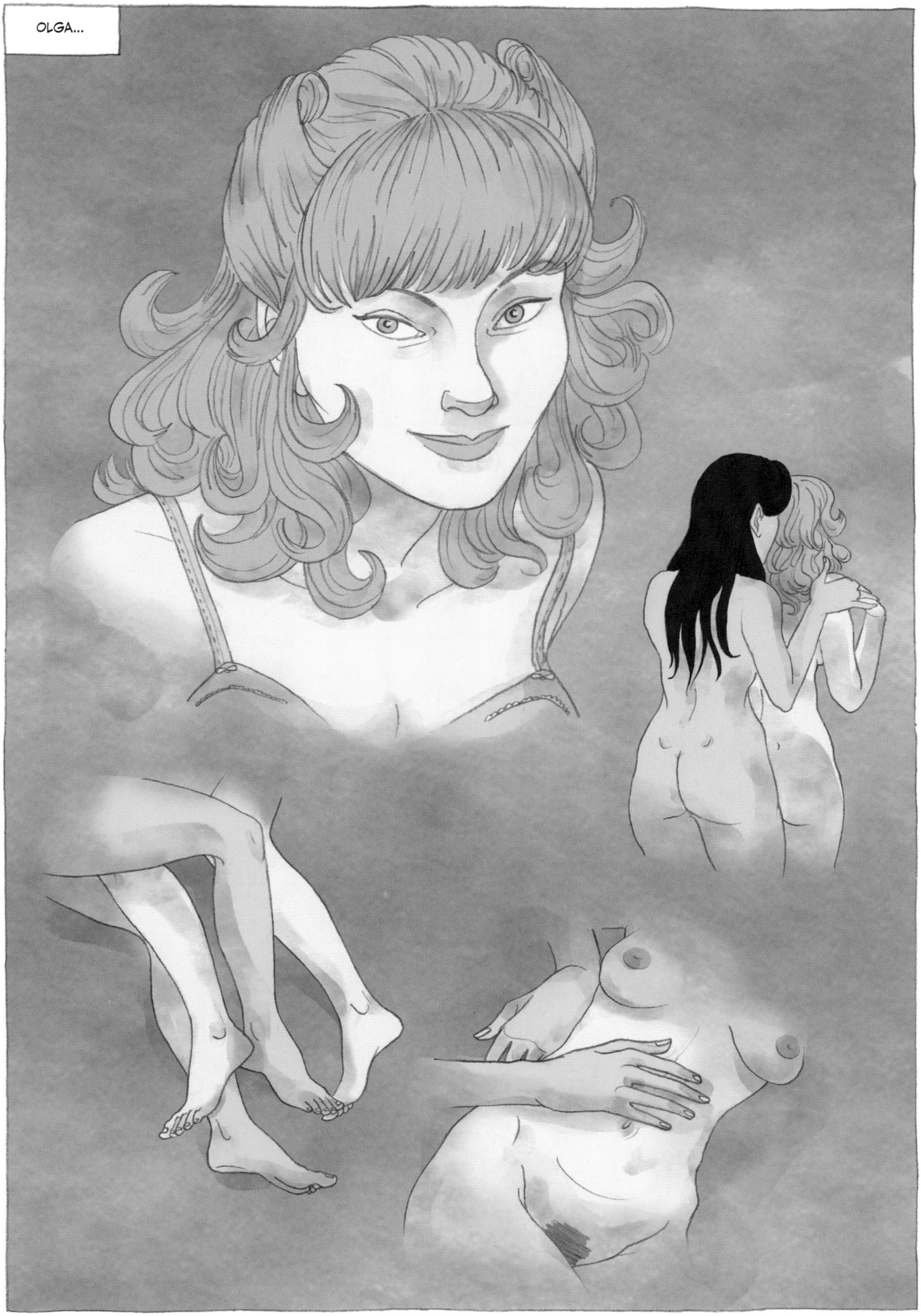
OLGA...

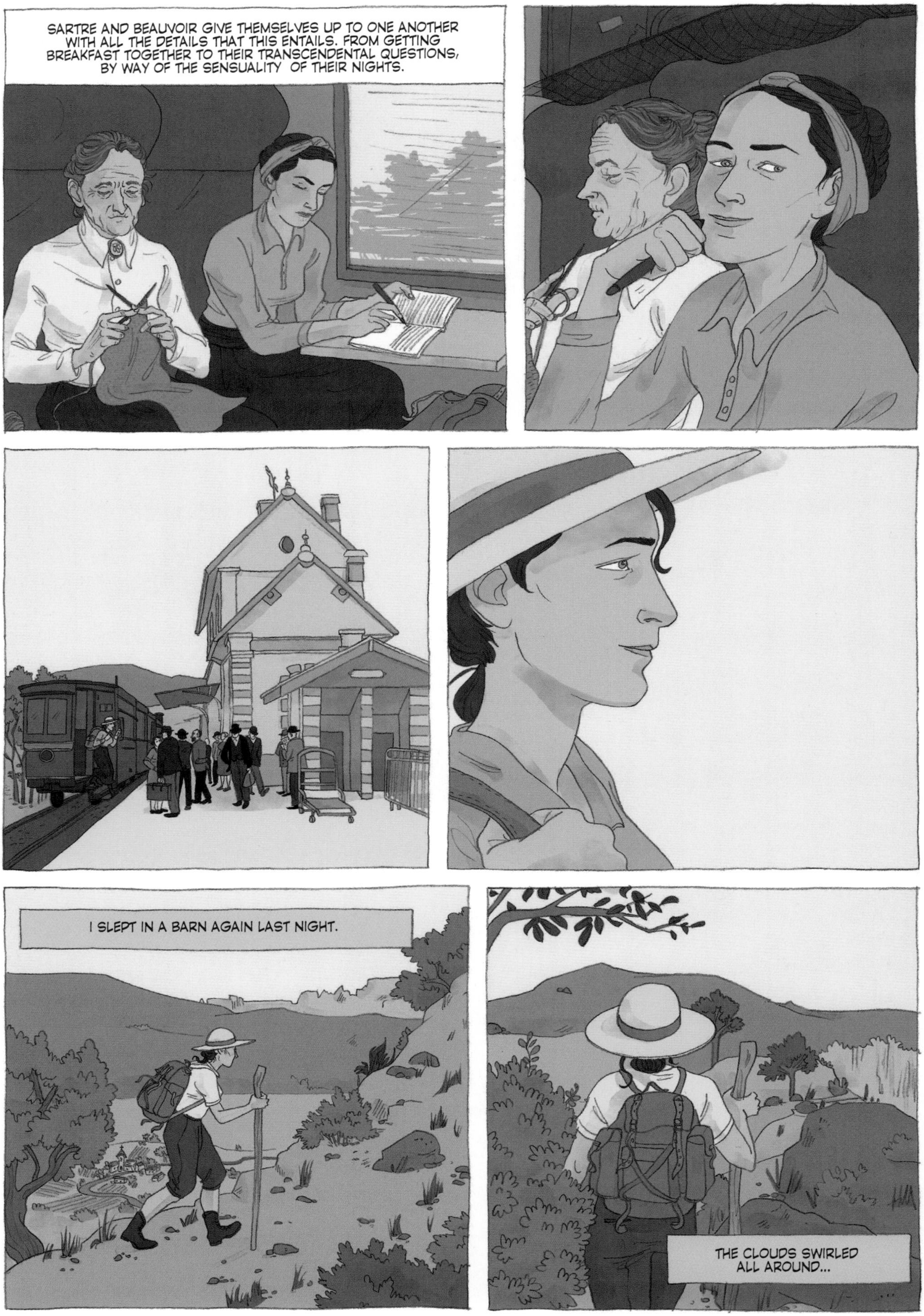

SARTRE AND BEAUVOIR GIVE THEMSELVES UP TO ONE ANOTHER WITH ALL THE DETAILS THAT THIS ENTAILS. FROM GETTING BREAKFAST TOGETHER TO THEIR TRANSCENDENTAL QUESTIONS, BY WAY OF THE SENSUALITY OF THEIR NIGHTS.
I SLEPT IN A BARN AGAIN LAST NIGHT.
THE CLOUDS SWIRLED ALL AROUND...

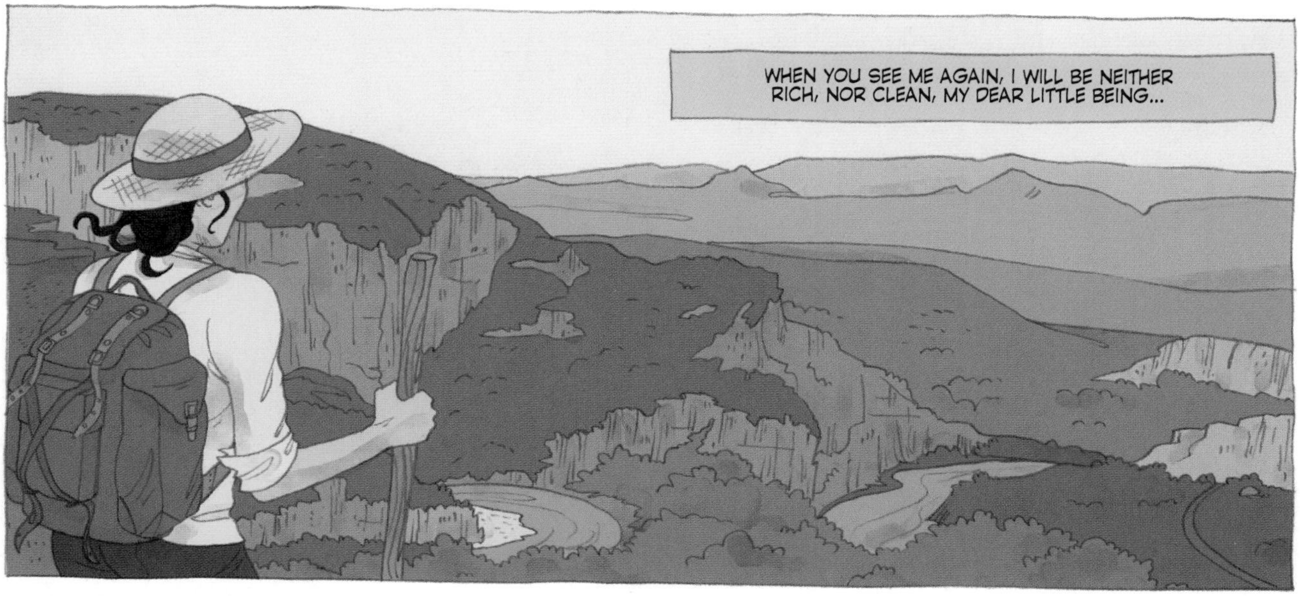
WHEN YOU SEE ME AGAIN, I WILL BE NEITHER RICH, NOR CLEAN, MY DEAR LITTLE BEING...

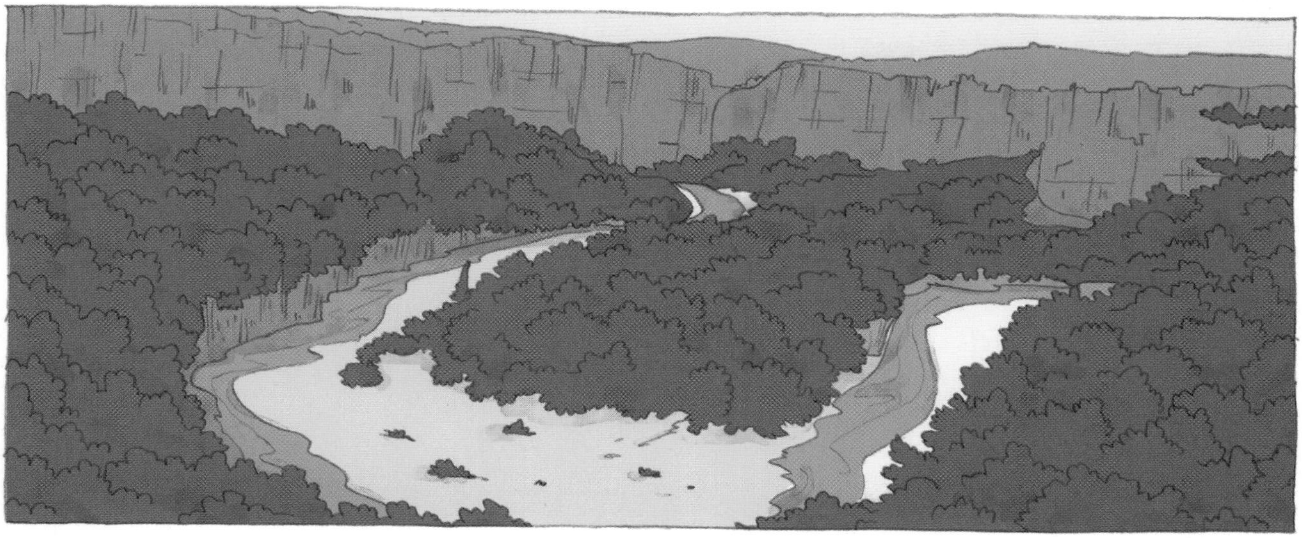

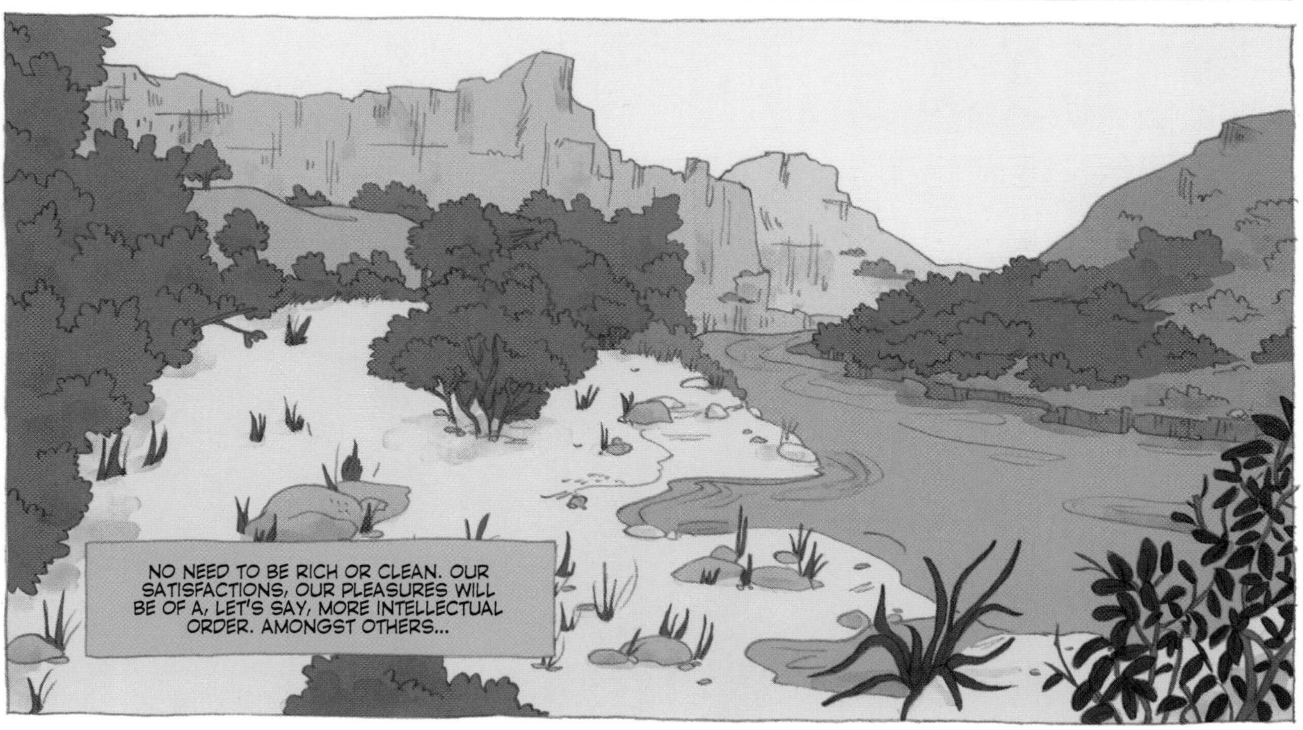
NO NEED TO BE RICH OR CLEAN. OUR SATISFACTIONS, OUR PLEASURES WILL BE OF A, LET'S SAY, MORE INTELLECTUAL ORDER. AMONGST OTHERS...

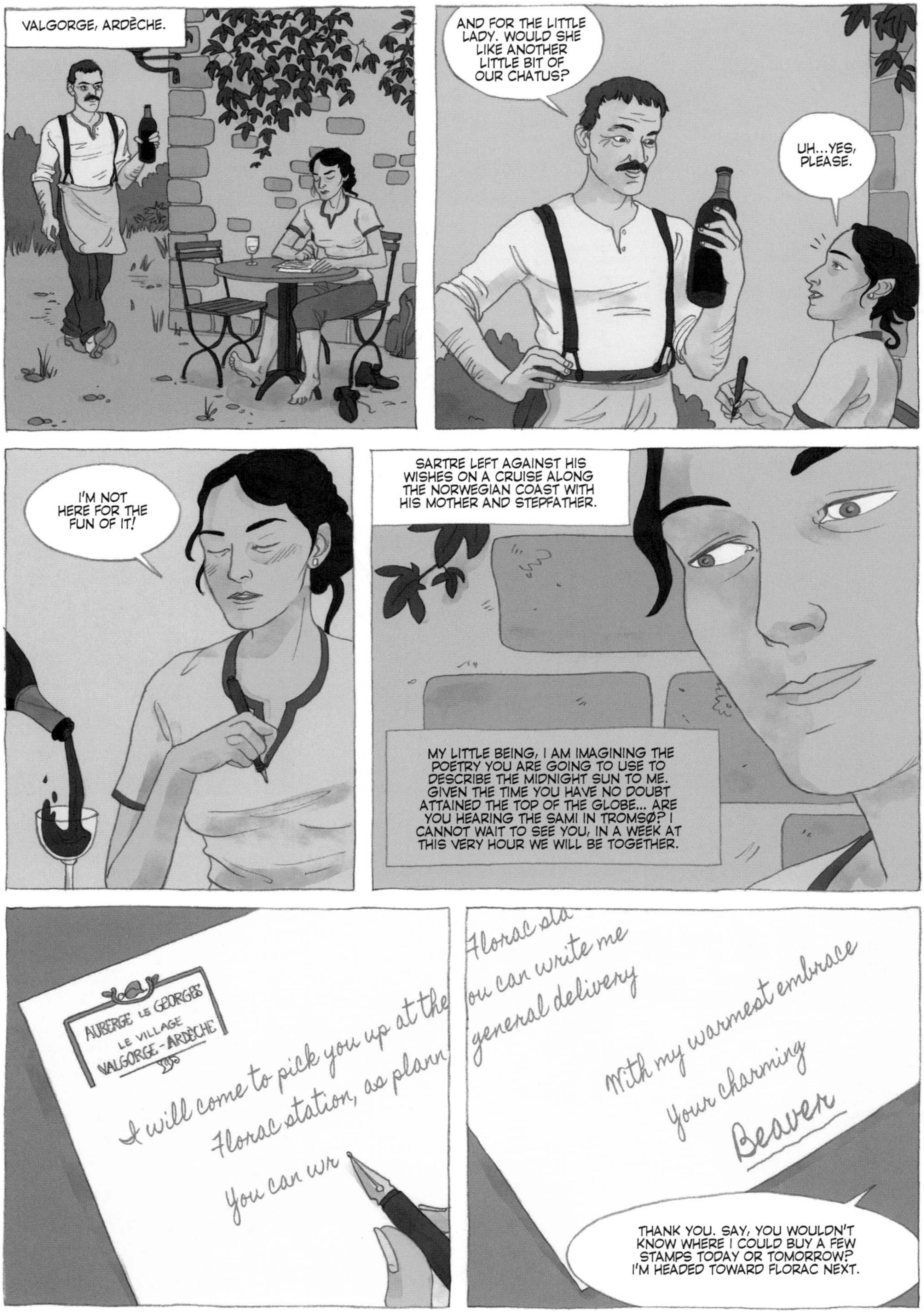
VALGORGE, ARDÈCHE.
AND FOR THE LITTLE LADY. WOULD SHE LIKE ANOTHER LITTLE BIT OF OUR CHATUS?
UH...YES, PLEASE.
I'M NOT HERE FOR THE FUN OF IT!
SARTRE LEFT AGAINST HIS WISHES ON A CRUISE ALONG THE NORWEGIAN COAST WITH HIS MOTHER AND STEPFATHER.
MY LITTLE BEING, I AM IMAGINING THE POETRY YOU ARE GOING TO USE TO DESCRIBE THE MIDNIGHT SUN TO ME. GIVEN THE TIME YOU HAVE NO DOUBT ATTAINED THE TOP OF THE GLOBE... ARE YOU HEARING THE SAMI IN TROMSØ? I CANNOT WAIT TO SEE YOU, IN A WEEK AT THIS VERY HOUR WE WILL BE TOGETHER.
AUBERGE LE GEORGES LE VILLAGE VALGORGE - ARDÈCHE
I will come to pick you up at the Florac station, as plann
You can wr
Florac sta
ou can write me general delivery
With my warmest embrace
Your charming
Beaver
THANK YOU. SAY, YOU WOULDN'T KNOW WHERE I COULD BUY A FEW STAMPS TODAY OR TOMORROW? I'M HEADED TOWARD FLORAC NEXT.

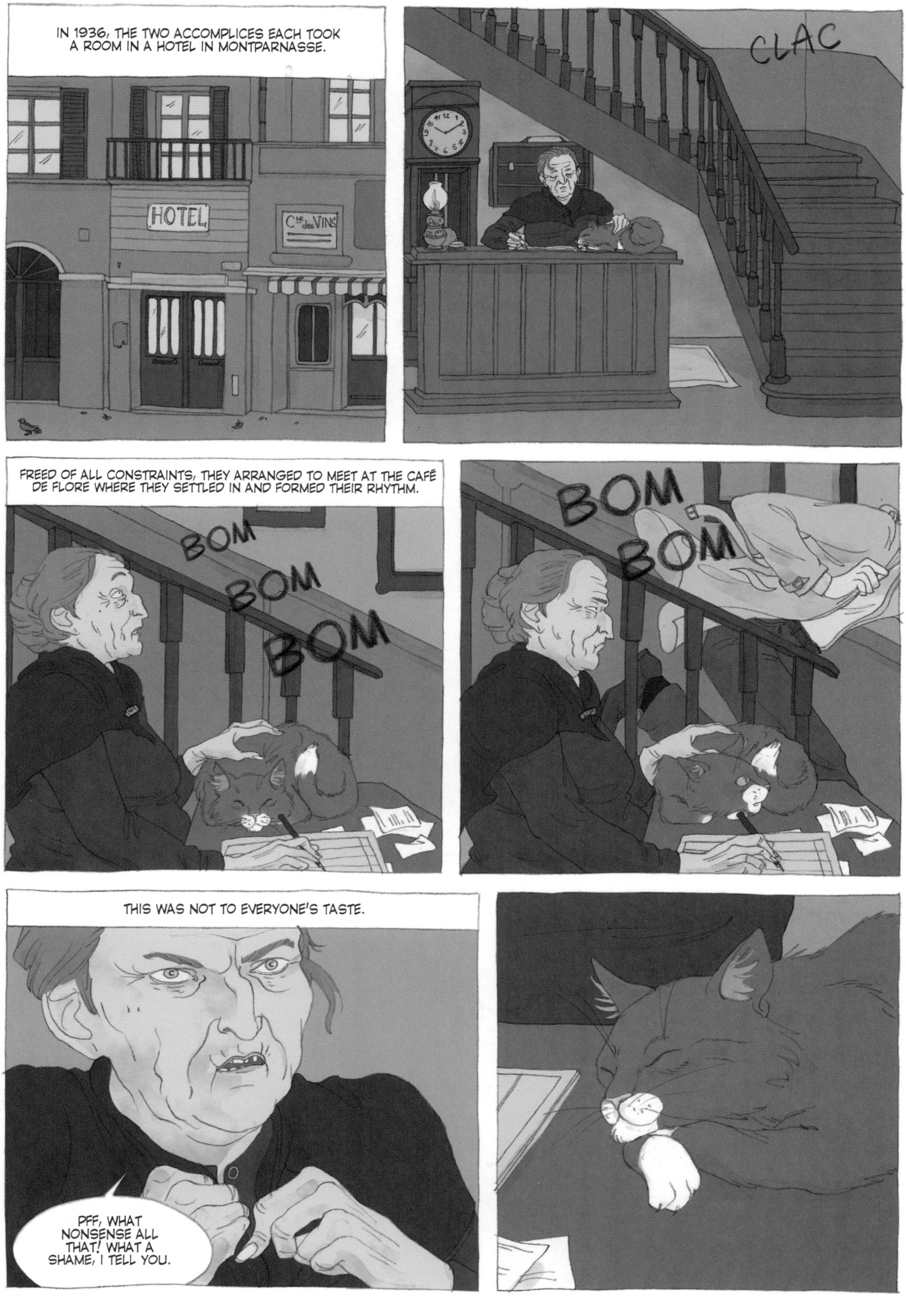

IN 1936, THE TWO ACCOMPLICES EACH TOOK A ROOM IN A HOTEL IN MONTPARNASSE.
HOTEL
Cie des VINS
CLAC
FREED OF ALL CONSTRAINTS, THEY ARRANGED TO MEET AT THE CAFÉ DE FLORE WHERE THEY SETTLED IN AND FORMED THEIR RHYTHM.
BOM BOM BOM
BOM BOM
THIS WAS NOT TO EVERYONE'S TASTE.
PFF, WHAT NONSENSE ALL THAT! WHAT A SHAME, I TELL YOU.

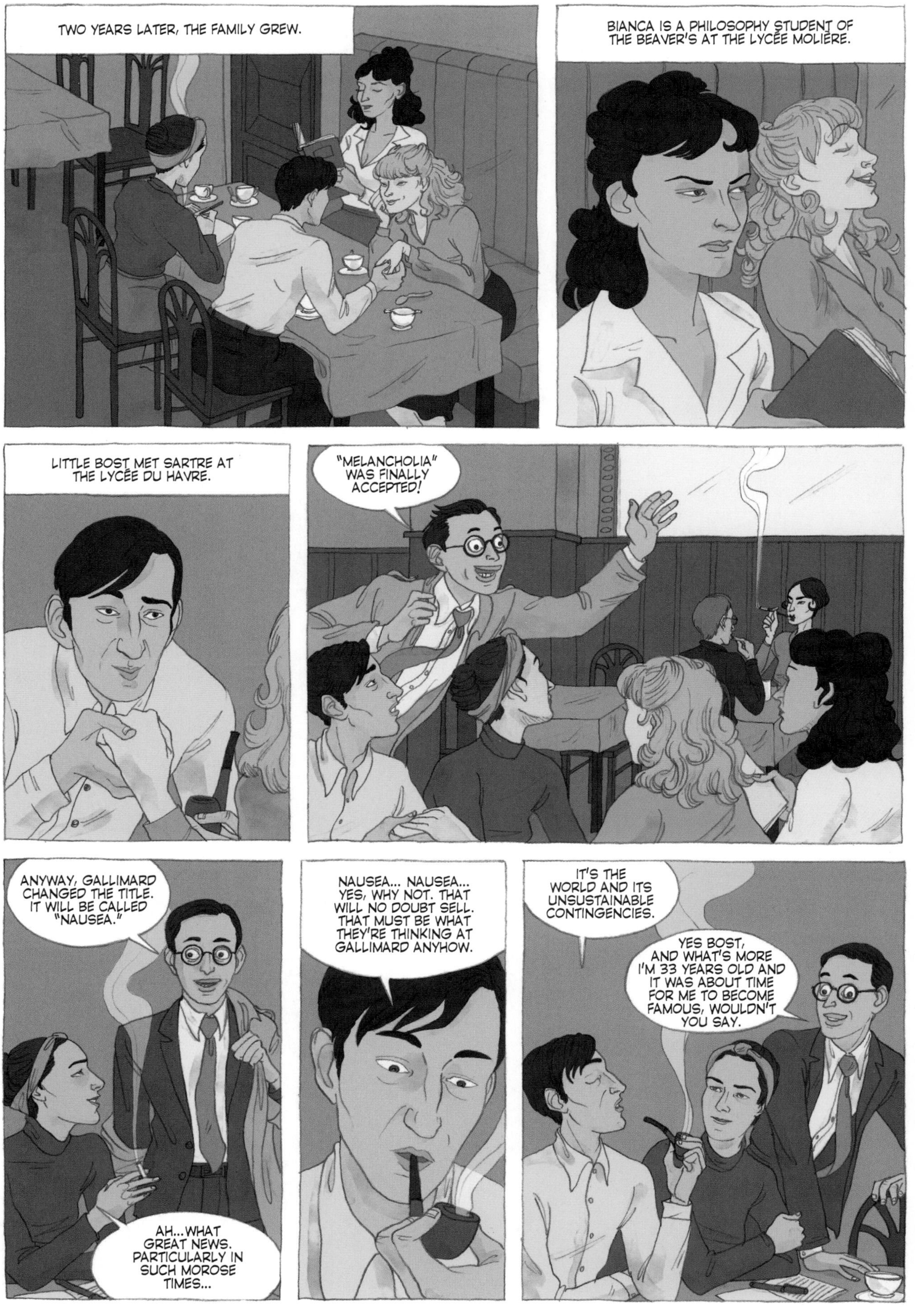
TWO YEARS LATER, THE FAMILY GREW.
BIANCA IS A PHILOSOPHY STUDENT OF THE BEAVER'S AT THE LYCÉE MOLIÈRE.
LITTLE BOST MET SARTRE AT THE LYCÉE DU HAVRE.
"MELANCHOLIA" WAS FINALLY ACCEPTED!
ANYWAY, GALLIMARD CHANGED THE TITLE. IT WILL BE CALLED "NAUSEA."
AH...WHAT GREAT NEWS. PARTICULARLY IN SUCH MOROSE TIMES...
NAUSEA... NAUSEA... YES, WHY NOT. THAT WILL NO DOUBT SELL. THAT MUST BE WHAT THEY'RE THINKING AT GALLIMARD ANYHOW.
IT'S THE WORLD AND ITS UNSUSTAINABLE CONTINGENCIES.
YES BOST, AND WHAT'S MORE I'M 33 YEARS OLD AND IT WAS ABOUT TIME FOR ME TO BECOME FAMOUS, WOULDN'T YOU SAY.

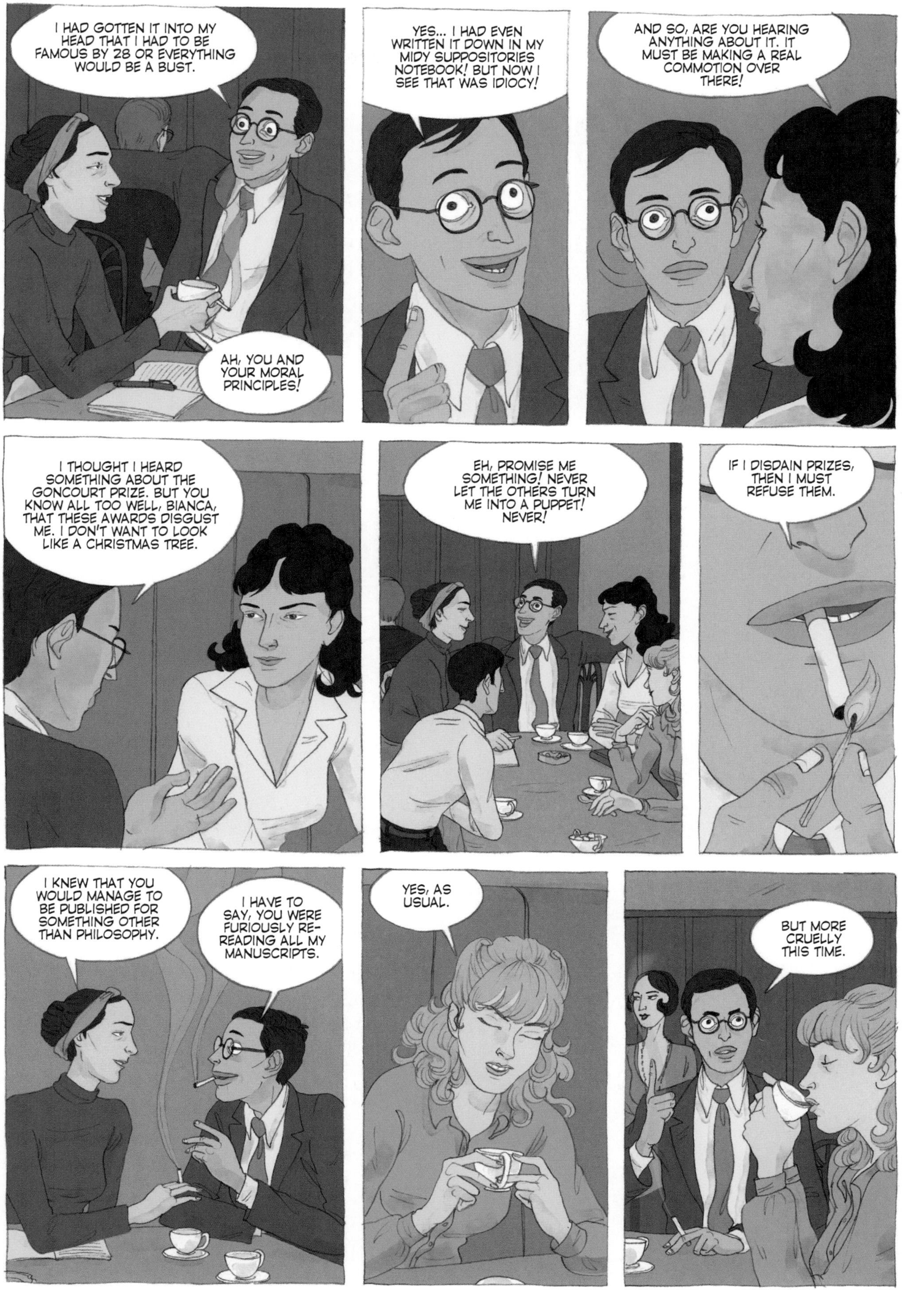
I HAD GOTTEN IT INTO MY HEAD THAT I HAD TO BE FAMOUS BY 28 OR EVERYTHING WOULD BE A BUST.
AH, YOU AND YOUR MORAL PRINCIPLES!
YES... I HAD EVEN WRITTEN IT DOWN IN MY MIDY SUPPOSITORIES NOTEBOOK! BUT NOW I SEE THAT WAS IDIOCY!
AND SO, ARE YOU HEARING ANYTHING ABOUT IT. IT MUST BE MAKING A REAL COMMOTION OVER THERE!
I THOUGHT I HEARD SOMETHING ABOUT THE GONCOURT PRIZE. BUT YOU KNOW ALL TOO WELL, BIANCA, THAT THESE AWARDS DISGUST ME. I DON'T WANT TO LOOK LIKE A CHRISTMAS TREE.
EH, PROMISE ME SOMETHING! NEVER LET THE OTHERS TURN ME INTO A PUPPET! NEVER!
IF I DISDAIN PRIZES, THEN I MUST REFUSE THEM.
I KNEW THAT YOU WOULD MANAGE TO BE PUBLISHED FOR SOMETHING OTHER THAN PHILOSOPHY.
I HAVE TO SAY, YOU WERE FURIOUSLY RE-READING ALL MY MANUSCRIPTS.
YES, AS USUAL.
BUT MORE CRUELLY THIS TIME.

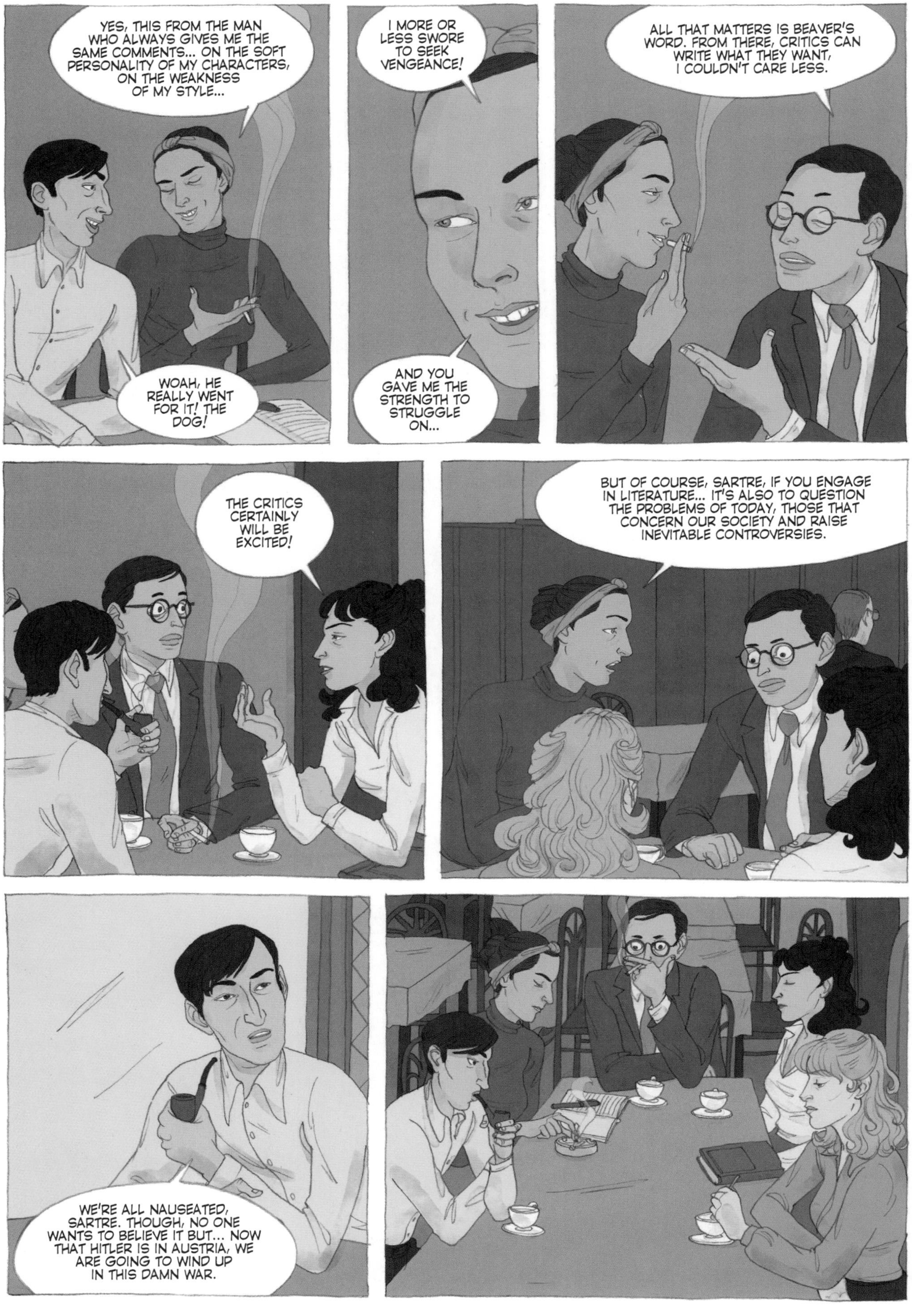
YES, THIS FROM THE MAN WHO ALWAYS GIVES ME THE SAME COMMENTS... ON THE SOFT PERSONALITY OF MY CHARACTERS, ON THE WEAKNESS OF MY STYLE...
WOAH, HE REALLY WENT FOR IT! THE DOG!
I MORE OR LESS SWORE TO SEEK VENGEANCE!
AND YOU GAVE ME THE STRENGTH TO STRUGGLE ON...
ALL THAT MATTERS IS BEAVER'S WORD. FROM THERE, CRITICS CAN WRITE WHAT THEY WANT, I COULDN'T CARE LESS.
THE CRITICS CERTAINLY WILL BE EXCITED!
BUT OF COURSE, SARTRE, IF YOU ENGAGE IN LITERATURE... IT'S ALSO TO QUESTION THE PROBLEMS OF TODAY, THOSE THAT CONCERN OUR SOCIETY AND RAISE INEVITABLE CONTROVERSIES.
WE'RE ALL NAUSEATED, SARTRE. THOUGH, NO ONE WANTS TO BELIEVE IT BUT... NOW THAT HITLER IS IN AUSTRIA, WE ARE GOING TO WIND UP IN THIS DAMN WAR.

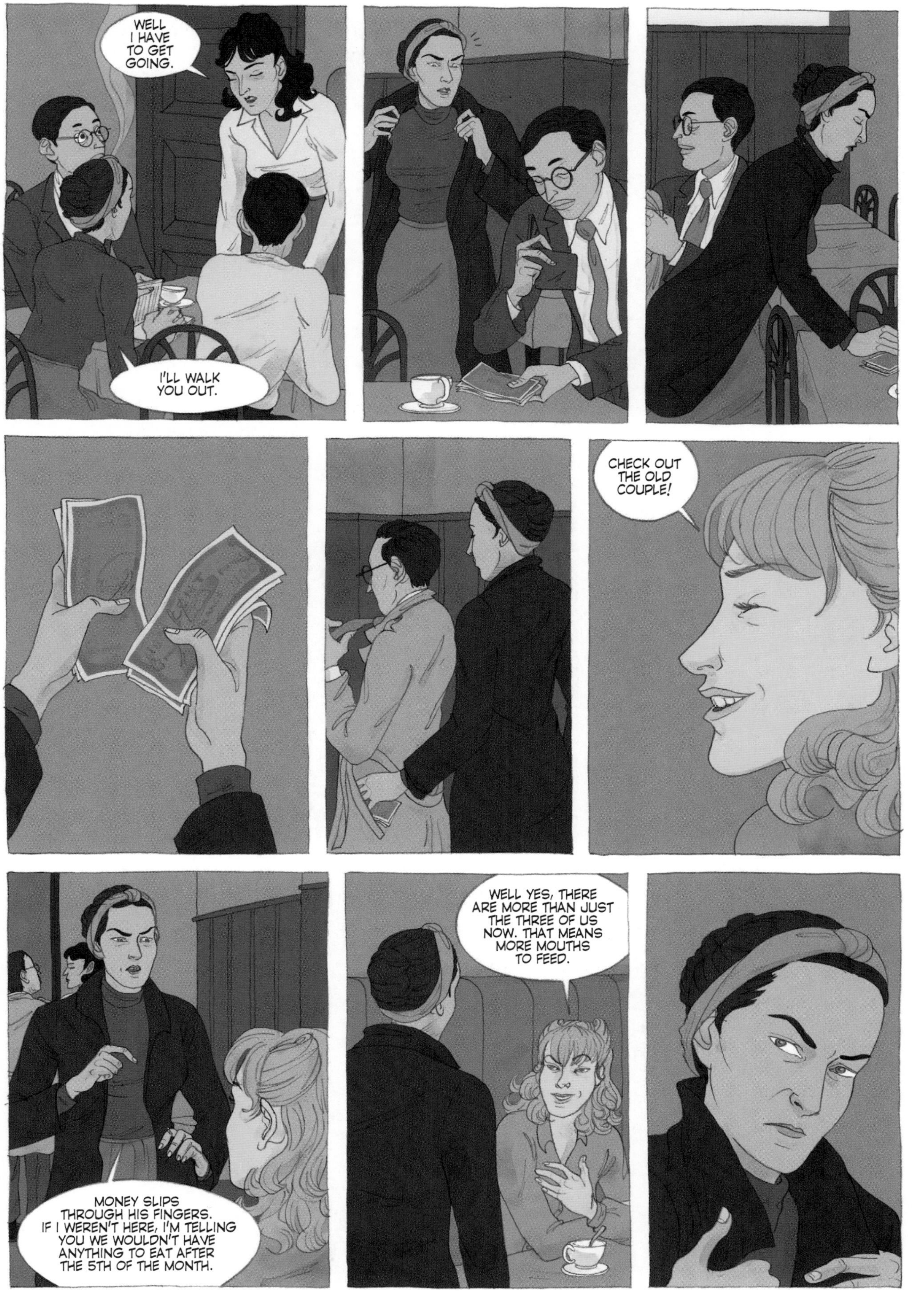
WELL I HAVE TO GET GOING.
I'LL WALK YOU OUT.
CHECK OUT THE OLD COUPLE!
MONEY SLIPS THROUGH HIS FINGERS. IF I WEREN'T HERE, I'M TELLING YOU WE WOULDN'T HAVE ANYTHING TO EAT AFTER THE 5TH OF THE MONTH.
WELL YES, THERE ARE MORE THAN JUST THE THREE OF US NOW. THAT MEANS MORE MOUTHS TO FEED.

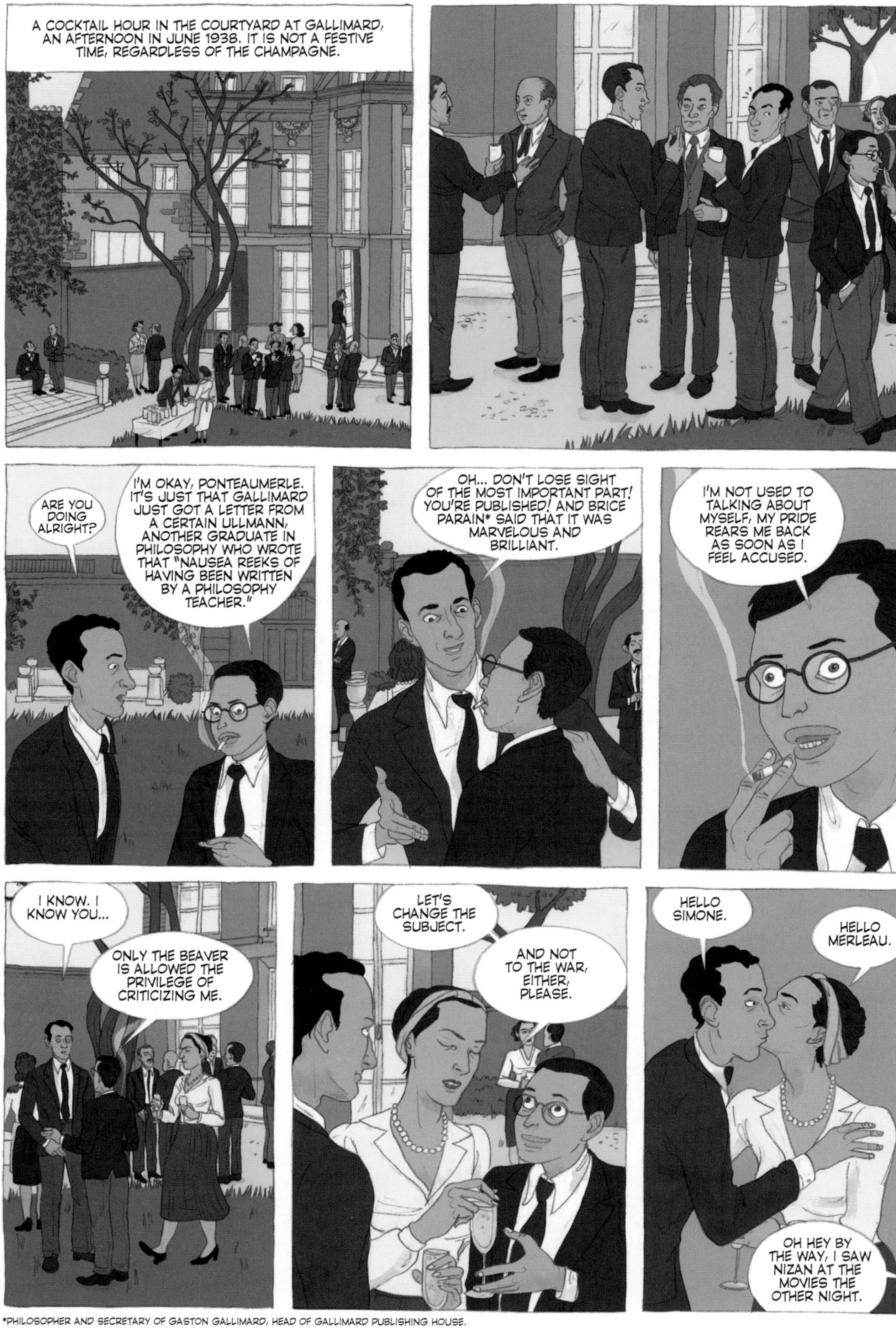
A COCKTAIL HOUR IN THE COURTYARD AT GALLIMARD, AN AFTERNOON IN JUNE 1938. IT IS NOT A FESTIVE TIME, REGARDLESS OF THE CHAMPAGNE.
ARE YOU DOING ALRIGHT?
I'M OKAY, PONTEAUMERLE. IT'S JUST THAT GALLIMARD JUST GOT A LETTER FROM A CERTAIN ULLMANN, ANOTHER GRADUATE IN PHILOSOPHY WHO WROTE THAT "NAUSEA REEKS OF HAVING BEEN WRITTEN BY A PHILOSOPHY TEACHER."
OH... DON'T LOSE SIGHT OF THE MOST IMPORTANT PART! YOU'RE PUBLISHED! AND BRICE PARAIN* SAID THAT IT WAS MARVELOUS AND BRILLIANT.
I'M NOT USED TO TALKING ABOUT MYSELF, MY PRIDE REARS ME BACK AS SOON AS I FEEL ACCUSED.
I KNOW. I KNOW YOU...
ONLY THE BEAVER IS ALLOWED THE PRIVILEGE OF CRITICIZING ME.
LET'S CHANGE THE SUBJECT.
AND NOT TO THE WAR, EITHER, PLEASE.
HELLO SIMONE.
HELLO MERLEAU.
OH HEY BY THE WAY, I SAW NIZAN AT THE MOVIES THE OTHER NIGHT.

*PHILOSOPHER AND SECRETARY OF GASTON GALLIMARD, HEAD OF GALLIMARD PUBLISHING HOUSE.

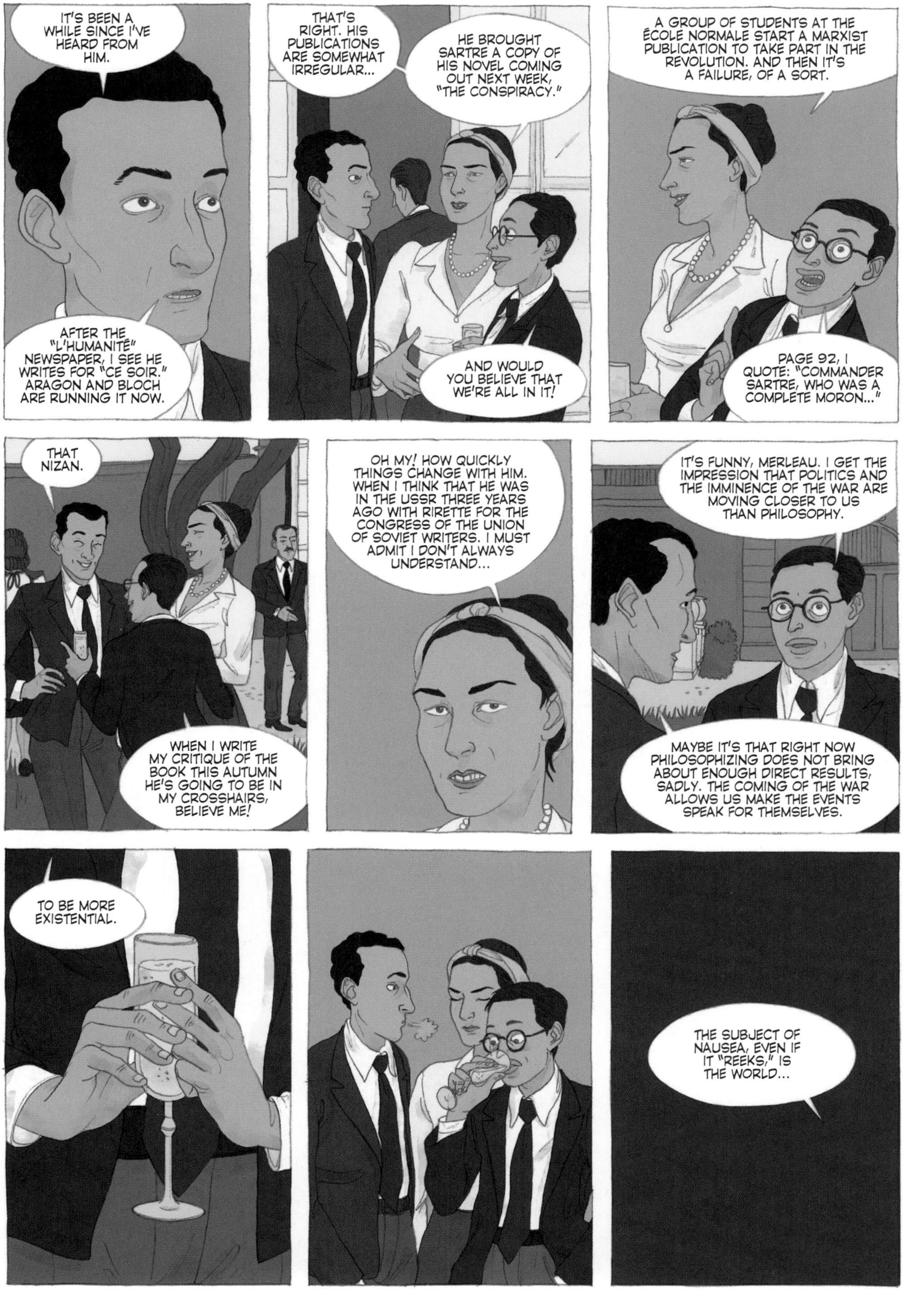
IT'S BEEN A WHILE SINCE I'VE HEARD FROM HIM.
AFTER THE "L'HUMANITÉ" NEWSPAPER, I SEE HE WRITES FOR "CE SOIR." ARAGON AND BLOCH ARE RUNNING IT NOW.
THAT'S RIGHT. HIS PUBLICATIONS ARE SOMEWHAT IRREGULAR...
HE BROUGHT SARTRE A COPY OF HIS NOVEL COMING OUT NEXT WEEK, "THE CONSPIRACY."
AND WOULD YOU BELIEVE THAT WE'RE ALL IN IT!
A GROUP OF STUDENTS AT THE ÉCOLE NORMALE START A MARXIST PUBLICATION TO TAKE PART IN THE REVOLUTION. AND THEN IT'S A FAILURE, OF A SORT.
PAGE 92, I QUOTE: "COMMANDER SARTRE, WHO WAS A COMPLETE MORON..."
THAT NIZAN.
WHEN I WRITE MY CRITIQUE OF THE BOOK THIS AUTUMN HE'S GOING TO BE IN MY CROSSHAIRS, BELIEVE ME!
OH MY! HOW QUICKLY THINGS CHANGE WITH HIM. WHEN I THINK THAT HE WAS IN THE USSR THREE YEARS AGO WITH RIRETTE FOR THE CONGRESS OF THE UNION OF SOVIET WRITERS. I MUST ADMIT I DON'T ALWAYS UNDERSTAND...
IT'S FUNNY, MERLEAU. I GET THE IMPRESSION THAT POLITICS AND THE IMMINENCE OF THE WAR ARE MOVING CLOSER TO US THAN PHILOSOPHY.
MAYBE IT'S THAT RIGHT NOW PHILOSOPHIZING DOES NOT BRING ABOUT ENOUGH DIRECT RESULTS, SADLY. THE COMING OF THE WAR ALLOWS US MAKE THE EVENTS SPEAK FOR THEMSELVES.
TO BE MORE EXISTENTIAL.
THE SUBJECT OF NAUSEA, EVEN IF IT "REEKS," IS THE WORLD...

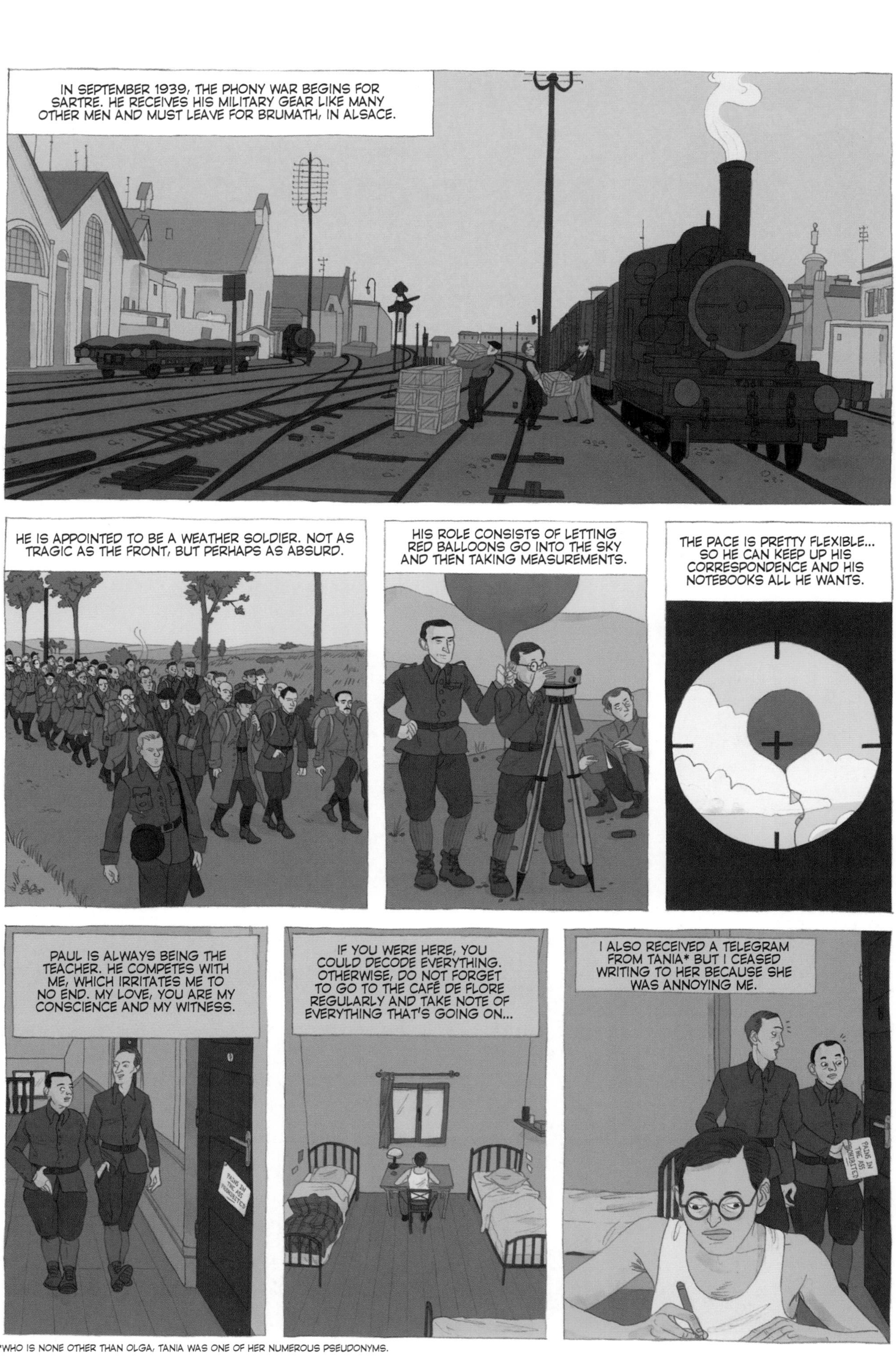
IN SEPTEMBER 1939, THE PHONY WAR BEGINS FOR SARTRE. HE RECEIVES HIS MILITARY GEAR LIKE MANY OTHER MEN AND MUST LEAVE FOR BRUMATH, IN ALSACE.
HE IS APPOINTED TO BE A WEATHER SOLDIER. NOT AS TRAGIC AS THE FRONT, BUT PERHAPS AS ABSURD.
HIS ROLE CONSISTS OF LETTING RED BALLOONS GO INTO THE SKY AND THEN TAKING MEASUREMENTS.
THE PACE IS PRETTY FLEXIBLE... SO HE CAN KEEP UP HIS CORRESPONDENCE AND HIS NOTEBOOKS ALL HE WANTS.
PAUL IS ALWAYS BEING THE TEACHER. HE COMPETES WITH ME, WHICH IRRITATES ME TO NO END. MY LOVE, YOU ARE MY CONSCIENCE AND MY WITNESS.
IF YOU WERE HERE, YOU COULD DECODE EVERYTHING. OTHERWISE, DO NOT FORGET TO GO TO THE CAFÉ DE FLORE REGULARLY AND TAKE NOTE OF EVERYTHING THAT'S GOING ON...
I ALSO RECEIVED A TELEGRAM FROM TANIA* BUT I CEASED WRITING TO HER BECAUSE SHE WAS ANNOYING ME.

*WHO IS NONE OTHER THAN OLGA, TANIA WAS ONE OF HER NUMEROUS PSEUDONYMS.

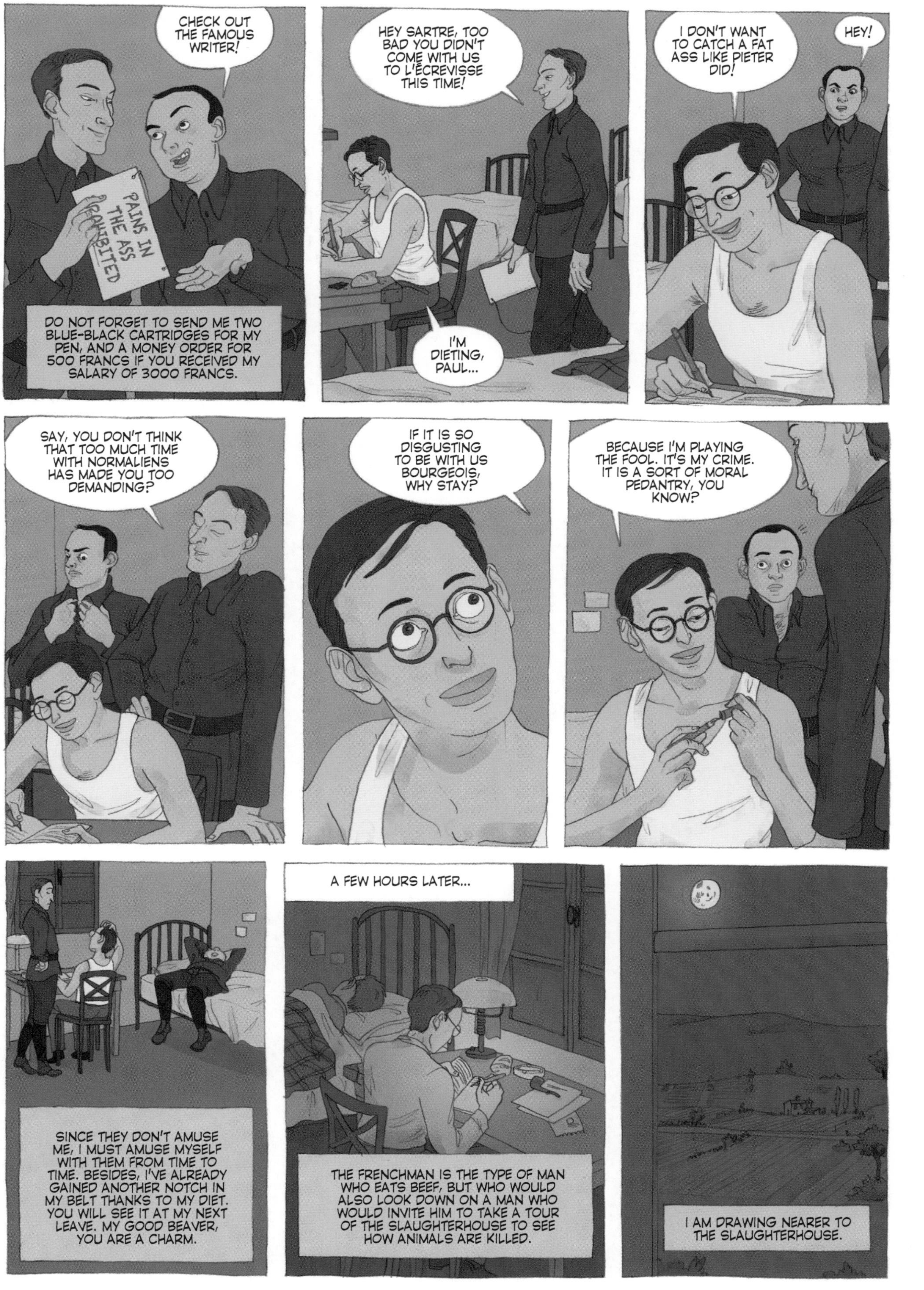
CHECK OUT THE FAMOUS WRITER!
PAINS IN THE ASS PROHIBITED
DO NOT FORGET TO SEND ME TWO BLUE-BLACK CARTRIDGES FOR MY PEN, AND A MONEY ORDER FOR 500 FRANCS IF YOU RECEIVED MY SALARY OF 3000 FRANCS.
HEY SARTRE, TOO BAD YOU DIDN'T COME WITH US TO L'ÉCREVISSE THIS TIME!
I'M DIETING, PAUL...
I DON'T WANT TO CATCH A FAT ASS LIKE PIETER DID!
HEY!
SAY, YOU DON'T THINK THAT TOO MUCH TIME WITH NORMALIENS HAS MADE YOU TOO DEMANDING?
IF IT IS SO DISGUSTING TO BE WITH US BOURGEOIS, WHY STAY?
BECAUSE I'M PLAYING THE FOOL. IT'S MY CRIME. IT IS A SORT OF MORAL PEDANTRY, YOU KNOW?
SINCE THEY DON'T AMUSE ME, I MUST AMUSE MYSELF WITH THEM FROM TIME TO TIME. BESIDES, I'VE ALREADY GAINED ANOTHER NOTCH IN MY BELT THANKS TO MY DIET. YOU WILL SEE IT AT MY NEXT LEAVE. MY GOOD BEAVER, YOU ARE A CHARM.
A FEW HOURS LATER...
THE FRENCHMAN IS THE TYPE OF MAN WHO EATS BEEF, BUT WHO WOULD ALSO LOOK DOWN ON A MAN WHO WOULD INVITE HIM TO TAKE A TOUR OF THE SLAUGHTERHOUSE TO SEE HOW ANIMALS ARE KILLED.
I AM DRAWING NEARER TO THE SLAUGHTERHOUSE.

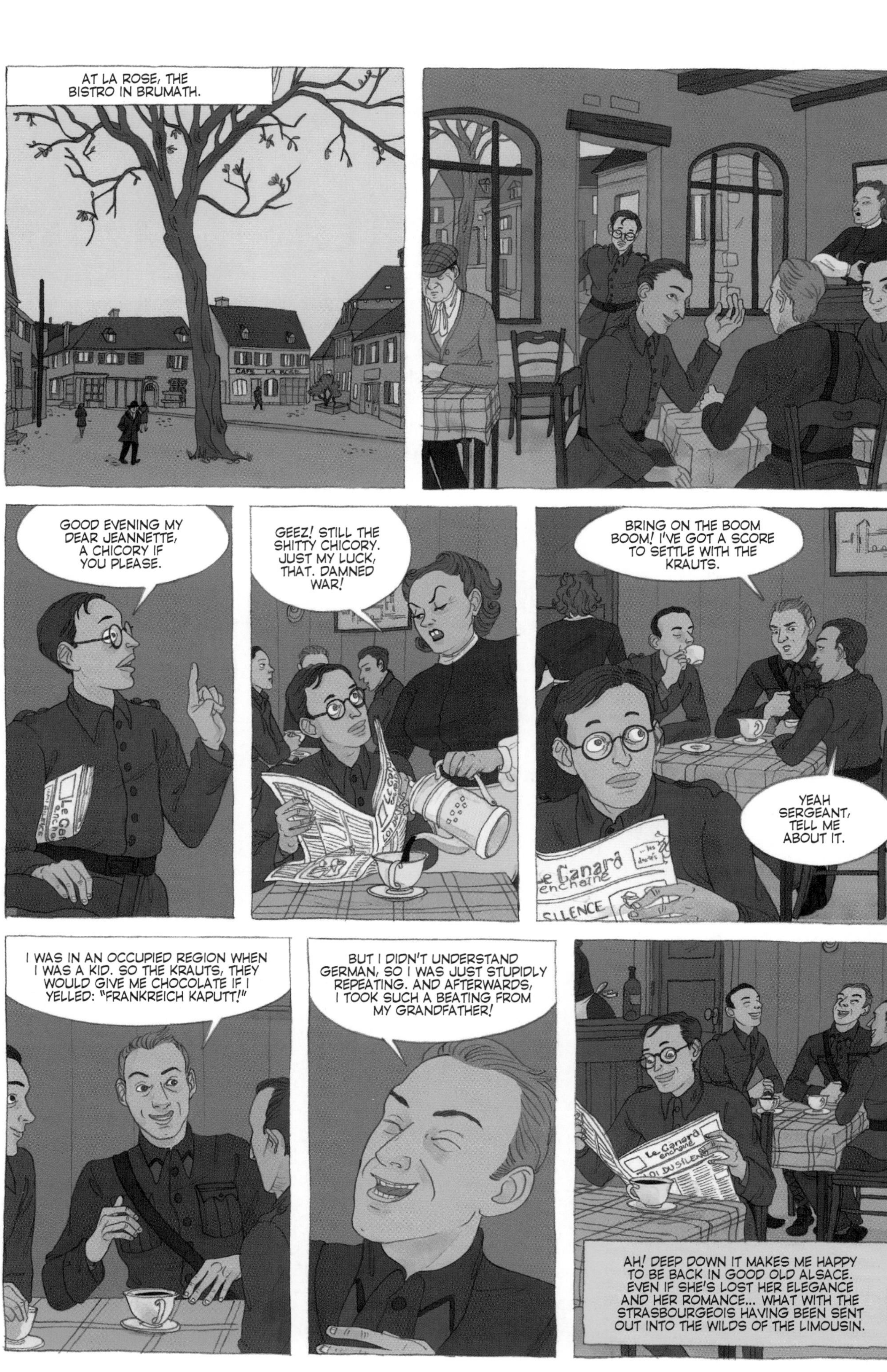
AT LA ROSE, THE BISTRO IN BRUMATH.
GOOD EVENING MY DEAR JEANNETTE, A CHICORY IF YOU PLEASE.
GEEZ! STILL THE SHITTY CHICORY. JUST MY LUCK, THAT. DAMNED WAR!
BRING ON THE BOOM BOOM! I'VE GOT A SCORE TO SETTLE WITH THE KRAUTS.
YEAH SERGEANT, TELL ME ABOUT IT.
I WAS IN AN OCCUPIED REGION WHEN I WAS A KID. SO THE KRAUTS, THEY WOULD GIVE ME CHOCOLATE IF I YELLED: "FRANKREICH KAPUTT!"
BUT I DIDN'T UNDERSTAND GERMAN, SO I WAS JUST STUPIDLY REPEATING. AND AFTERWARDS, I TOOK SUCH A BEATING FROM MY GRANDFATHER!
AH! DEEP DOWN IT MAKES ME HAPPY TO BE BACK IN GOOD OLD ALSACE. EVEN IF SHE'S LOST HER ELEGANCE AND HER ROMANCE... WHAT WITH THE STRASBOURGEOIS HAVING BEEN SENT OUT INTO THE WILDS OF THE LIMOUSIN.

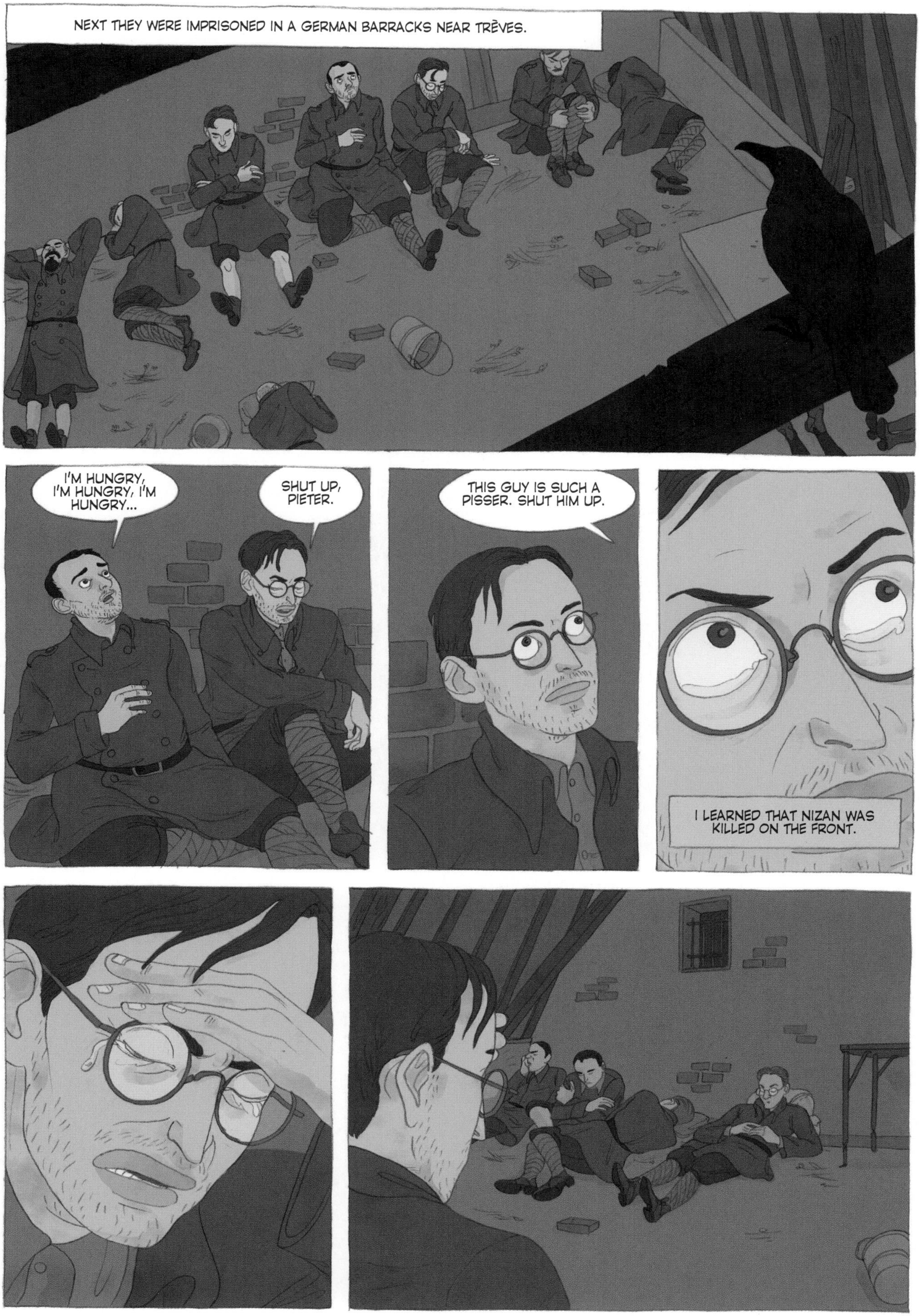
NEXT THEY WERE IMPRISONED IN A GERMAN BARRACKS NEAR TRÈVES.
I'M HUNGRY, I'M HUNGRY, I'M HUNGRY...
SHUT UP, PIETER.
THIS GUY IS SUCH A PISSER. SHUT HIM UP.
I LEARNED THAT NIZAN WAS KILLED ON THE FRONT.

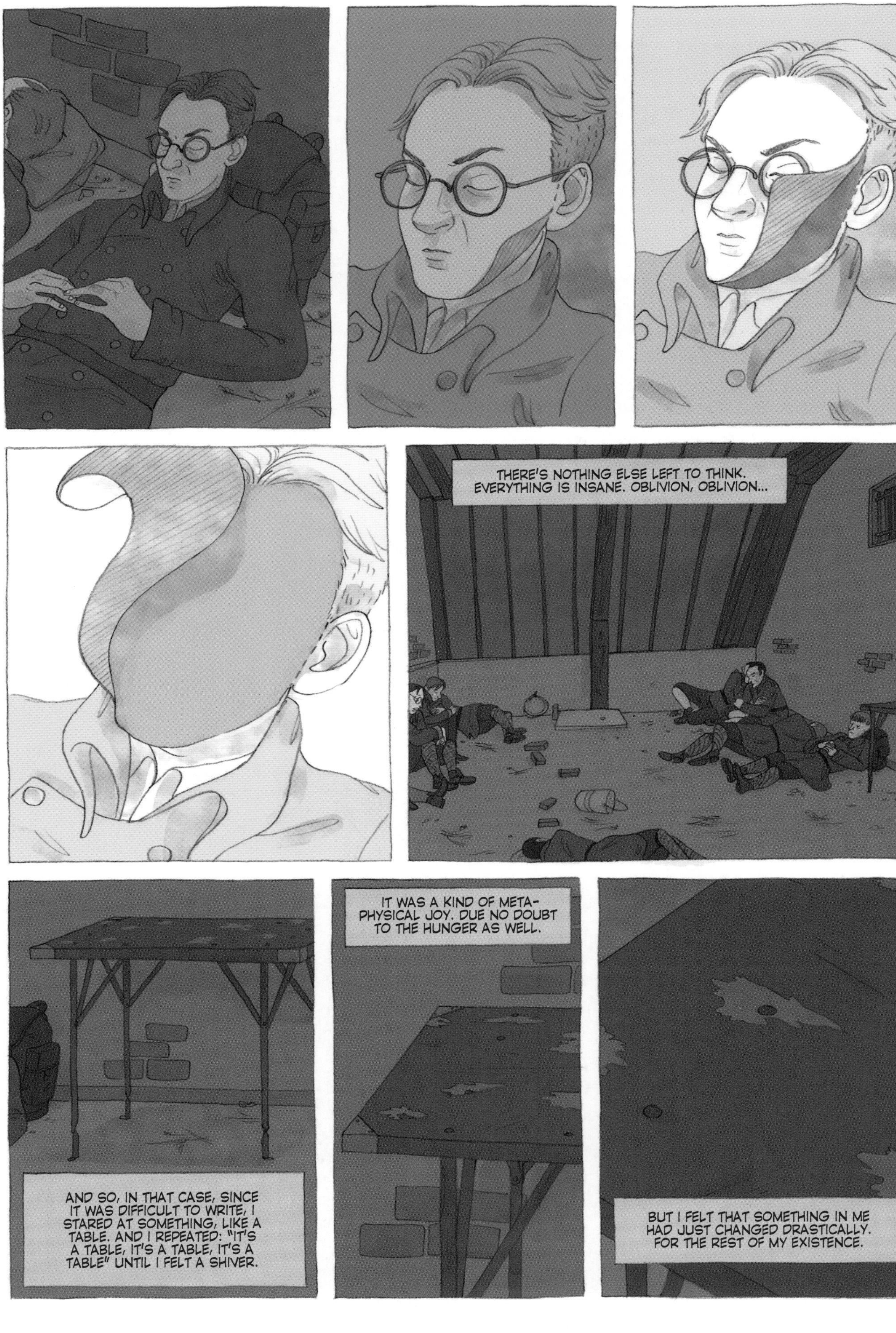
THERE'S NOTHING ELSE LEFT TO THINK. EVERYTHING IS INSANE. OBLIVION, OBLIVION...
AND SO, IN THAT CASE, SINCE IT WAS DIFFICULT TO WRITE, I STARED AT SOMETHING, LIKE A TABLE. AND I REPEATED: "IT'S A TABLE, IT'S A TABLE, IT'S A TABLE" UNTIL I FELT A SHIVER.
IT WAS A KIND OF META-PHYSICAL JOY. DUE NO DOUBT TO THE HUNGER AS WELL.
BUT I FELT THAT SOMETHING IN ME HAD JUST CHANGED DRASTICALLY. FOR THE REST OF MY EXISTENCE.

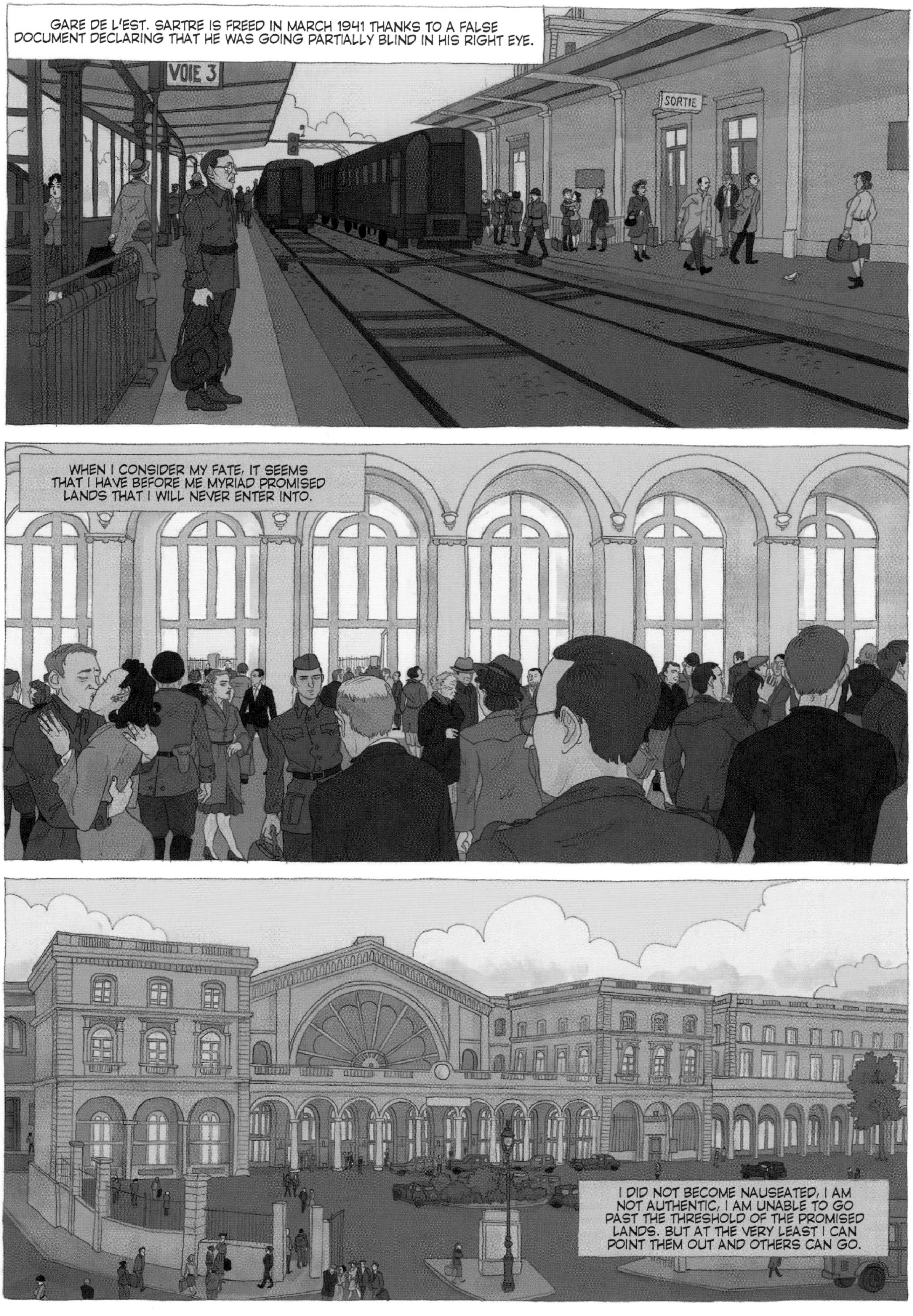
GARE DE L'EST. SARTRE IS FREED IN MARCH 1941 THANKS TO A FALSE DOCUMENT DECLARING THAT HE WAS GOING PARTIALLY BLIND IN HIS RIGHT EYE.
VOIE 3
SORTIE
WHEN I CONSIDER MY FATE, IT SEEMS THAT I HAVE BEFORE ME MYRIAD PROMISED LANDS THAT I WILL NEVER ENTER INTO.
I DID NOT BECOME NAUSEATED, I AM NOT AUTHENTIC, I AM UNABLE TO GO PAST THE THRESHOLD OF THE PROMISED LANDS. BUT AT THE VERY LEAST I CAN POINT THEM OUT AND OTHERS CAN GO.

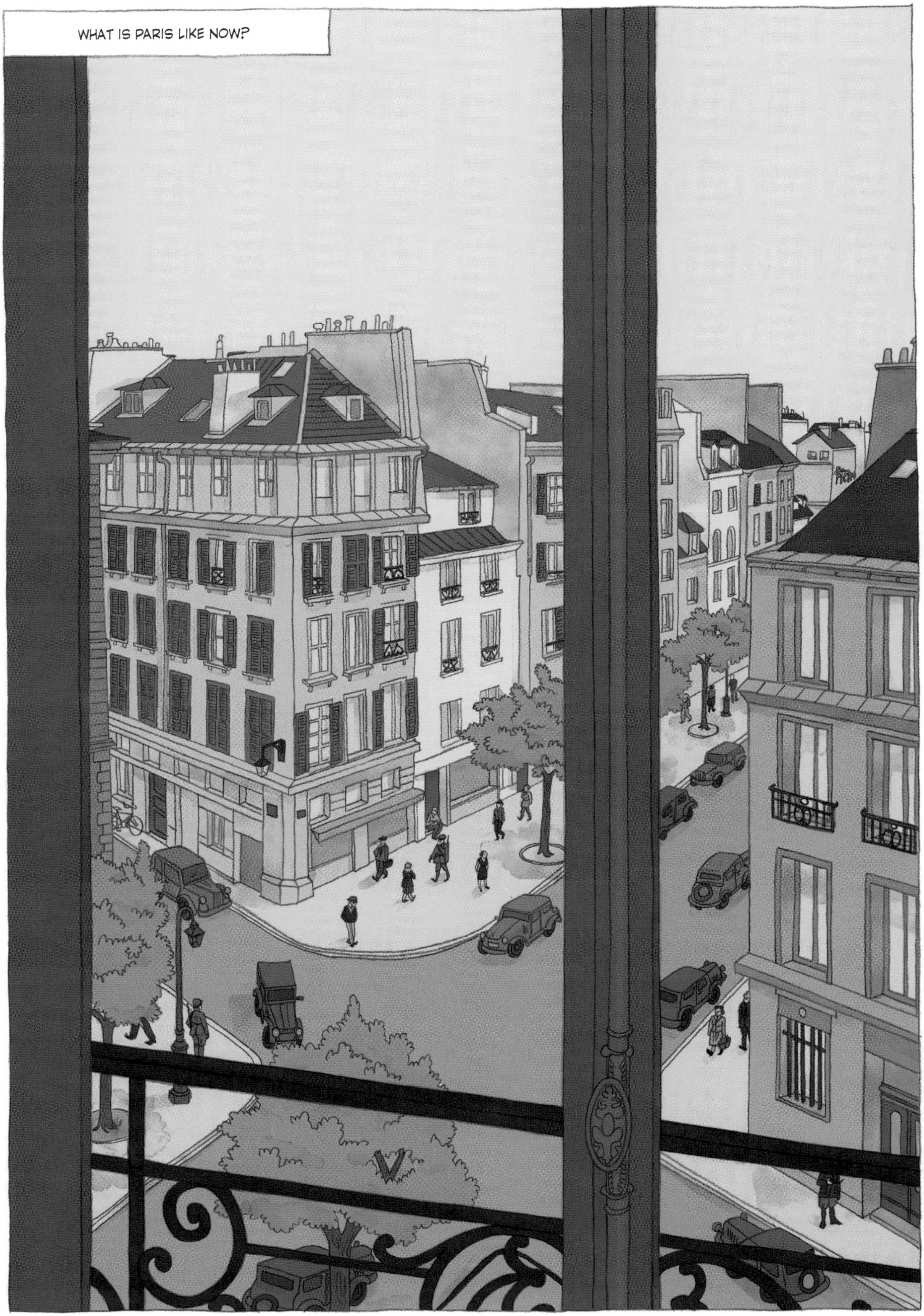
WHAT IS PARIS LIKE NOW?

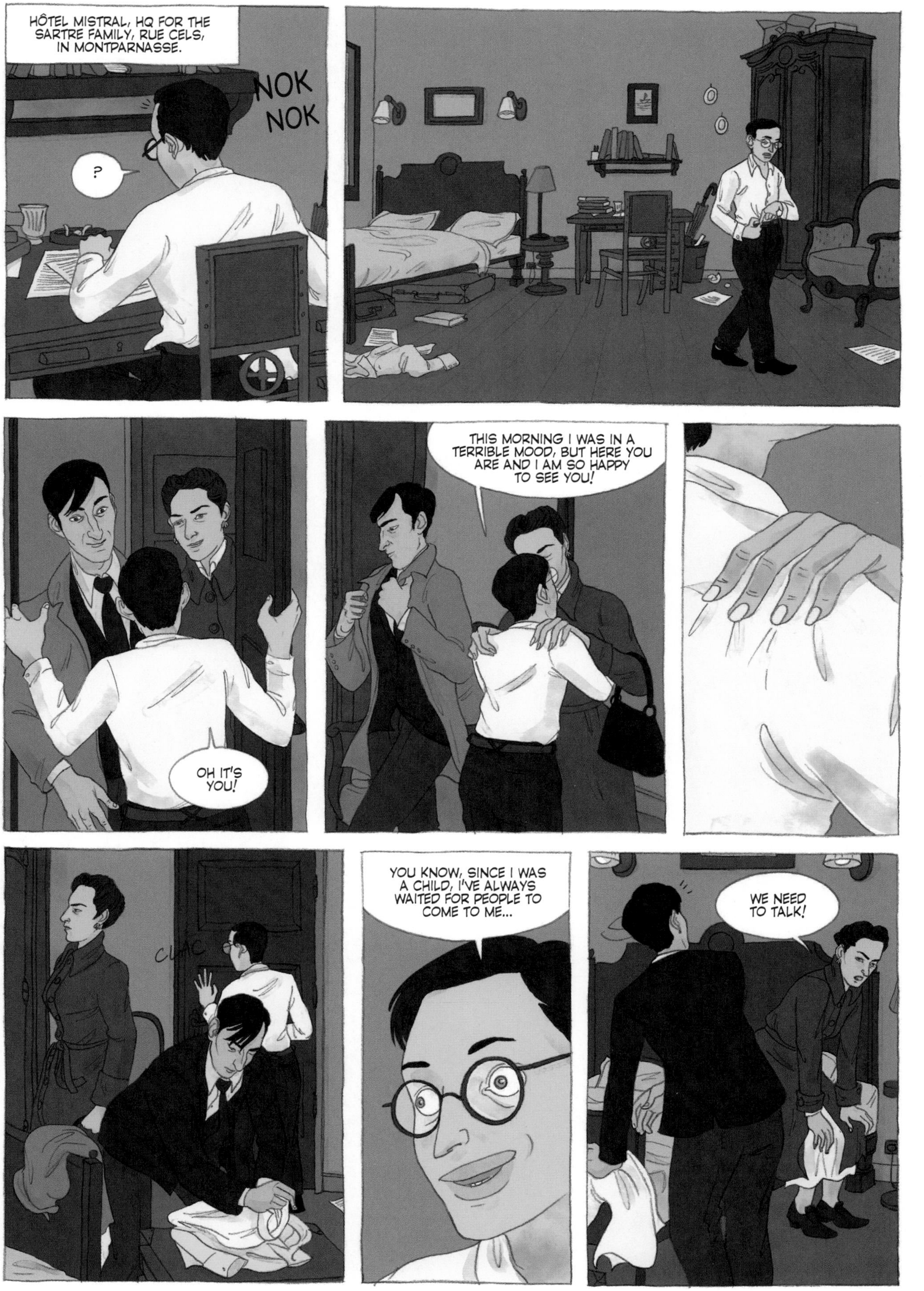
HÔTEL MISTRAL, HQ FOR THE SARTRE FAMILY, RUE CELS, IN MONTPARNASSE.
NOK NOK
?
OH IT'S YOU!
THIS MORNING I WAS IN A TERRIBLE MOOD, BUT HERE YOU ARE AND I AM SO HAPPY TO SEE YOU!
CLAC
YOU KNOW, SINCE I WAS A CHILD, I'VE ALWAYS WAITED FOR PEOPLE TO COME TO ME...
WE NEED TO TALK!

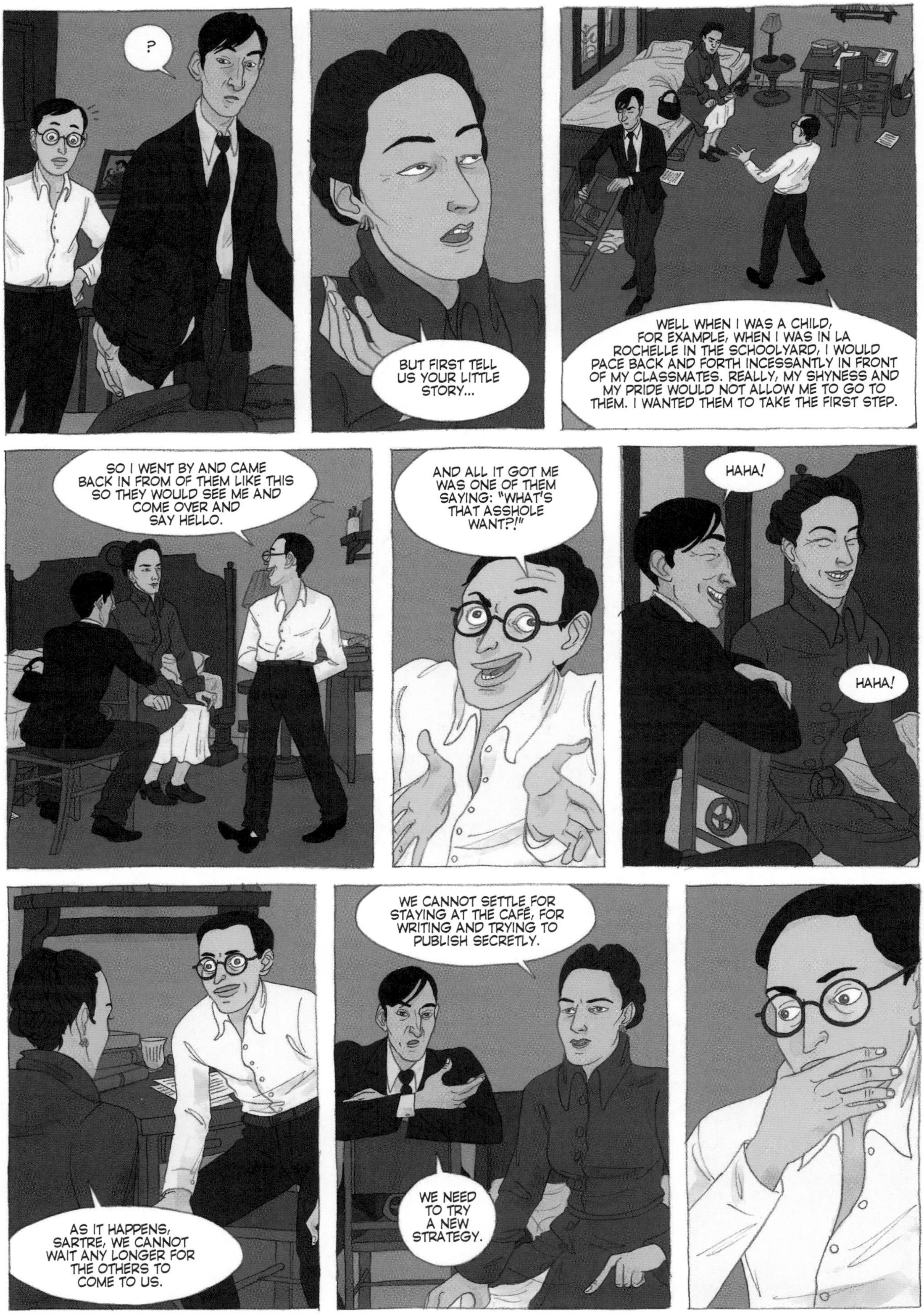
?
BUT FIRST TELL US YOUR LITTLE STORY...
WELL WHEN I WAS A CHILD, FOR EXAMPLE, WHEN I WAS IN LA ROCHELLE IN THE SCHOOLYARD, I WOULD PACE BACK AND FORTH INCESSANTLY IN FRONT OF MY CLASSMATES. REALLY, MY SHYNESS AND MY PRIDE WOULD NOT ALLOW ME TO GO TO THEM. I WANTED THEM TO TAKE THE FIRST STEP.
SO I WENT BY AND CAME BACK IN FROM OF THEM LIKE THIS SO THEY WOULD SEE ME AND COME OVER AND SAY HELLO.
AND ALL IT GOT ME WAS ONE OF THEM SAYING: "WHAT'S THAT ASSHOLE WANT?!"
HAHA!
HAHA!
AS IT HAPPENS, SARTRE, WE CANNOT WAIT ANY LONGER FOR THE OTHERS TO COME TO US.
WE CANNOT SETTLE FOR STAYING AT THE CAFÉ, FOR WRITING AND TRYING TO PUBLISH SECRETLY.
WE NEED TO TRY A NEW STRATEGY.

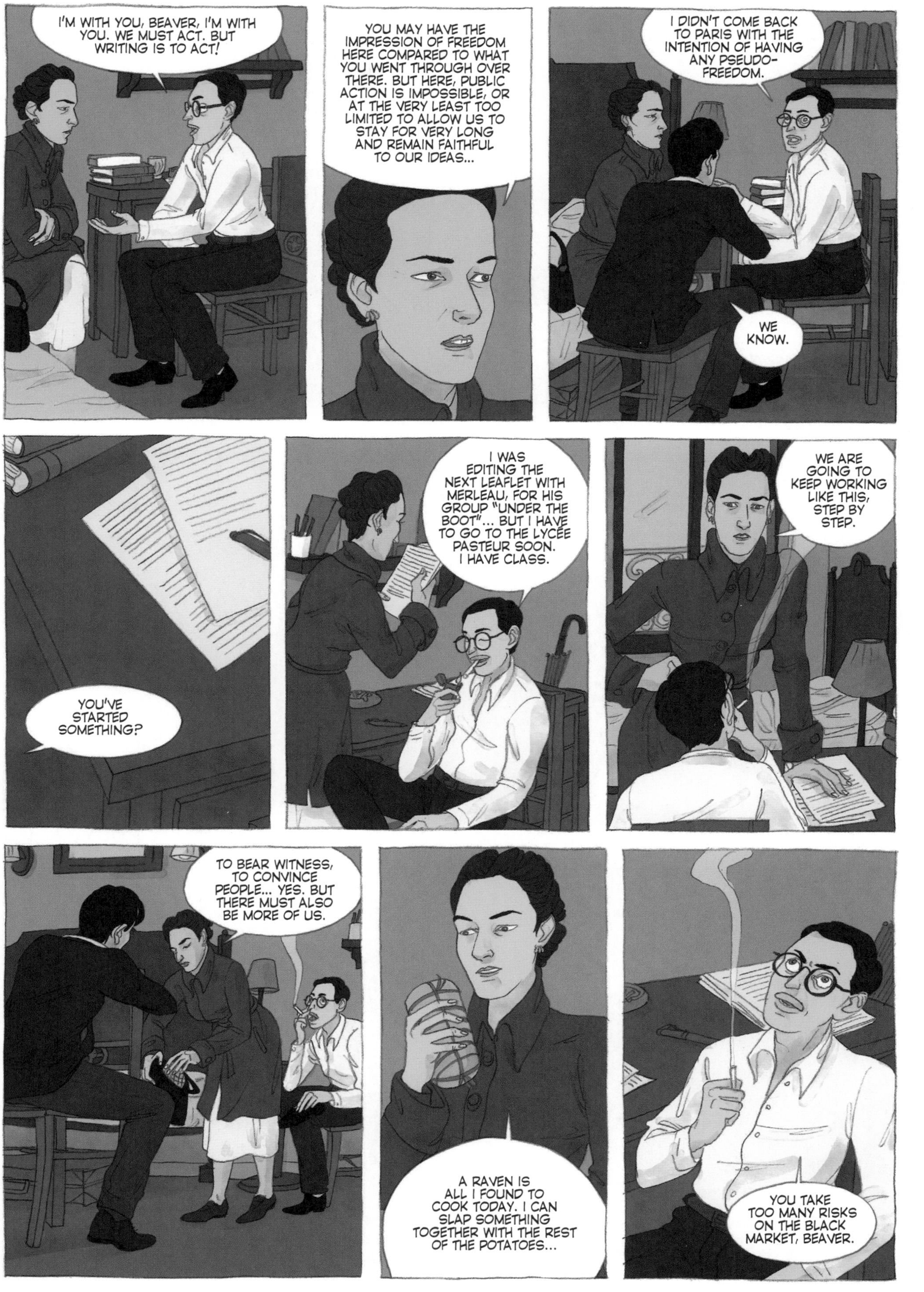
I'M WITH YOU, BEAVER, I'M WITH YOU. WE MUST ACT. BUT WRITING IS TO ACT!
YOU MAY HAVE THE IMPRESSION OF FREEDOM HERE COMPARED TO WHAT YOU WENT THROUGH OVER THERE. BUT HERE, PUBLIC ACTION IS IMPOSSIBLE, OR AT THE VERY LEAST TOO LIMITED TO ALLOW US TO STAY FOR VERY LONG AND REMAIN FAITHFUL TO OUR IDEAS...
I DIDN'T COME BACK TO PARIS WITH THE INTENTION OF HAVING ANY PSEUDO-FREEDOM.
WE KNOW.
YOU'VE STARTED SOMETHING?
I WAS EDITING THE NEXT LEAFLET WITH MERLEAU, FOR HIS GROUP "UNDER THE BOOT"... BUT I HAVE TO GO TO THE LYCÉE PASTEUR SOON. I HAVE CLASS.
WE ARE GOING TO KEEP WORKING LIKE THIS, STEP BY STEP.
TO BEAR WITNESS, TO CONVINCE PEOPLE... YES. BUT THERE MUST ALSO BE MORE OF US.
A RAVEN IS ALL I FOUND TO COOK TODAY. I CAN SLAP SOMETHING TOGETHER WITH THE REST OF THE POTATOES...
YOU TAKE TOO MANY RISKS ON THE BLACK MARKET, BEAVER.

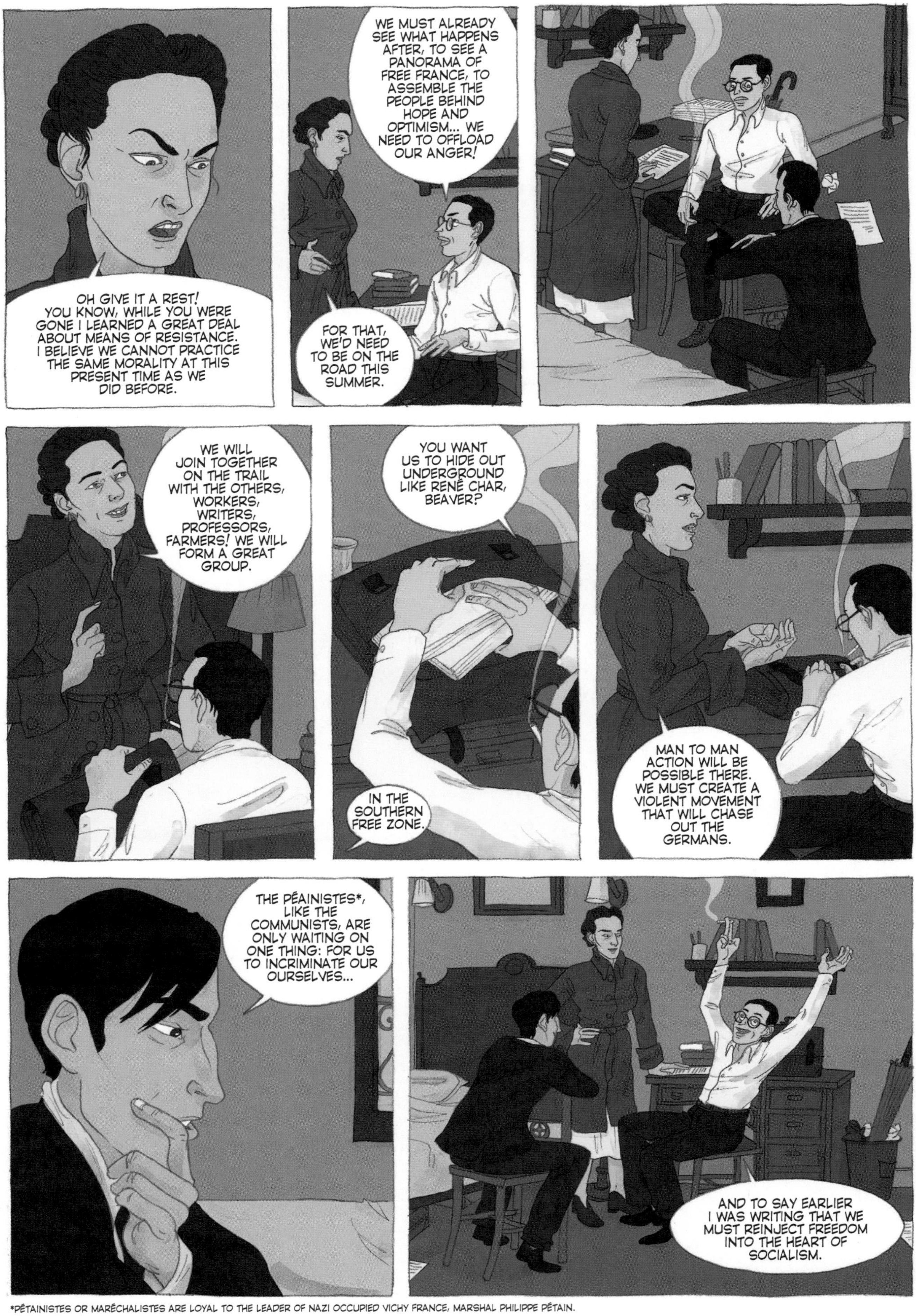
OH GIVE IT A REST! YOU KNOW, WHILE YOU WERE GONE I LEARNED A GREAT DEAL ABOUT MEANS OF RESISTANCE. I BELIEVE WE CANNOT PRACTICE THE SAME MORALITY AT THIS PRESENT TIME AS WE DID BEFORE.
WE MUST ALREADY SEE WHAT HAPPENS AFTER, TO SEE A PANORAMA OF FREE FRANCE, TO ASSEMBLE THE PEOPLE BEHIND HOPE AND OPTIMISM... WE NEED TO OFFLOAD OUR ANGER!
FOR THAT, WE'D NEED TO BE ON THE ROAD THIS SUMMER.
WE WILL JOIN TOGETHER ON THE TRAIL WITH THE OTHERS, WORKERS, WRITERS, PROFESSORS, FARMERS! WE WILL FORM A GREAT GROUP.
YOU WANT US TO HIDE OUT UNDERGROUND LIKE RENÉ CHAR, BEAVER?
IN THE SOUTHERN FREE ZONE.
MAN TO MAN ACTION WILL BE POSSIBLE THERE. WE MUST CREATE A VIOLENT MOVEMENT THAT WILL CHASE OUT THE GERMANS.
THE PÉAINISTES*, LIKE THE COMMUNISTS, ARE ONLY WAITING ON ONE THING: FOR US TO INCRIMINATE OUR OURSELVES...
AND TO SAY EARLIER I WAS WRITING THAT WE MUST REINJECT FREEDOM INTO THE HEART OF SOCIALISM.

*PÉTAINISTES OR MARÉCHALISTES ARE LOYAL TO THE LEADER OF NAZI OCCUPIED VICHY FRANCE, MARSHAL PHILIPPE PÉTAIN.

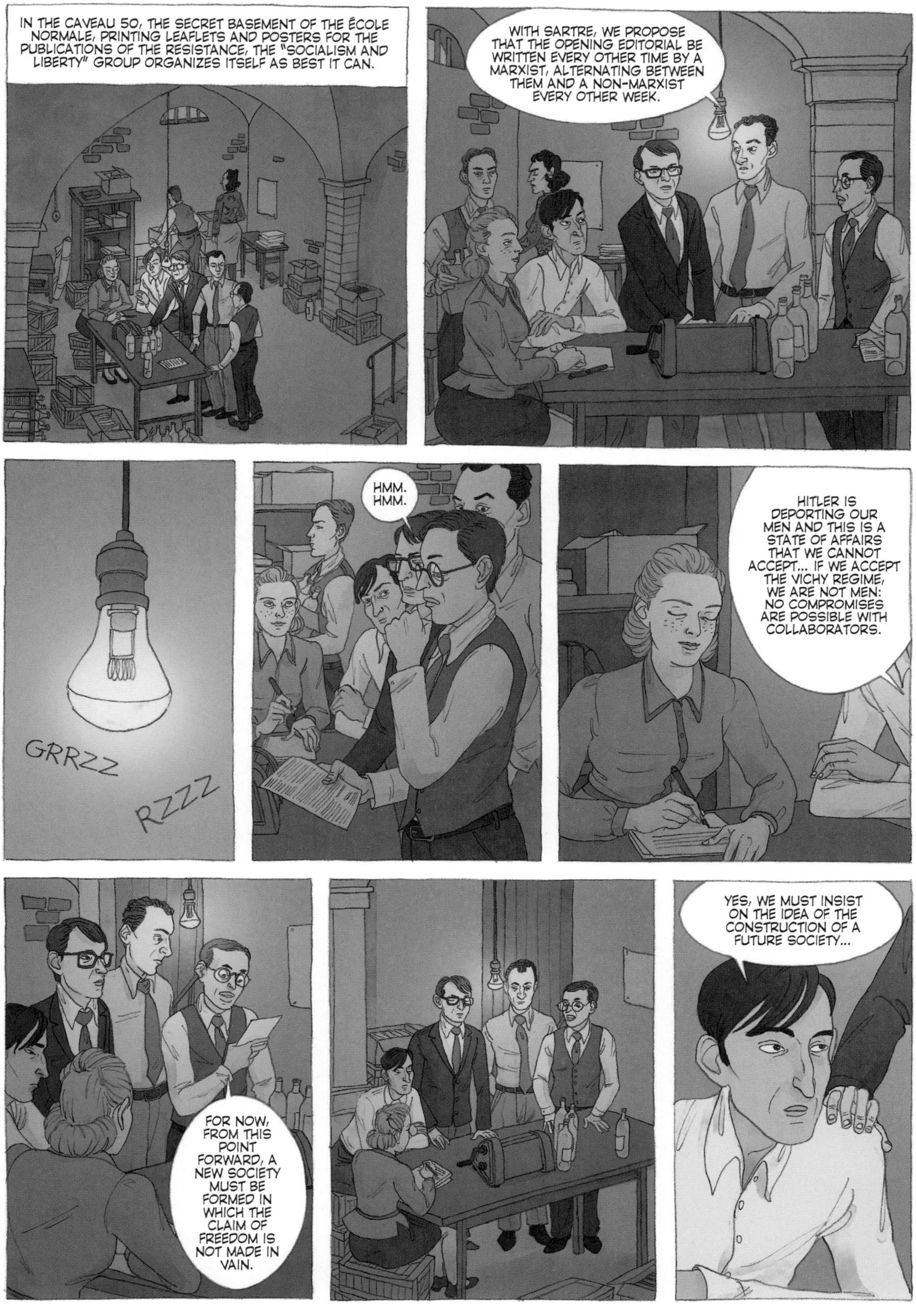
IN THE CAVEAU 50, THE SECRET BASEMENT OF THE ÉCOLE NORMALE, PRINTING LEAFLETS AND POSTERS FOR THE PUBLICATIONS OF THE RESISTANCE, THE "SOCIALISM AND LIBERTY" GROUP ORGANIZES ITSELF AS BEST IT CAN.
WITH SARTRE, WE PROPOSE THAT THE OPENING EDITORIAL BE WRITTEN EVERY OTHER TIME BY A MARXIST, ALTERNATING BETWEEN THEM AND A NON-MARXIST EVERY OTHER WEEK.
GRRZZ
RZZZ
HMM. HMM.
HITLER IS DEPORTING OUR MEN AND THIS IS A STATE OF AFFAIRS THAT WE CANNOT ACCEPT... IF WE ACCEPT THE VICHY REGIME, WE ARE NOT MEN: NO COMPROMISES ARE POSSIBLE WITH COLLABORATORS.
FOR NOW, FROM THIS POINT FORWARD, A NEW SOCIETY MUST BE FORMED IN WHICH THE CLAIM OF FREEDOM IS NOT MADE IN VAIN.
YES, WE MUST INSIST ON THE IDEA OF THE CONSTRUCTION OF A FUTURE SOCIETY...

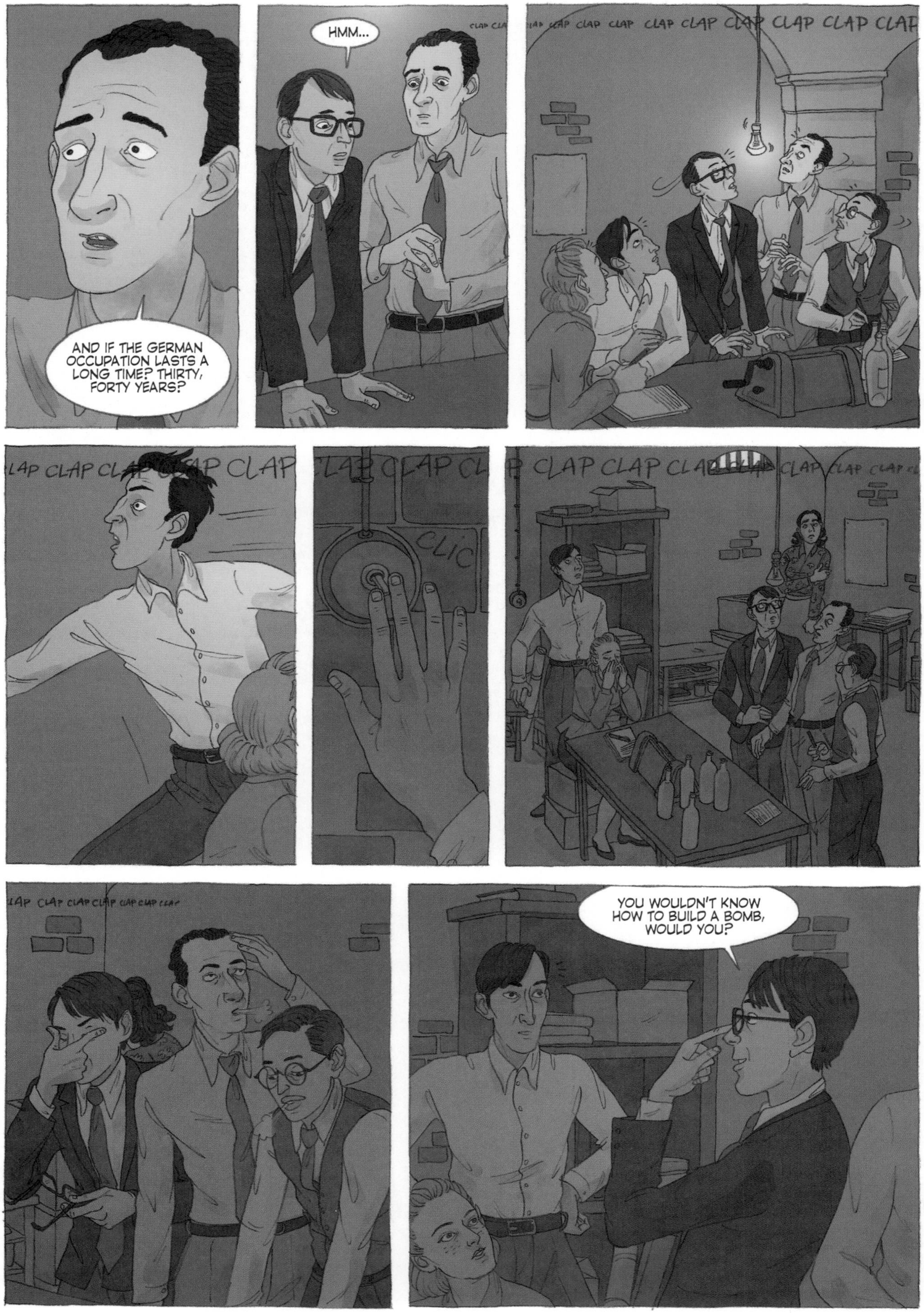

AND IF THE GERMAN OCCUPATION LASTS A LONG TIME? THIRTY, FORTY YEARS?
HMM...
CLAP CLAP CLAP CLAP CLAP CLAP CLAP CLAP CLAP CLAP
CLAP CLAP CLAP CLAP CLAP
CLIC
CLAP CLAP CLAP CLAP CLAP CLAP
CLAP CLAP CLAP CLAP CLAP CLAP CLAP
YOU WOULDN'T KNOW HOW TO BUILD A BOMB, WOULD YOU?

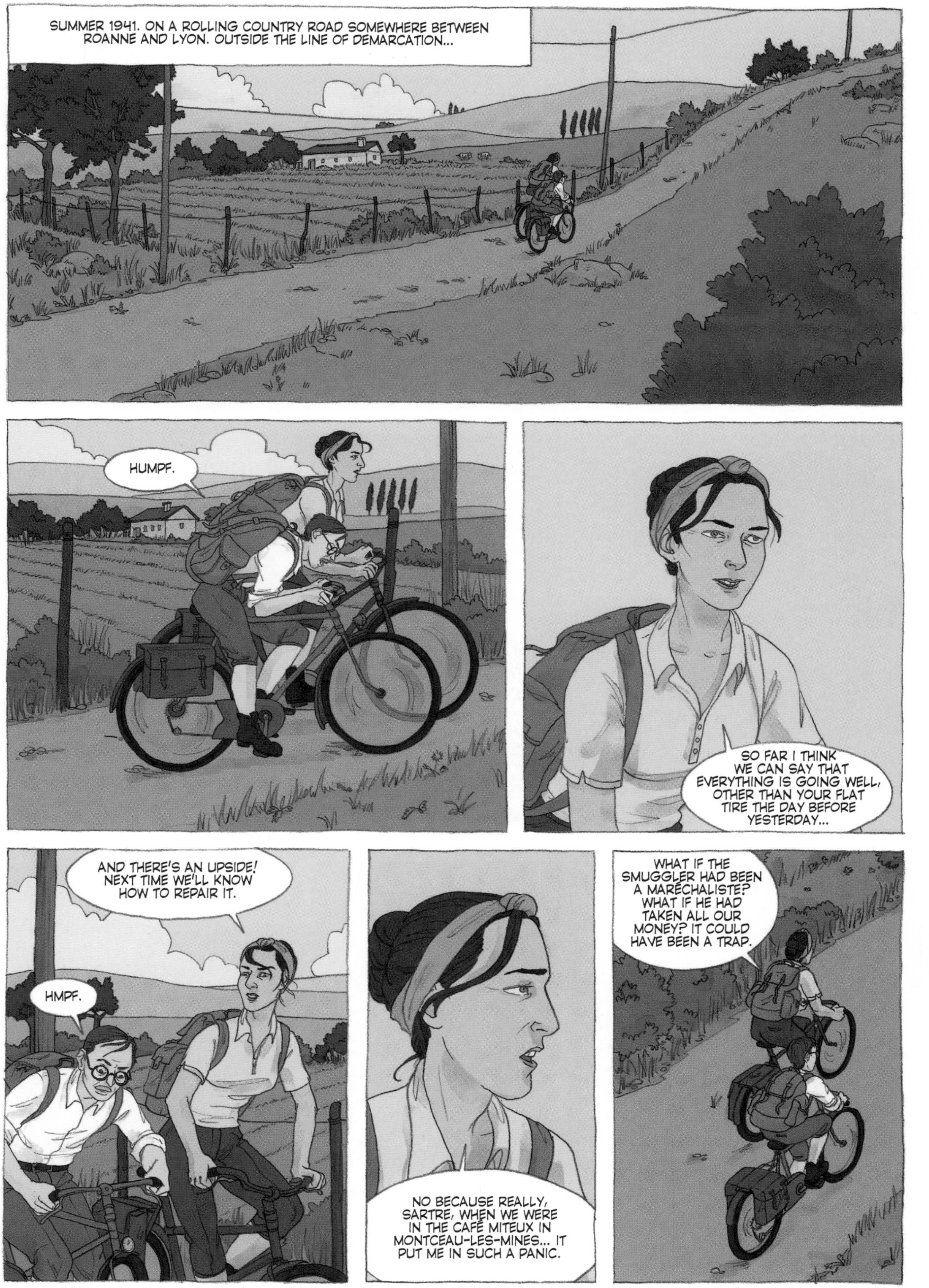
SUMMER 1941. ON A ROLLING COUNTRY ROAD SOMEWHERE BETWEEN ROANNE AND LYON. OUTSIDE THE LINE OF DEMARCATION...
HUMPF.
SO FAR I THINK WE CAN SAY THAT EVERYTHING IS GOING WELL, OTHER THAN YOUR FLAT TIRE THE DAY BEFORE YESTERDAY...
AND THERE'S AN UPSIDE! NEXT TIME WE'LL KNOW HOW TO REPAIR IT.
HMPF.
NO BECAUSE REALLY, SARTRE, WHEN WE WERE IN THE CAFÉ MITEUX IN MONTCEAU-LES-MINES... IT PUT ME IN SUCH A PANIC.
WHAT IF THE SMUGGLER HAD BEEN A MARÉCHALISTE? WHAT IF HE HAD TAKEN ALL OUR MONEY? IT COULD HAVE BEEN A TRAP.

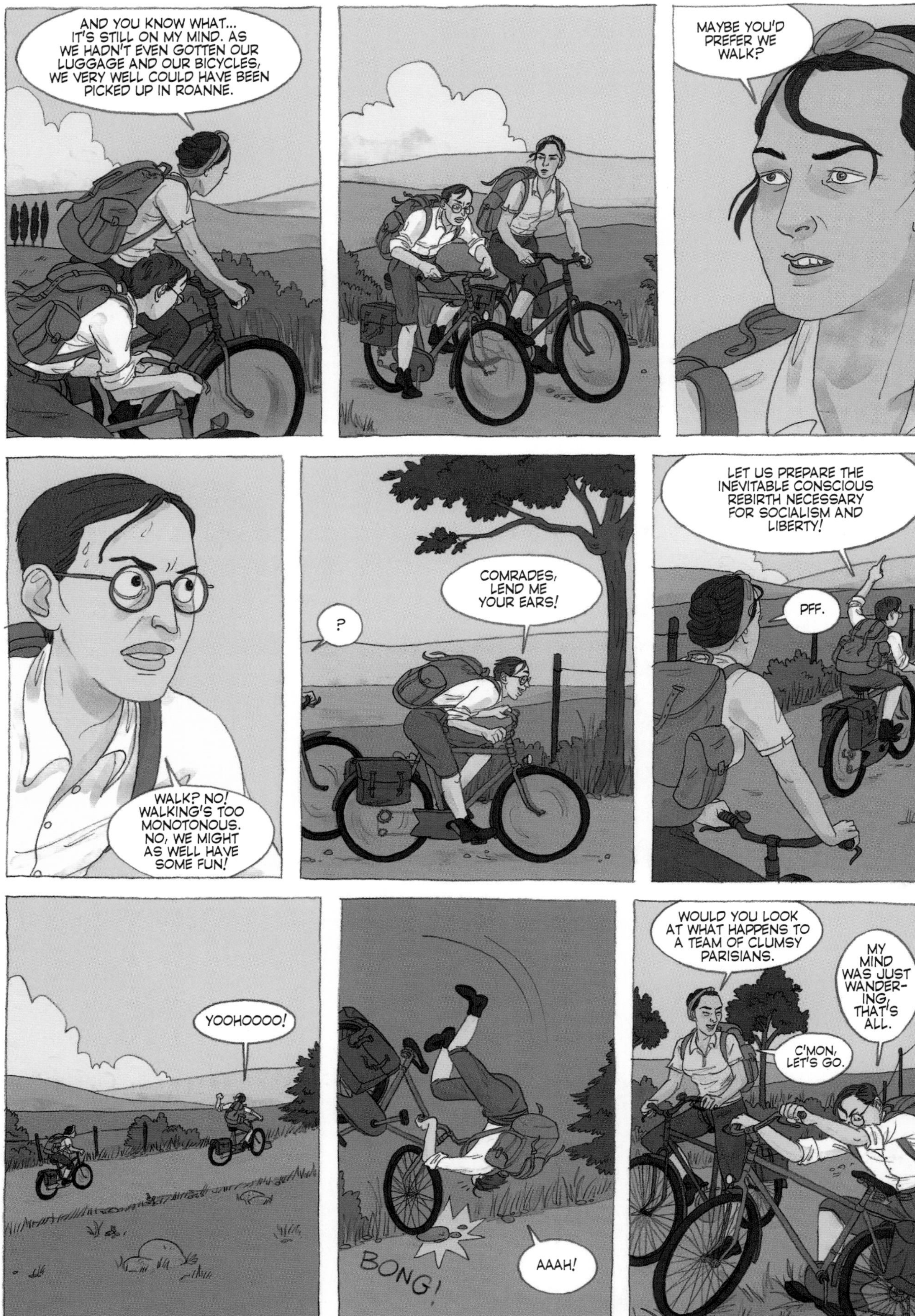
AND YOU KNOW WHAT... IT'S STILL ON MY MIND. AS WE HADN'T EVEN GOTTEN OUR LUGGAGE AND OUR BICYCLES, WE VERY WELL COULD HAVE BEEN PICKED UP IN ROANNE.
MAYBE YOU'D PREFER WE WALK?
WALK? NO! WALKING'S TOO MONOTONOUS. NO, WE MIGHT AS WELL HAVE SOME FUN!
?
COMRADES, LEND ME YOUR EARS!
LET US PREPARE THE INEVITABLE CONSCIOUS REBIRTH NECESSARY FOR SOCIALISM AND LIBERTY!
PFF.
YOOHOOOO!
BONG!
AAAH!
WOULD YOU LOOK AT WHAT HAPPENS TO A TEAM OF CLUMSY PARISIANS.
MY MIND WAS JUST WANDER-ING, THAT'S ALL.
C'MON, LET'S GO.

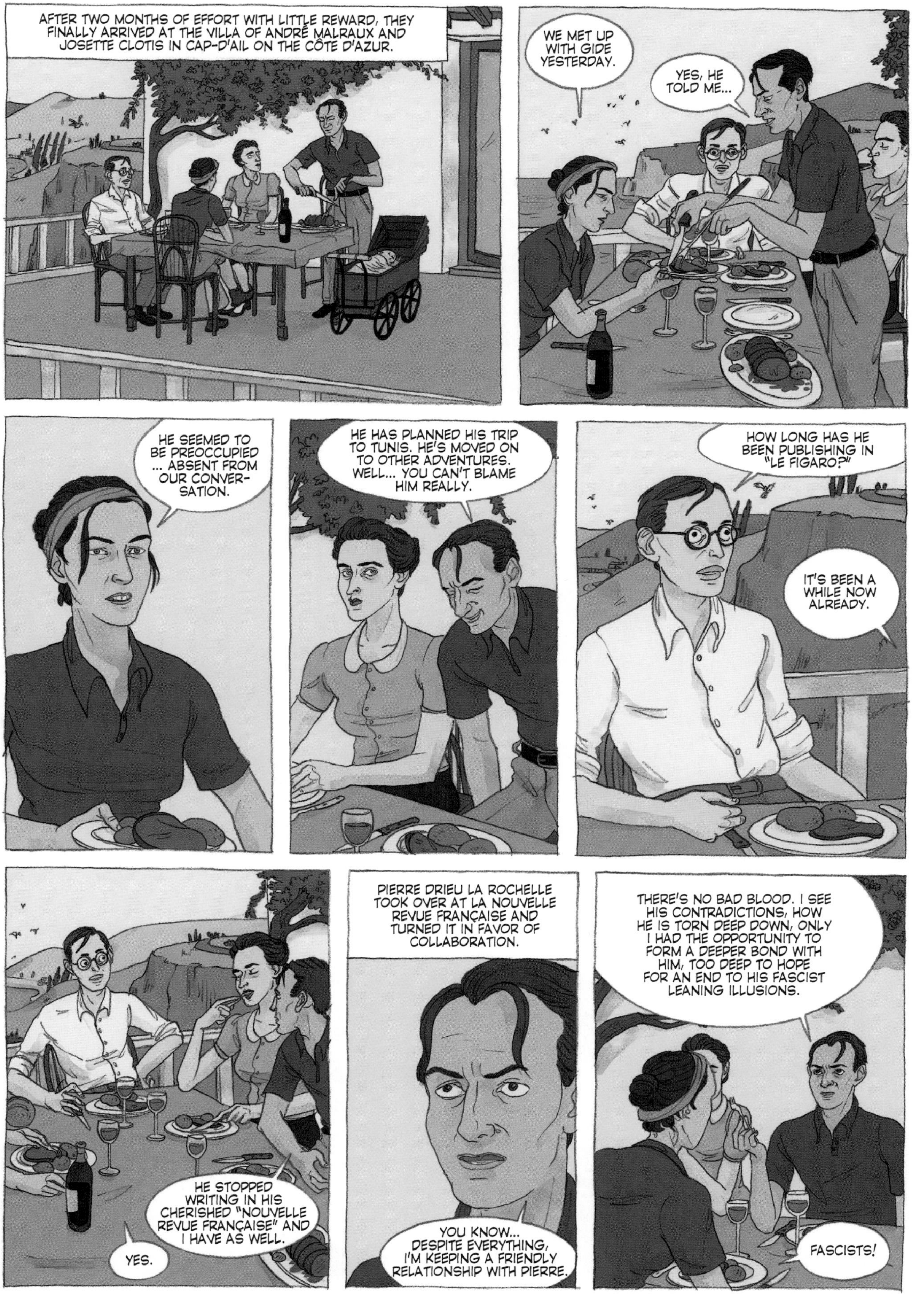
AFTER TWO MONTHS OF EFFORT WITH LITTLE REWARD, THEY FINALLY ARRIVED AT THE VILLA OF ANDRÉ MALRAUX AND JOSETTE CLOTIS IN CAP-D'AIL ON THE CÔTE D'AZUR.
WE MET UP WITH GIDE YESTERDAY.
YES, HE TOLD ME...
HE SEEMED TO BE PREOCCUPIED ... ABSENT FROM OUR CONVER-SATION.
HE HAS PLANNED HIS TRIP TO TUNIS. HE'S MOVED ON TO OTHER ADVENTURES. WELL... YOU CAN'T BLAME HIM REALLY.
HOW LONG HAS HE BEEN PUBLISHING IN "LE FIGARO?"
IT'S BEEN A WHILE NOW ALREADY.
HE STOPPED WRITING IN HIS CHERISHED "NOUVELLE REVUE FRANÇAISE" AND I HAVE AS WELL.
YES.
PIERRE DRIEU LA ROCHELLE TOOK OVER AT LA NOUVELLE REVUE FRANÇAISE AND TURNED IT IN FAVOR OF COLLABORATION.
YOU KNOW... DESPITE EVERYTHING, I'M KEEPING A FRIENDLY RELATIONSHIP WITH PIERRE.
THERE'S NO BAD BLOOD. I SEE HIS CONTRADICTIONS, HOW HE IS TORN DEEP DOWN, ONLY I HAD THE OPPORTUNITY TO FORM A DEEPER BOND WITH HIM, TOO DEEP TO HOPE FOR AN END TO HIS FASCIST LEANING ILLUSIONS.
FASCISTS!

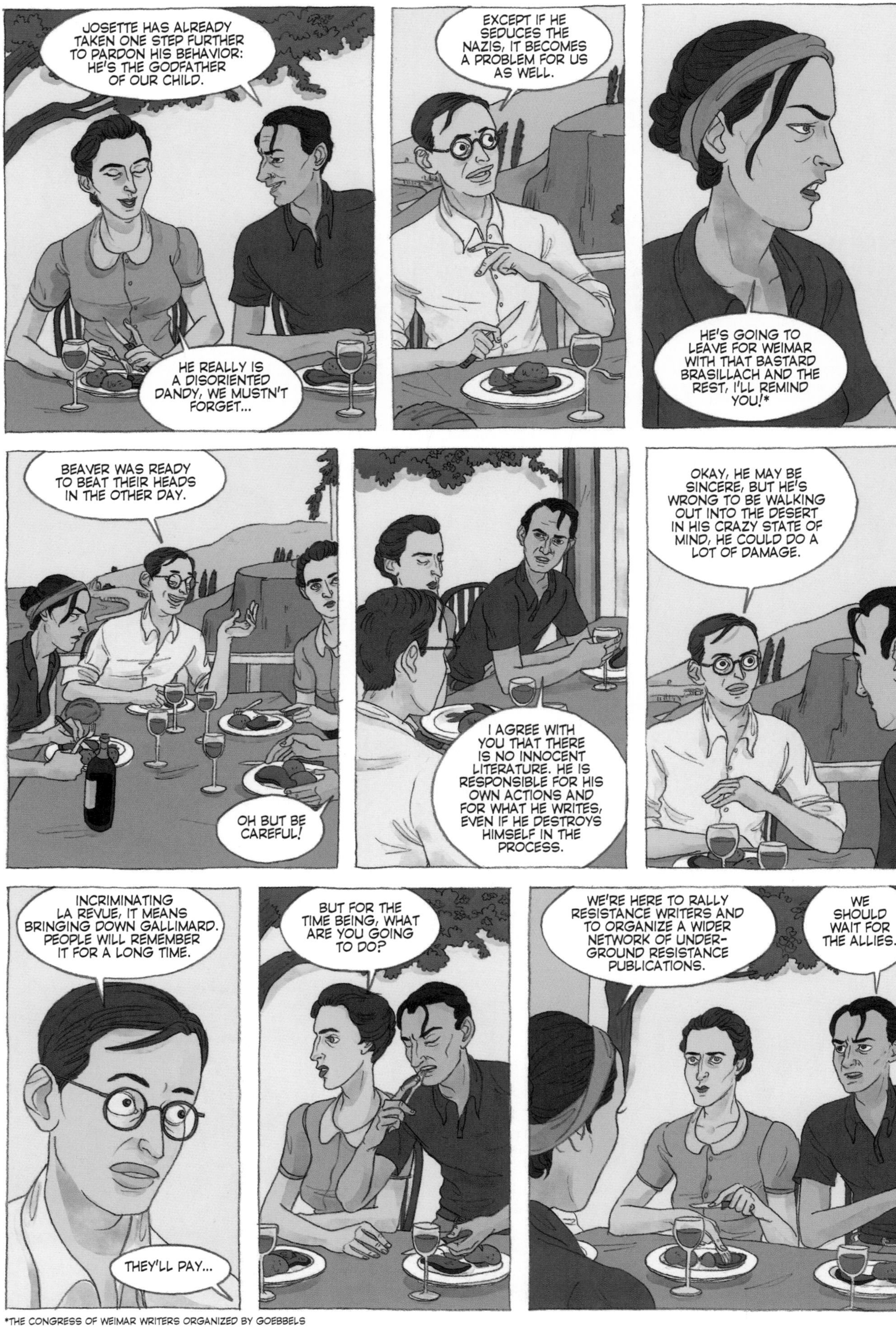
JOSETTE HAS ALREADY TAKEN ONE STEP FURTHER TO PARDON HIS BEHAVIOR: HE'S THE GODFATHER OF OUR CHILD.
HE REALLY IS A DISORIENTED DANDY, WE MUSTN'T FORGET...
EXCEPT IF HE SEDUCES THE NAZIS, IT BECOMES A PROBLEM FOR US AS WELL.
HE'S GOING TO LEAVE FOR WEIMAR WITH THAT BASTARD BRASILLACH AND THE REST, I'LL REMIND YOU!*
BEAVER WAS READY TO BEAT THEIR HEADS IN THE OTHER DAY.
OH BUT BE CAREFUL!
I AGREE WITH YOU THAT THERE IS NO INNOCENT LITERATURE. HE IS RESPONSIBLE FOR HIS OWN ACTIONS AND FOR WHAT HE WRITES, EVEN IF HE DESTROYS HIMSELF IN THE PROCESS.
OKAY, HE MAY BE SINCERE, BUT HE'S WRONG TO BE WALKING OUT INTO THE DESERT IN HIS CRAZY STATE OF MIND, HE COULD DO A LOT OF DAMAGE.
INCRIMINATING LA REVUE, IT MEANS BRINGING DOWN GALLIMARD. PEOPLE WILL REMEMBER IT FOR A LONG TIME.
THEY'LL PAY...
BUT FOR THE TIME BEING, WHAT ARE YOU GOING TO DO?
WE'RE HERE TO RALLY RESISTANCE WRITERS AND TO ORGANIZE A WIDER NETWORK OF UNDER-GROUND RESISTANCE PUBLICATIONS.
WE SHOULD WAIT FOR THE ALLIES.

*THE CONGRESS OF WEIMAR WRITERS ORGANIZED BY GOEBBELS

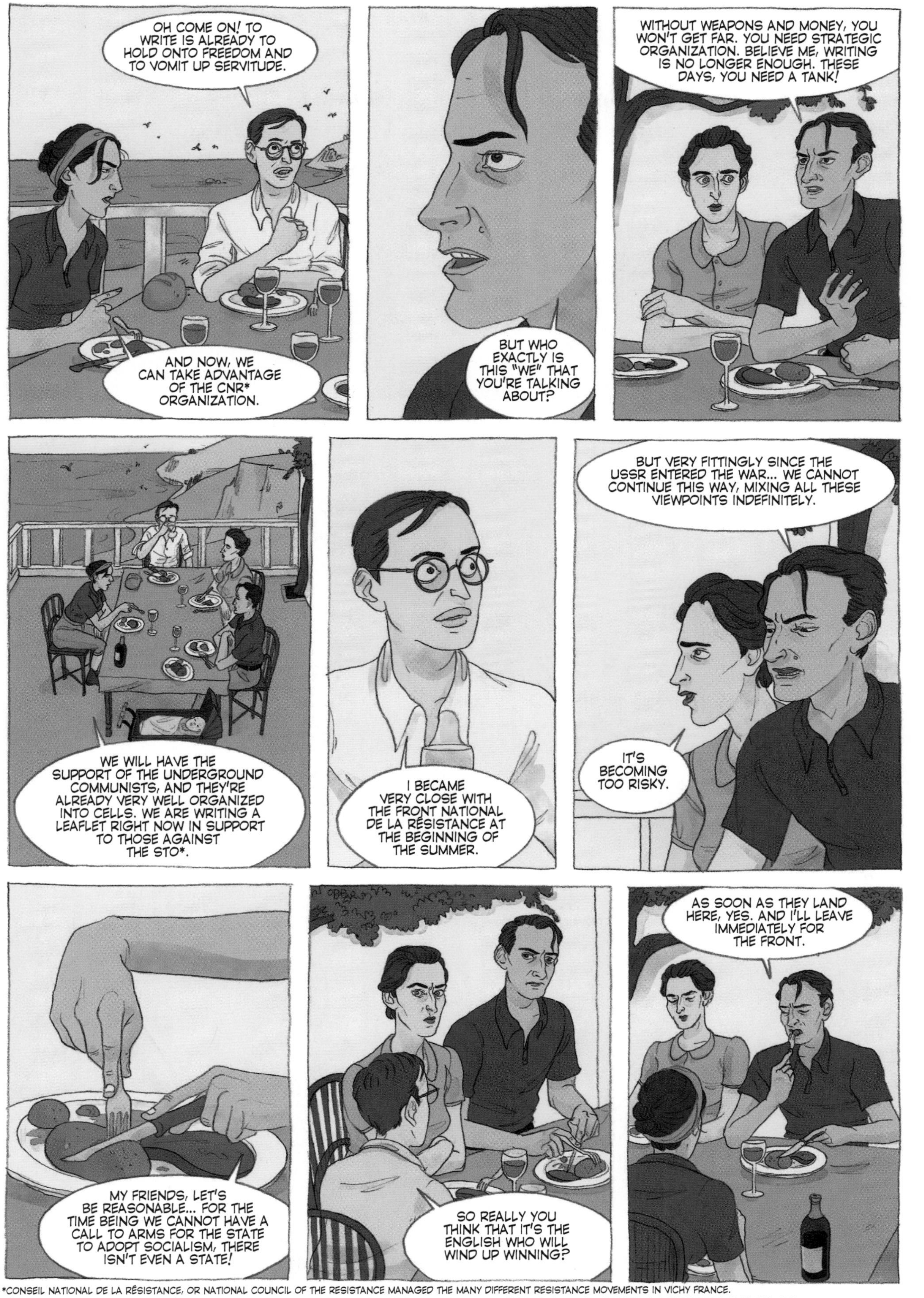
OH COME ON! TO WRITE IS ALREADY TO HOLD ONTO FREEDOM AND TO VOMIT UP SERVITUDE.
AND NOW, WE CAN TAKE ADVANTAGE OF THE CNR* ORGANIZATION.
BUT WHO EXACTLY IS THIS "WE" THAT YOU'RE TALKING ABOUT?
WITHOUT WEAPONS AND MONEY, YOU WON'T GET FAR. YOU NEED STRATEGIC ORGANIZATION. BELIEVE ME, WRITING IS NO LONGER ENOUGH. THESE DAYS, YOU NEED A TANK!
WE WILL HAVE THE SUPPORT OF THE UNDERGROUND COMMUNISTS, AND THEY'RE ALREADY VERY WELL ORGANIZED INTO CELLS. WE ARE WRITING A LEAFLET RIGHT NOW IN SUPPORT TO THOSE AGAINST THE STO*.
I BECAME VERY CLOSE WITH THE FRONT NATIONAL DE LA RÉSISTANCE AT THE BEGINNING OF THE SUMMER.
BUT VERY FITTINGLY SINCE THE USSR ENTERED THE WAR... WE CANNOT CONTINUE THIS WAY, MIXING ALL THESE VIEWPOINTS INDEFINITELY.
IT'S BECOMING TOO RISKY.
MY FRIENDS, LET'S BE REASONABLE... FOR THE TIME BEING WE CANNOT HAVE A CALL TO ARMS FOR THE STATE TO ADOPT SOCIALISM, THERE ISN'T EVEN A STATE!
SO REALLY YOU THINK THAT IT'S THE ENGLISH WHO WILL WIND UP WINNING?
AS SOON AS THEY LAND HERE, YES. AND I'LL LEAVE IMMEDIATELY FOR THE FRONT.

*CONSEIL NATIONAL DE LA RÉSISTANCE, OR NATIONAL COUNCIL OF THE RESISTANCE MANAGED THE MANY DIFFERENT RESISTANCE MOVEMENTS IN VICHY FRANCE.
**"SERVICE DU TRAVAIL OBLIGATOIRE," OR COMPULSORY WORK SERVICE WHICH FORCED FRENCHMEN INTO WORK CAMPS ALL OVER NAZI GERMAN TERRITORY DURING THE WAR.

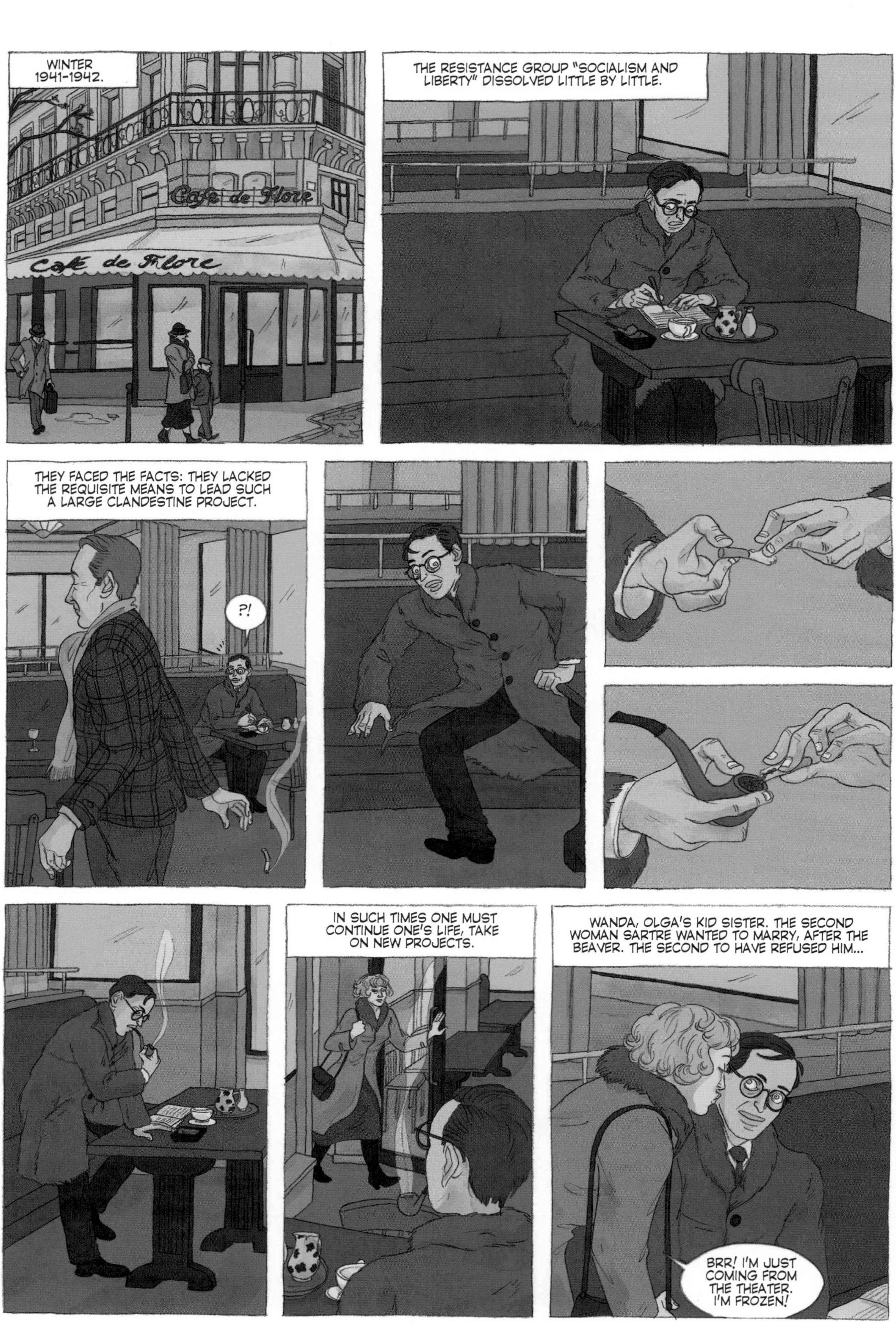
WINTER 1941-1942.
Café de Flore
Café de Flore
THE RESISTANCE GROUP "SOCIALISM AND LIBERTY" DISSOLVED LITTLE BY LITTLE.
THEY FACED THE FACTS: THEY LACKED THE REQUISITE MEANS TO LEAD SUCH A LARGE CLANDESTINE PROJECT.
?!
IN SUCH TIMES ONE MUST CONTINUE ONE'S LIFE, TAKE ON NEW PROJECTS.
WANDA, OLGA'S KID SISTER. THE SECOND WOMAN SARTRE WANTED TO MARRY, AFTER THE BEAVER. THE SECOND TO HAVE REFUSED HIM...
BRR! I'M JUST COMING FROM THE THEATER. I'M FROZEN!

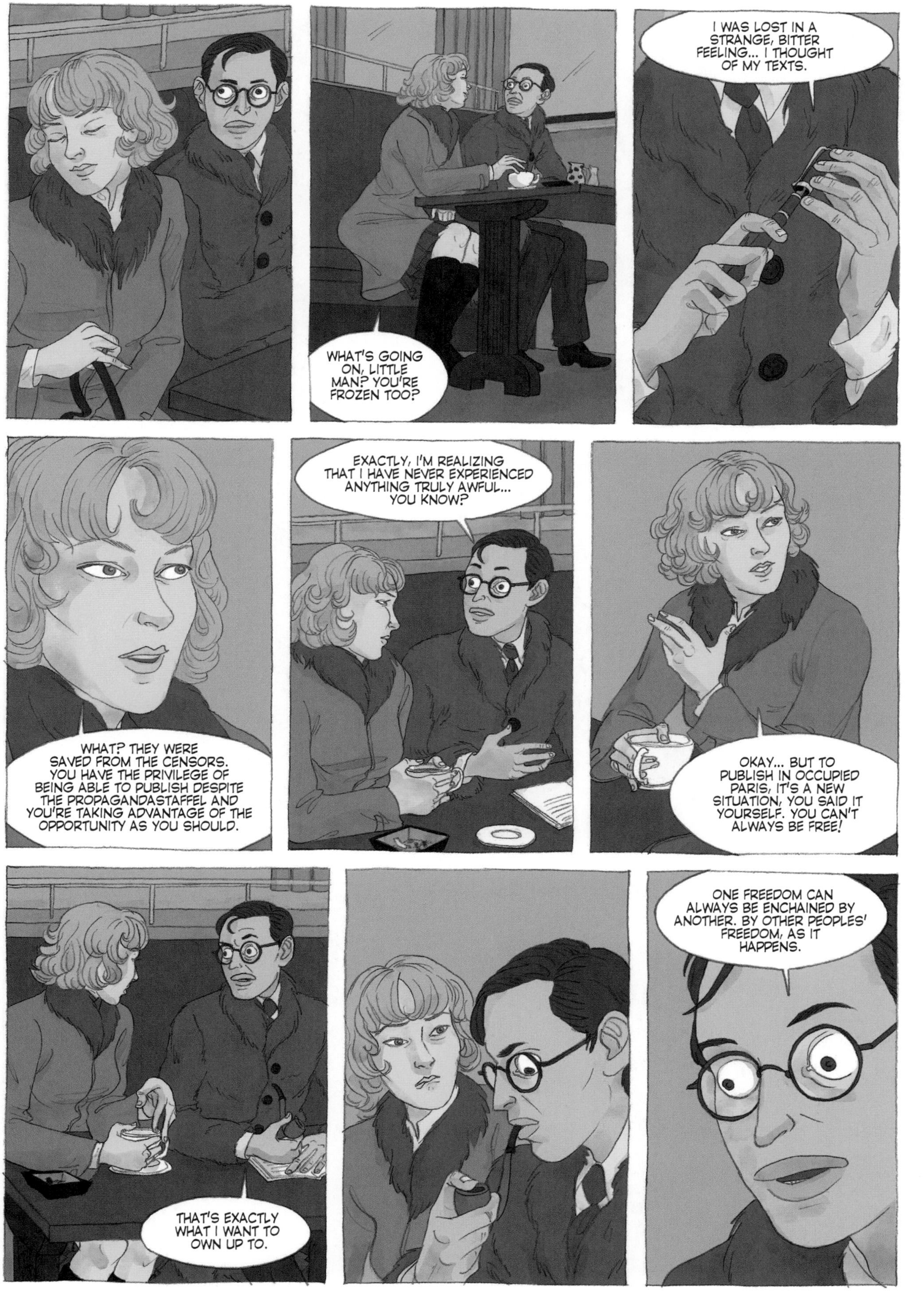
WHAT'S GOING ON, LITTLE MAN? YOU'RE FROZEN TOO?
I WAS LOST IN A STRANGE, BITTER FEELING... I THOUGHT OF MY TEXTS.
WHAT? THEY WERE SAVED FROM THE CENSORS. YOU HAVE THE PRIVILEGE OF BEING ABLE TO PUBLISH DESPITE THE PROPAGANDASTAFFEL AND YOU'RE TAKING ADVANTAGE OF THE OPPORTUNITY AS YOU SHOULD.
EXACTLY, I'M REALIZING THAT I HAVE NEVER EXPERIENCED ANYTHING TRULY AWFUL... YOU KNOW?
OKAY... BUT TO PUBLISH IN OCCUPIED PARIS, IT'S A NEW SITUATION, YOU SAID IT YOURSELF. YOU CAN'T ALWAYS BE FREE!
THAT'S EXACTLY WHAT I WANT TO OWN UP TO.
ONE FREEDOM CAN ALWAYS BE ENCHAINED BY ANOTHER. BY OTHER PEOPLES' FREEDOM, AS IT HAPPENS.

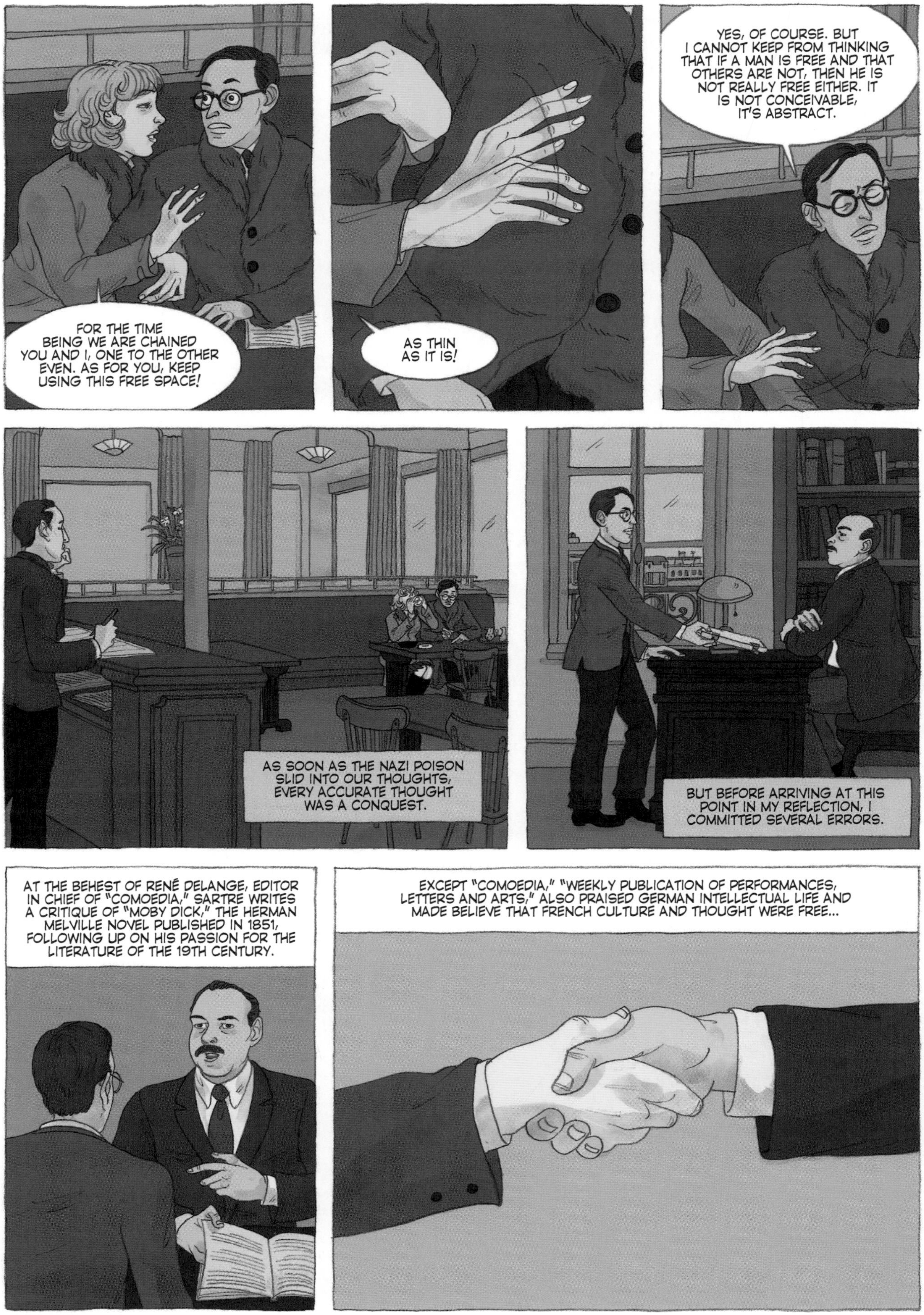
FOR THE TIME BEING WE ARE CHAINED YOU AND I, ONE TO THE OTHER EVEN. AS FOR YOU, KEEP USING THIS FREE SPACE!
AS THIN AS IT IS!
YES, OF COURSE. BUT I CANNOT KEEP FROM THINKING THAT IF A MAN IS FREE AND THAT OTHERS ARE NOT, THEN HE IS NOT REALLY FREE EITHER. IT IS NOT CONCEIVABLE, IT'S ABSTRACT.
AS SOON AS THE NAZI POISON SLID INTO OUR THOUGHTS, EVERY ACCURATE THOUGHT WAS A CONQUEST.
BUT BEFORE ARRIVING AT THIS POINT IN MY REFLECTION, I COMMITTED SEVERAL ERRORS.
AT THE BEHEST OF RENÉ DELANGE, EDITOR IN CHIEF OF "COMOEDIA," SARTRE WRITES A CRITIQUE OF "MOBY DICK," THE HERMAN MELVILLE NOVEL PUBLISHED IN 1851, FOLLOWING UP ON HIS PASSION FOR THE LITERATURE OF THE 19TH CENTURY.
EXCEPT "COMOEDIA," "WEEKLY PUBLICATION OF PERFORMANCES, LETTERS AND ARTS," ALSO PRAISED GERMAN INTELLECTUAL LIFE AND MADE BELIEVE THAT FRENCH CULTURE AND THOUGHT WERE FREE...

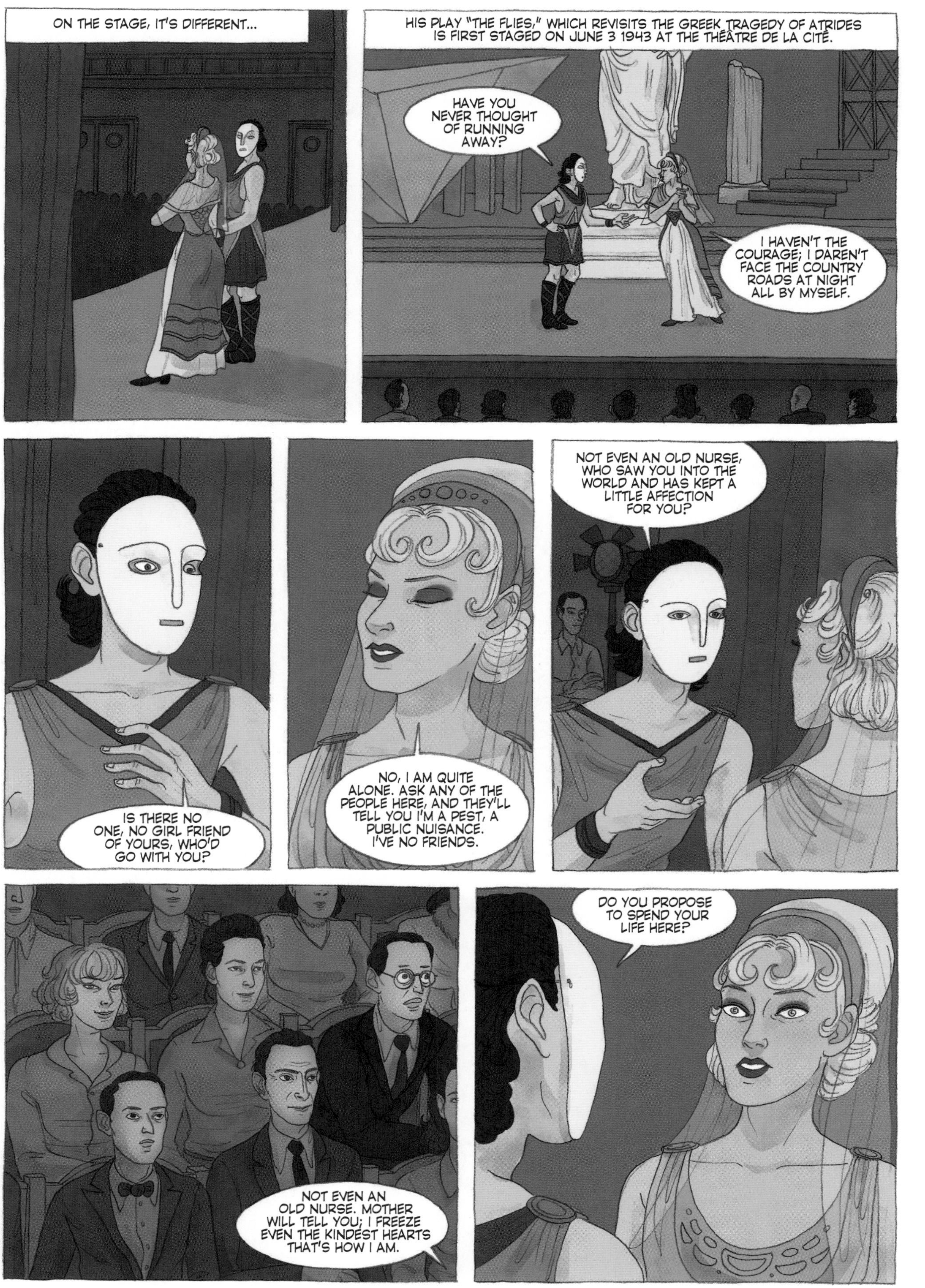
ON THE STAGE, IT'S DIFFERENT...
HIS PLAY "THE FLIES," WHICH REVISITS THE GREEK TRAGEDY OF ATRIDES IS FIRST STAGED ON JUNE 3 1943 AT THE THÉÂTRE DE LA CITÉ.
HAVE YOU NEVER THOUGHT OF RUNNING AWAY?
I HAVEN'T THE COURAGE; I DAREN'T FACE THE COUNTRY ROADS AT NIGHT ALL BY MYSELF.
IS THERE NO ONE, NO GIRL FRIEND OF YOURS, WHO'D GO WITH YOU?
NO, I AM QUITE ALONE. ASK ANY OF THE PEOPLE HERE, AND THEY'LL TELL YOU I'M A PEST, A PUBLIC NUISANCE. I'VE NO FRIENDS.
NOT EVEN AN OLD NURSE, WHO SAW YOU INTO THE WORLD AND HAS KEPT A LITTLE AFFECTION FOR YOU?
NOT EVEN AN OLD NURSE. MOTHER WILL TELL YOU; I FREEZE EVEN THE KINDEST HEARTS THAT'S HOW I AM.
DO YOU PROPOSE TO SPEND YOUR LIFE HERE?

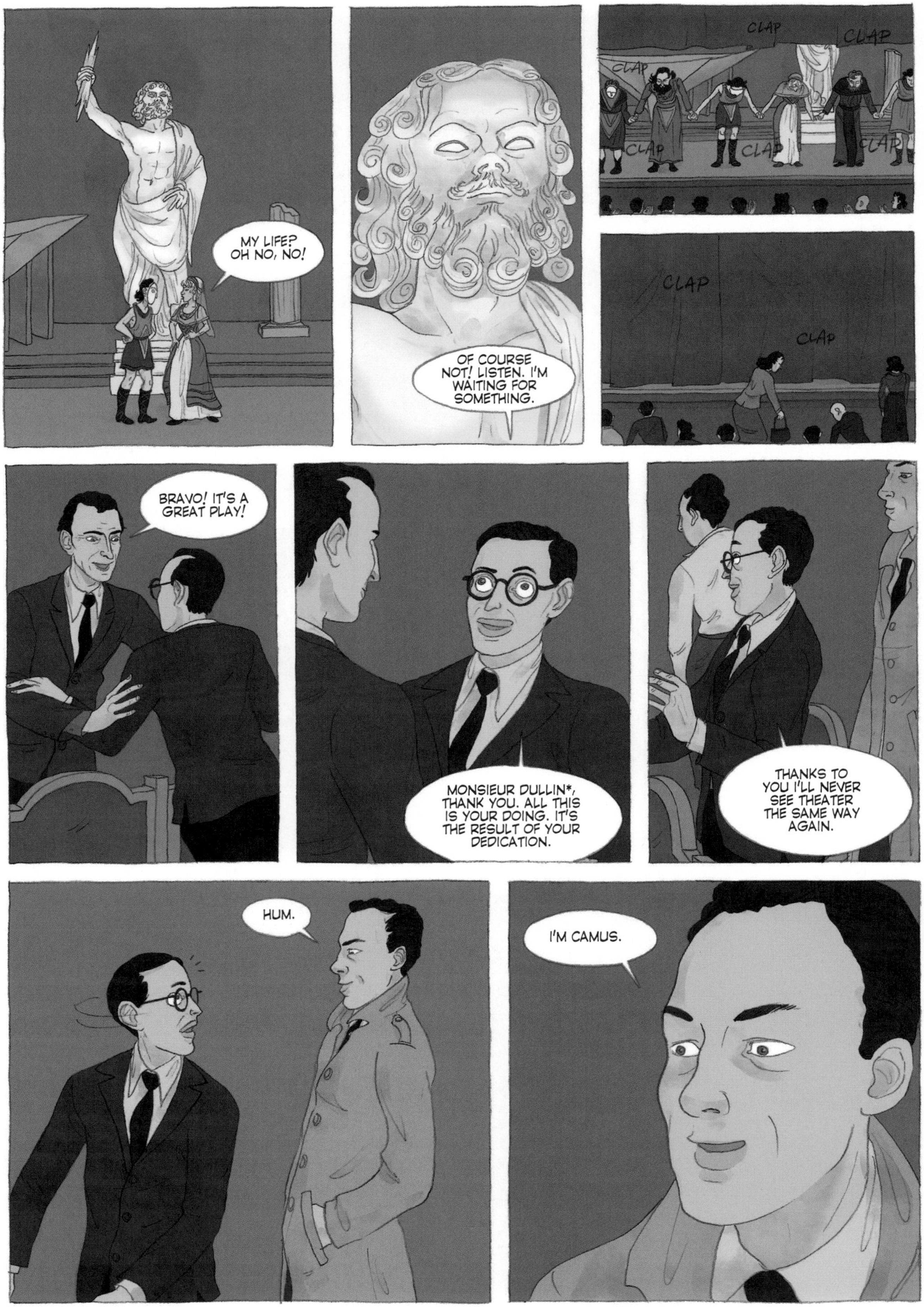
MY LIFE? OH NO, NO!
OF COURSE NOT! LISTEN. I'M WAITING FOR SOMETHING.
CLAP
CLAP
CLAP
CLAP
CLAP
CLAP
CLAP
CLAP
BRAVO! IT'S A GREAT PLAY!
MONSIEUR DULLIN*, THANK YOU. ALL THIS IS YOUR DOING. IT'S THE RESULT OF YOUR DEDICATION.
THANKS TO YOU I'LL NEVER SEE THEATER THE SAME WAY AGAIN.
HUM.
I'M CAMUS.

*CHARLES DULLIN, THEATER DIRECTOR AND PRODUCER

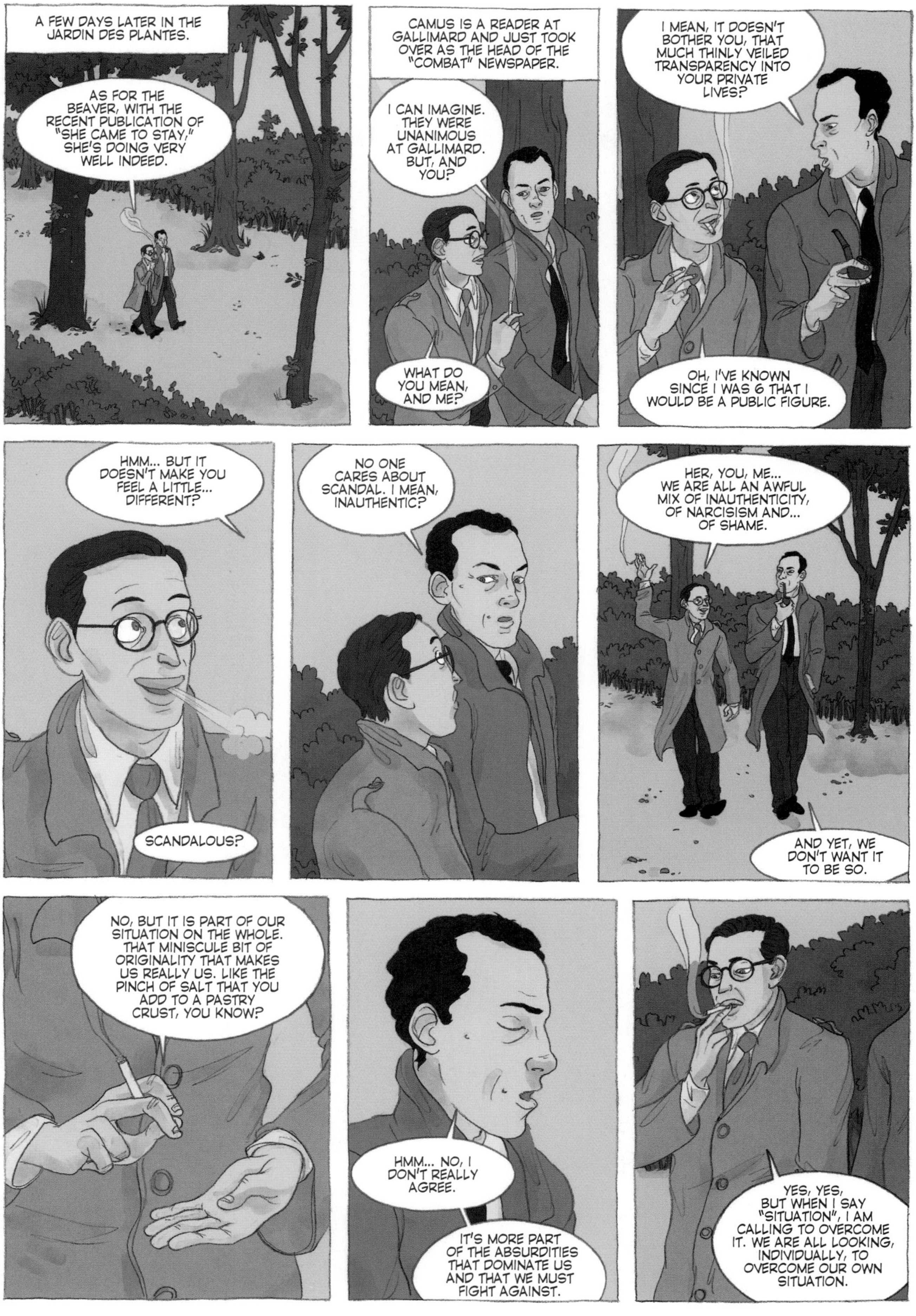
A FEW DAYS LATER IN THE JARDIN DES PLANTES.
AS FOR THE BEAVER, WITH THE RECENT PUBLICATION OF "SHE CAME TO STAY," SHE'S DOING VERY WELL INDEED.
CAMUS IS A READER AT GALLIMARD AND JUST TOOK OVER AS THE HEAD OF THE "COMBAT" NEWSPAPER.
I CAN IMAGINE. THEY WERE UNANIMOUS AT GALLIMARD. BUT, AND YOU?
WHAT DO YOU MEAN, AND ME?
I MEAN, IT DOESN'T BOTHER YOU, THAT MUCH THINLY VEILED TRANSPARENCY INTO YOUR PRIVATE LIVES?
OH, I'VE KNOWN SINCE I WAS 6 THAT I WOULD BE A PUBLIC FIGURE.
HMM... BUT IT DOESN'T MAKE YOU FEEL A LITTLE... DIFFERENT?
SCANDALOUS?
NO ONE CARES ABOUT SCANDAL. I MEAN, INAUTHENTIC?
HER, YOU, ME... WE ARE ALL AN AWFUL MIX OF INAUTHENTICITY, OF NARCISISM AND... OF SHAME.
AND YET, WE DON'T WANT IT TO BE SO.
NO, BUT IT IS PART OF OUR SITUATION ON THE WHOLE. THAT MINISCULE BIT OF ORIGINALITY THAT MAKES US REALLY US. LIKE THE PINCH OF SALT THAT YOU ADD TO A PASTRY CRUST, YOU KNOW?
HMM... NO, I DON'T REALLY AGREE.
IT'S MORE PART OF THE ABSURDITIES THAT DOMINATE US AND THAT WE MUST FIGHT AGAINST.
YES, YES, BUT WHEN I SAY "SITUATION", I AM CALLING TO OVERCOME IT. WE ARE ALL LOOKING, INDIVIDUALLY, TO OVERCOME OUR OWN SITUATION.

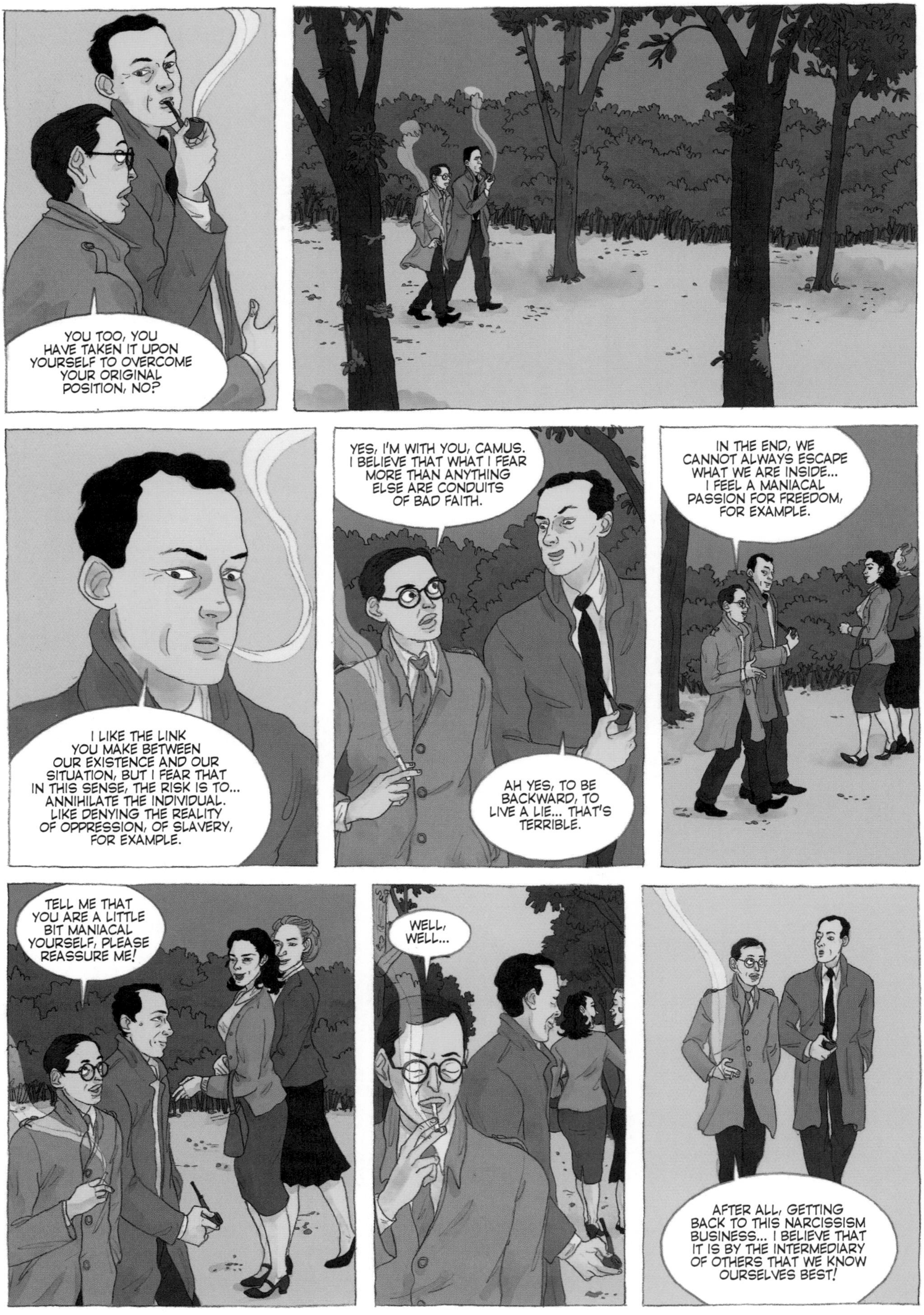
YOU TOO, YOU HAVE TAKEN IT UPON YOURSELF TO OVERCOME YOUR ORIGINAL POSITION, NO?
I LIKE THE LINK YOU MAKE BETWEEN OUR EXISTENCE AND OUR SITUATION, BUT I FEAR THAT IN THIS SENSE, THE RISK IS TO... ANNIHILATE THE INDIVIDUAL. LIKE DENYING THE REALITY OF OPPRESSION, OF SLAVERY, FOR EXAMPLE.
YES, I'M WITH YOU, CAMUS. I BELIEVE THAT WHAT I FEAR MORE THAN ANYTHING ELSE ARE CONDUITS OF BAD FAITH.
AH YES, TO BE BACKWARD, TO LIVE A LIE... THAT'S TERRIBLE.
IN THE END, WE CANNOT ALWAYS ESCAPE WHAT WE ARE INSIDE... I FEEL A MANIACAL PASSION FOR FREEDOM, FOR EXAMPLE.
TELL ME THAT YOU ARE A LITTLE BIT MANIACAL YOURSELF, PLEASE REASSURE ME!
WELL, WELL...
AFTER ALL, GETTING BACK TO THIS NARCISSISM BUSINESS... I BELIEVE THAT IT IS BY THE INTERMEDIARY OF OTHERS THAT WE KNOW OURSELVES BEST!

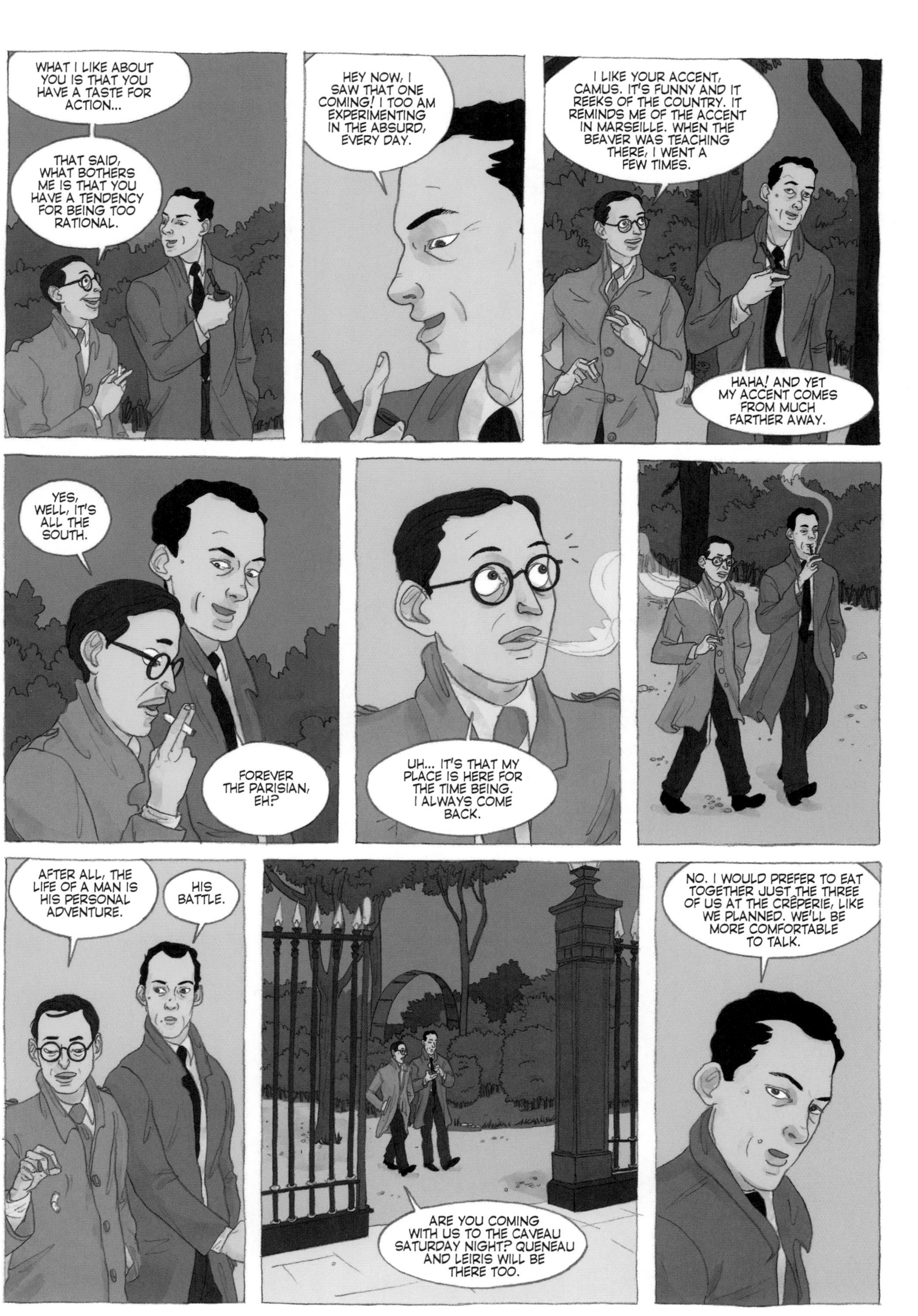
WHAT I LIKE ABOUT YOU IS THAT YOU HAVE A TASTE FOR ACTION...
THAT SAID, WHAT BOTHERS ME IS THAT YOU HAVE A TENDENCY FOR BEING TOO RATIONAL.
HEY NOW, I SAW THAT ONE COMING! I TOO AM EXPERIMENTING IN THE ABSURD, EVERY DAY.
I LIKE YOUR ACCENT, CAMUS. IT'S FUNNY AND IT REEKS OF THE COUNTRY. IT REMINDS ME OF THE ACCENT IN MARSEILLE. WHEN THE BEAVER WAS TEACHING THERE, I WENT A FEW TIMES.
HAHA! AND YET MY ACCENT COMES FROM MUCH FARTHER AWAY.
YES, WELL, IT'S ALL THE SOUTH.
FOREVER THE PARISIAN, EH?
UH... IT'S THAT MY PLACE IS HERE FOR THE TIME BEING. I ALWAYS COME BACK.
AFTER ALL, THE LIFE OF A MAN IS HIS PERSONAL ADVENTURE.
HIS BATTLE.
ARE YOU COMING WITH US TO THE CAVEAU SATURDAY NIGHT? QUENEAU AND LEIRIS WILL BE THERE TOO.
NO. I WOULD PREFER TO EAT TOGETHER JUST THE THREE OF US AT THE CRÊPERIE, LIKE WE PLANNED. WE'LL BE MORE COMFORTABLE TO TALK.

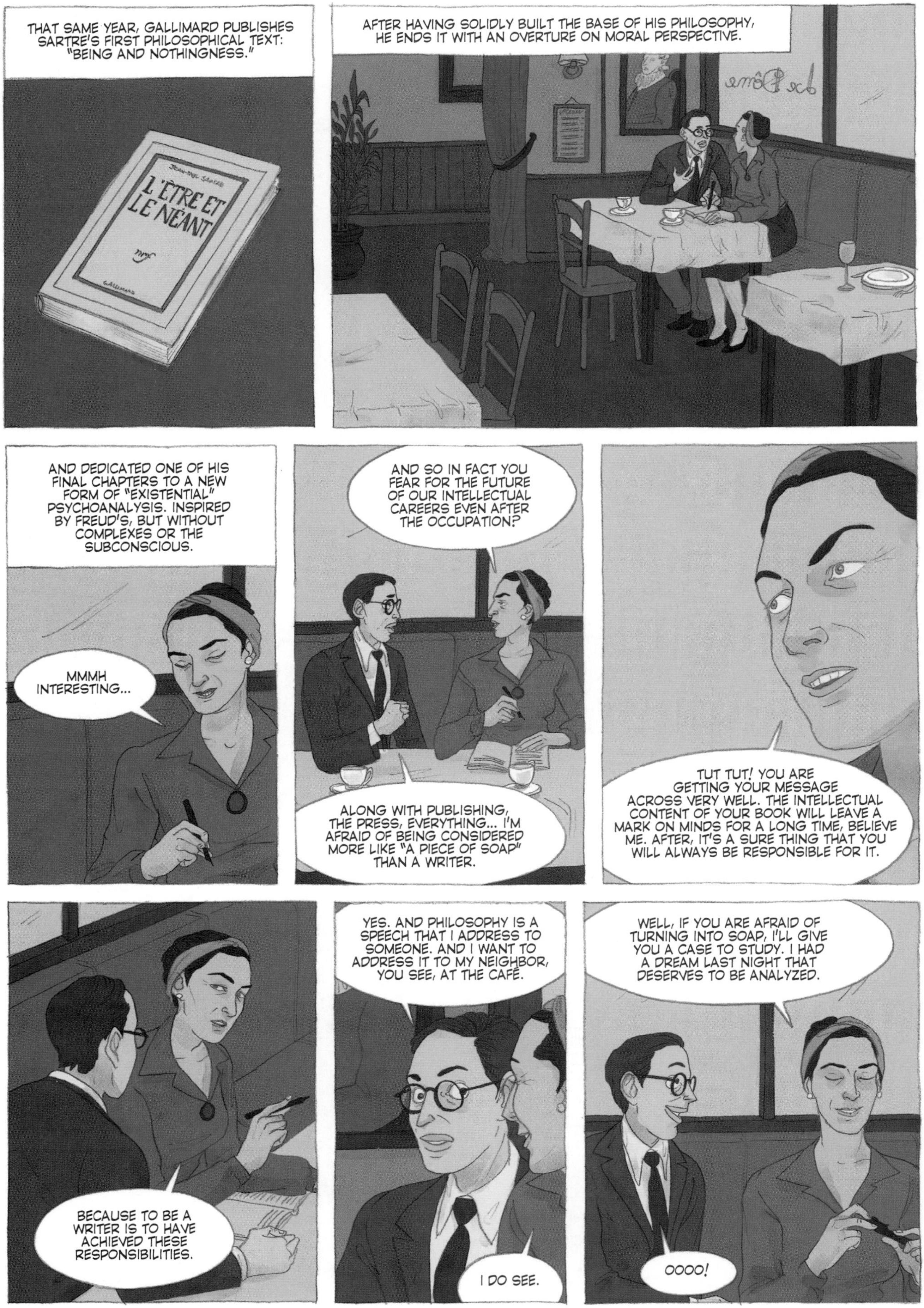
THAT SAME YEAR, GALLIMARD PUBLISHES SARTRE'S FIRST PHILOSOPHICAL TEXT: "BEING AND NOTHINGNESS."
L'ÊTRE ET LE NÉANT
GALLIMARD
AFTER HAVING SOLIDLY BUILT THE BASE OF HIS PHILOSOPHY, HE ENDS IT WITH AN OVERTURE ON MORAL PERSPECTIVE.
AND DEDICATED ONE OF HIS FINAL CHAPTERS TO A NEW FORM OF "EXISTENTIAL" PSYCHOANALYSIS. INSPIRED BY FREUD'S, BUT WITHOUT COMPLEXES OR THE SUBCONSCIOUS.
MMMH INTERESTING...
AND SO IN FACT YOU FEAR FOR THE FUTURE OF OUR INTELLECTUAL CAREERS EVEN AFTER THE OCCUPATION?
ALONG WITH PUBLISHING, THE PRESS, EVERYTHING... I'M AFRAID OF BEING CONSIDERED MORE LIKE "A PIECE OF SOAP" THAN A WRITER.
TUT TUT! YOU ARE GETTING YOUR MESSAGE ACROSS VERY WELL. THE INTELLECTUAL CONTENT OF YOUR BOOK WILL LEAVE A MARK ON MINDS FOR A LONG TIME, BELIEVE ME. AFTER, IT'S A SURE THING THAT YOU WILL ALWAYS BE RESPONSIBLE FOR IT.
BECAUSE TO BE A WRITER IS TO HAVE ACHIEVED THESE RESPONSIBILITIES.
YES. AND PHILOSOPHY IS A SPEECH THAT I ADDRESS TO SOMEONE. AND I WANT TO ADDRESS IT TO MY NEIGHBOR, YOU SEE, AT THE CAFÉ.
I DO SEE.
WELL, IF YOU ARE AFRAID OF TURNING INTO SOAP, I'LL GIVE YOU A CASE TO STUDY. I HAD A DREAM LAST NIGHT THAT DESERVES TO BE ANALYZED.
OOOO!

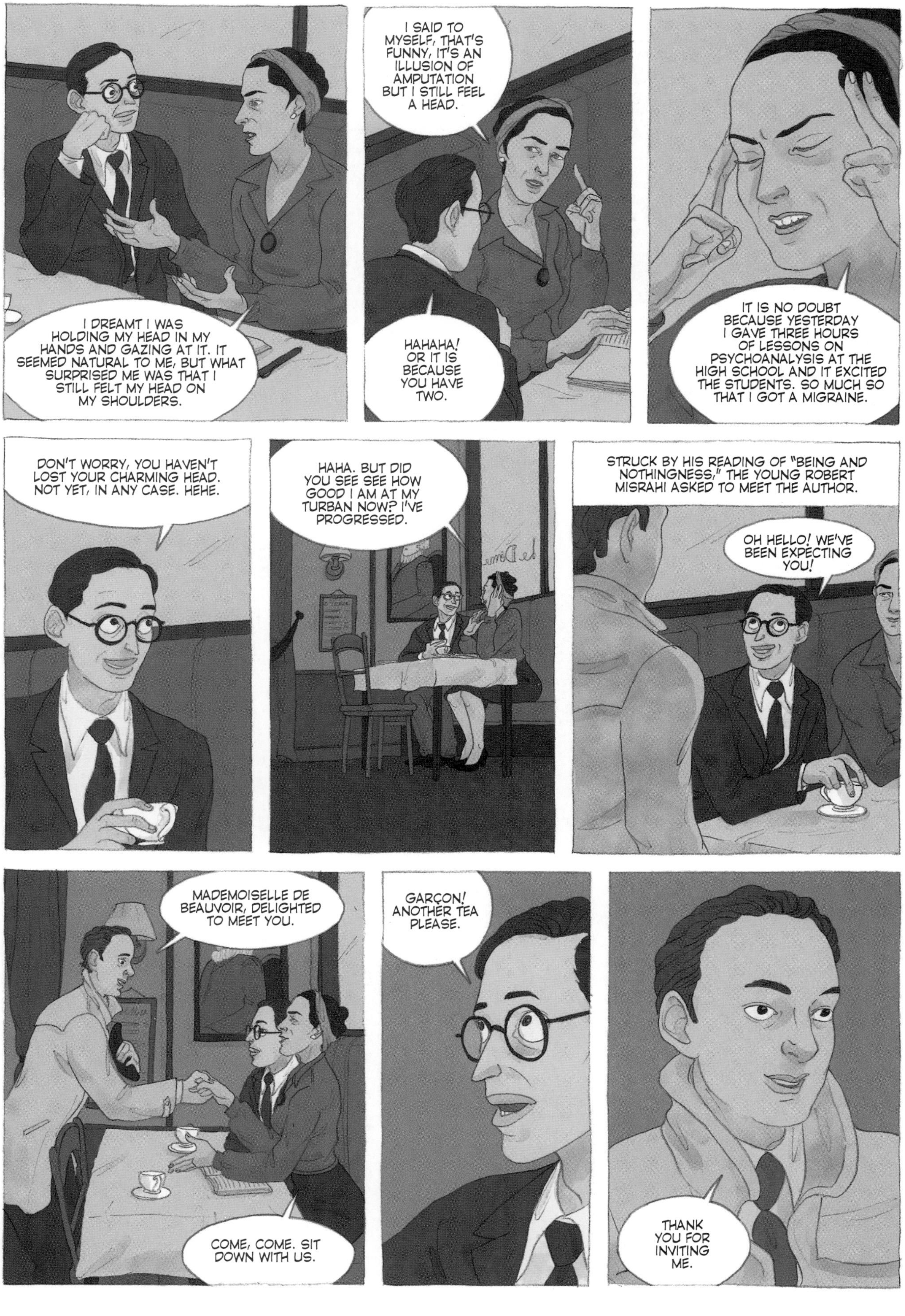
I DREAMT I WAS HOLDING MY HEAD IN MY HANDS AND GAZING AT IT. IT SEEMED NATURAL TO ME, BUT WHAT SURPRISED ME WAS THAT I STILL FELT MY HEAD ON MY SHOULDERS.
I SAID TO MYSELF, THAT'S FUNNY, IT'S AN ILLUSION OF AMPUTATION BUT I STILL FEEL A HEAD.
HAHAHA! OR IT IS BECAUSE YOU HAVE TWO.
IT IS NO DOUBT BECAUSE YESTERDAY I GAVE THREE HOURS OF LESSONS ON PSYCHOANALYSIS AT THE HIGH SCHOOL AND IT EXCITED THE STUDENTS. SO MUCH SO THAT I GOT A MIGRAINE.
DON'T WORRY, YOU HAVEN'T LOST YOUR CHARMING HEAD. NOT YET, IN ANY CASE. HEHE.
HAHA. BUT DID YOU SEE SEE HOW GOOD I AM AT MY TURBAN NOW? I'VE PROGRESSED.
STRUCK BY HIS READING OF "BEING AND NOTHINGNESS," THE YOUNG ROBERT MISRAHI ASKED TO MEET THE AUTHOR.
OH HELLO! WE'VE BEEN EXPECTING YOU!
MADEMOISELLE DE BEAUVOIR, DELIGHTED TO MEET YOU.
COME, COME. SIT DOWN WITH US.
GARÇON! ANOTHER TEA PLEASE.
THANK YOU FOR INVITING ME.

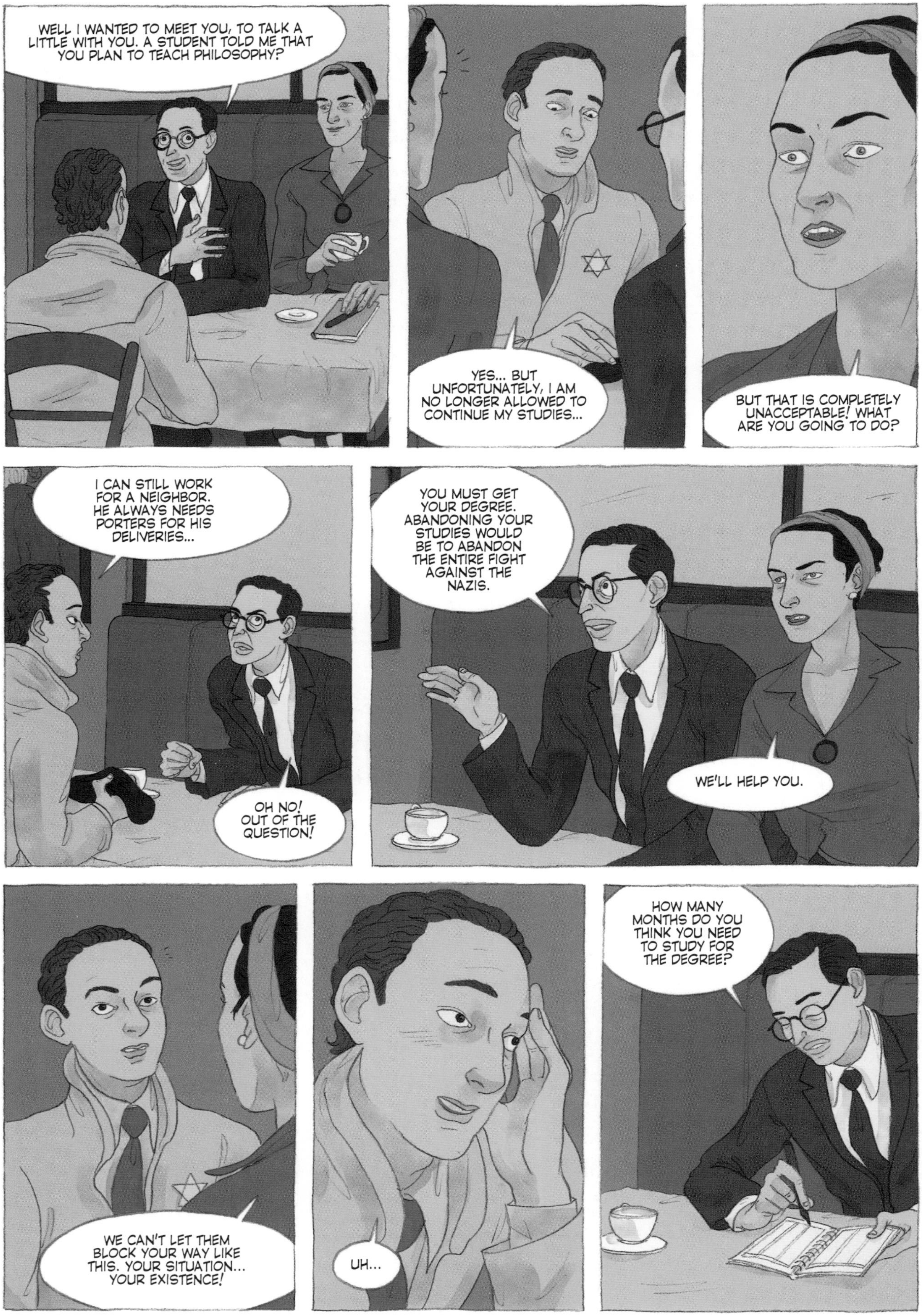
WELL I WANTED TO MEET YOU, TO TALK A LITTLE WITH YOU. A STUDENT TOLD ME THAT YOU PLAN TO TEACH PHILOSOPHY?
YES... BUT UNFORTUNATELY, I AM NO LONGER ALLOWED TO CONTINUE MY STUDIES...
BUT THAT IS COMPLETELY UNACCEPTABLE! WHAT ARE YOU GOING TO DO?
I CAN STILL WORK FOR A NEIGHBOR. HE ALWAYS NEEDS PORTERS FOR HIS DELIVERIES...
OH NO! OUT OF THE QUESTION!
YOU MUST GET YOUR DEGREE. ABANDONING YOUR STUDIES WOULD BE TO ABANDON THE ENTIRE FIGHT AGAINST THE NAZIS.
WE'LL HELP YOU.
WE CAN'T LET THEM BLOCK YOUR WAY LIKE THIS. YOUR SITUATION... YOUR EXISTENCE!
UH...
HOW MANY MONTHS DO YOU THINK YOU NEED TO STUDY FOR THE DEGREE?

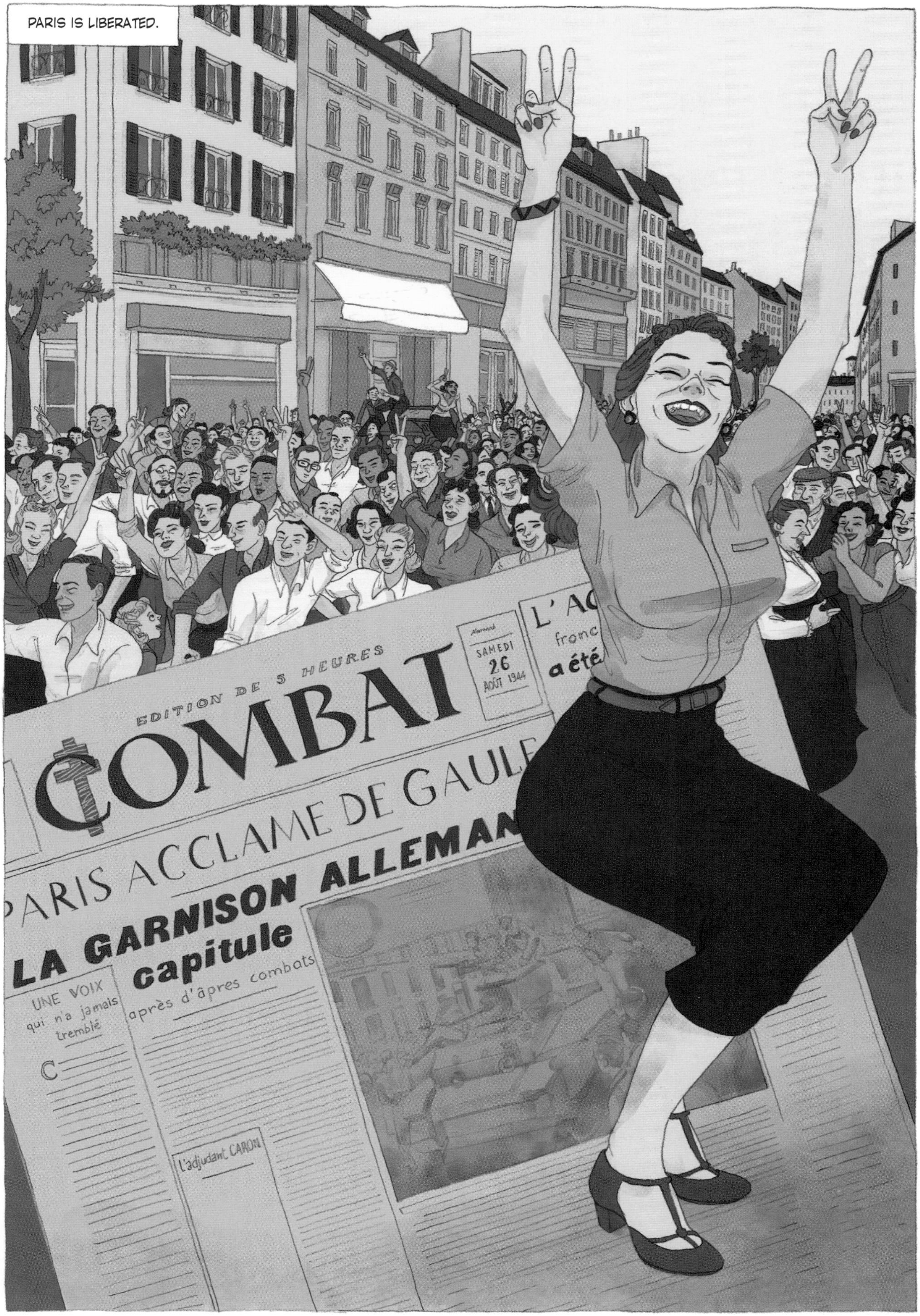
PARIS IS LIBERATED.
EDITION DE 5 HEURES
COMBAT
SAMEDI 26 AOÛT 1944
LA GARNISON
capitule
après d'âpres combats
UNE VOIX qui n'a jamais tremblé
L'adjudant CARON

RECRUITED BY ALBERT CAMUS FOR "COMBAT," SARTRE LEAVES FOR NEW YORK IN JANUARY 1945 ON A DC-8.

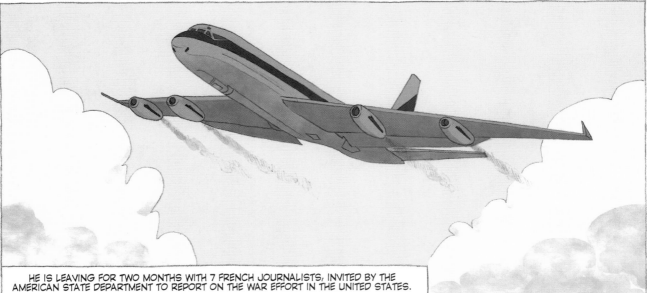

HE IS LEAVING FOR TWO MONTHS WITH 7 FRENCH JOURNALISTS, INVITED BY THE AMERICAN STATE DEPARTMENT TO REPORT ON THE WAR EFFORT IN THE UNITED STATES.

I WAS FINALLY GOING TO STAND ON THE GROUND OF THE GREATEST OF FREE COUNTRIES. THE ONE THAT MADE ME DREAM OF BUFFALO BILL!

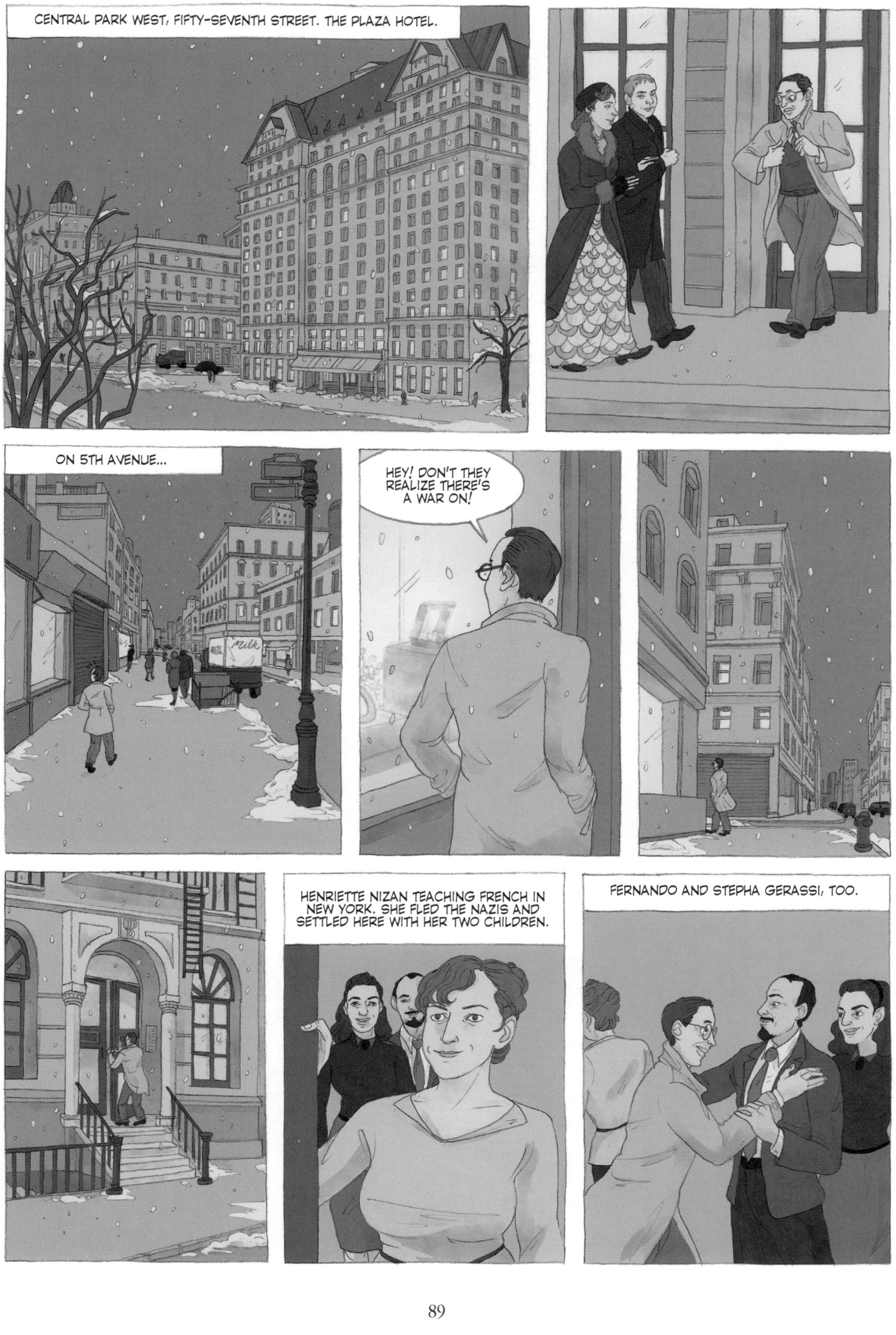

CENTRAL PARK WEST, FIFTY-SEVENTH STREET. THE PLAZA HOTEL.
ON 5TH AVENUE...
HEY! DON'T THEY REALIZE THERE'S A WAR ON!
HENRIETTE NIZAN TEACHING FRENCH IN NEW YORK. SHE FLED THE NAZIS AND SETTLED HERE WITH HER TWO CHILDREN.
FERNANDO AND STEPHA GERASSI, TOO.

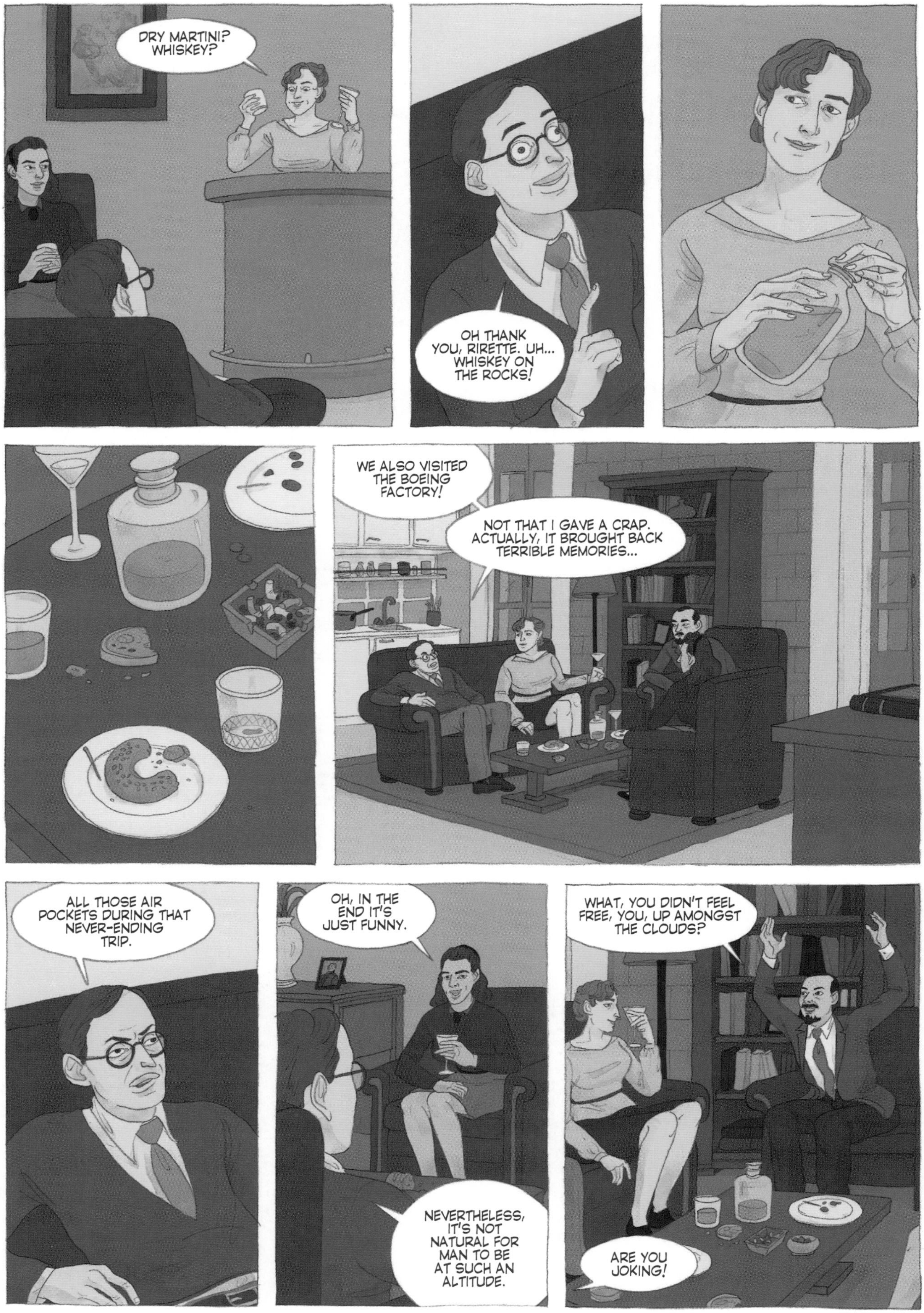
DRY MARTINI? WHISKEY?
OH THANK YOU, RIRETTE. UH... WHISKEY ON THE ROCKS!
WE ALSO VISITED THE BOEING FACTORY!
NOT THAT I GAVE A CRAP. ACTUALLY, IT BROUGHT BACK TERRIBLE MEMORIES...
ALL THOSE AIR POCKETS DURING THAT NEVER-ENDING TRIP.
OH, IN THE END IT'S JUST FUNNY.
NEVERTHELESS, IT'S NOT NATURAL FOR MAN TO BE AT SUCH AN ALTITUDE.
WHAT, YOU DIDN'T FEEL FREE, YOU, UP AMONGST THE CLOUDS?
ARE YOU JOKING!

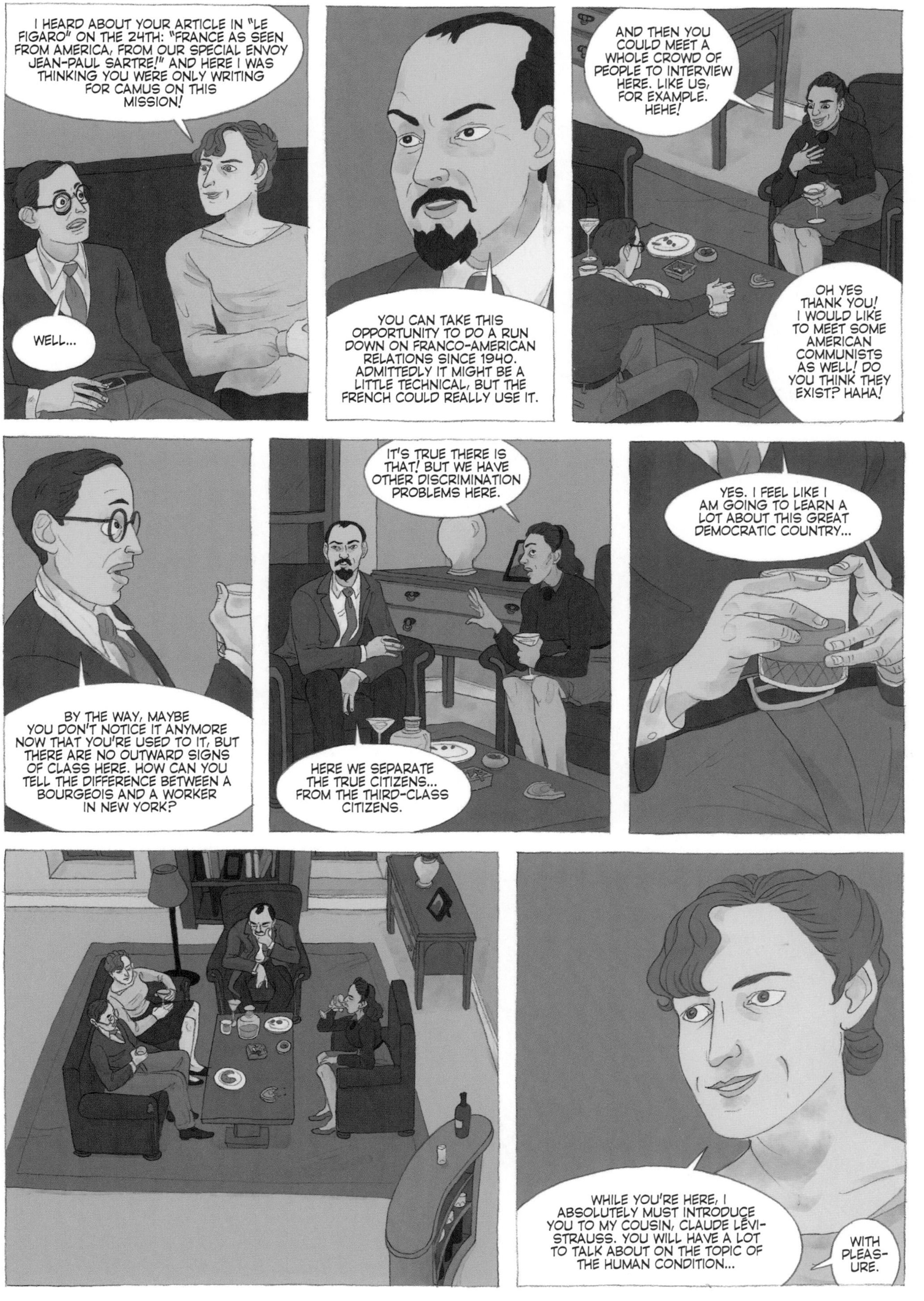

I HEARD ABOUT YOUR ARTICLE IN "LE FIGARO" ON THE 24TH: "FRANCE AS SEEN FROM AMERICA, FROM OUR SPECIAL ENVOY JEAN-PAUL SARTRE!" AND HERE I WAS THINKING YOU WERE ONLY WRITING FOR CAMUS ON THIS MISSION!
WELL...
YOU CAN TAKE THIS OPPORTUNITY TO DO A RUN DOWN ON FRANCO-AMERICAN RELATIONS SINCE 1940. ADMITTEDLY IT MIGHT BE A LITTLE TECHNICAL, BUT THE FRENCH COULD REALLY USE IT.
AND THEN YOU COULD MEET A WHOLE CROWD OF PEOPLE TO INTERVIEW HERE. LIKE US, FOR EXAMPLE. HEHE!
OH YES THANK YOU! I WOULD LIKE TO MEET SOME AMERICAN COMMUNISTS AS WELL! DO YOU THINK THEY EXIST? HAHA!
BY THE WAY, MAYBE YOU DON'T NOTICE IT ANYMORE NOW THAT YOU'RE USED TO IT, BUT THERE ARE NO OUTWARD SIGNS OF CLASS HERE. HOW CAN YOU TELL THE DIFFERENCE BETWEEN A BOURGEOIS AND A WORKER IN NEW YORK?
IT'S TRUE THERE IS THAT! BUT WE HAVE OTHER DISCRIMINATION PROBLEMS HERE.
HERE WE SEPARATE THE TRUE CITIZENS... FROM THE THIRD-CLASS CITIZENS.
YES. I FEEL LIKE I AM GOING TO LEARN A LOT ABOUT THIS GREAT DEMOCRATIC COUNTRY...
WHILE YOU'RE HERE, I ABSOLUTELY MUST INTRODUCE YOU TO MY COUSIN, CLAUDE LÉVI-STRAUSS. YOU WILL HAVE A LOT TO TALK ABOUT ON THE TOPIC OF THE HUMAN CONDITION...
WITH PLEAS-URE.

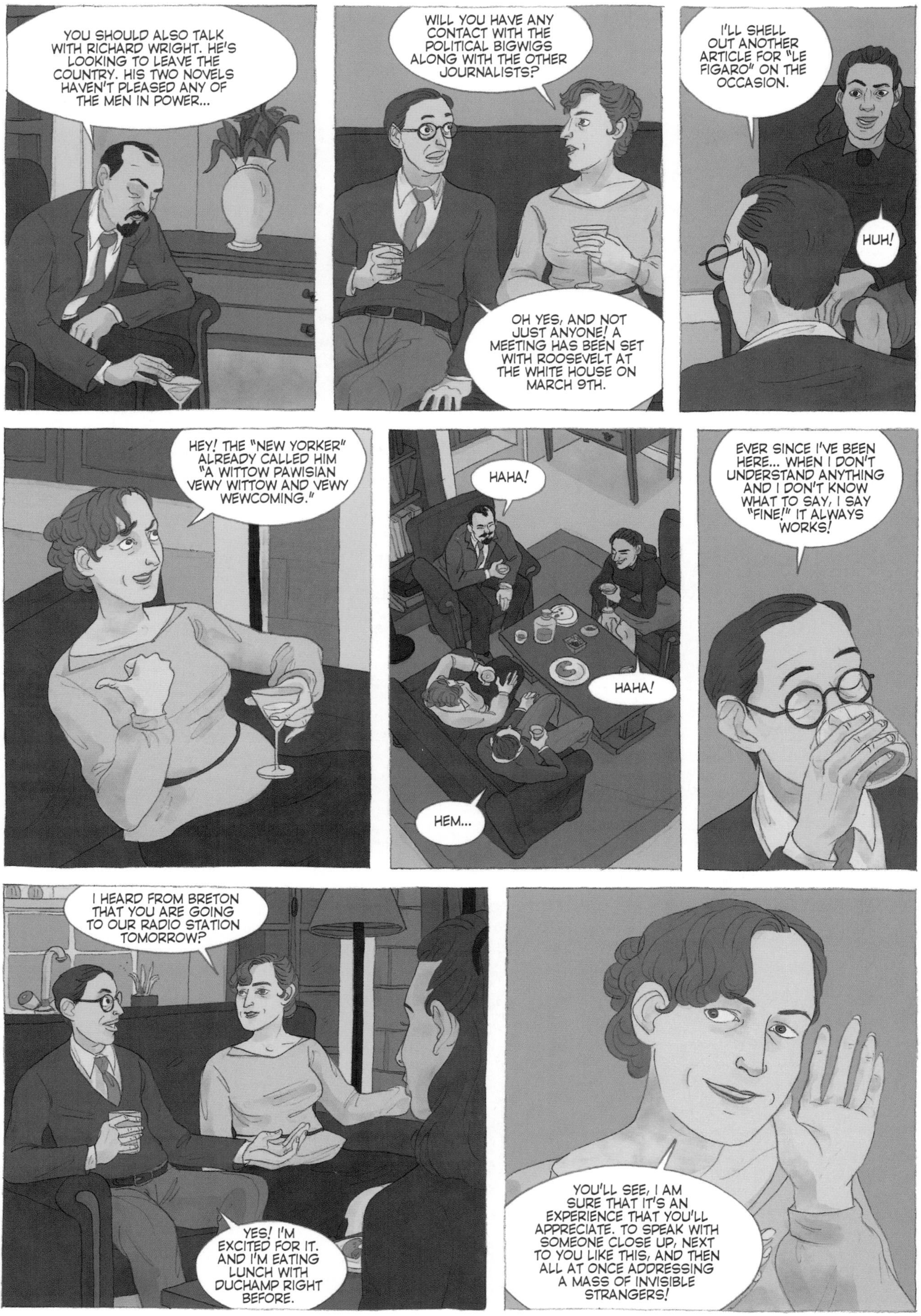
YOU SHOULD ALSO TALK WITH RICHARD WRIGHT. HE'S LOOKING TO LEAVE THE COUNTRY. HIS TWO NOVELS HAVEN'T PLEASED ANY OF THE MEN IN POWER...
WILL YOU HAVE ANY CONTACT WITH THE POLITICAL BIGWIGS ALONG WITH THE OTHER JOURNALISTS?
OH YES, AND NOT JUST ANYONE! A MEETING HAS BEEN SET WITH ROOSEVELT AT THE WHITE HOUSE ON MARCH 9TH.
I'LL SHELL OUT ANOTHER ARTICLE FOR "LE FIGARO" ON THE OCCASION.
HUH!
HEY! THE "NEW YORKER" ALREADY CALLED HIM "A WITTOW PAWISIAN VEWY WITTOW AND VEWY WEWCOMING."
HAHA!
HAHA!
HEM...
EVER SINCE I'VE BEEN HERE... WHEN I DON'T UNDERSTAND ANYTHING AND I DON'T KNOW WHAT TO SAY, I SAY "FINE!" IT ALWAYS WORKS!
I HEARD FROM BRETON THAT YOU ARE GOING TO OUR RADIO STATION TOMORROW?
YES! I'M EXCITED FOR IT. AND I'M EATING LUNCH WITH DUCHAMP RIGHT BEFORE.
YOU'LL SEE, I AM SURE THAT IT'S AN EXPERIENCE THAT YOU'LL APPRECIATE. TO SPEAK WITH SOMEONE CLOSE UP, NEXT TO YOU LIKE THIS, AND THEN ALL AT ONCE ADDRESSING A MASS OF INVISIBLE STRANGERS!

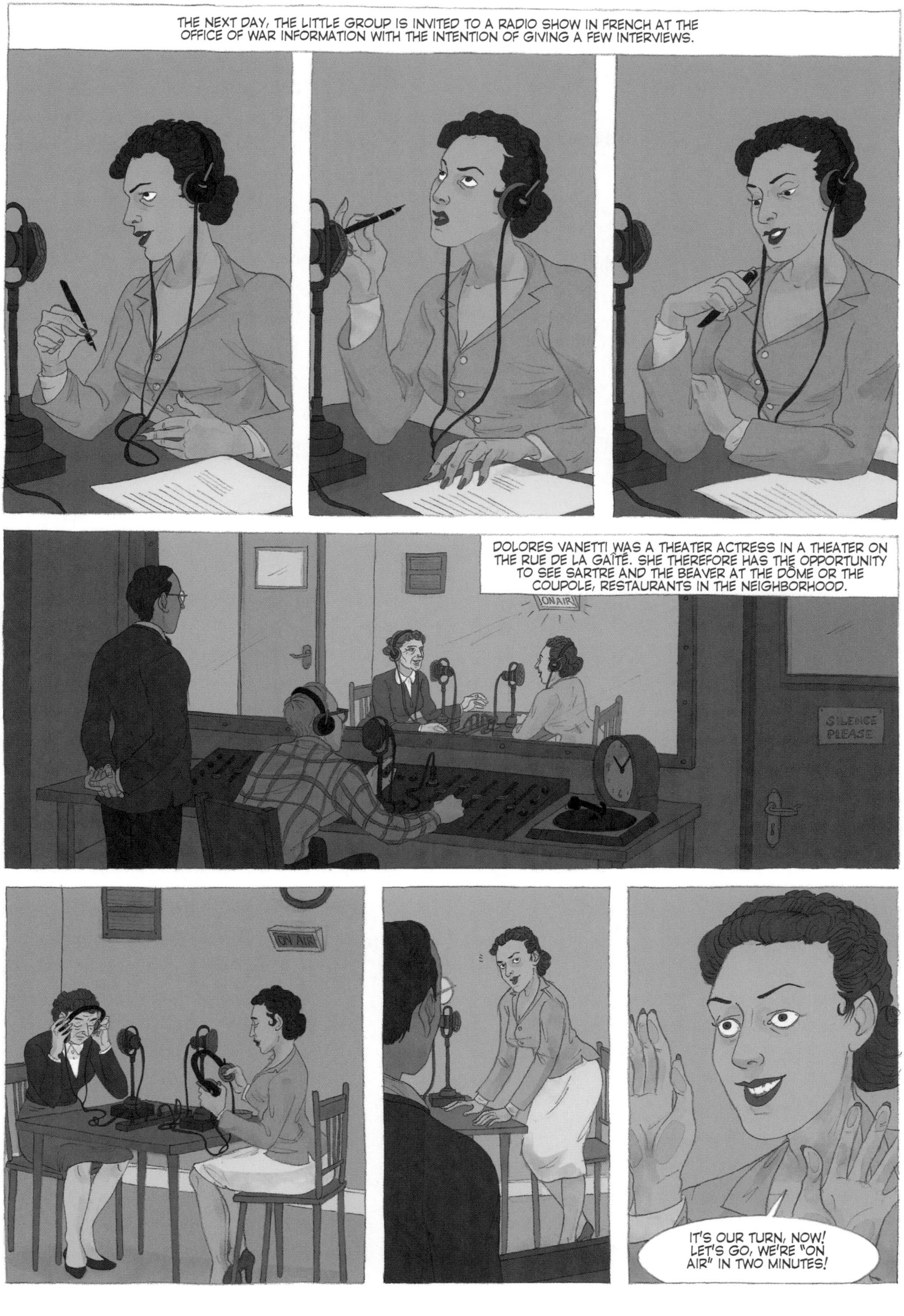
THE NEXT DAY, THE LITTLE GROUP IS INVITED TO A RADIO SHOW IN FRENCH AT THE OFFICE OF WAR INFORMATION WITH THE INTENTION OF GIVING A FEW INTERVIEWS.
DOLORES VANETTI WAS A THEATER ACTRESS IN A THEATER ON THE RUE DE LA GAÎTÉ. SHE THEREFORE HAS THE OPPORTUNITY TO SEE SARTRE AND THE BEAVER AT THE DÔME OR THE COUPOLE, RESTAURANTS IN THE NEIGHBORHOOD.
ON AIR
SILENCE PLEASE
ON AIR
IT'S OUR TURN, NOW! LET'S GO, WE'RE "ON AIR" IN TWO MINUTES!

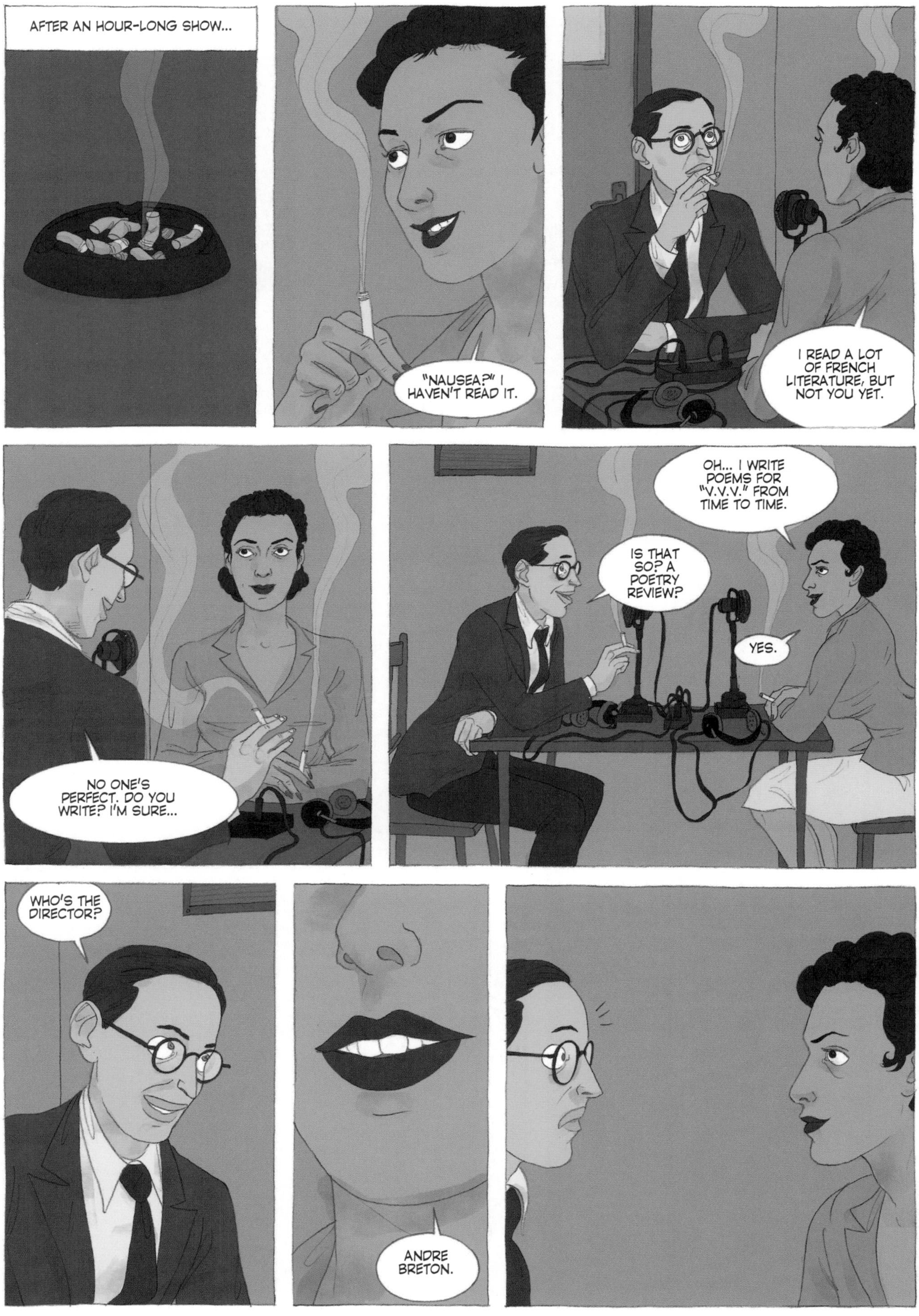
AFTER AN HOUR-LONG SHOW...
"NAUSEA?" I HAVEN'T READ IT.
I READ A LOT OF FRENCH LITERATURE, BUT NOT YOU YET.
NO ONE'S PERFECT. DO YOU WRITE? I'M SURE...
OH... I WRITE POEMS FOR "V.V.V." FROM TIME TO TIME.
IS THAT SO? A POETRY REVIEW?
YES.
WHO'S THE DIRECTOR?
ANDRE BRETON.

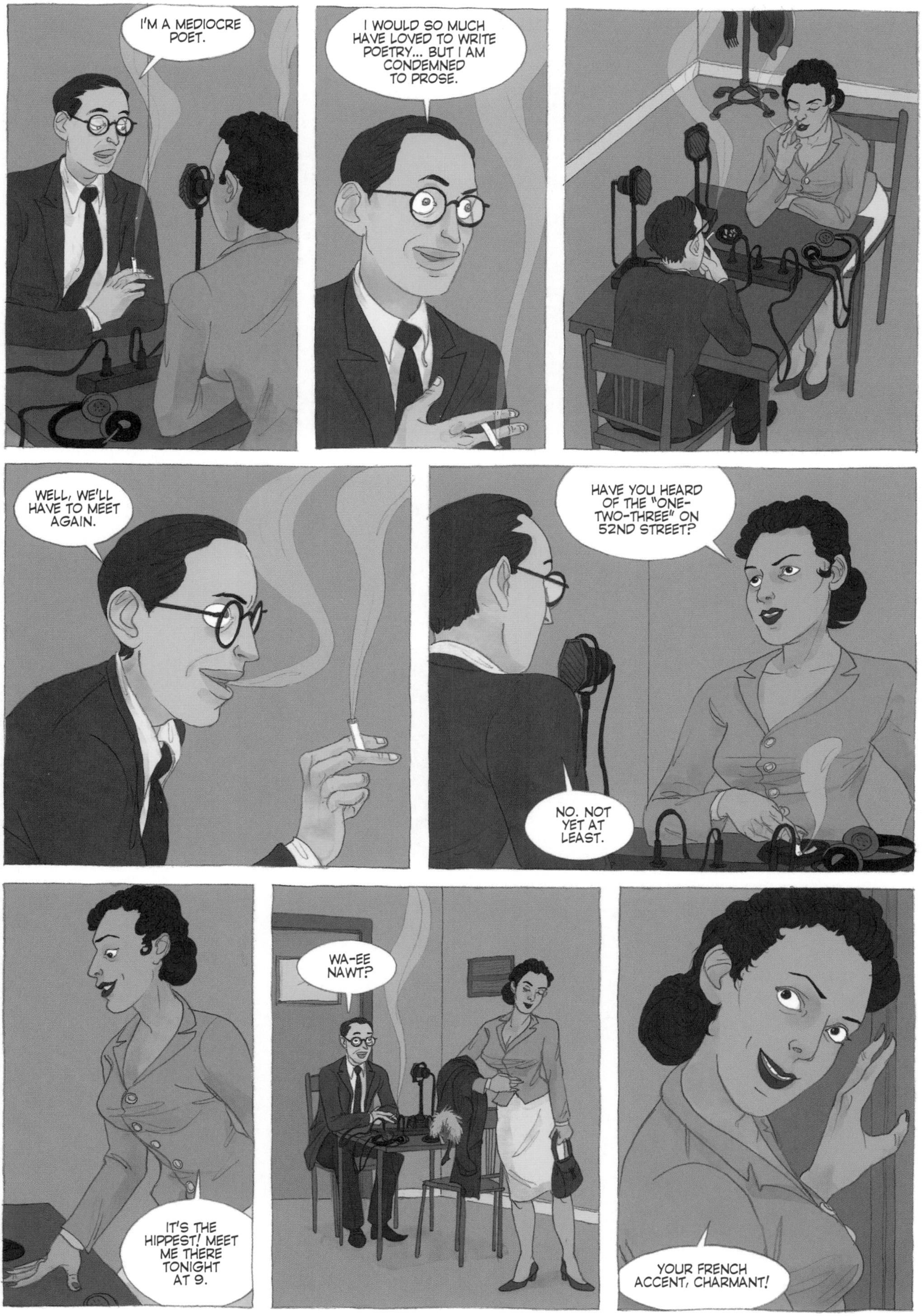
I'M A MEDIOCRE POET.
I WOULD SO MUCH HAVE LOVED TO WRITE POETRY... BUT I AM CONDEMNED TO PROSE.
WELL, WE'LL HAVE TO MEET AGAIN.
HAVE YOU HEARD OF THE "ONE-TWO-THREE" ON 52ND STREET?
NO. NOT YET AT LEAST.
IT'S THE HIPPEST! MEET ME THERE TONIGHT AT 9.
WA-EE NAWT?
YOUR FRENCH ACCENT, CHARMANT!

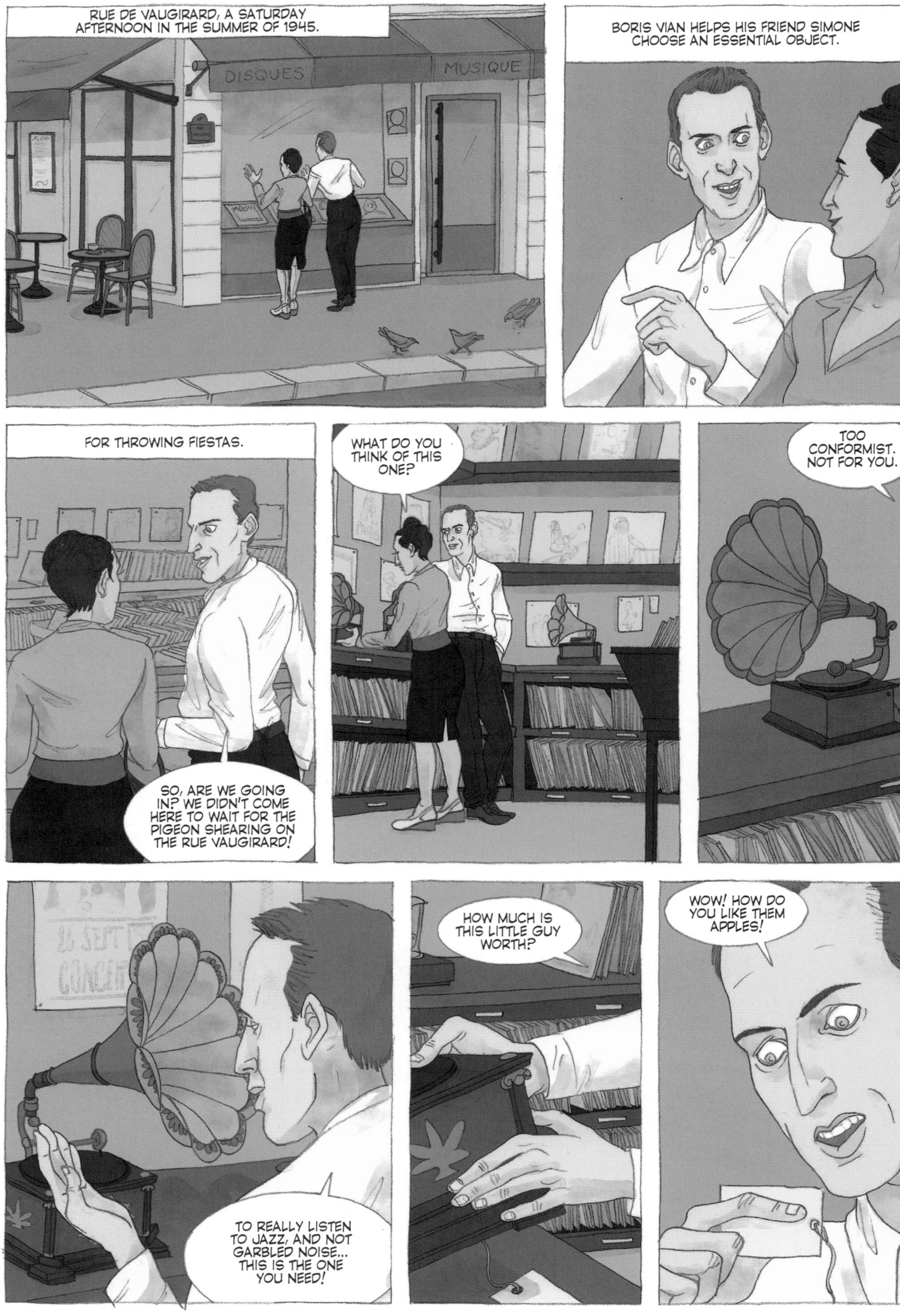
RUE DE VAUGIRARD, A SATURDAY AFTERNOON IN THE SUMMER OF 1945.
DISQUES
MUSIQUE
BORIS VIAN HELPS HIS FRIEND SIMONE CHOOSE AN ESSENTIAL OBJECT.
FOR THROWING FIESTAS.
SO, ARE WE GOING IN? WE DIDN'T COME HERE TO WAIT FOR THE PIGEON SHEARING ON THE RUE VAUGIRARD!
WHAT DO YOU THINK OF THIS ONE?
TOO CONFORMIST. NOT FOR YOU.
TO REALLY LISTEN TO JAZZ, AND NOT GARBLED NOISE... THIS IS THE ONE YOU NEED!
HOW MUCH IS THIS LITTLE GUY WORTH?
WOW! HOW DO YOU LIKE THEM APPLES!

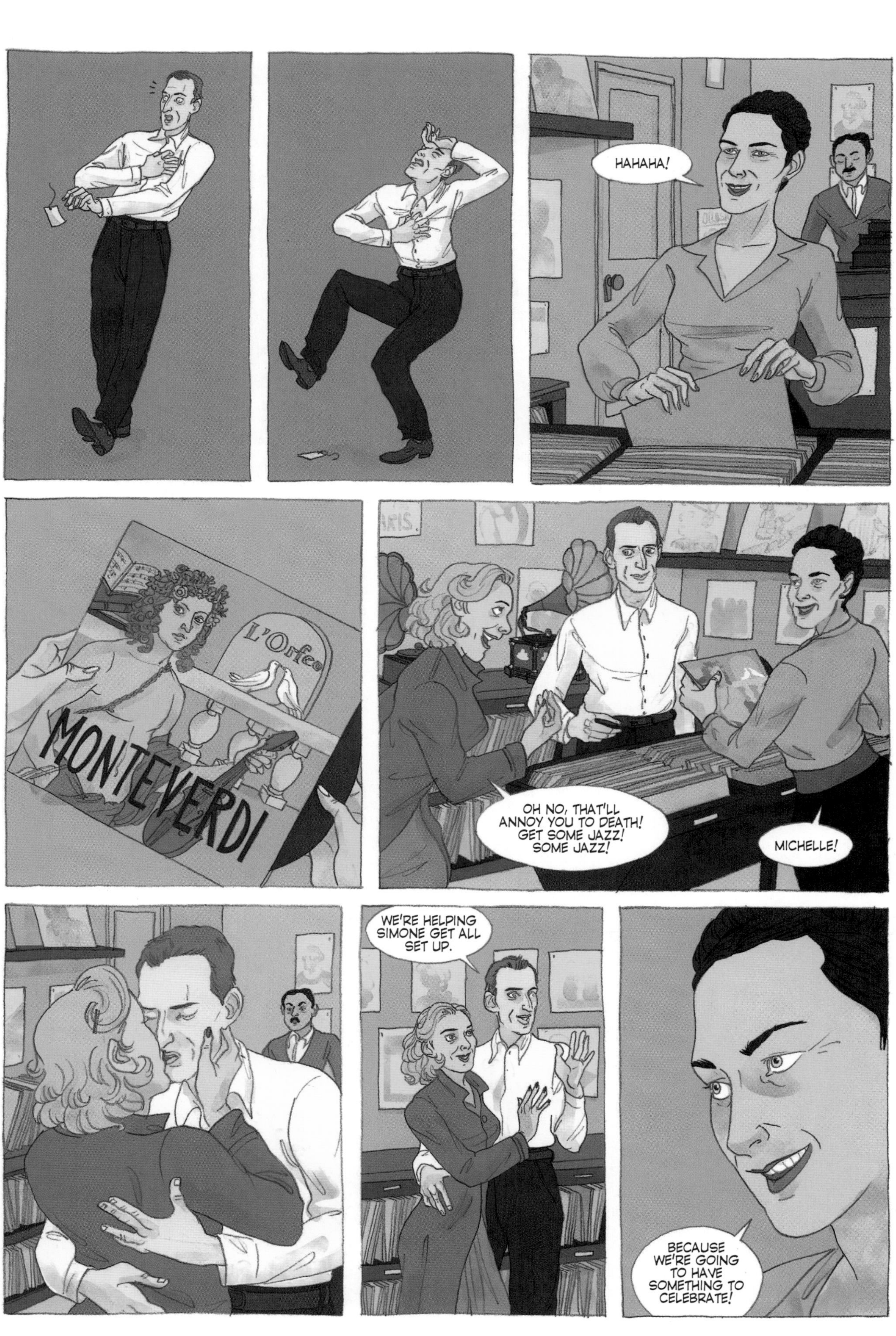

HAHAHA!
L'Orfeo
MONTEVERDI
OH NO, THAT'LL ANNOY YOU TO DEATH! GET SOME JAZZ! SOME JAZZ!
MICHELLE!
WE'RE HELPING SIMONE GET ALL SET UP.
BECAUSE WE'RE GOING TO HAVE SOMETHING TO CELEBRATE!

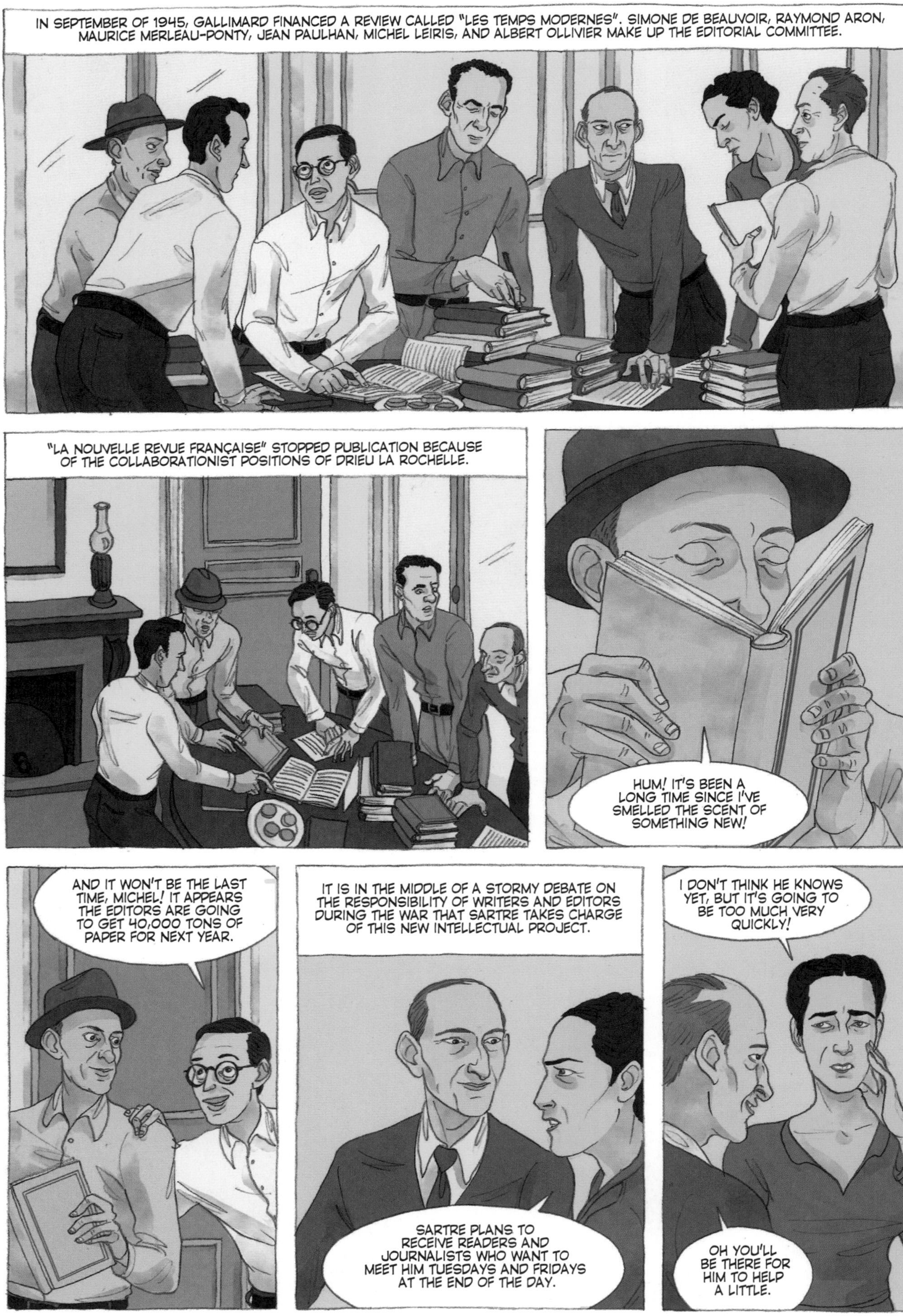

IN SEPTEMBER OF 1945, GALLIMARD FINANCED A REVIEW CALLED "LES TEMPS MODERNES". SIMONE DE BEAUVOIR, RAYMOND ARON, MAURICE MERLEAU-PONTY, JEAN PAULHAN, MICHEL LEIRIS, AND ALBERT OLLIVIER MAKE UP THE EDITORIAL COMMITTEE.
"LA NOUVELLE REVUE FRANÇAISE" STOPPED PUBLICATION BECAUSE OF THE COLLABORATIONIST POSITIONS OF DRIEU LA ROCHELLE.
HUM! IT'S BEEN A LONG TIME SINCE I'VE SMELLED THE SCENT OF SOMETHING NEW!
AND IT WON'T BE THE LAST TIME, MICHEL! IT APPEARS THE EDITORS ARE GOING TO GET 40,000 TONS OF PAPER FOR NEXT YEAR.
IT IS IN THE MIDDLE OF A STORMY DEBATE ON THE RESPONSIBILITY OF WRITERS AND EDITORS DURING THE WAR THAT SARTRE TAKES CHARGE OF THIS NEW INTELLECTUAL PROJECT.
SARTRE PLANS TO RECEIVE READERS AND JOURNALISTS WHO WANT TO MEET HIM TUESDAYS AND FRIDAYS AT THE END OF THE DAY.
I DON'T THINK HE KNOWS YET, BUT IT'S GOING TO BE TOO MUCH VERY QUICKLY!
OH YOU'LL BE THERE FOR HIM TO HELP A LITTLE.

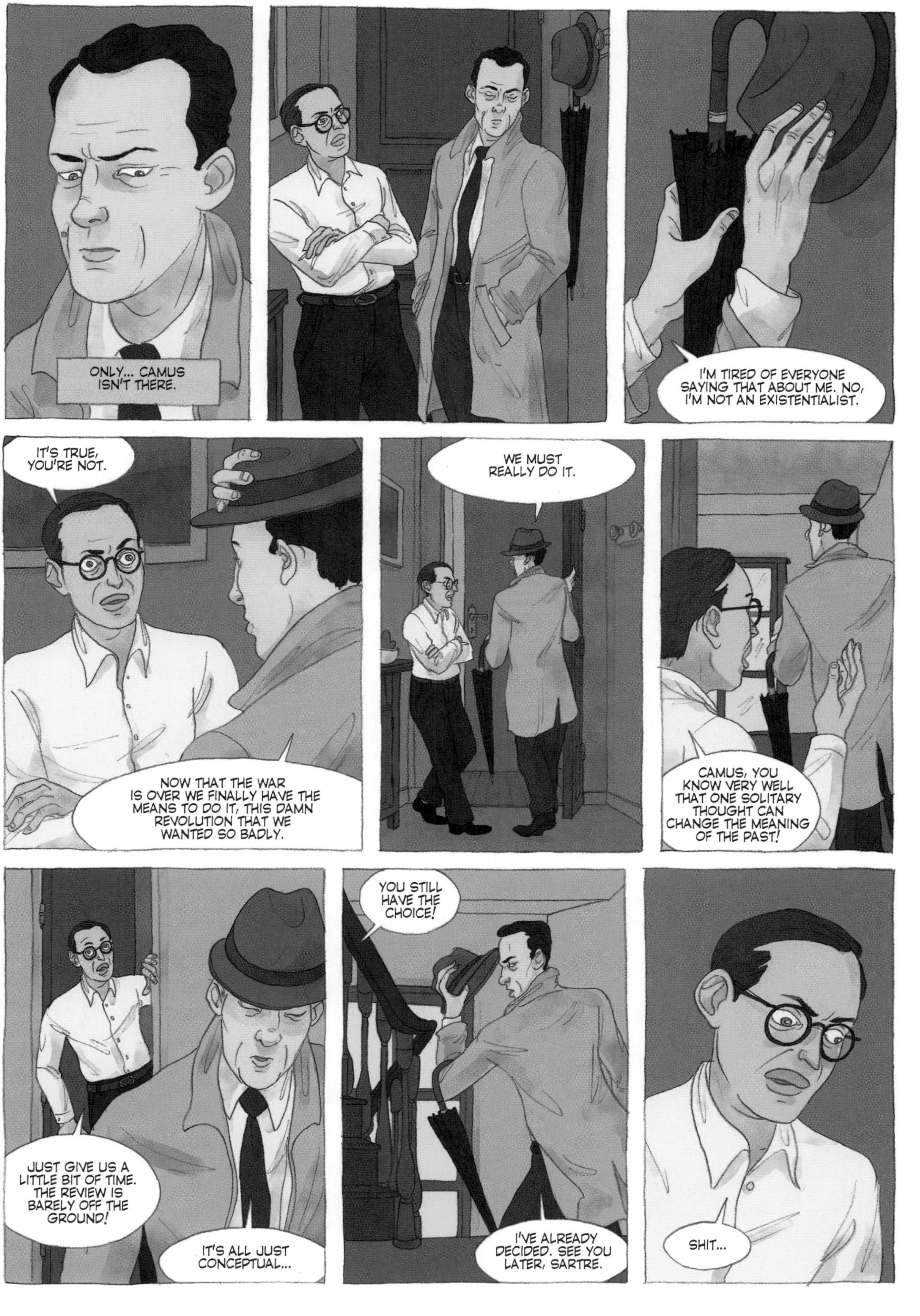
ONLY... CAMUS ISN'T THERE.
I'M TIRED OF EVERYONE SAYING THAT ABOUT ME. NO, I'M NOT AN EXISTENTIALIST.
IT'S TRUE, YOU'RE NOT.
NOW THAT THE WAR IS OVER WE FINALLY HAVE THE MEANS TO DO IT, THIS DAMN REVOLUTION THAT WE WANTED SO BADLY.
WE MUST REALLY DO IT.
CAMUS, YOU KNOW VERY WELL THAT ONE SOLITARY THOUGHT CAN CHANGE THE MEANING OF THE PAST!
JUST GIVE US A LITTLE BIT OF TIME. THE REVIEW IS BARELY OFF THE GROUND!
IT'S ALL JUST CONCEPTUAL...
YOU STILL HAVE THE CHOICE!
I'VE ALREADY DECIDED. SEE YOU LATER, SARTRE.
SHIT...

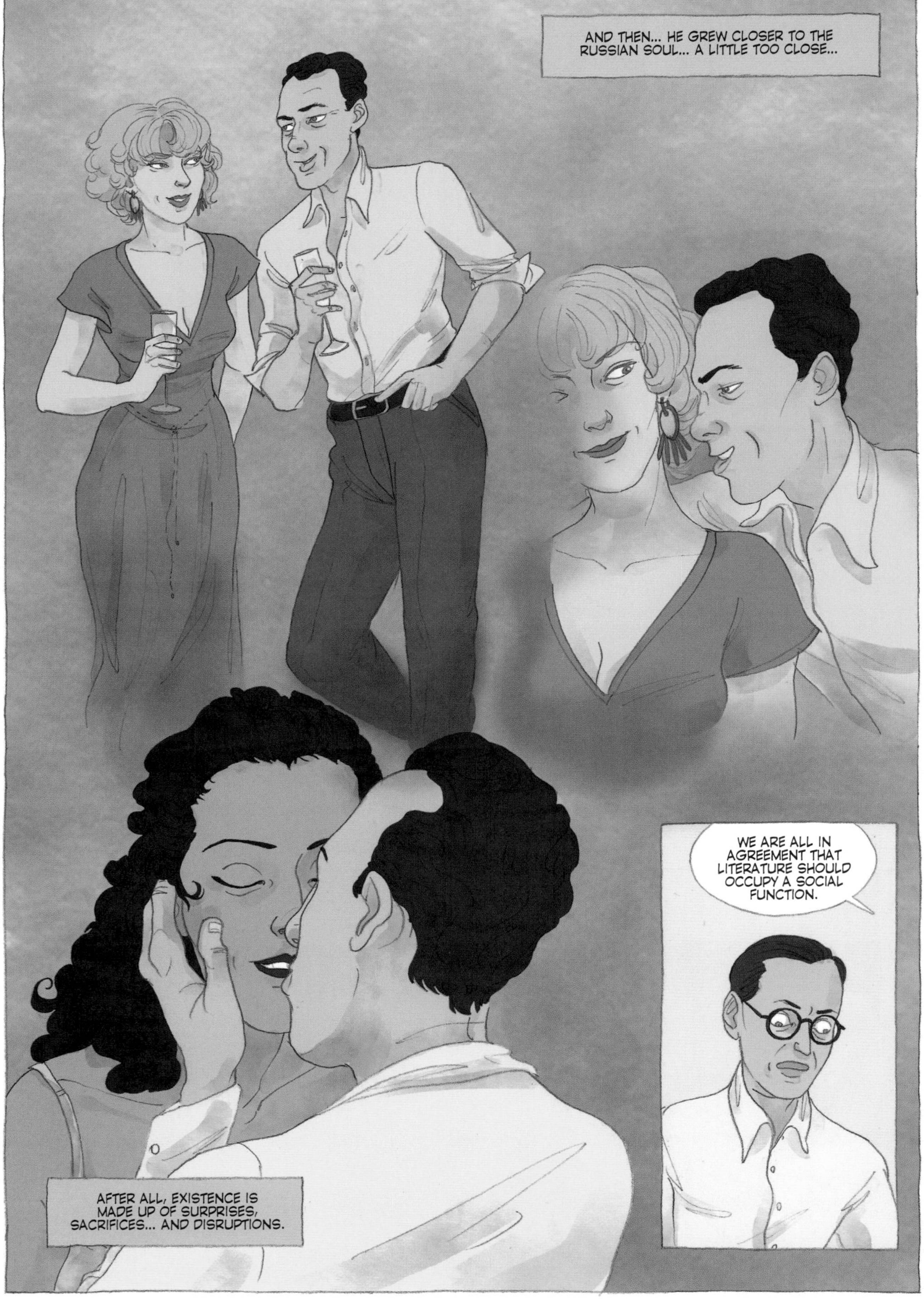
AND THEN... HE GREW CLOSER TO THE RUSSIAN SOUL... A LITTLE TOO CLOSE...
WE ARE ALL IN AGREEMENT THAT LITERATURE SHOULD OCCUPY A SOCIAL FUNCTION.
AFTER ALL, EXISTENCE IS MADE UP OF SURPRISES, SACRIFICES... AND DISRUPTIONS.

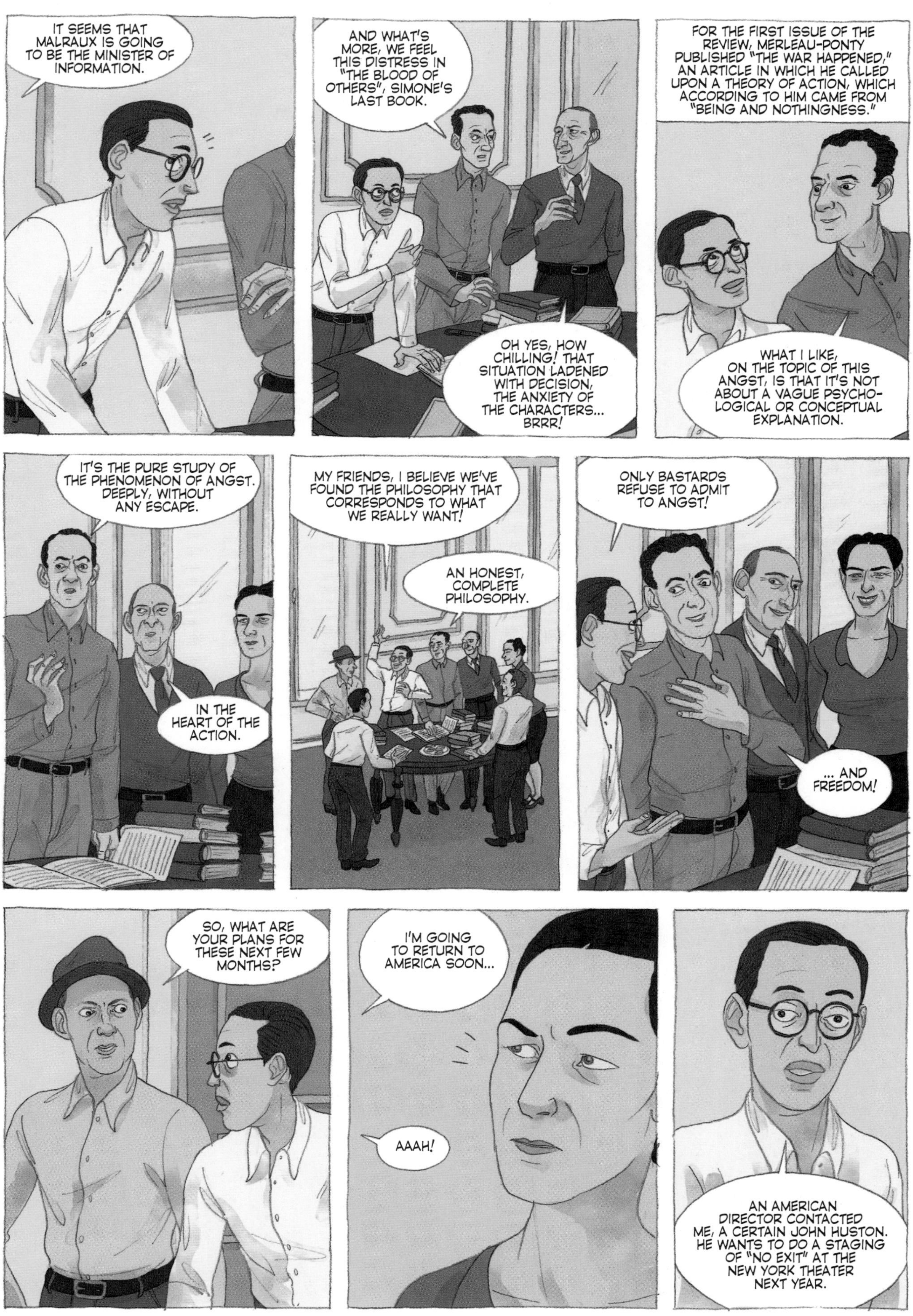
IT SEEMS THAT MALRAUX IS GOING TO BE THE MINISTER OF INFORMATION.
AND WHAT'S MORE, WE FEEL THIS DISTRESS IN "THE BLOOD OF OTHERS", SIMONE'S LAST BOOK.
OH YES, HOW CHILLING! THAT SITUATION LADENED WITH DECISION, THE ANXIETY OF THE CHARACTERS... BRRR!
FOR THE FIRST ISSUE OF THE REVIEW, MERLEAU-PONTY PUBLISHED "THE WAR HAPPENED," AN ARTICLE IN WHICH HE CALLED UPON A THEORY OF ACTION, WHICH ACCORDING TO HIM CAME FROM "BEING AND NOTHINGNESS."
WHAT I LIKE, ON THE TOPIC OF THIS ANGST, IS THAT IT'S NOT ABOUT A VAGUE PSYCHOLOGICAL OR CONCEPTUAL EXPLANATION.
IT'S THE PURE STUDY OF THE PHENOMENON OF ANGST. DEEPLY, WITHOUT ANY ESCAPE.
IN THE HEART OF THE ACTION.
MY FRIENDS, I BELIEVE WE'VE FOUND THE PHILOSOPHY THAT CORRESPONDS TO WHAT WE REALLY WANT!
AN HONEST, COMPLETE PHILOSOPHY.
ONLY BASTARDS REFUSE TO ADMIT TO ANGST!
... AND FREEDOM!
SO, WHAT ARE YOUR PLANS FOR THESE NEXT FEW MONTHS?
I'M GOING TO RETURN TO AMERICA SOON...
AAAH!
AN AMERICAN DIRECTOR CONTACTED ME, A CERTAIN JOHN HUSTON. HE WANTS TO DO A STAGING OF "NO EXIT" AT THE NEW YORK THEATER NEXT YEAR.

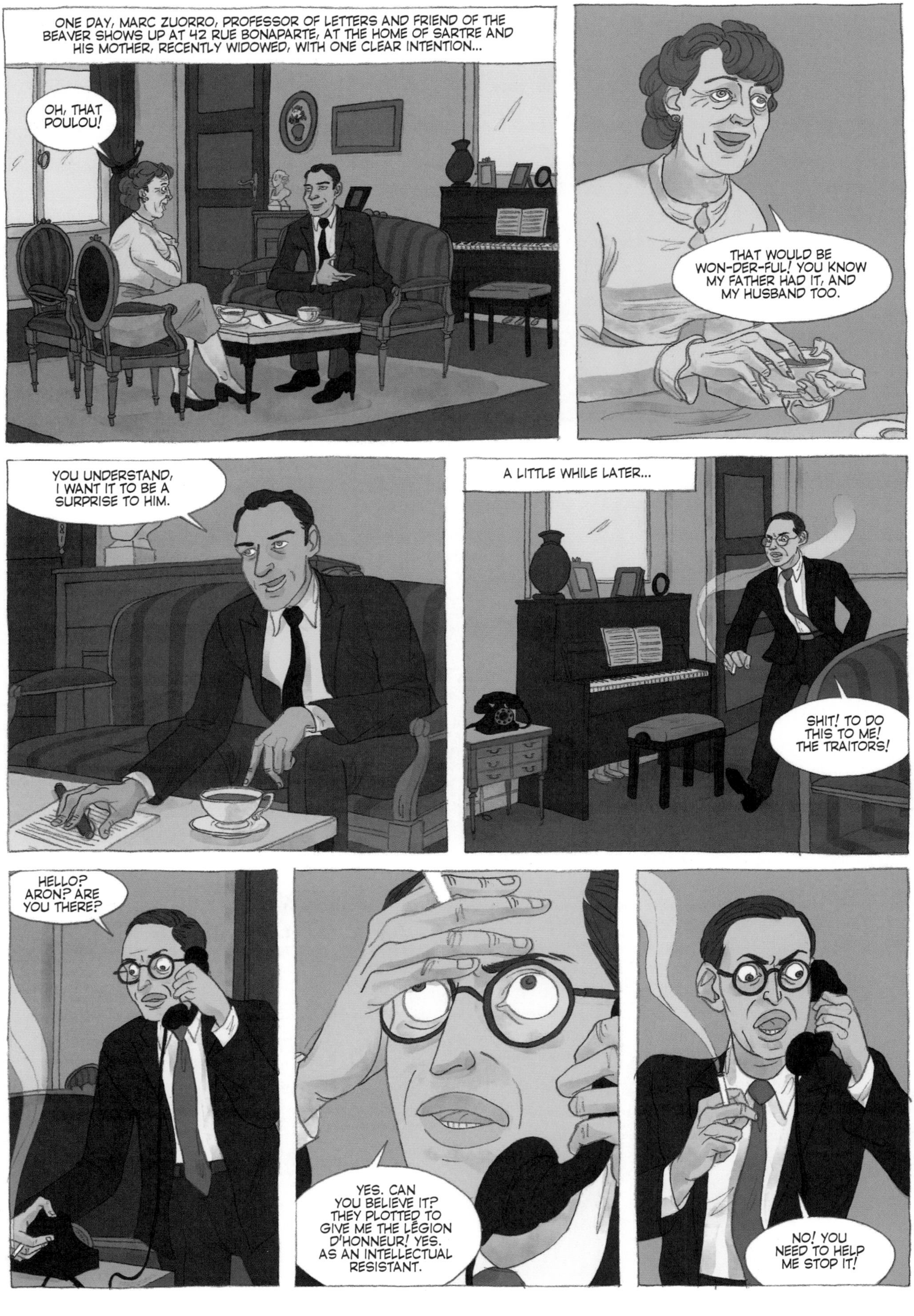
ONE DAY, MARC ZUORRO, PROFESSOR OF LETTERS AND FRIEND OF THE BEAVER SHOWS UP AT 42 RUE BONAPARTE, AT THE HOME OF SARTRE AND HIS MOTHER, RECENTLY WIDOWED, WITH ONE CLEAR INTENTION...
OH, THAT POULOU!
THAT WOULD BE WON-DER-FUL! YOU KNOW MY FATHER HAD IT, AND MY HUSBAND TOO.
YOU UNDERSTAND, I WANT IT TO BE A SURPRISE TO HIM.
A LITTLE WHILE LATER...
SHIT! TO DO THIS TO ME! THE TRAITORS!
HELLO? ARON? ARE YOU THERE?
YES. CAN YOU BELIEVE IT? THEY PLOTTED TO GIVE ME THE LÉGION D'HONNEUR! YES. AS AN INTELLECTUAL RESISTANT.
NO! YOU NEED TO HELP ME STOP IT!

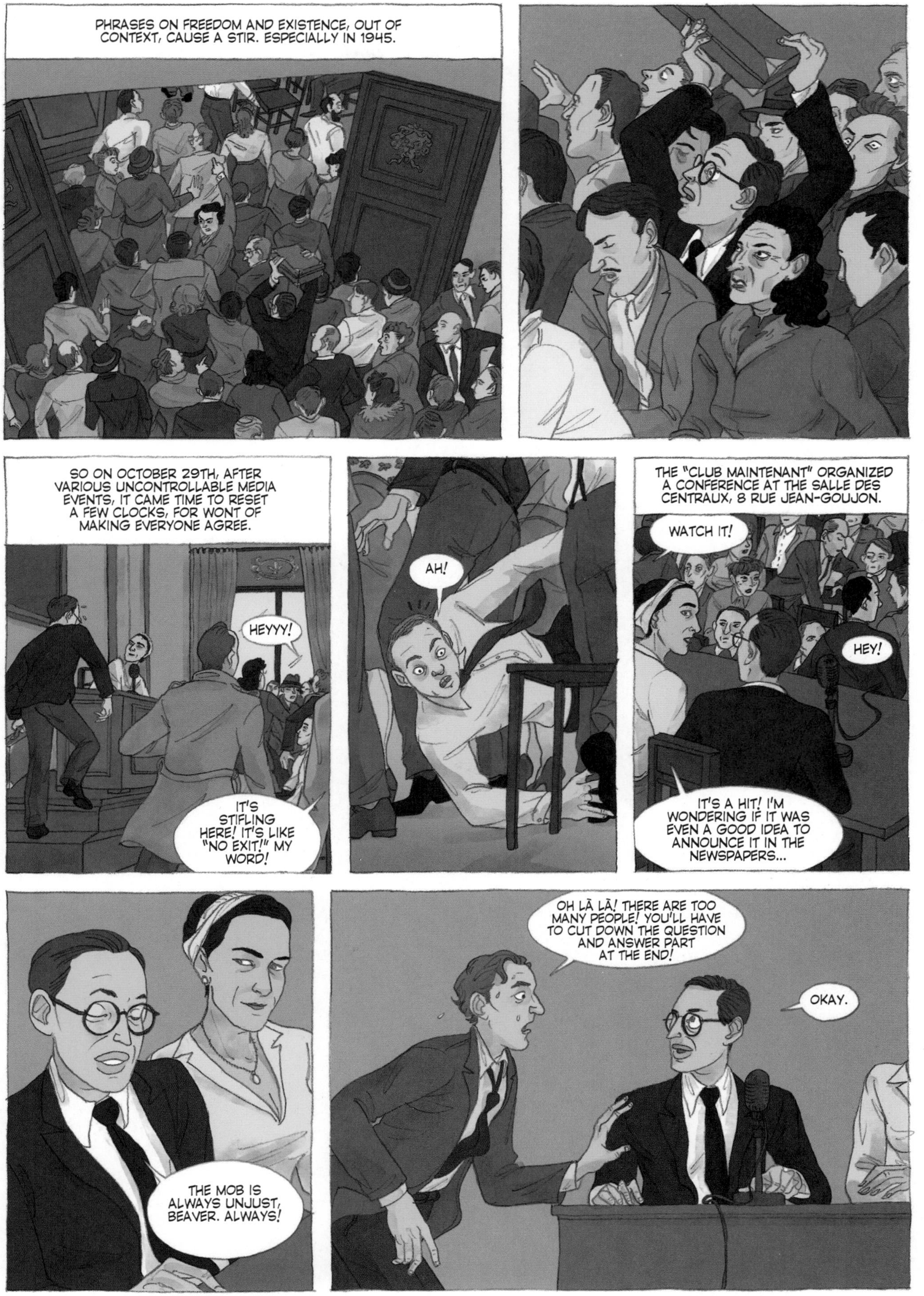
PHRASES ON FREEDOM AND EXISTENCE, OUT OF CONTEXT, CAUSE A STIR. ESPECIALLY IN 1945.
SO ON OCTOBER 29TH, AFTER VARIOUS UNCONTROLLABLE MEDIA EVENTS, IT CAME TIME TO RESET A FEW CLOCKS, FOR WONT OF MAKING EVERYONE AGREE.
HEYYY!
IT'S STIFLING HERE! IT'S LIKE "NO EXIT!" MY WORD!
AH!
THE "CLUB MAINTENANT" ORGANIZED A CONFERENCE AT THE SALLE DES CENTRAUX, 8 RUE JEAN-GOUJON.
WATCH IT!
HEY!
IT'S A HIT! I'M WONDERING IF IT WAS EVEN A GOOD IDEA TO ANNOUNCE IT IN THE NEWSPAPERS...
THE MOB IS ALWAYS UNJUST, BEAVER. ALWAYS!
OH LÃ LÃ! THERE ARE TOO MANY PEOPLE! YOU'LL HAVE TO CUT DOWN THE QUESTION AND ANSWER PART AT THE END!
OKAY.

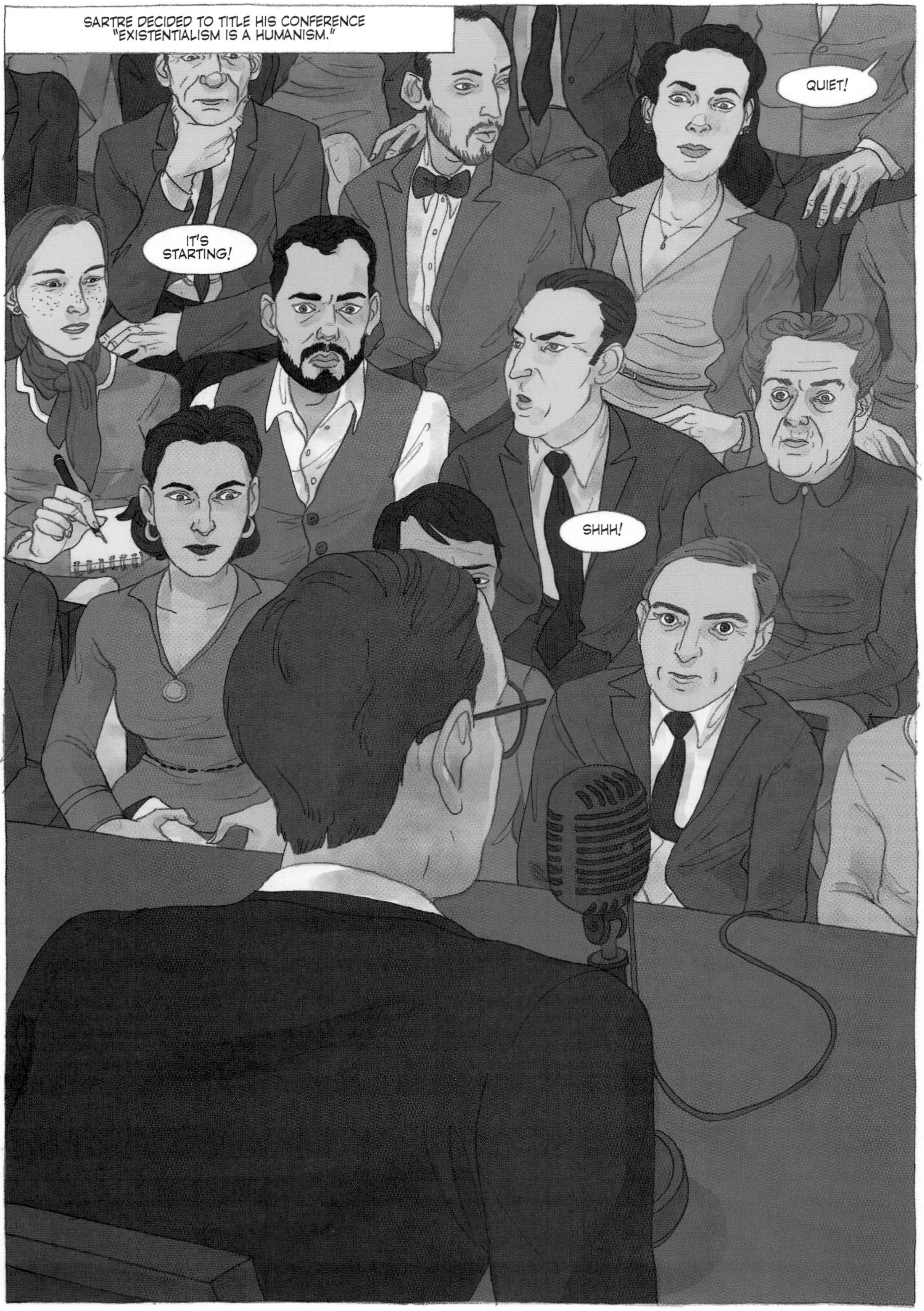
SARTRE DECIDED TO TITLE HIS CONFERENCE "EXISTENTIALISM IS A HUMANISM."
QUIET!
IT'S STARTING!
SHHH!

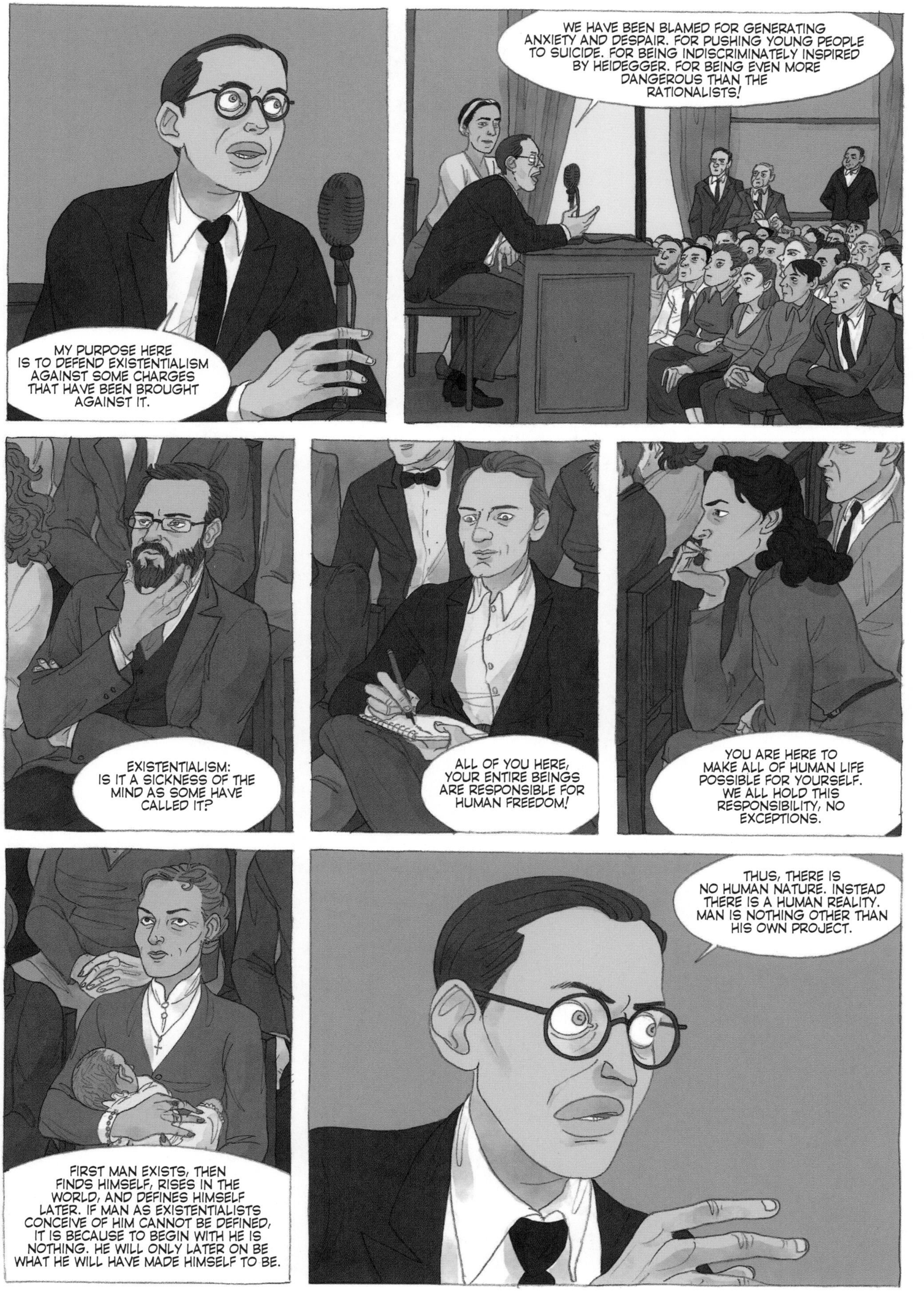
MY PURPOSE HERE IS TO DEFEND EXISTENTIALISM AGAINST SOME CHARGES THAT HAVE BEEN BROUGHT AGAINST IT.
WE HAVE BEEN BLAMED FOR GENERATING ANXIETY AND DESPAIR. FOR PUSHING YOUNG PEOPLE TO SUICIDE. FOR BEING INDISCRIMINATELY INSPIRED BY HEIDEGGER. FOR BEING EVEN MORE DANGEROUS THAN THE RATIONALISTS!
EXISTENTIALISM: IS IT A SICKNESS OF THE MIND AS SOME HAVE CALLED IT?
ALL OF YOU HERE, YOUR ENTIRE BEINGS ARE RESPONSIBLE FOR HUMAN FREEDOM!
YOU ARE HERE TO MAKE ALL OF HUMAN LIFE POSSIBLE FOR YOURSELF. WE ALL HOLD THIS RESPONSIBILITY, NO EXCEPTIONS.
FIRST MAN EXISTS, THEN FINDS HIMSELF, RISES IN THE WORLD, AND DEFINES HIMSELF LATER. IF MAN AS EXISTENTIALISTS CONCEIVE OF HIM CANNOT BE DEFINED, IT IS BECAUSE TO BEGIN WITH HE IS NOTHING. HE WILL ONLY LATER ON BE WHAT HE WILL HAVE MADE HIMSELF TO BE.
THUS, THERE IS NO HUMAN NATURE. INSTEAD THERE IS A HUMAN REALITY. MAN IS NOTHING OTHER THAN HIS OWN PROJECT.

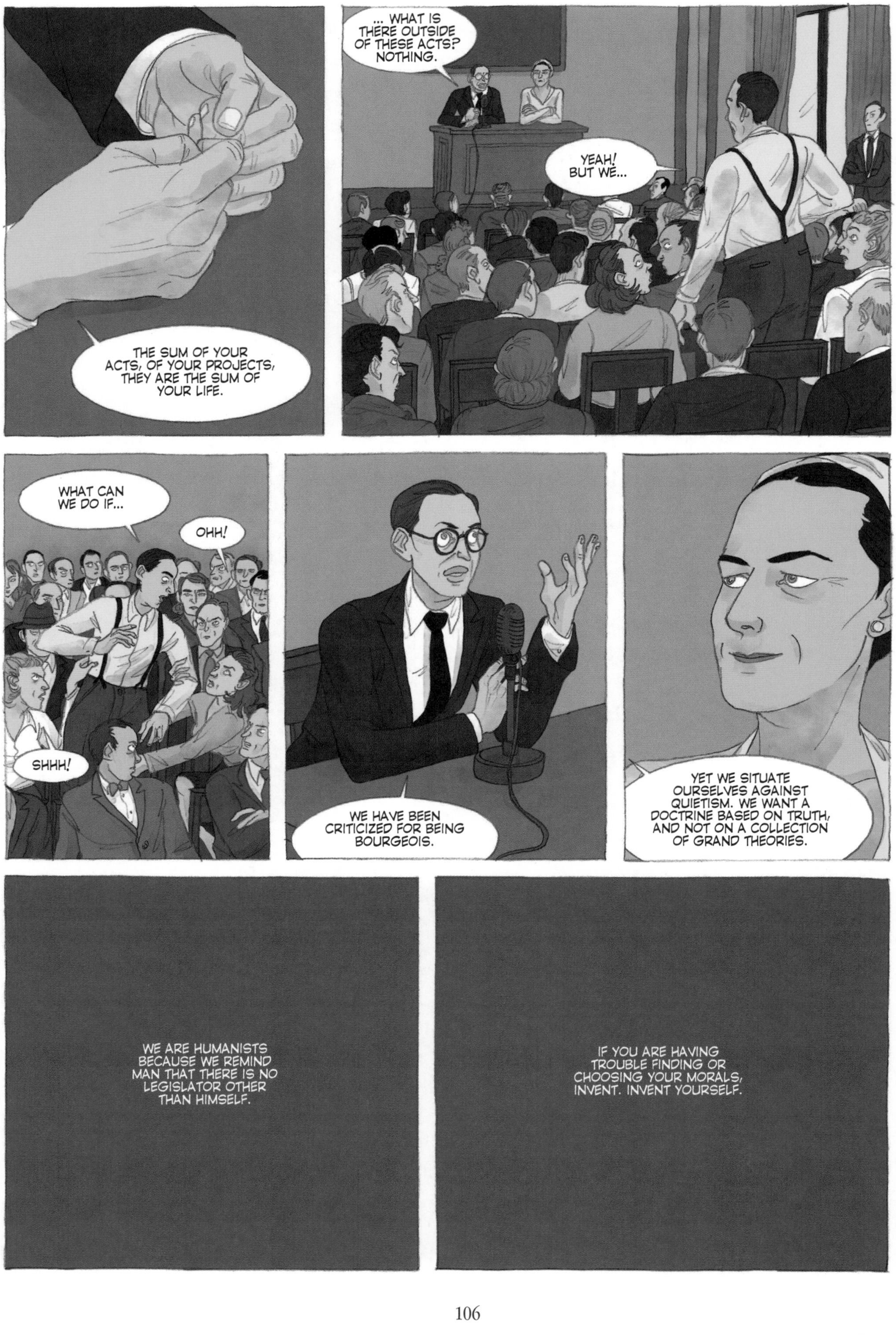
THE SUM OF YOUR ACTS, OF YOUR PROJECTS, THEY ARE THE SUM OF YOUR LIFE.
... WHAT IS THERE OUTSIDE OF THESE ACTS? NOTHING.
YEAH! BUT WE...
WHAT CAN WE DO IF...
OHH!
SHHH!
WE HAVE BEEN CRITICIZED FOR BEING BOURGEOIS.
YET WE SITUATE OURSELVES AGAINST QUIETISM. WE WANT A DOCTRINE BASED ON TRUTH, AND NOT ON A COLLECTION OF GRAND THEORIES.
WE ARE HUMANISTS BECAUSE WE REMIND MAN THAT THERE IS NO LEGISLATOR OTHER THAN HIMSELF.
IF YOU ARE HAVING TROUBLE FINDING OR CHOOSING YOUR MORALS, INVENT. INVENT YOURSELF.

PART THREE :
"PASSIONS AND IMPOSSIBILITY"

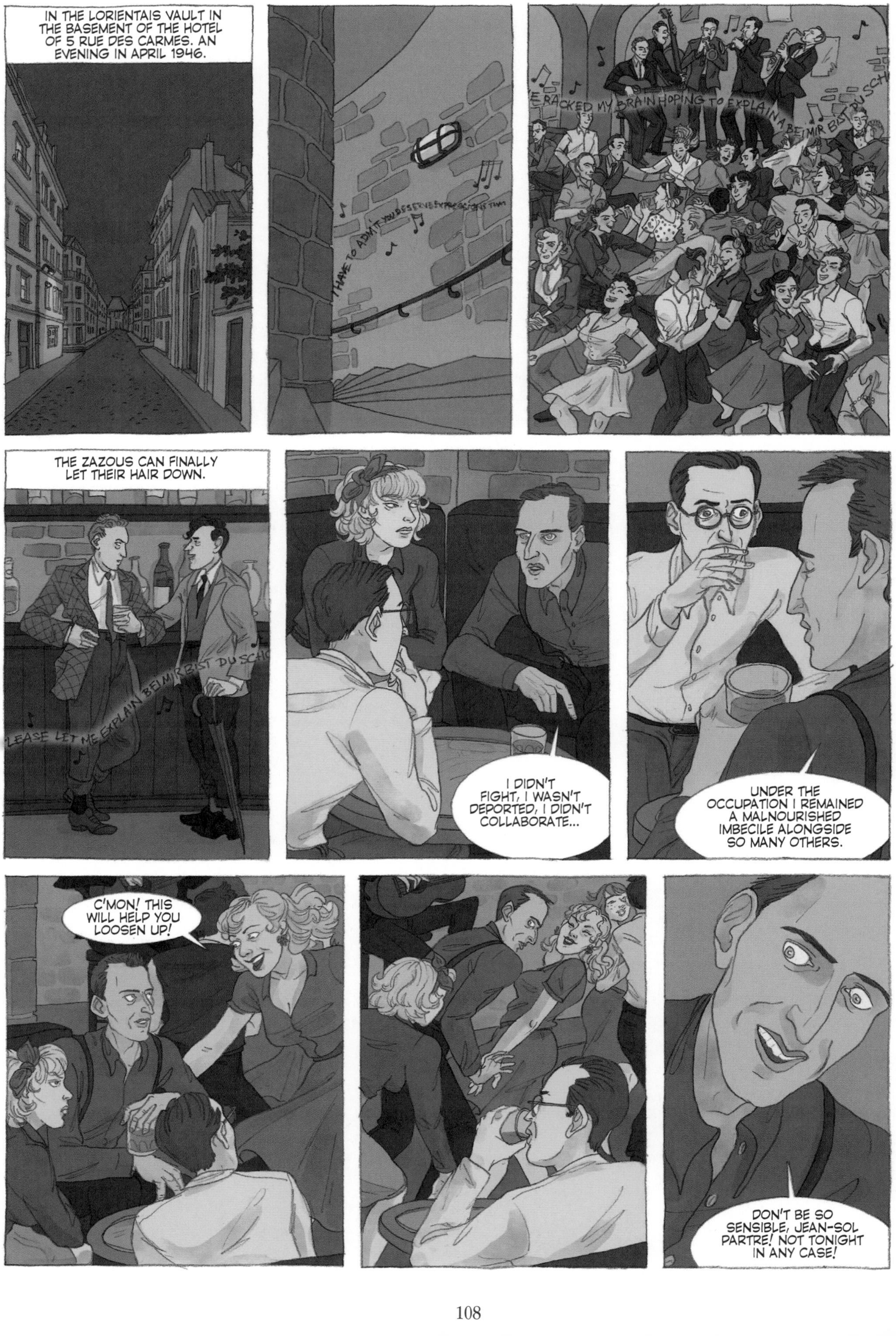
IN THE LORIENTAIS VAULT IN THE BASEMENT OF THE HOTEL OF 5 RUE DES CARMES. AN EVENING IN APRIL 1946.
RACKED MY BRAIN HOPING TO EXPLAIN A BEI MIR BIST DU SCH
THE ZAZOUS CAN FINALLY LET THEIR HAIR DOWN.
LEASE LET ME EXPLAIN BEI MIR BIST DU SCH
I DIDN'T FIGHT, I WASN'T DEPORTED, I DIDN'T COLLABORATE...
UNDER THE OCCUPATION I REMAINED A MALNOURISHED IMBECILE ALONGSIDE SO MANY OTHERS.
C'MON! THIS WILL HELP YOU LOOSEN UP!
DON'T BE SO SENSIBLE, JEAN-SOL PARTRE! NOT TONIGHT IN ANY CASE!

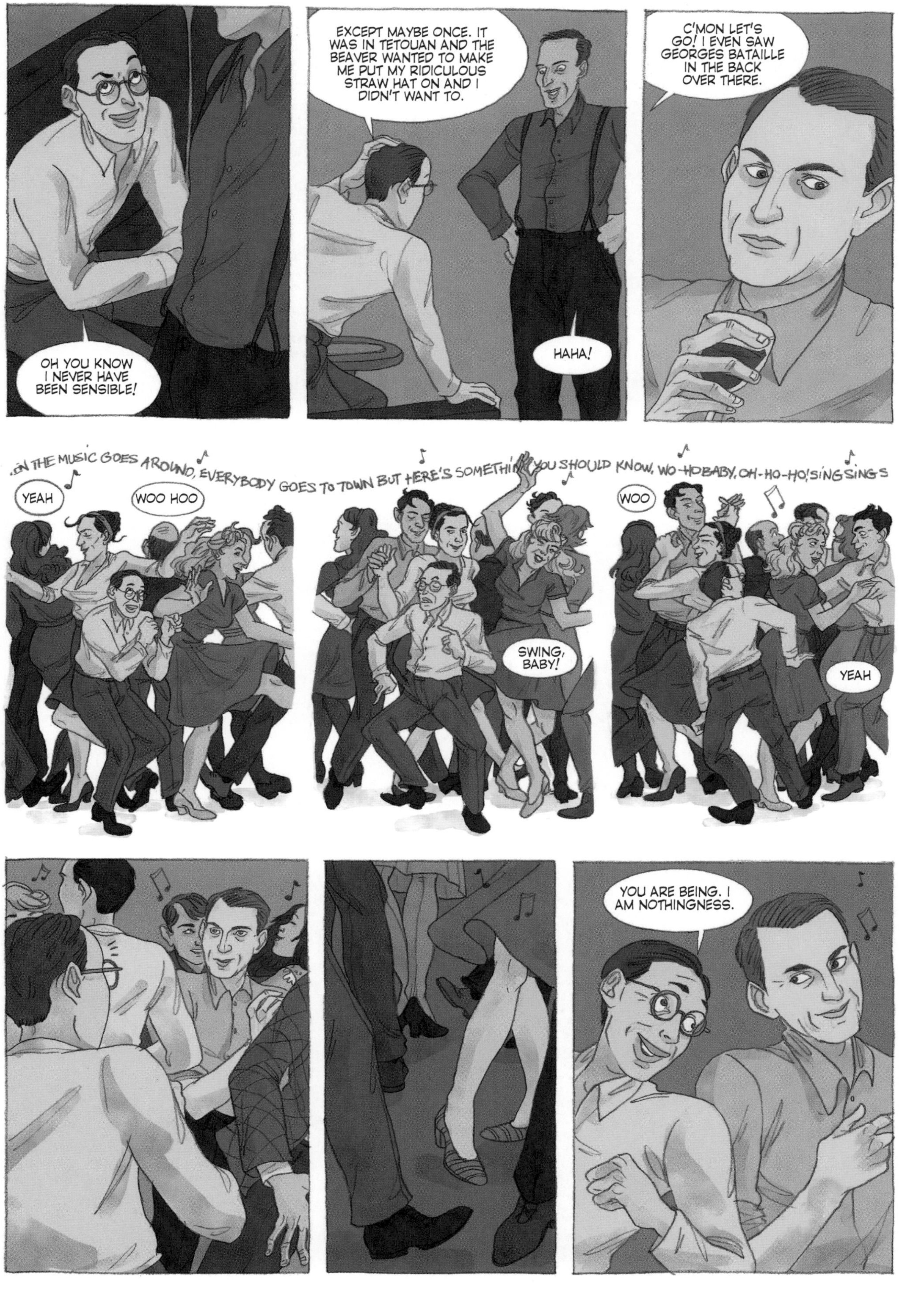
OH YOU KNOW I NEVER HAVE BEEN SENSIBLE!
EXCEPT MAYBE ONCE. IT WAS IN TETOUAN AND THE BEAVER WANTED TO MAKE ME PUT MY RIDICULOUS STRAW HAT ON AND I DIDN'T WANT TO.
HAHA!
C'MON LET'S GO! I EVEN SAW GEORGES BATAILLE IN THE BACK OVER THERE.
..IN THE MUSIC GOES AROUND, EVERYBODY GOES TO TOWN BUT HERE'S SOMETHI YOU SHOULD KNOW, WO-HO BABY, OH-HO-HO! SING SINGS
YEAH
WOO HOO
SWING, BABY!
WOO
YEAH
YOU ARE BEING. I AM NOTHINGNESS.

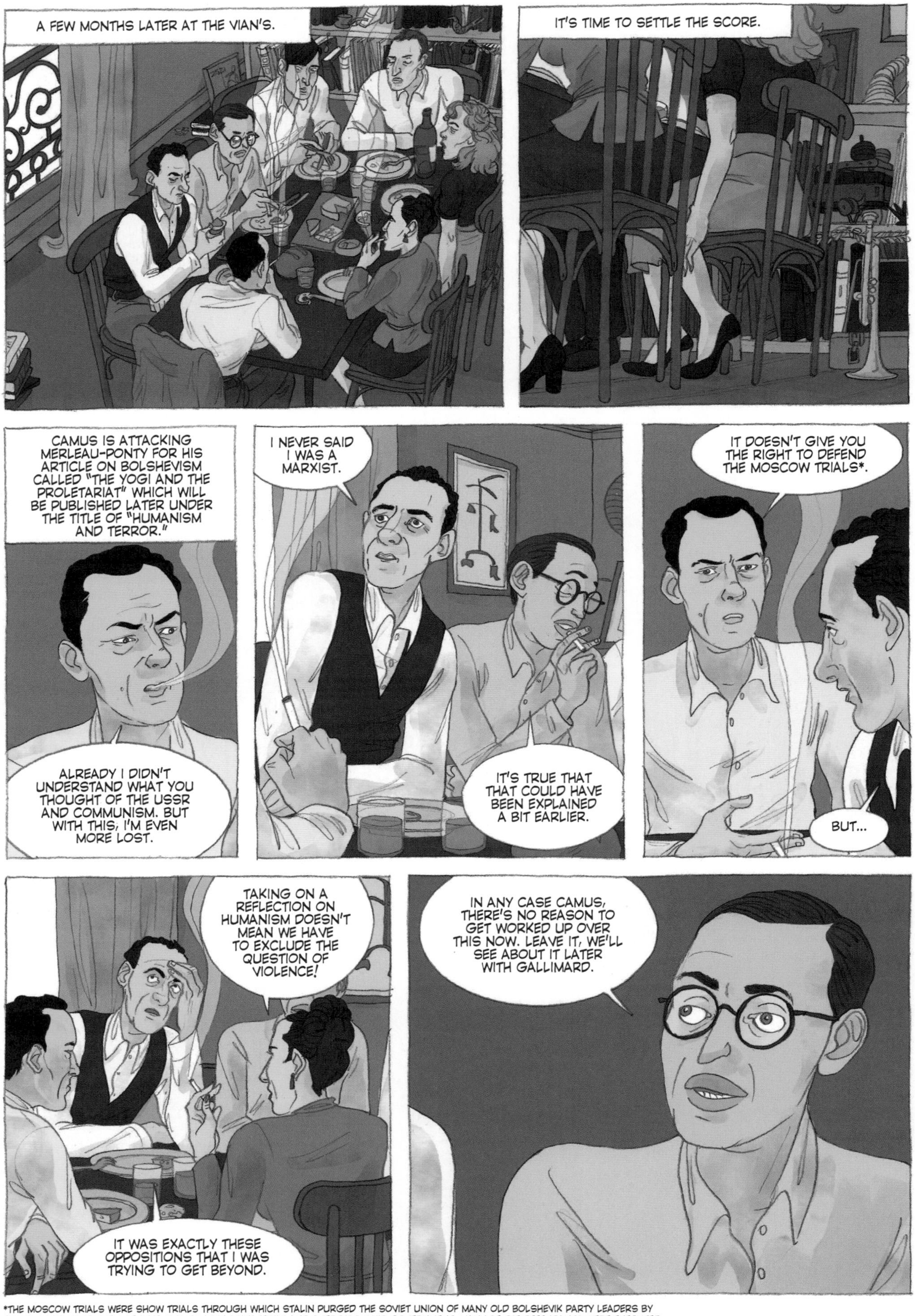
A FEW MONTHS LATER AT THE VIAN'S.
IT'S TIME TO SETTLE THE SCORE.
CAMUS IS ATTACKING MERLEAU-PONTY FOR HIS ARTICLE ON BOLSHEVISM CALLED "THE YOGI AND THE PROLETARIAT" WHICH WILL BE PUBLISHED LATER UNDER THE TITLE OF "HUMANISM AND TERROR."
ALREADY I DIDN'T UNDERSTAND WHAT YOU THOUGHT OF THE USSR AND COMMUNISM. BUT WITH THIS, I'M EVEN MORE LOST.
I NEVER SAID I WAS A MARXIST.
IT'S TRUE THAT THAT COULD HAVE BEEN EXPLAINED A BIT EARLIER.
IT DOESN'T GIVE YOU THE RIGHT TO DEFEND THE MOSCOW TRIALS*.
BUT...
TAKING ON A REFLECTION ON HUMANISM DOESN'T MEAN WE HAVE TO EXCLUDE THE QUESTION OF VIOLENCE!
IT WAS EXACTLY THESE OPPOSITIONS THAT I WAS TRYING TO GET BEYOND.
IN ANY CASE CAMUS, THERE'S NO REASON TO GET WORKED UP OVER THIS NOW. LEAVE IT, WE'LL SEE ABOUT IT LATER WITH GALLIMARD.

*THE MOSCOW TRIALS WERE SHOW TRIALS THROUGH WHICH STALIN PURGED THE SOVIET UNION OF MANY OLD BOLSHEVIK PARTY LEADERS BY FALSELY ACCUSING THEM OF ATTEMPTS TO ASSASSINATE HIM AND OVERTHROW HIS GOVERNMENT. MANY OF THE DEFENDANTS WERE EXECUTED.

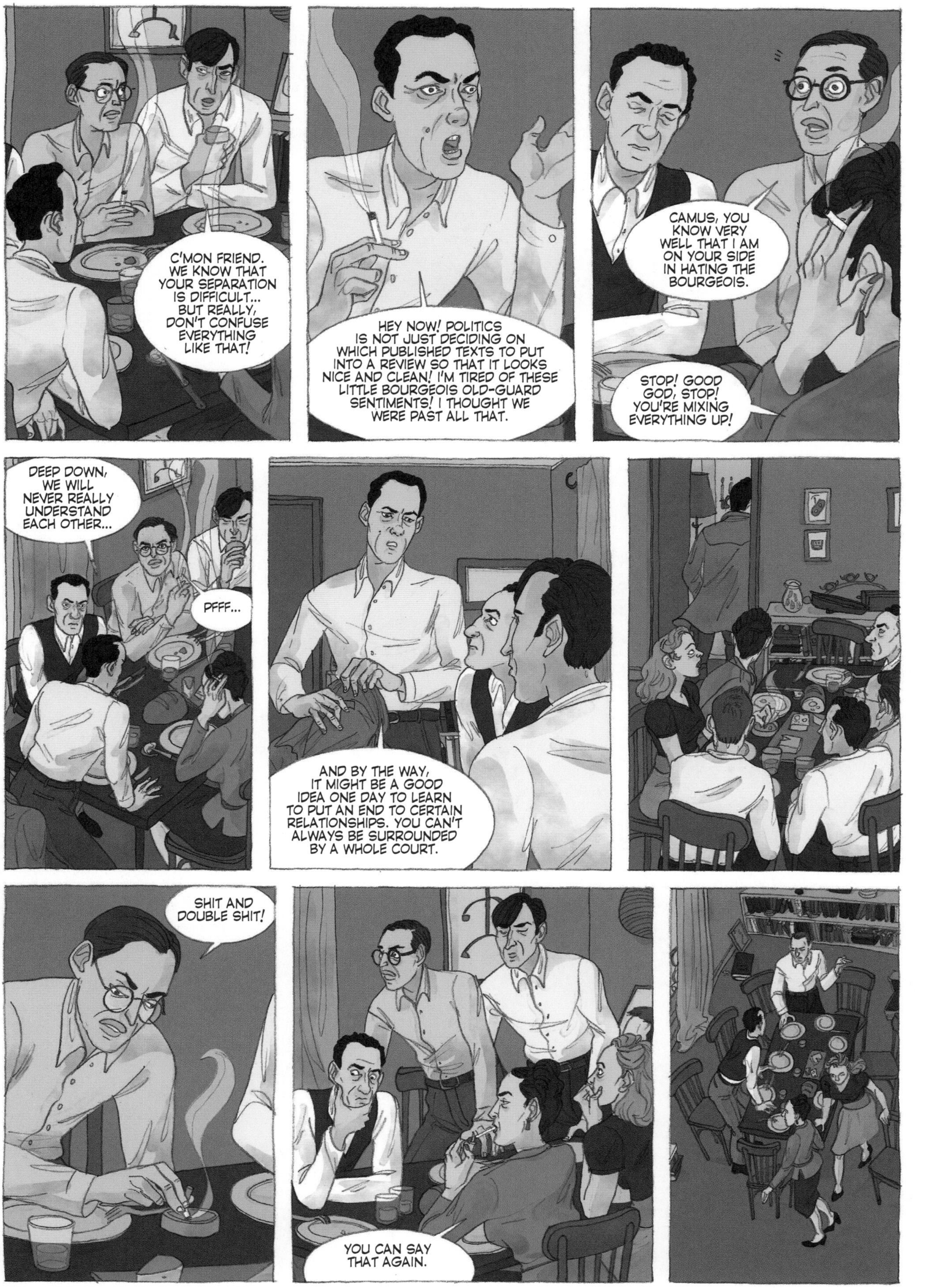
C'MON FRIEND. WE KNOW THAT YOUR SEPARATION IS DIFFICULT... BUT REALLY, DON'T CONFUSE EVERYTHING LIKE THAT!
HEY NOW! POLITICS IS NOT JUST DECIDING ON WHICH PUBLISHED TEXTS TO PUT INTO A REVIEW SO THAT IT LOOKS NICE AND CLEAN! I'M TIRED OF THESE LITTLE BOURGEOIS OLD-GUARD SENTIMENTS! I THOUGHT WE WERE PAST ALL THAT.
CAMUS, YOU KNOW VERY WELL THAT I AM ON YOUR SIDE IN HATING THE BOURGEOIS.
STOP! GOOD GOD, STOP! YOU'RE MIXING EVERYTHING UP!
DEEP DOWN, WE WILL NEVER REALLY UNDERSTAND EACH OTHER...
PFFF...
AND BY THE WAY, IT MIGHT BE A GOOD IDEA ONE DAY TO LEARN TO PUT AN END TO CERTAIN RELATIONSHIPS. YOU CAN'T ALWAYS BE SURROUNDED BY A WHOLE COURT.
SHIT AND DOUBLE SHIT!
YOU CAN SAY THAT AGAIN.

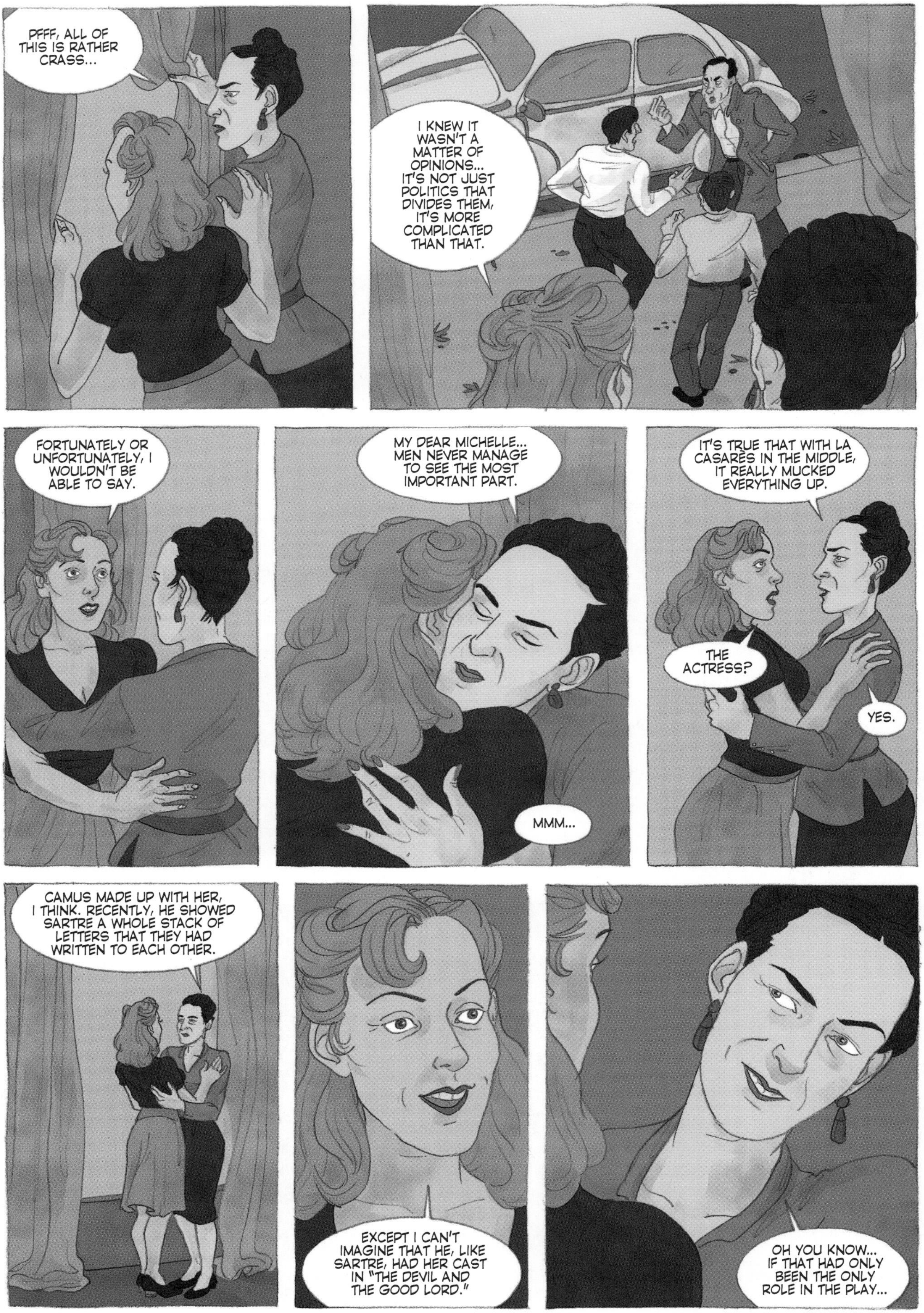
PFFF, ALL OF THIS IS RATHER CRASS...
I KNEW IT WASN'T A MATTER OF OPINIONS... IT'S NOT JUST POLITICS THAT DIVIDES THEM, IT'S MORE COMPLICATED THAN THAT.
FORTUNATELY OR UNFORTUNATELY, I WOULDN'T BE ABLE TO SAY.
MY DEAR MICHELLE... MEN NEVER MANAGE TO SEE THE MOST IMPORTANT PART.
MMM...
IT'S TRUE THAT WITH LA CASARÈS IN THE MIDDLE, IT REALLY MUCKED EVERYTHING UP.
THE ACTRESS?
YES.
CAMUS MADE UP WITH HER, I THINK. RECENTLY, HE SHOWED SARTRE A WHOLE STACK OF LETTERS THAT THEY HAD WRITTEN TO EACH OTHER.
EXCEPT I CAN'T IMAGINE THAT HE, LIKE SARTRE, HAD HER CAST IN "THE DEVIL AND THE GOOD LORD."
OH YOU KNOW... IF THAT HAD ONLY BEEN THE ONLY ROLE IN THE PLAY...

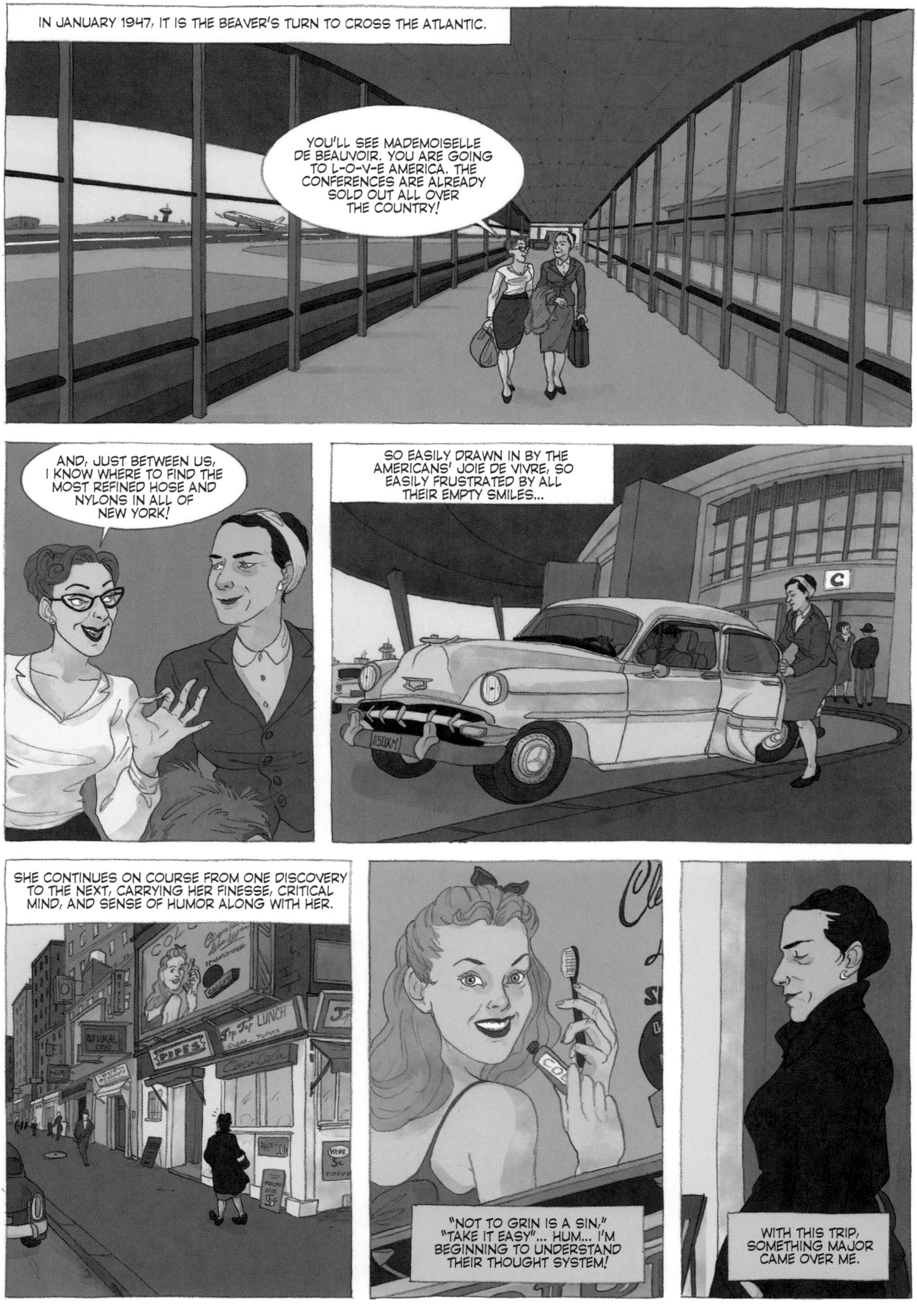
IN JANUARY 1947, IT IS THE BEAVER'S TURN TO CROSS THE ATLANTIC.
YOU'LL SEE MADEMOISELLE DE BEAUVOIR. YOU ARE GOING TO L-O-V-E AMERICA. THE CONFERENCES ARE ALREADY SOLD OUT ALL OVER THE COUNTRY!
AND, JUST BETWEEN US, I KNOW WHERE TO FIND THE MOST REFINED HOSE AND NYLONS IN ALL OF NEW YORK!
SO EASILY DRAWN IN BY THE AMERICANS' JOIE DE VIVRE, SO EASILY FRUSTRATED BY ALL THEIR EMPTY SMILES...
SHE CONTINUES ON COURSE FROM ONE DISCOVERY TO THE NEXT, CARRYING HER FINESSE, CRITICAL MIND, AND SENSE OF HUMOR ALONG WITH HER.
LUNCH
PIPES
"NOT TO GRIN IS A SIN," "TAKE IT EASY"... HUM... I'M BEGINNING TO UNDERSTAND THEIR THOUGHT SYSTEM!
WITH THIS TRIP, SOMETHING MAJOR CAME OVER ME.

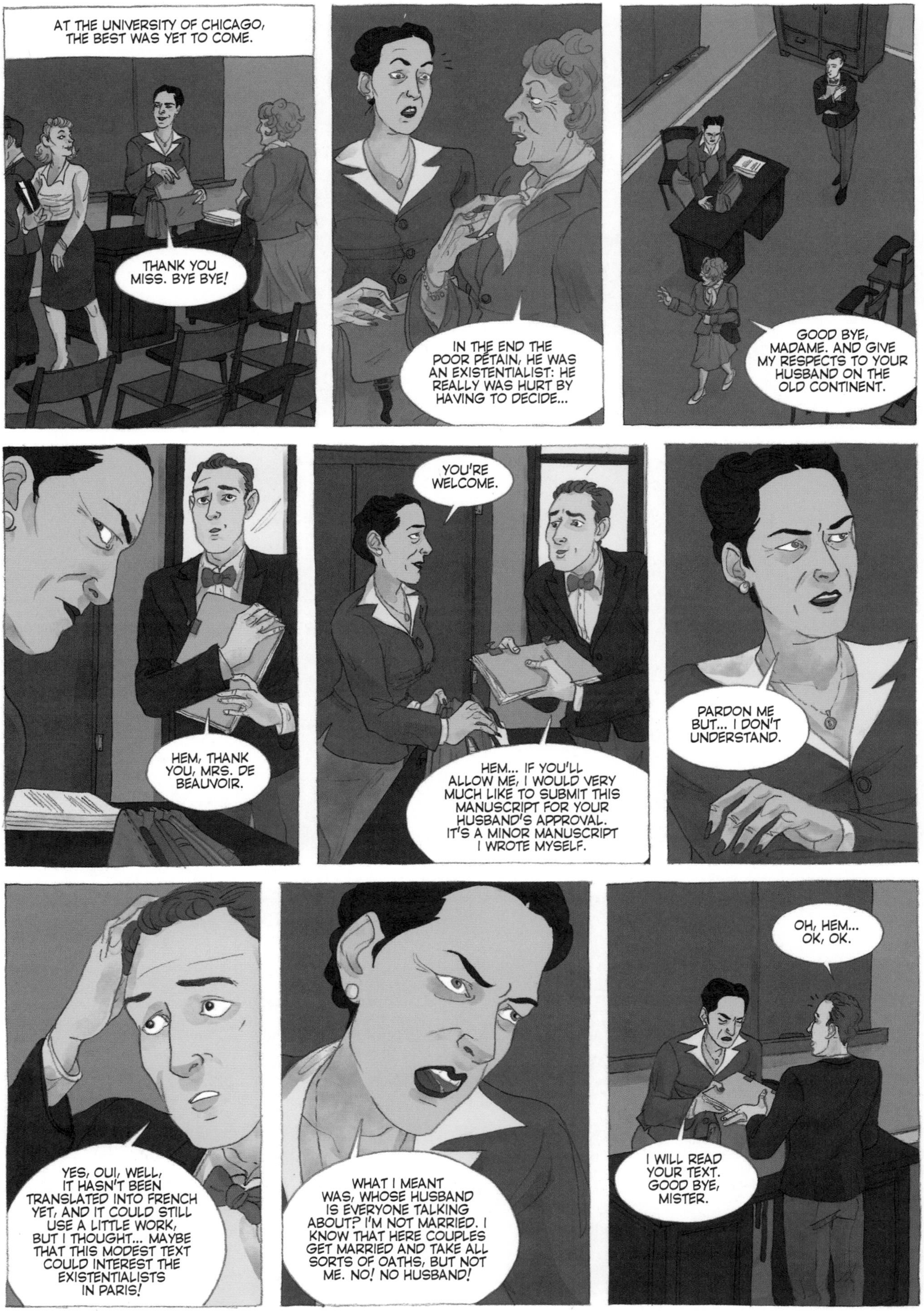
AT THE UNIVERSITY OF CHICAGO, THE BEST WAS YET TO COME.
THANK YOU MISS. BYE BYE!
IN THE END THE POOR PÉTAIN, HE WAS AN EXISTENTIALIST: HE REALLY WAS HURT BY HAVING TO DECIDE...
GOOD BYE, MADAME. AND GIVE MY RESPECTS TO YOUR HUSBAND ON THE OLD CONTINENT.
HEM, THANK YOU, MRS. DE BEAUVOIR.
YOU'RE WELCOME.
HEM... IF YOU'LL ALLOW ME, I WOULD VERY MUCH LIKE TO SUBMIT THIS MANUSCRIPT FOR YOUR HUSBAND'S APPROVAL. IT'S A MINOR MANUSCRIPT I WROTE MYSELF.
PARDON ME BUT... I DON'T UNDERSTAND.
YES, OUI, WELL, IT HASN'T BEEN TRANSLATED INTO FRENCH YET, AND IT COULD STILL USE A LITTLE WORK, BUT I THOUGHT... MAYBE THAT THIS MODEST TEXT COULD INTEREST THE EXISTENTIALISTS IN PARIS!
WHAT I MEANT WAS, WHOSE HUSBAND IS EVERYONE TALKING ABOUT? I'M NOT MARRIED. I KNOW THAT HERE COUPLES GET MARRIED AND TAKE ALL SORTS OF OATHS, BUT NOT ME. NO! NO HUSBAND!
OH, HEM... OK, OK.
I WILL READ YOUR TEXT. GOOD BYE, MISTER.

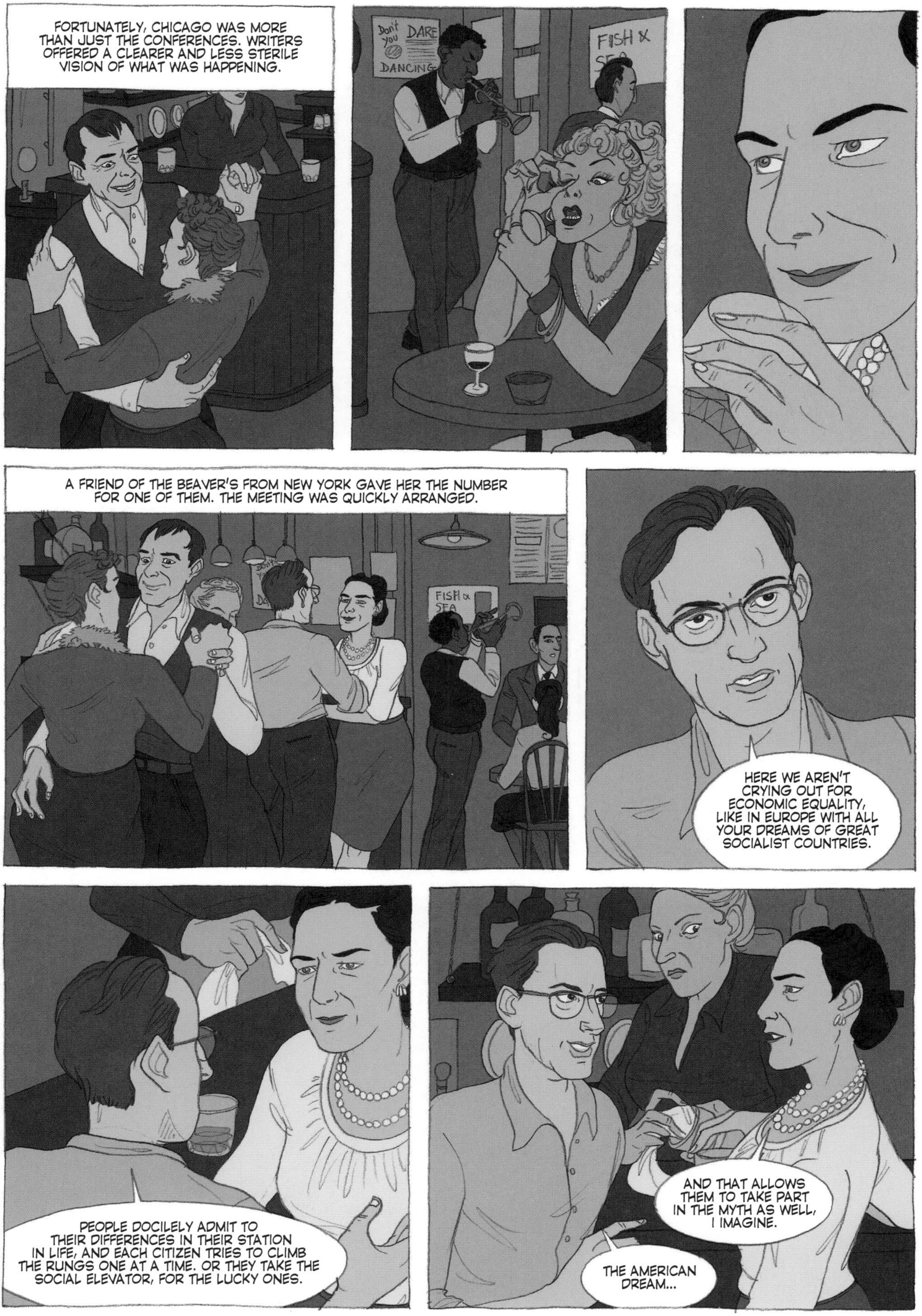
FORTUNATELY, CHICAGO WAS MORE THAN JUST THE CONFERENCES. WRITERS OFFERED A CLEARER AND LESS STERILE VISION OF WHAT WAS HAPPENING.
Don't you DARE DANCING
FISH & SEA
A FRIEND OF THE BEAVER'S FROM NEW YORK GAVE HER THE NUMBER FOR ONE OF THEM. THE MEETING WAS QUICKLY ARRANGED.
FISH & SEA
HERE WE AREN'T CRYING OUT FOR ECONOMIC EQUALITY, LIKE IN EUROPE WITH ALL YOUR DREAMS OF GREAT SOCIALIST COUNTRIES.
PEOPLE DOCILELY ADMIT TO THEIR DIFFERENCES IN THEIR STATION IN LIFE, AND EACH CITIZEN TRIES TO CLIMB THE RUNGS ONE AT A TIME. OR THEY TAKE THE SOCIAL ELEVATOR, FOR THE LUCKY ONES.
AND THAT ALLOWS THEM TO TAKE PART IN THE MYTH AS WELL, I IMAGINE.
THE AMERICAN DREAM...

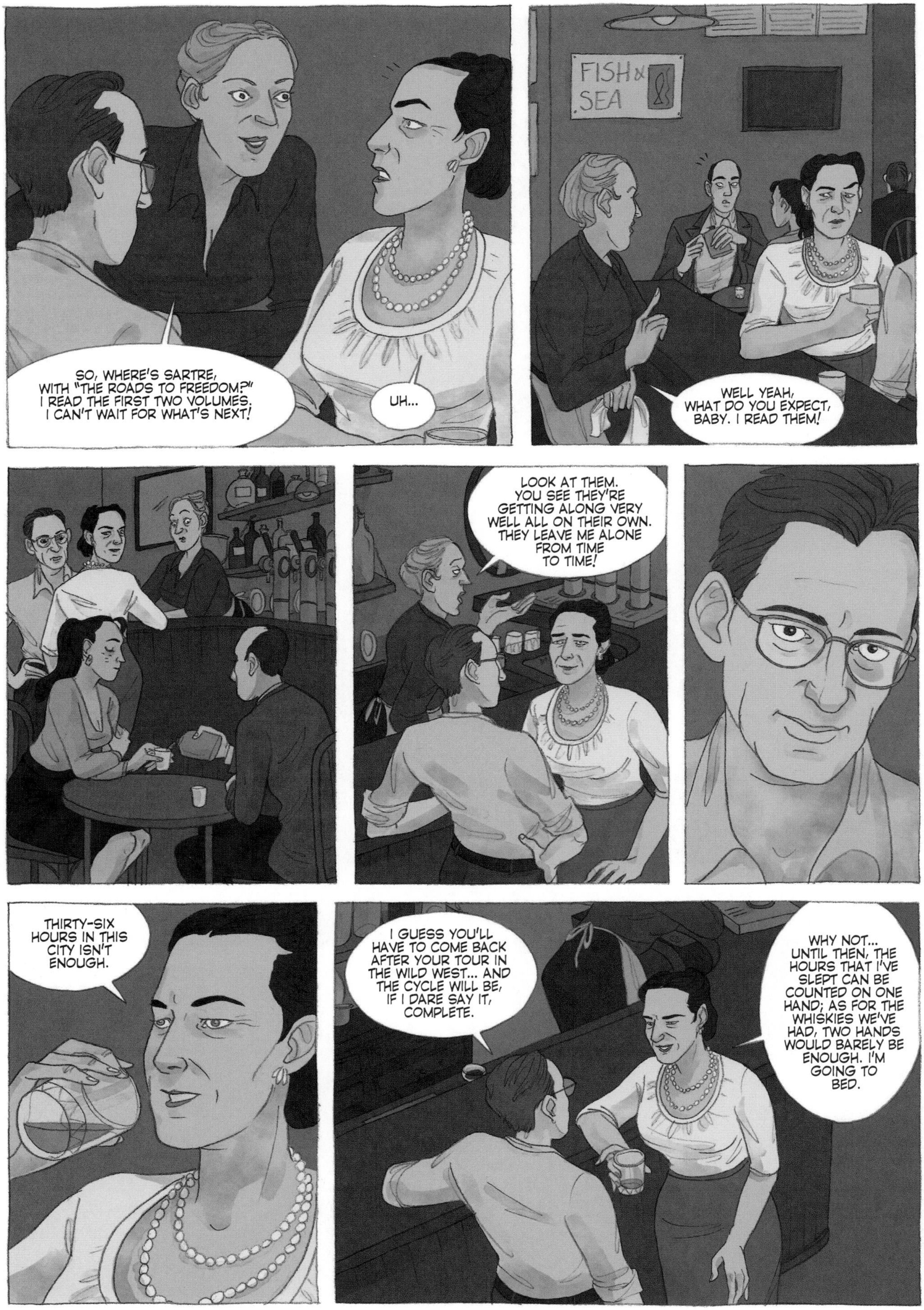

SO, WHERE'S SARTRE, WITH "THE ROADS TO FREEDOM?" I READ THE FIRST TWO VOLUMES. I CAN'T WAIT FOR WHAT'S NEXT!
UH...
WELL YEAH, WHAT DO YOU EXPECT, BABY. I READ THEM!
FISH & SEA
LOOK AT THEM. YOU SEE THEY'RE GETTING ALONG VERY WELL ALL ON THEIR OWN. THEY LEAVE ME ALONE FROM TIME TO TIME!
THIRTY-SIX HOURS IN THIS CITY ISN'T ENOUGH.
I GUESS YOU'LL HAVE TO COME BACK AFTER YOUR TOUR IN THE WILD WEST... AND THE CYCLE WILL BE, IF I DARE SAY IT, COMPLETE.
WHY NOT... UNTIL THEN, THE HOURS THAT I'VE SLEPT CAN BE COUNTED ON ONE HAND; AS FOR THE WHISKIES WE'VE HAD, TWO HANDS WOULD BARELY BE ENOUGH. I'M GOING TO BED.

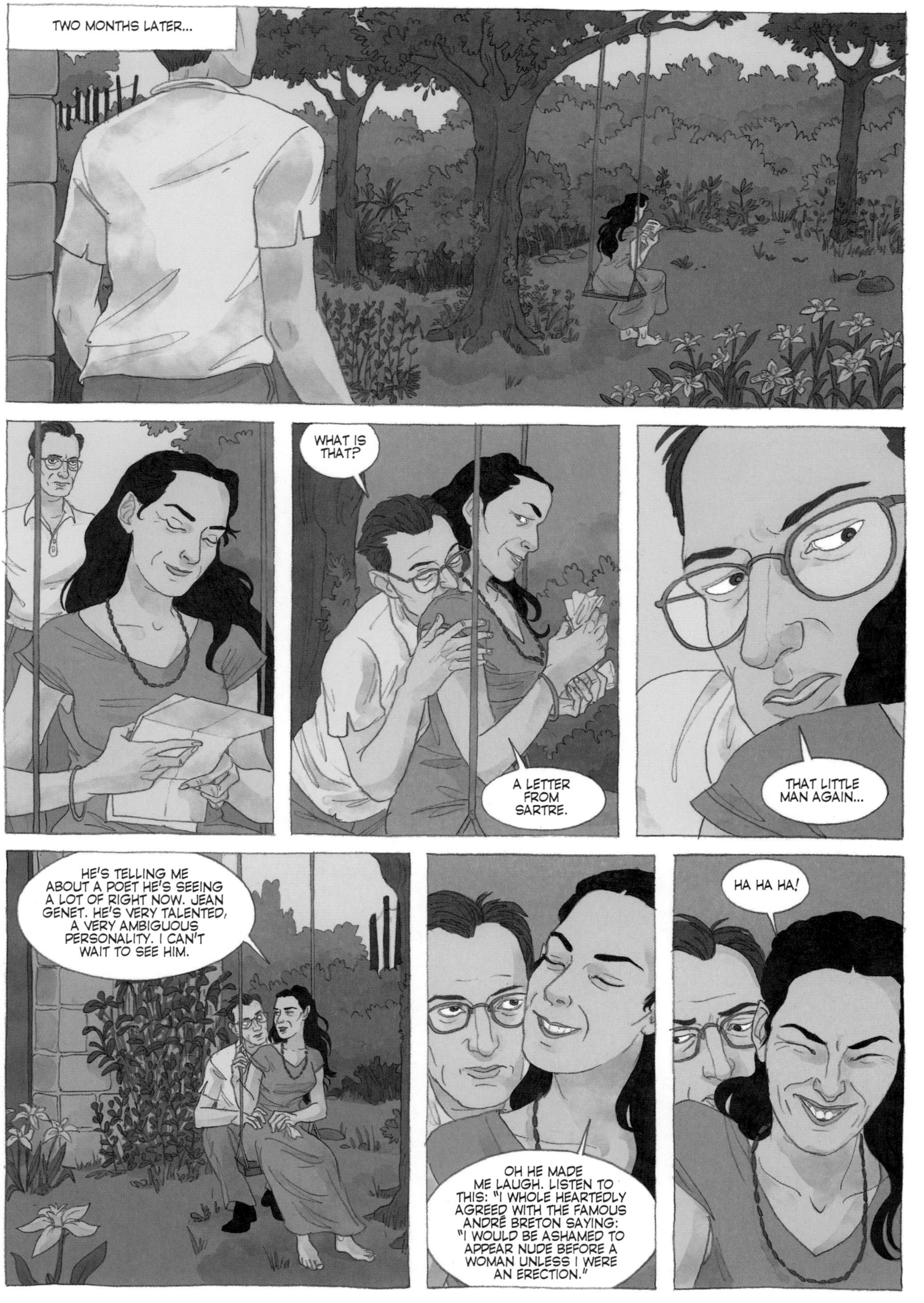
TWO MONTHS LATER...
WHAT IS THAT?
A LETTER FROM SARTRE.
THAT LITTLE MAN AGAIN...
HE'S TELLING ME ABOUT A POET HE'S SEEING A LOT OF RIGHT NOW. JEAN GENET. HE'S VERY TALENTED, A VERY AMBIGUOUS PERSONALITY. I CAN'T WAIT TO SEE HIM.
OH HE MADE ME LAUGH. LISTEN TO THIS: "I WHOLE HEARTEDLY AGREED WITH THE FAMOUS ANDRÉ BRETON SAYING: "I WOULD BE ASHAMED TO APPEAR NUDE BEFORE A WOMAN UNLESS I WERE AN ERECTION."
HA HA HA!

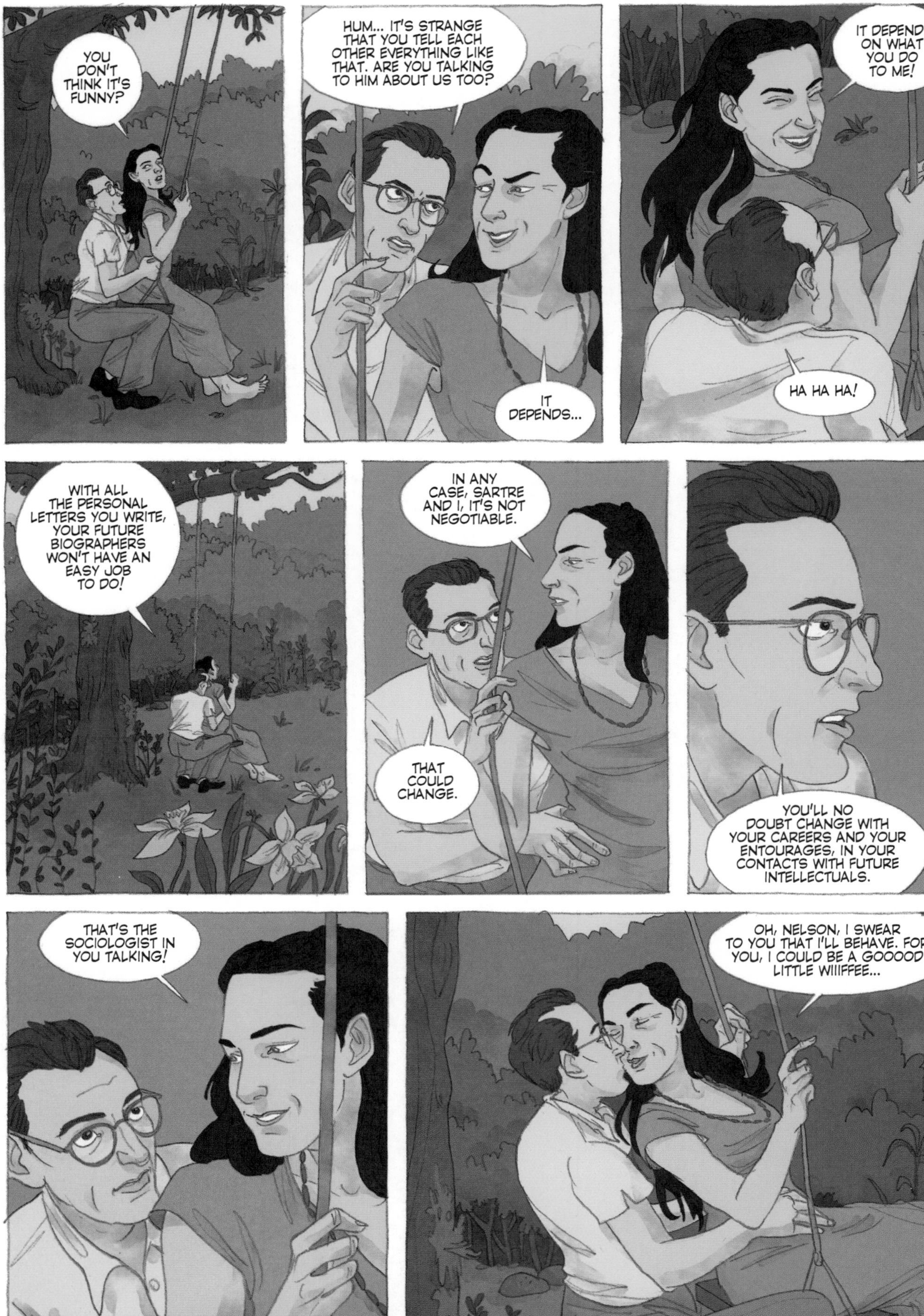
YOU DON'T THINK IT'S FUNNY?
HUM... IT'S STRANGE THAT YOU TELL EACH OTHER EVERYTHING LIKE THAT. ARE YOU TALKING TO HIM ABOUT US TOO?
IT DEPENDS...
IT DEPENDS ON WHAT YOU DO TO ME!
HA HA HA!
WITH ALL THE PERSONAL LETTERS YOU WRITE, YOUR FUTURE BIOGRAPHERS WON'T HAVE AN EASY JOB TO DO!
IN ANY CASE, SARTRE AND I, IT'S NOT NEGOTIABLE.
THAT COULD CHANGE.
YOU'LL NO DOUBT CHANGE WITH YOUR CAREERS AND YOUR ENTOURAGES, IN YOUR CONTACTS WITH FUTURE INTELLECTUALS.
THAT'S THE SOCIOLOGIST IN YOU TALKING!
OH, NELSON, I SWEAR TO YOU THAT I'LL BEHAVE. FOR YOU, I COULD BE A GOOOOD LITTLE WIIIFFEE...

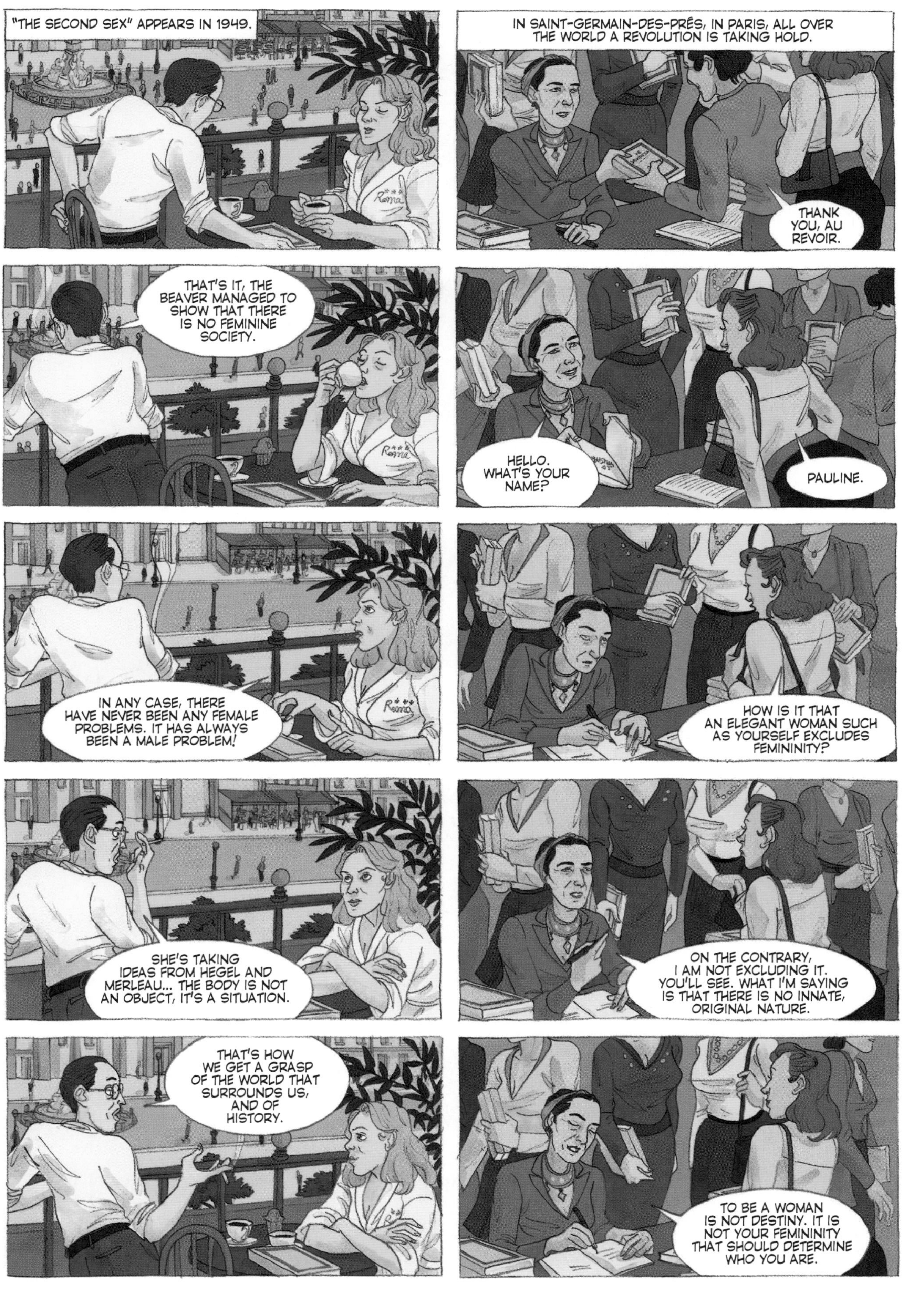
"THE SECOND SEX" APPEARS IN 1949.
IN SAINT-GERMAIN-DES-PRÉS, IN PARIS, ALL OVER THE WORLD A REVOLUTION IS TAKING HOLD.
THANK YOU, AU REVOIR.
THAT'S IT, THE BEAVER MANAGED TO SHOW THAT THERE IS NO FEMININE SOCIETY.
HELLO. WHAT'S YOUR NAME?
PAULINE.
IN ANY CASE, THERE HAVE NEVER BEEN ANY FEMALE PROBLEMS. IT HAS ALWAYS BEEN A MALE PROBLEM!
HOW IS IT THAT AN ELEGANT WOMAN SUCH AS YOURSELF EXCLUDES FEMININITY?
SHE'S TAKING IDEAS FROM HEGEL AND MERLEAU... THE BODY IS NOT AN OBJECT, IT'S A SITUATION.
ON THE CONTRARY, I AM NOT EXCLUDING IT. YOU'LL SEE. WHAT I'M SAYING IS THAT THERE IS NO INNATE, ORIGINAL NATURE.
THAT'S HOW WE GET A GRASP OF THE WORLD THAT SURROUNDS US, AND OF HISTORY.
TO BE A WOMAN IS NOT DESTINY. IT IS NOT YOUR FEMININITY THAT SHOULD DETERMINE WHO YOU ARE.

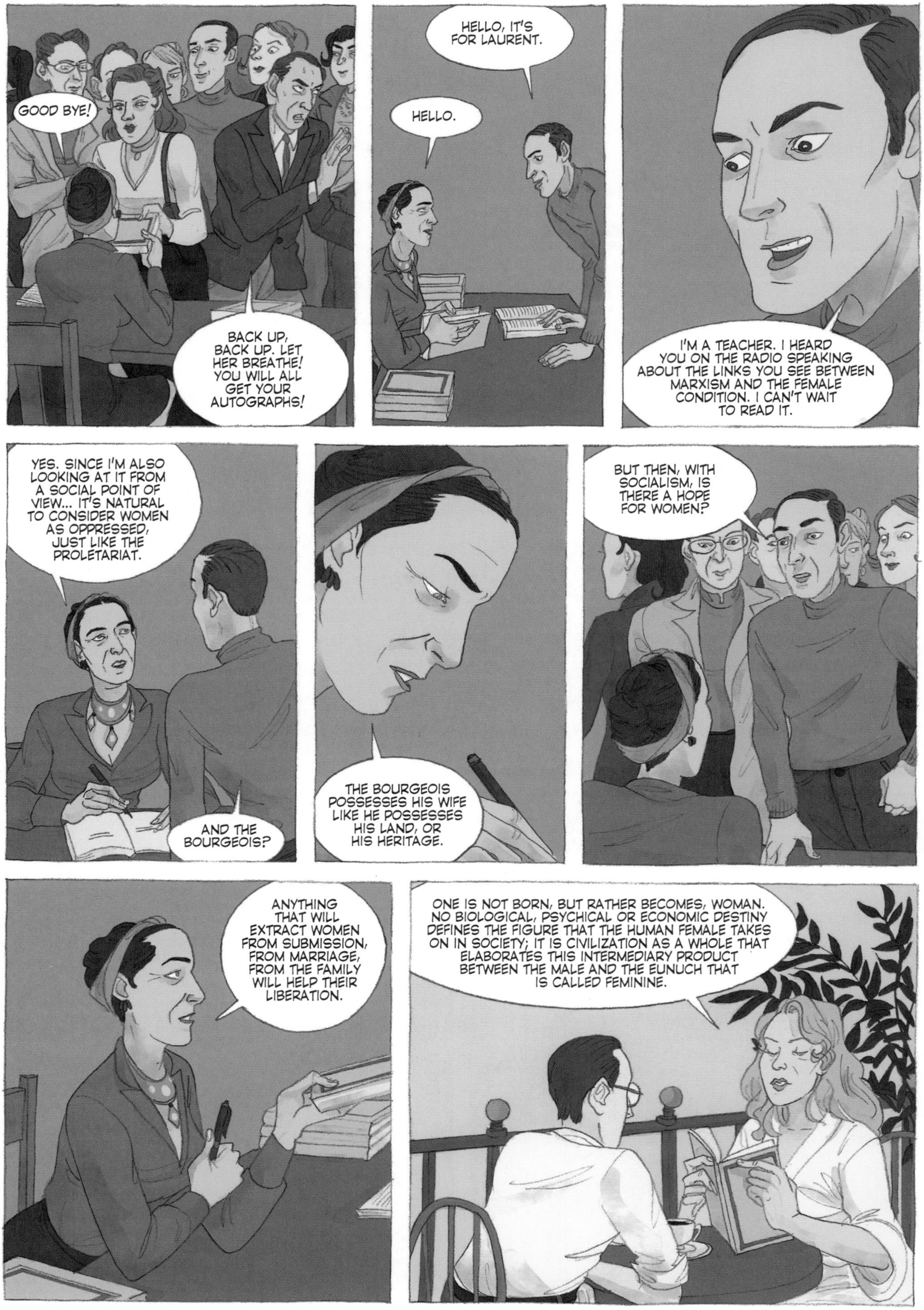
GOOD BYE!
BACK UP, BACK UP. LET HER BREATHE! YOU WILL ALL GET YOUR AUTOGRAPHS!
HELLO, IT'S FOR LAURENT.
HELLO.
I'M A TEACHER. I HEARD YOU ON THE RADIO SPEAKING ABOUT THE LINKS YOU SEE BETWEEN MARXISM AND THE FEMALE CONDITION. I CAN'T WAIT TO READ IT.
YES. SINCE I'M ALSO LOOKING AT IT FROM A SOCIAL POINT OF VIEW... IT'S NATURAL TO CONSIDER WOMEN AS OPPRESSED, JUST LIKE THE PROLETARIAT.
AND THE BOURGEOIS?
THE BOURGEOIS POSSESSES HIS WIFE LIKE HE POSSESSES HIS LAND, OR HIS HERITAGE.
BUT THEN, WITH SOCIALISM, IS THERE A HOPE FOR WOMEN?
ANYTHING THAT WILL EXTRACT WOMEN FROM SUBMISSION, FROM MARRIAGE, FROM THE FAMILY WILL HELP THEIR LIBERATION.
ONE IS NOT BORN, BUT RATHER BECOMES, WOMAN. NO BIOLOGICAL, PSYCHICAL OR ECONOMIC DESTINY DEFINES THE FIGURE THAT THE HUMAN FEMALE TAKES ON IN SOCIETY; IT IS CIVILIZATION AS A WHOLE THAT ELABORATES THIS INTERMEDIARY PRODUCT BETWEEN THE MALE AND THE EUNUCH THAT IS CALLED FEMININE.

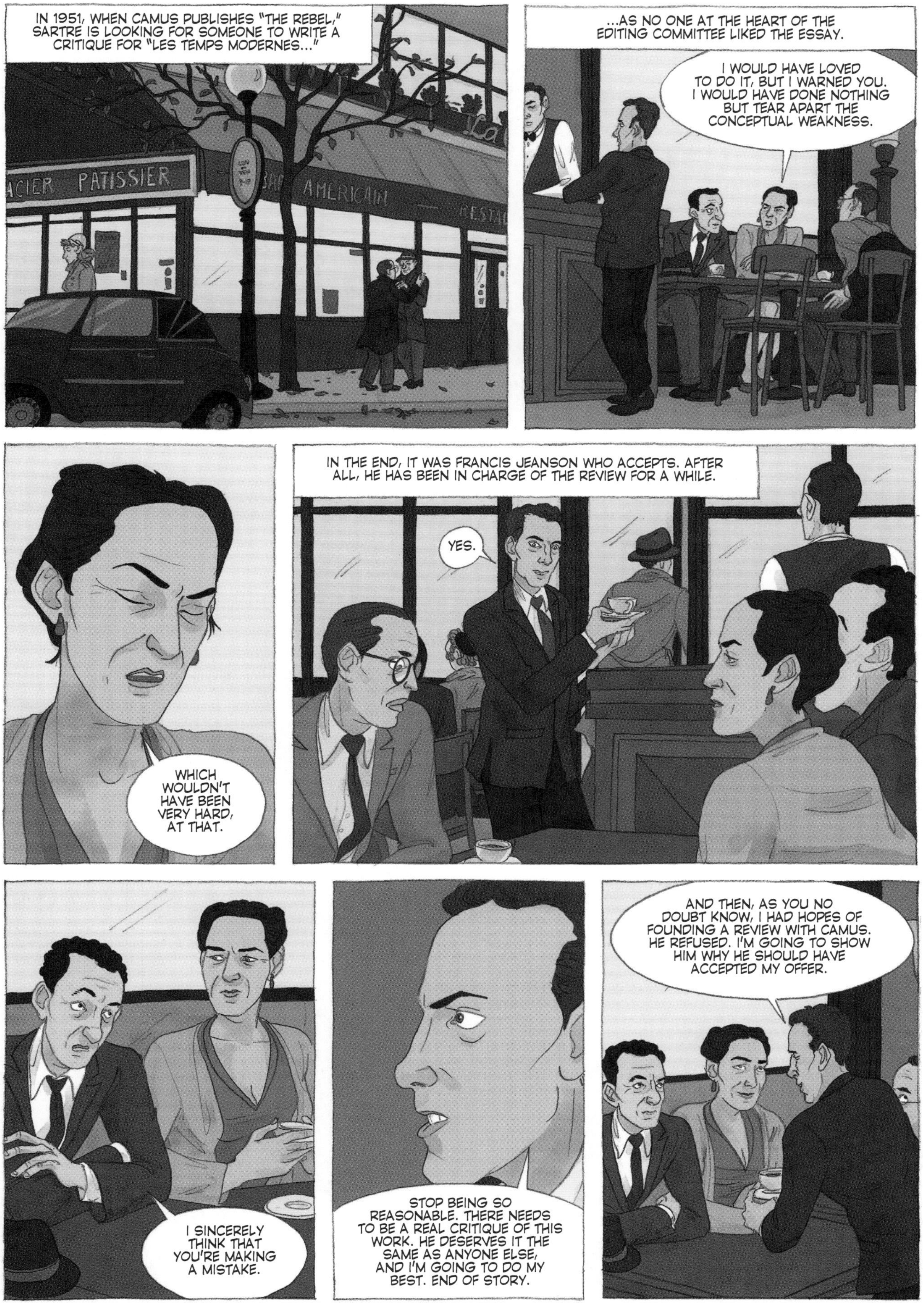
IN 1951, WHEN CAMUS PUBLISHES "THE REBEL," SARTRE IS LOOKING FOR SOMEONE TO WRITE A CRITIQUE FOR "LES TEMPS MODERNES..."
PATISSIER
AMERICAIN
...AS NO ONE AT THE HEART OF THE EDITING COMMITTEE LIKED THE ESSAY.
I WOULD HAVE LOVED TO DO IT, BUT I WARNED YOU. I WOULD HAVE DONE NOTHING BUT TEAR APART THE CONCEPTUAL WEAKNESS.
WHICH WOULDN'T HAVE BEEN VERY HARD, AT THAT.
IN THE END, IT WAS FRANCIS JEANSON WHO ACCEPTS. AFTER ALL, HE HAS BEEN IN CHARGE OF THE REVIEW FOR A WHILE.
YES.
I SINCERELY THINK THAT YOU'RE MAKING A MISTAKE.
STOP BEING SO REASONABLE. THERE NEEDS TO BE A REAL CRITIQUE OF THIS WORK. HE DESERVES IT THE SAME AS ANYONE ELSE, AND I'M GOING TO DO MY BEST. END OF STORY.
AND THEN, AS YOU NO DOUBT KNOW, I HAD HOPES OF FOUNDING A REVIEW WITH CAMUS. HE REFUSED. I'M GOING TO SHOW HIM WHY HE SHOULD HAVE ACCEPTED MY OFFER.

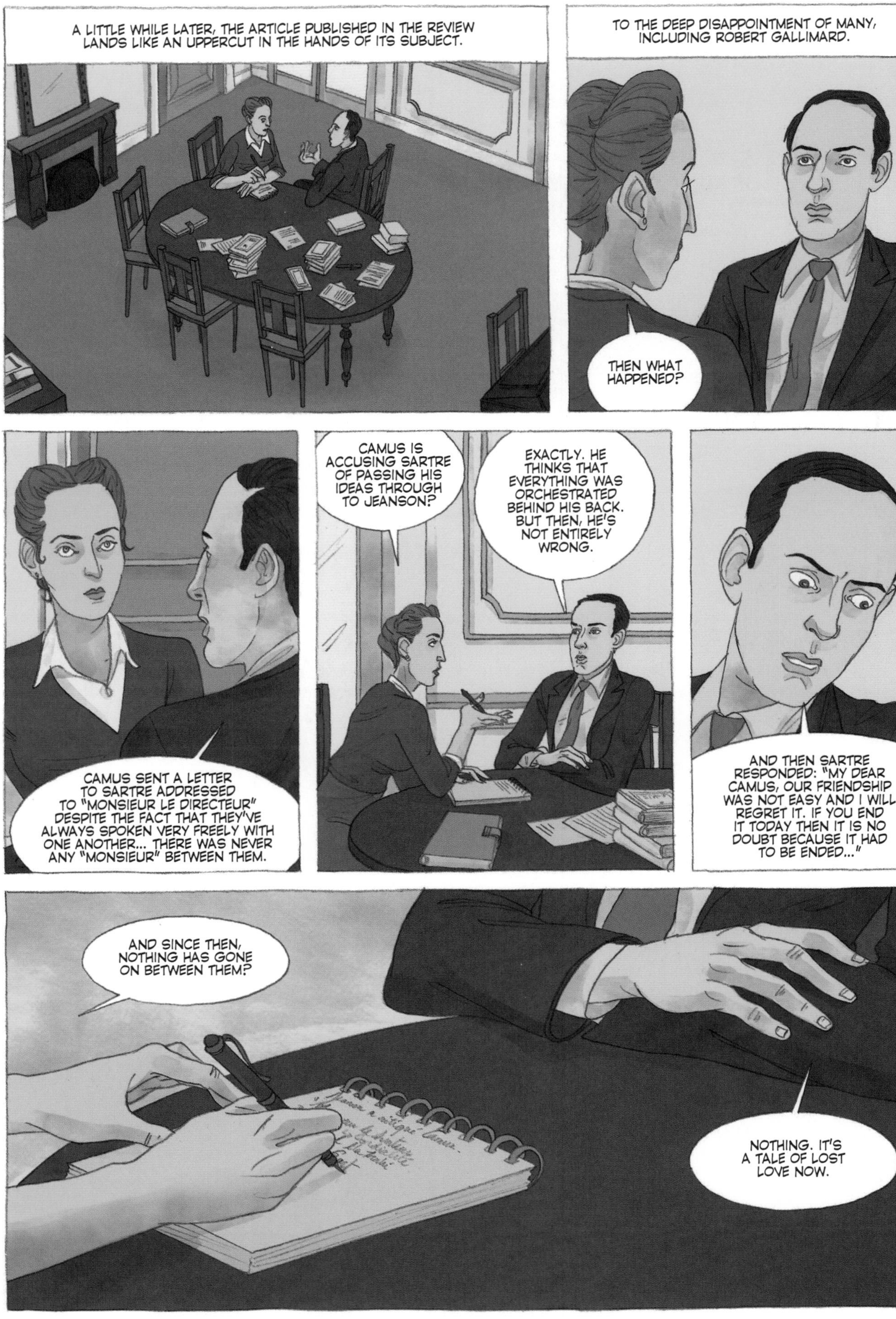
A LITTLE WHILE LATER, THE ARTICLE PUBLISHED IN THE REVIEW LANDS LIKE AN UPPERCUT IN THE HANDS OF ITS SUBJECT.
TO THE DEEP DISAPPOINTMENT OF MANY, INCLUDING ROBERT GALLIMARD.
THEN WHAT HAPPENED?
CAMUS SENT A LETTER TO SARTRE ADDRESSED TO "MONSIEUR LE DIRECTEUR" DESPITE THE FACT THAT THEY'VE ALWAYS SPOKEN VERY FREELY WITH ONE ANOTHER... THERE WAS NEVER ANY "MONSIEUR" BETWEEN THEM.
CAMUS IS ACCUSING SARTRE OF PASSING HIS IDEAS THROUGH TO JEANSON?
EXACTLY. HE THINKS THAT EVERYTHING WAS ORCHESTRATED BEHIND HIS BACK. BUT THEN, HE'S NOT ENTIRELY WRONG.
AND THEN SARTRE RESPONDED: "MY DEAR CAMUS, OUR FRIENDSHIP WAS NOT EASY AND I WILL REGRET IT. IF YOU END IT TODAY THEN IT IS NO DOUBT BECAUSE IT HAD TO BE ENDED..."
AND SINCE THEN, NOTHING HAS GONE ON BETWEEN THEM?
NOTHING. IT'S A TALE OF LOST LOVE NOW.

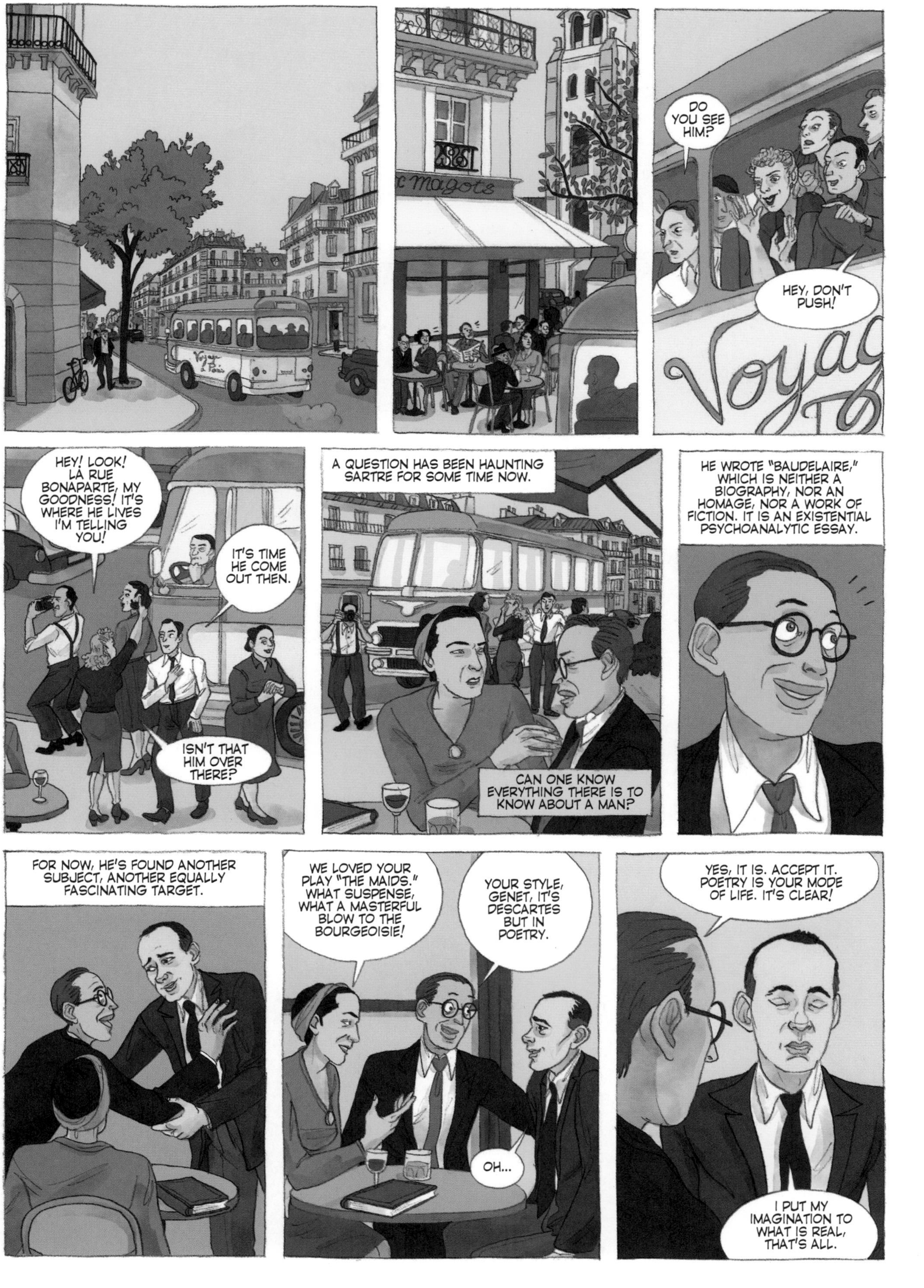

DO YOU SEE HIM?
HEY, DON'T PUSH!
HEY! LOOK! LÀ RUE BONAPARTE, MY GOODNESS! IT'S WHERE HE LIVES I'M TELLING YOU!
IT'S TIME HE COME OUT THEN.
ISN'T THAT HIM OVER THERE?
A QUESTION HAS BEEN HAUNTING SARTRE FOR SOME TIME NOW.
CAN ONE KNOW EVERYTHING THERE IS TO KNOW ABOUT A MAN?
HE WROTE "BAUDELAIRE," WHICH IS NEITHER A BIOGRAPHY, NOR AN HOMAGE, NOR A WORK OF FICTION. IT IS AN EXISTENTIAL PSYCHOANALYTIC ESSAY.
FOR NOW, HE'S FOUND ANOTHER SUBJECT, ANOTHER EQUALLY FASCINATING TARGET.
WE LOVED YOUR PLAY "THE MAIDS." WHAT SUSPENSE, WHAT A MASTERFUL BLOW TO THE BOURGEOISIE!
YOUR STYLE, GENET, IT'S DESCARTES BUT IN POETRY.
OH...
YES, IT IS. ACCEPT IT. POETRY IS YOUR MODE OF LIFE. IT'S CLEAR!
I PUT MY IMAGINATION TO WHAT IS REAL, THAT'S ALL.

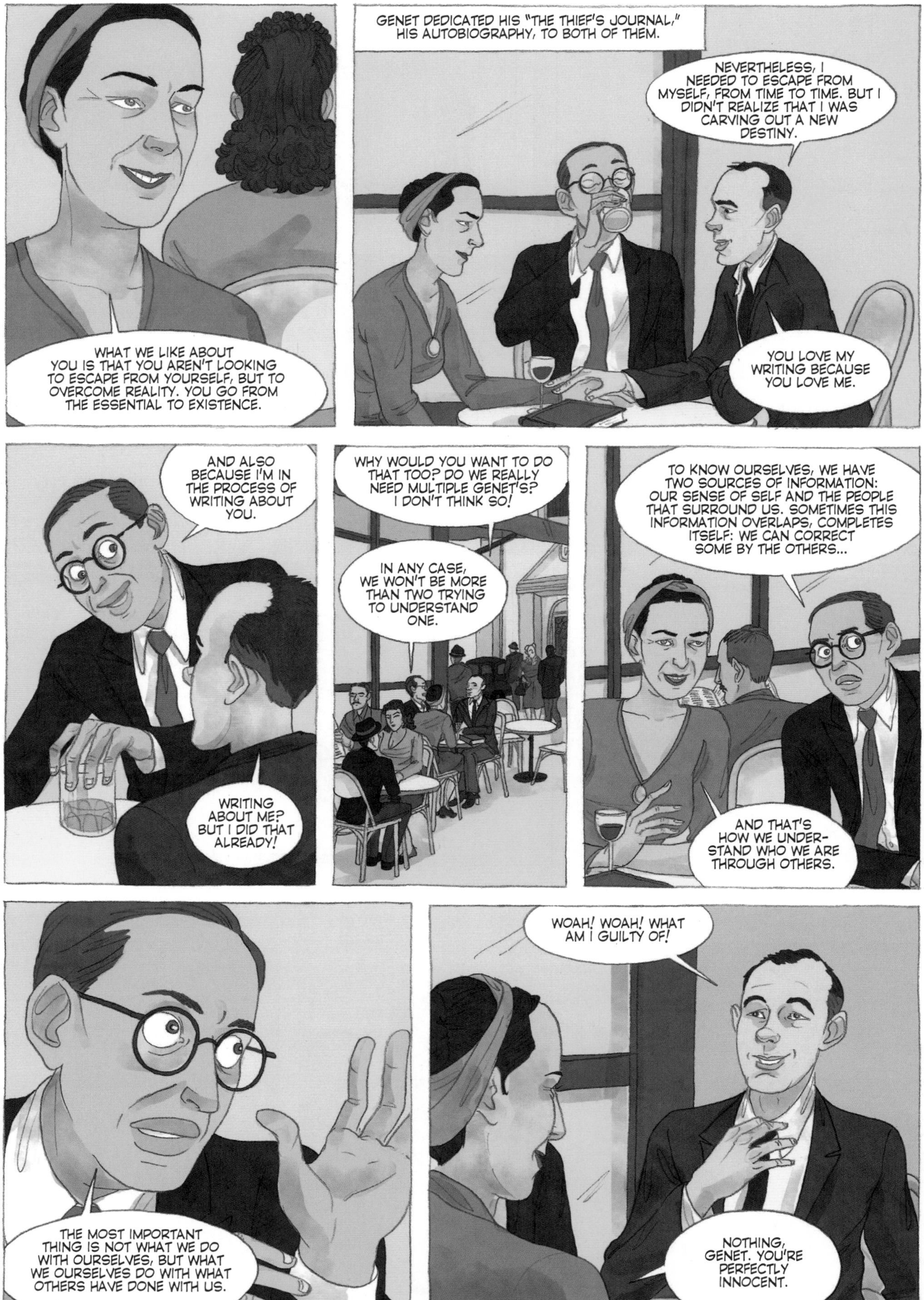
WHAT WE LIKE ABOUT YOU IS THAT YOU AREN'T LOOKING TO ESCAPE FROM YOURSELF, BUT TO OVERCOME REALITY. YOU GO FROM THE ESSENTIAL TO EXISTENCE.
GENET DEDICATED HIS "THE THIEF'S JOURNAL," HIS AUTOBIOGRAPHY, TO BOTH OF THEM.
NEVERTHELESS, I NEEDED TO ESCAPE FROM MYSELF, FROM TIME TO TIME. BUT I DIDN'T REALIZE THAT I WAS CARVING OUT A NEW DESTINY.
YOU LOVE MY WRITING BECAUSE YOU LOVE ME.
AND ALSO BECAUSE I'M IN THE PROCESS OF WRITING ABOUT YOU.
WRITING ABOUT ME? BUT I DID THAT ALREADY!
WHY WOULD YOU WANT TO DO THAT TOO? DO WE REALLY NEED MULTIPLE GENET'S? I DON'T THINK SO!
IN ANY CASE, WE WON'T BE MORE THAN TWO TRYING TO UNDERSTAND ONE.
TO KNOW OURSELVES, WE HAVE TWO SOURCES OF INFORMATION: OUR SENSE OF SELF AND THE PEOPLE THAT SURROUND US. SOMETIMES THIS INFORMATION OVERLAPS, COMPLETES ITSELF: WE CAN CORRECT SOME BY THE OTHERS...
AND THAT'S HOW WE UNDERSTAND WHO WE ARE THROUGH OTHERS.
THE MOST IMPORTANT THING IS NOT WHAT WE DO WITH OURSELVES, BUT WHAT WE OURSELVES DO WITH WHAT OTHERS HAVE DONE WITH US.
WOAH! WOAH! WHAT AM I GUILTY OF!
NOTHING, GENET. YOU'RE PERFECTLY INNOCENT.

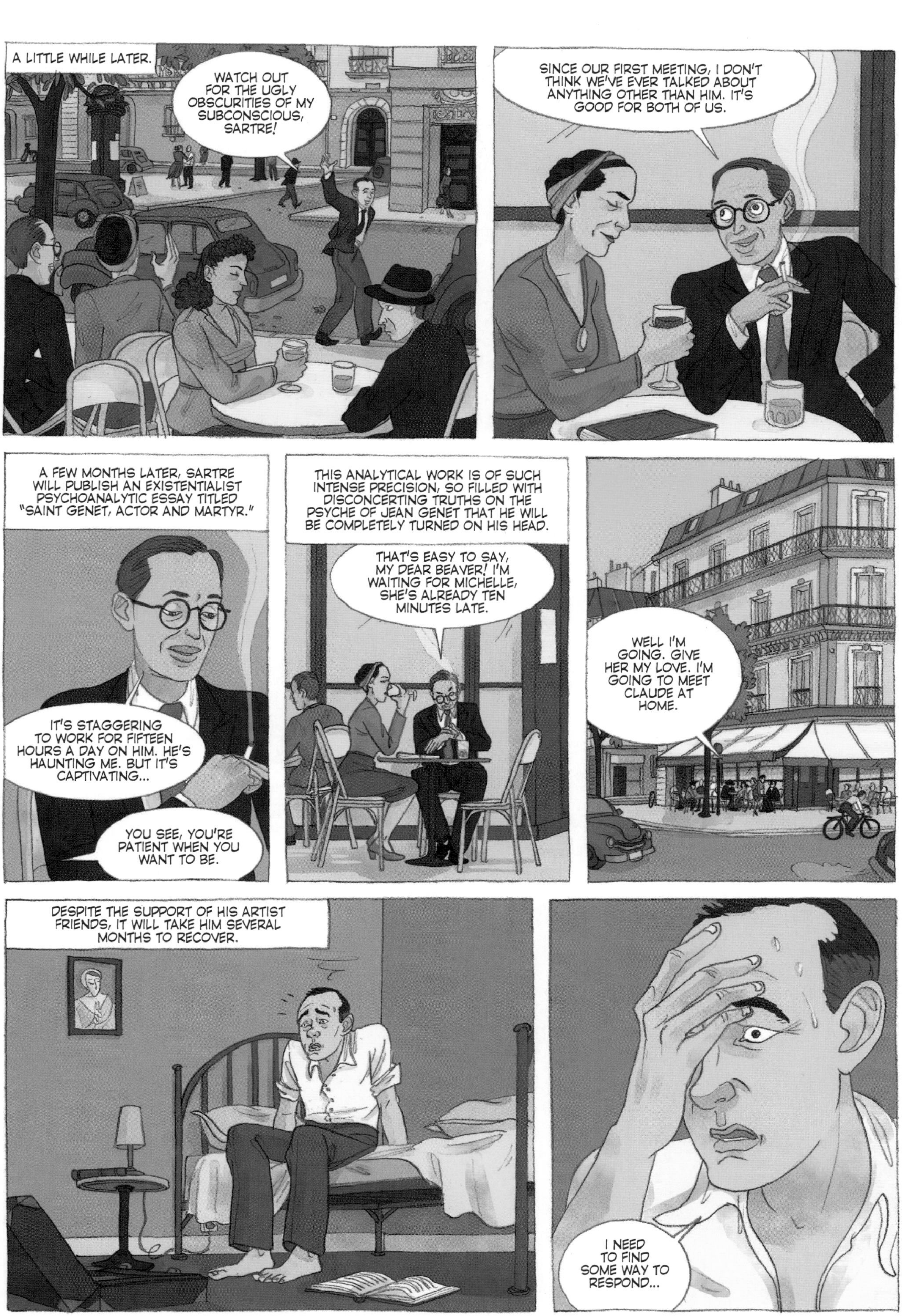

A LITTLE WHILE LATER.
WATCH OUT FOR THE UGLY OBSCURITIES OF MY SUBCONSCIOUS, SARTRE!
SINCE OUR FIRST MEETING, I DON'T THINK WE'VE EVER TALKED ABOUT ANYTHING OTHER THAN HIM. IT'S GOOD FOR BOTH OF US.
A FEW MONTHS LATER, SARTRE WILL PUBLISH AN EXISTENTIALIST PSYCHOANALYTIC ESSAY TITLED "SAINT GENET, ACTOR AND MARTYR."
IT'S STAGGERING TO WORK FOR FIFTEEN HOURS A DAY ON HIM. HE'S HAUNTING ME. BUT IT'S CAPTIVATING...
YOU SEE, YOU'RE PATIENT WHEN YOU WANT TO BE.
THIS ANALYTICAL WORK IS OF SUCH INTENSE PRECISION, SO FILLED WITH DISCONCERTING TRUTHS ON THE PSYCHE OF JEAN GENET THAT HE WILL BE COMPLETELY TURNED ON HIS HEAD.
THAT'S EASY TO SAY, MY DEAR BEAVER! I'M WAITING FOR MICHELLE, SHE'S ALREADY TEN MINUTES LATE.
WELL I'M GOING. GIVE HER MY LOVE. I'M GOING TO MEET CLAUDE AT HOME.
DESPITE THE SUPPORT OF HIS ARTIST FRIENDS, IT WILL TAKE HIM SEVERAL MONTHS TO RECOVER.
I NEED TO FIND SOME WAY TO RESPOND...

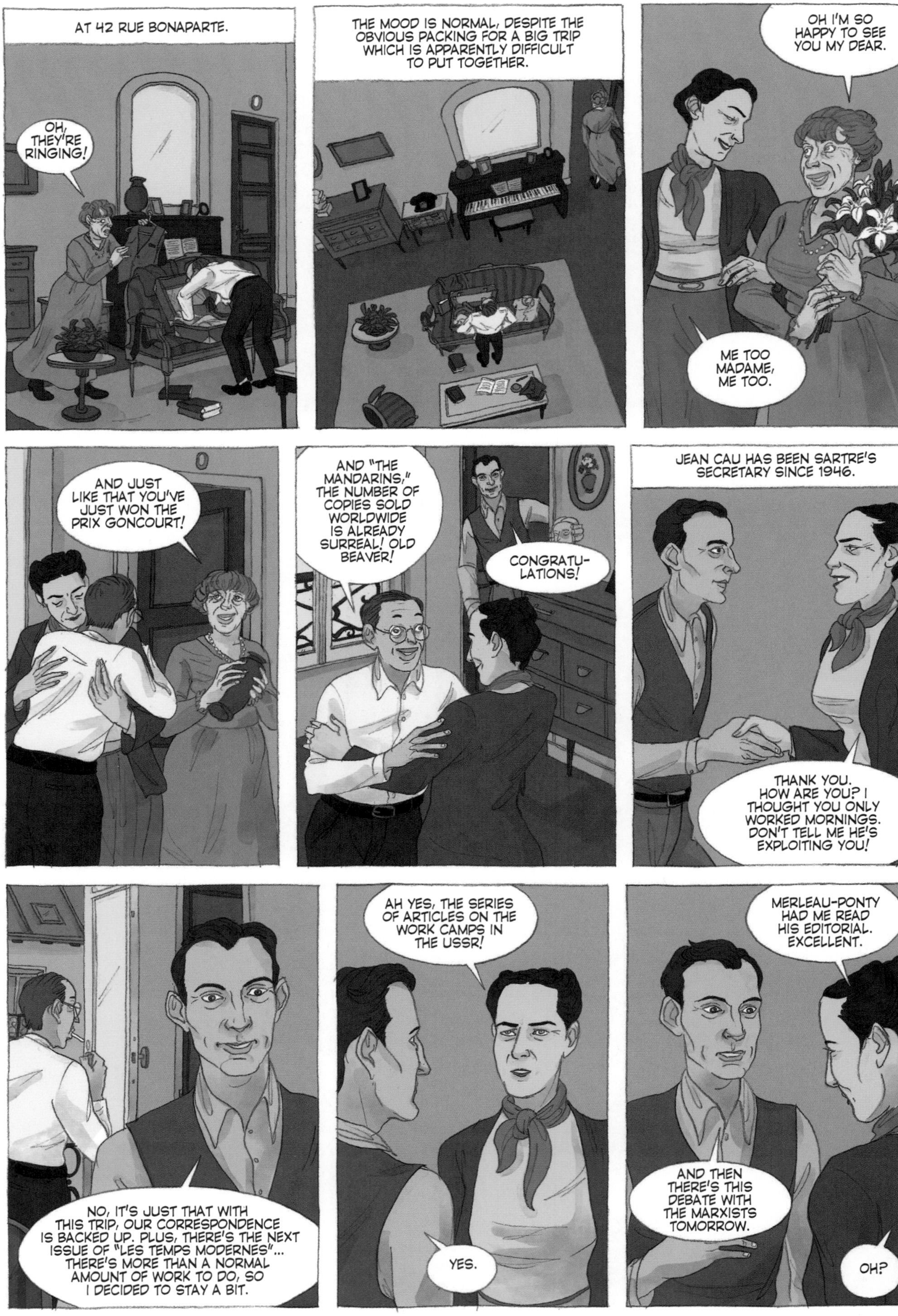
AT 42 RUE BONAPARTE.
OH, THEY'RE RINGING!
THE MOOD IS NORMAL, DESPITE THE OBVIOUS PACKING FOR A BIG TRIP WHICH IS APPARENTLY DIFFICULT TO PUT TOGETHER.
OH I'M SO HAPPY TO SEE YOU MY DEAR.
ME TOO MADAME, ME TOO.
AND JUST LIKE THAT YOU'VE JUST WON THE PRIX GONCOURT!
AND "THE MANDARINS," THE NUMBER OF COPIES SOLD WORLDWIDE IS ALREADY SURREAL! OLD BEAVER!
CONGRATU-LATIONS!
JEAN CAU HAS BEEN SARTRE'S SECRETARY SINCE 1946.
THANK YOU. HOW ARE YOU? I THOUGHT YOU ONLY WORKED MORNINGS. DON'T TELL ME HE'S EXPLOITING YOU!
NO, IT'S JUST THAT WITH THIS TRIP, OUR CORRESPONDENCE IS BACKED UP. PLUS, THERE'S THE NEXT ISSUE OF "LES TEMPS MODERNES"... THERE'S MORE THAN A NORMAL AMOUNT OF WORK TO DO, SO I DECIDED TO STAY A BIT.
AH YES, THE SERIES OF ARTICLES ON THE WORK CAMPS IN THE USSR!
YES.
MERLEAU-PONTY HAD ME READ HIS EDITORIAL. EXCELLENT.
AND THEN THERE'S THIS DEBATE WITH THE MARXISTS TOMORROW.
OH?

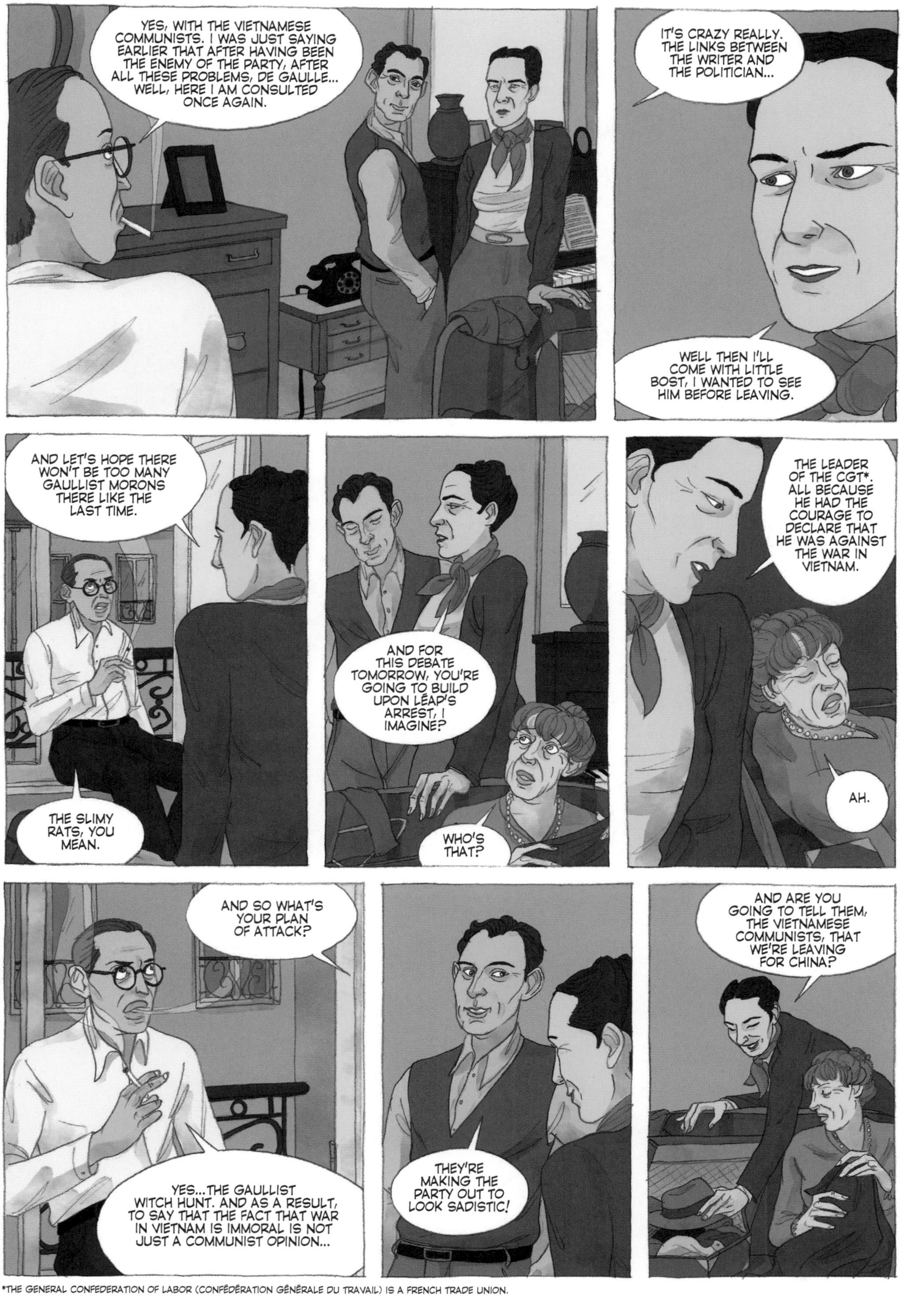
YES, WITH THE VIETNAMESE COMMUNISTS. I WAS JUST SAYING EARLIER THAT AFTER HAVING BEEN THE ENEMY OF THE PARTY, AFTER ALL THESE PROBLEMS, DE GAULLE... WELL, HERE I AM CONSULTED ONCE AGAIN.
IT'S CRAZY REALLY. THE LINKS BETWEEN THE WRITER AND THE POLITICIAN...
WELL THEN I'LL COME WITH LITTLE BOST, I WANTED TO SEE HIM BEFORE LEAVING.
AND LET'S HOPE THERE WON'T BE TOO MANY GAULLIST MORONS THERE LIKE THE LAST TIME.
THE SLIMY RATS, YOU MEAN.
AND FOR THIS DEBATE TOMORROW, YOU'RE GOING TO BUILD UPON LÉAP'S ARREST, I IMAGINE?
WHO'S THAT?
THE LEADER OF THE CGT*. ALL BECAUSE HE HAD THE COURAGE TO DECLARE THAT HE WAS AGAINST THE WAR IN VIETNAM.
AH.
AND SO WHAT'S YOUR PLAN OF ATTACK?
YES...THE GAULLIST WITCH HUNT. AND AS A RESULT, TO SAY THAT THE FACT THAT WAR IN VIETNAM IS IMMORAL IS NOT JUST A COMMUNIST OPINION...
THEY'RE MAKING THE PARTY OUT TO LOOK SADISTIC!
AND ARE YOU GOING TO TELL THEM, THE VIETNAMESE COMMUNISTS, THAT WE'RE LEAVING FOR CHINA?

*THE GENERAL CONFEDERATION OF LABOR (CONFÉDÉRATION GÉNÉRALE DU TRAVAIL) IS A FRENCH TRADE UNION.

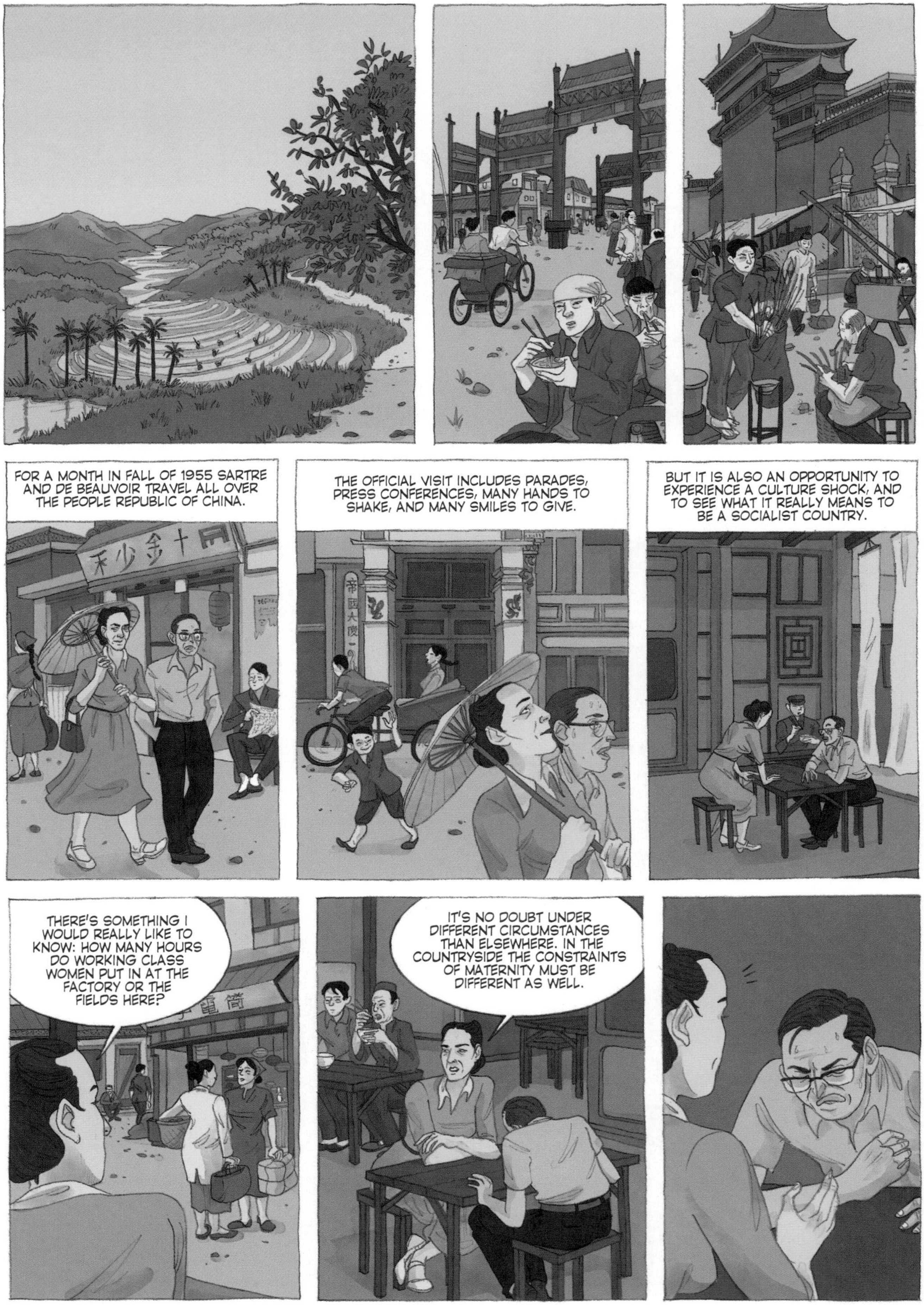
FOR A MONTH IN FALL OF 1955 SARTRE AND DE BEAUVOIR TRAVEL ALL OVER THE PEOPLE REPUBLIC OF CHINA.
THE OFFICIAL VISIT INCLUDES PARADES, PRESS CONFERENCES, MANY HANDS TO SHAKE, AND MANY SMILES TO GIVE.
BUT IT IS ALSO AN OPPORTUNITY TO EXPERIENCE A CULTURE SHOCK, AND TO SEE WHAT IT REALLY MEANS TO BE A SOCIALIST COUNTRY.
THERE'S SOMETHING I WOULD REALLY LIKE TO KNOW: HOW MANY HOURS DO WORKING CLASS WOMEN PUT IN AT THE FACTORY OR THE FIELDS HERE?
IT'S NO DOUBT UNDER DIFFERENT CIRCUMSTANCES THAN ELSEWHERE. IN THE COUNTRYSIDE THE CONSTRAINTS OF MATERNITY MUST BE DIFFERENT AS WELL.

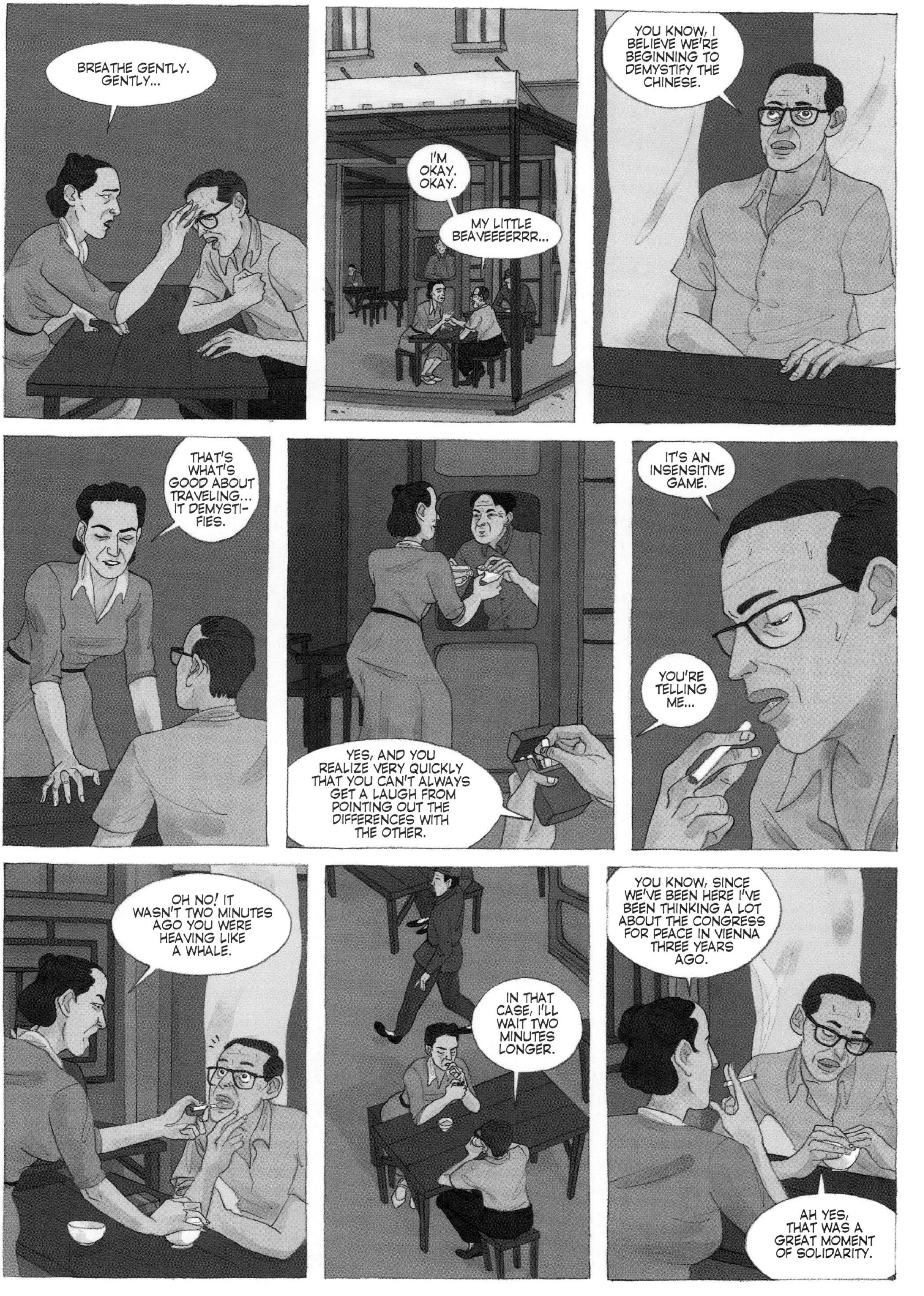
BREATHE GENTLY. GENTLY...
I'M OKAY. OKAY.
MY LITTLE BEAVEEEERRR...
YOU KNOW, I BELIEVE WE'RE BEGINNING TO DEMYSTIFY THE CHINESE.
THAT'S WHAT'S GOOD ABOUT TRAVELING... IT DEMYSTI-FIES.
YES, AND YOU REALIZE VERY QUICKLY THAT YOU CAN'T ALWAYS GET A LAUGH FROM POINTING OUT THE DIFFERENCES WITH THE OTHER.
IT'S AN INSENSITIVE GAME.
YOU'RE TELLING ME...
OH NO! IT WASN'T TWO MINUTES AGO YOU WERE HEAVING LIKE A WHALE.
IN THAT CASE, I'LL WAIT TWO MINUTES LONGER.
YOU KNOW, SINCE WE'VE BEEN HERE I'VE BEEN THINKING A LOT ABOUT THE CONGRESS FOR PEACE IN VIENNA THREE YEARS AGO.
AH YES, THAT WAS A GREAT MOMENT OF SOLIDARITY.

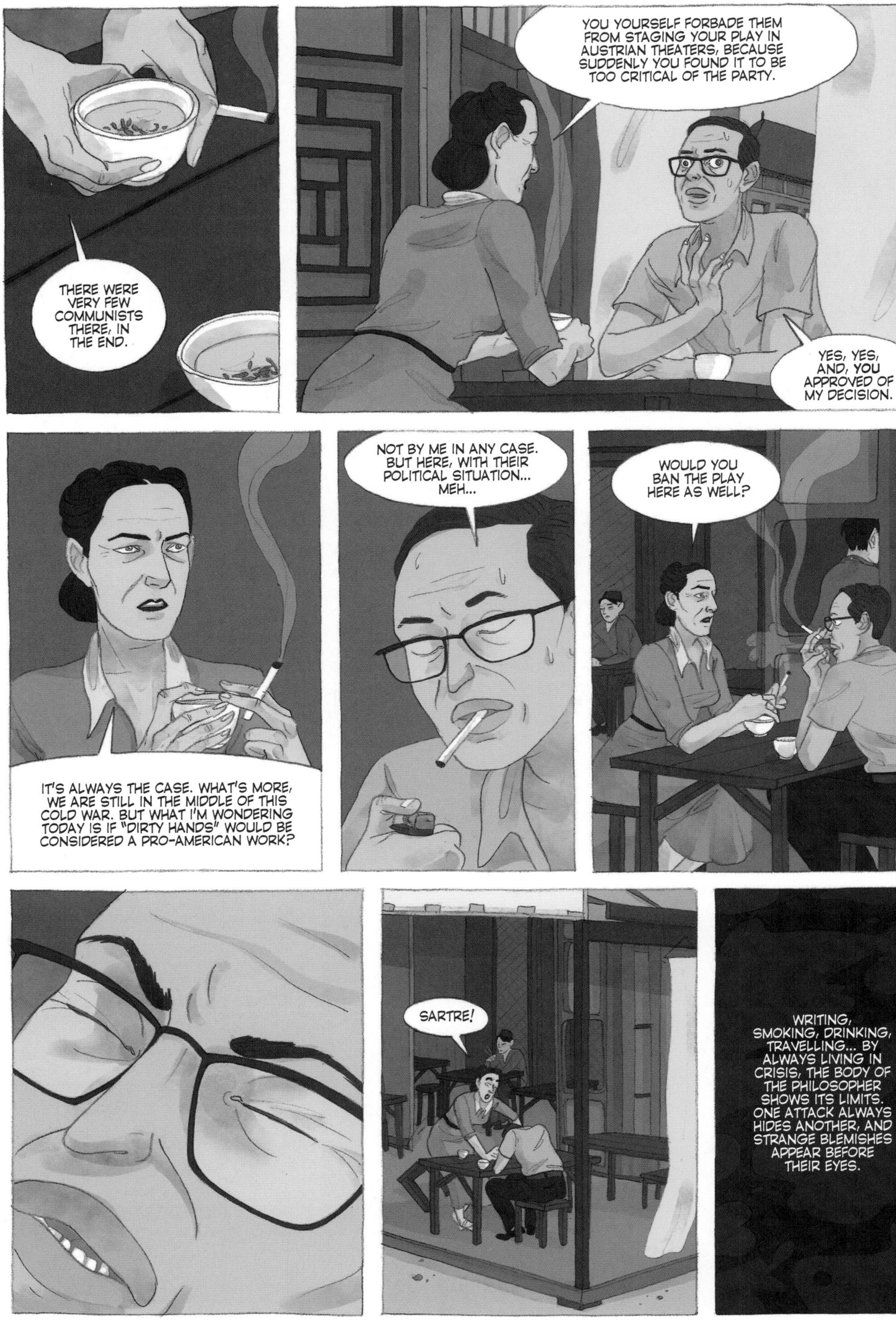
THERE WERE VERY FEW COMMUNISTS THERE, IN THE END.
YOU YOURSELF FORBADE THEM FROM STAGING YOUR PLAY IN AUSTRIAN THEATERS, BECAUSE SUDDENLY YOU FOUND IT TO BE TOO CRITICAL OF THE PARTY.
YES, YES, AND, YOU APPROVED OF MY DECISION.
IT'S ALWAYS THE CASE. WHAT'S MORE, WE ARE STILL IN THE MIDDLE OF THIS COLD WAR. BUT WHAT I'M WONDERING TODAY IS IF "DIRTY HANDS" WOULD BE CONSIDERED A PRO-AMERICAN WORK?
NOT BY ME IN ANY CASE. BUT HERE, WITH THEIR POLITICAL SITUATION... MEH...
WOULD YOU BAN THE PLAY HERE AS WELL?
SARTRE!
WRITING, SMOKING, DRINKING, TRAVELLING... BY ALWAYS LIVING IN CRISIS, THE BODY OF THE PHILOSOPHER SHOWS ITS LIMITS. ONE ATTACK ALWAYS HIDES ANOTHER, AND STRANGE BLEMISHES APPEAR BEFORE THEIR EYES.

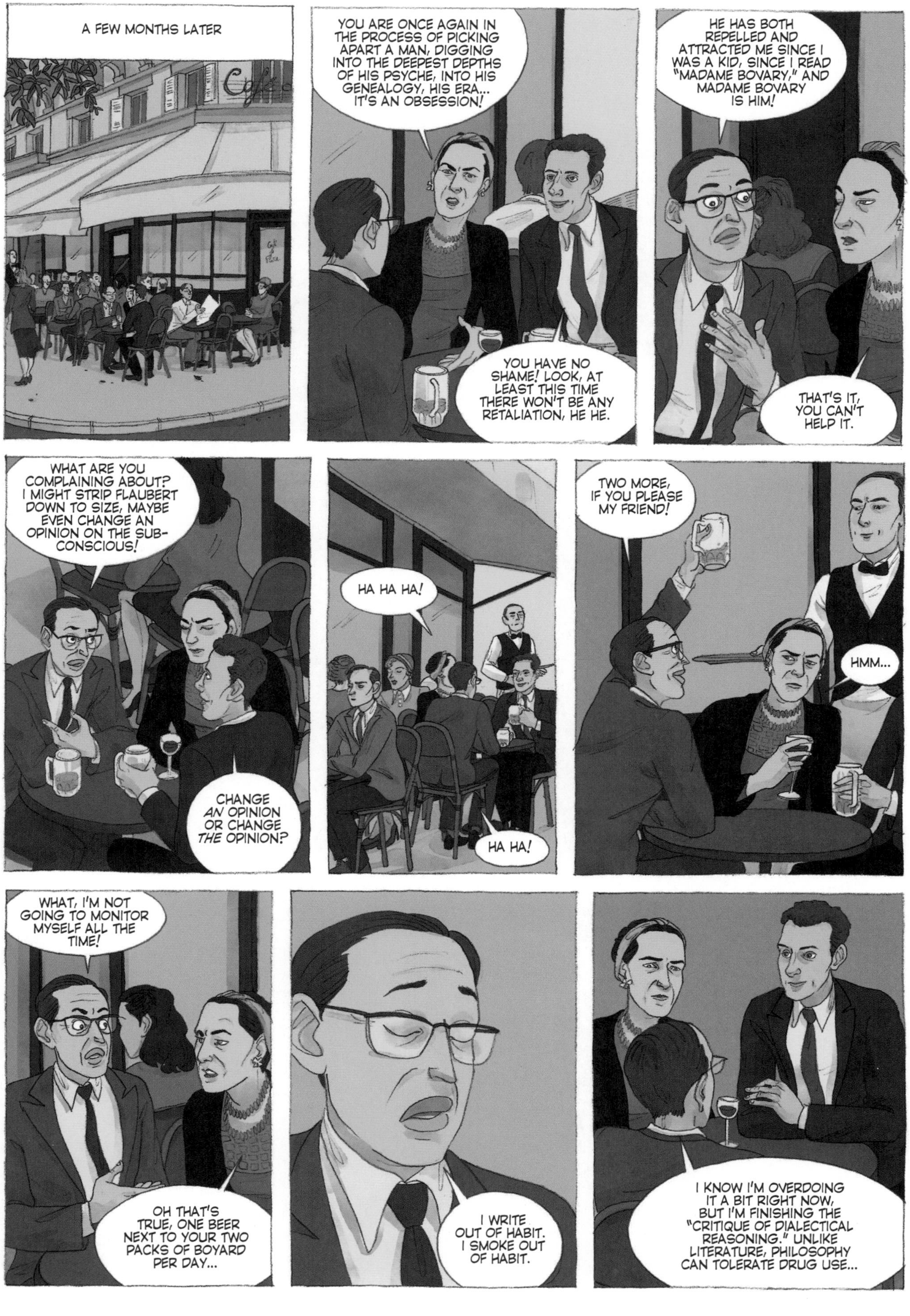
A FEW MONTHS LATER
YOU ARE ONCE AGAIN IN THE PROCESS OF PICKING APART A MAN, DIGGING INTO THE DEEPEST DEPTHS OF HIS PSYCHE, INTO HIS GENEALOGY, HIS ERA... IT'S AN OBSESSION!
YOU HAVE NO SHAME! LOOK, AT LEAST THIS TIME THERE WON'T BE ANY RETALIATION, HE HE.
HE HAS BOTH REPELLED AND ATTRACTED ME SINCE I WAS A KID, SINCE I READ "MADAME BOVARY," AND MADAME BOVARY IS HIM!
THAT'S IT, YOU CAN'T HELP IT.
WHAT ARE YOU COMPLAINING ABOUT? I MIGHT STRIP FLAUBERT DOWN TO SIZE, MAYBE EVEN CHANGE AN OPINION ON THE SUB-CONSCIOUS!
CHANGE *AN* OPINION OR CHANGE *THE* OPINION?
HA HA HA!
HA HA!
TWO MORE, IF YOU PLEASE MY FRIEND!
HMM...
WHAT, I'M NOT GOING TO MONITOR MYSELF ALL THE TIME!
OH THAT'S TRUE, ONE BEER NEXT TO YOUR TWO PACKS OF BOYARD PER DAY...
I WRITE OUT OF HABIT. I SMOKE OUT OF HABIT.
I KNOW I'M OVERDOING IT A BIT RIGHT NOW, BUT I'M FINISHING THE "CRITIQUE OF DIALECTICAL REASONING." UNLIKE LITERATURE, PHILOSOPHY CAN TOLERATE DRUG USE...

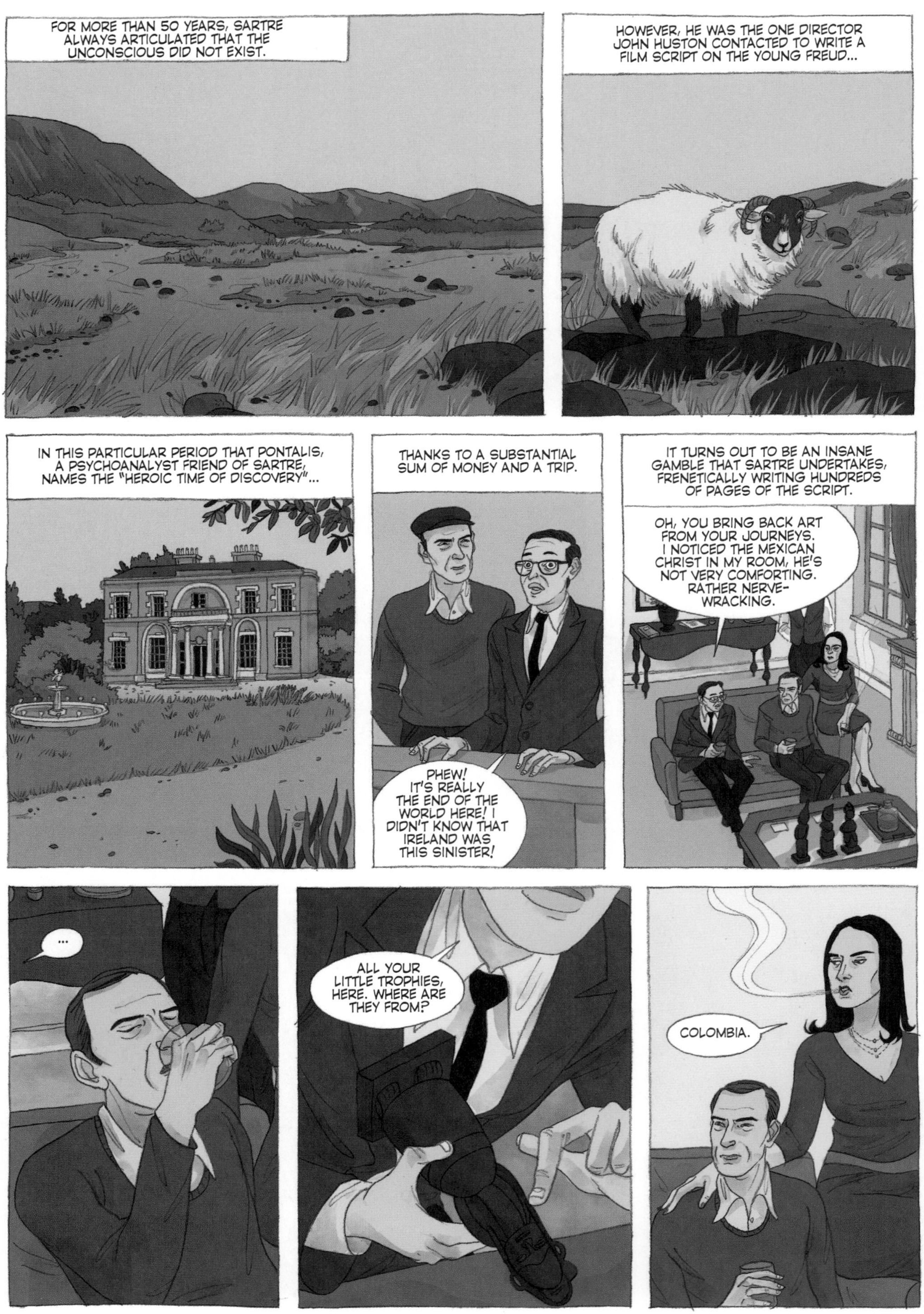
FOR MORE THAN 50 YEARS, SARTRE ALWAYS ARTICULATED THAT THE UNCONSCIOUS DID NOT EXIST.
HOWEVER, HE WAS THE ONE DIRECTOR JOHN HUSTON CONTACTED TO WRITE A FILM SCRIPT ON THE YOUNG FREUD...
IN THIS PARTICULAR PERIOD THAT PONTALIS, A PSYCHOANALYST FRIEND OF SARTRE, NAMES THE "HEROIC TIME OF DISCOVERY"...
THANKS TO A SUBSTANTIAL SUM OF MONEY AND A TRIP.
PHEW! IT'S REALLY THE END OF THE WORLD HERE! I DIDN'T KNOW THAT IRELAND WAS THIS SINISTER!
IT TURNS OUT TO BE AN INSANE GAMBLE THAT SARTRE UNDERTAKES, FRENETICALLY WRITING HUNDREDS OF PAGES OF THE SCRIPT.
OH, YOU BRING BACK ART FROM YOUR JOURNEYS. I NOTICED THE MEXICAN CHRIST IN MY ROOM, HE'S NOT VERY COMFORTING. RATHER NERVE-WRACKING.
...
ALL YOUR LITTLE TROPHIES, HERE. WHERE ARE THEY FROM?
COLOMBIA.

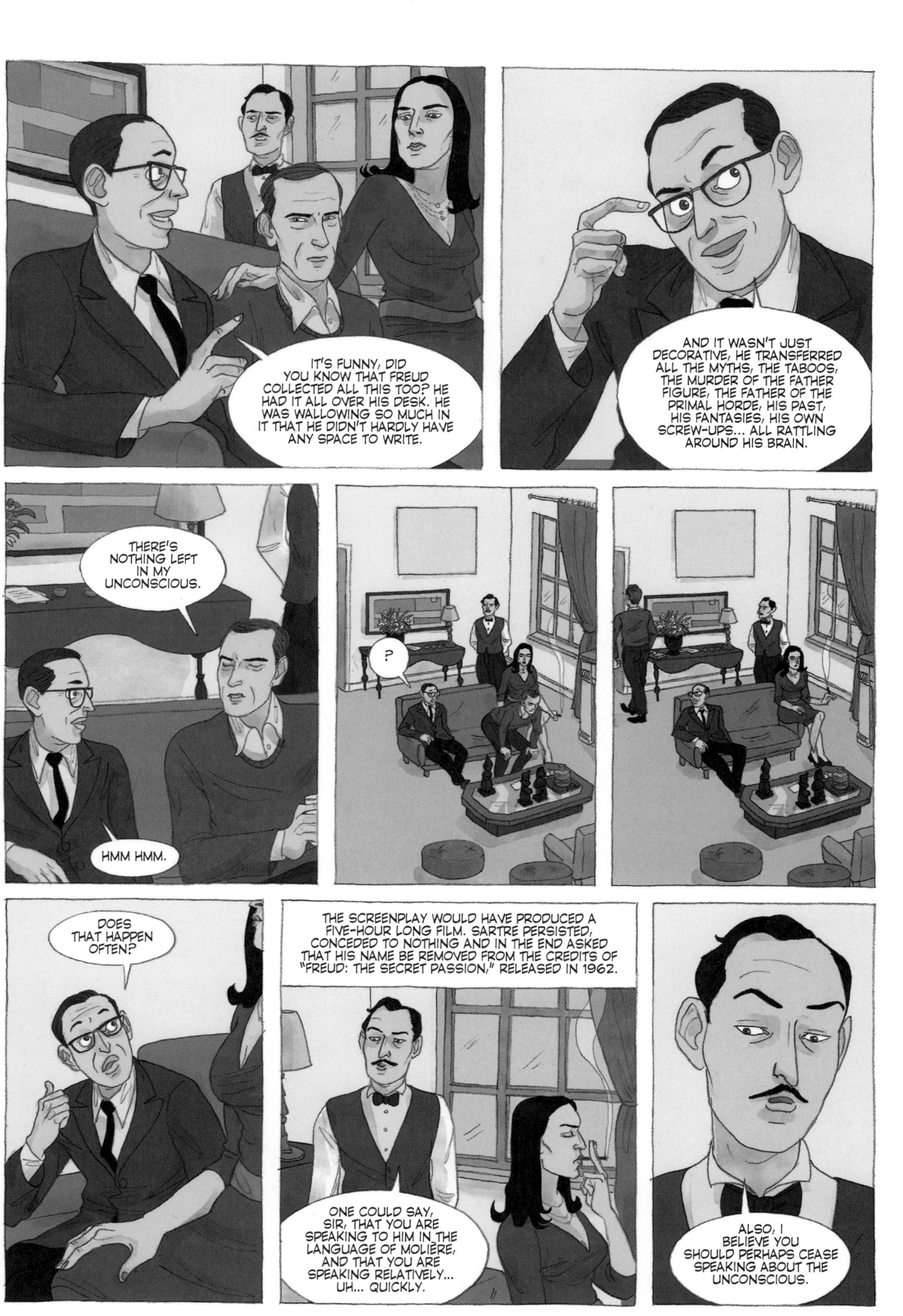
IT'S FUNNY, DID YOU KNOW THAT FREUD COLLECTED ALL THIS TOO? HE HAD IT ALL OVER HIS DESK. HE WAS WALLOWING SO MUCH IN IT THAT HE DIDN'T HARDLY HAVE ANY SPACE TO WRITE.
AND IT WASN'T JUST DECORATIVE, HE TRANSFERRED ALL THE MYTHS, THE TABOOS, THE MURDER OF THE FATHER FIGURE, THE FATHER OF THE PRIMAL HORDE, HIS PAST, HIS FANTASIES, HIS OWN SCREW-UPS... ALL RATTLING AROUND HIS BRAIN.
THERE'S NOTHING LEFT IN MY UNCONSCIOUS.
HMM HMM.
?
DOES THAT HAPPEN OFTEN?
THE SCREENPLAY WOULD HAVE PRODUCED A FIVE-HOUR LONG FILM. SARTRE PERSISTED, CONCEDED TO NOTHING AND IN THE END ASKED THAT HIS NAME BE REMOVED FROM THE CREDITS OF "FREUD: THE SECRET PASSION," RELEASED IN 1962.
ONE COULD SAY, SIR, THAT YOU ARE SPEAKING TO HIM IN THE LANGUAGE OF MOLIÈRE, AND THAT YOU ARE SPEAKING RELATIVELY... UH... QUICKLY.
ALSO, I BELIEVE YOU SHOULD PERHAPS CEASE SPEAKING ABOUT THE UNCONSCIOUS.

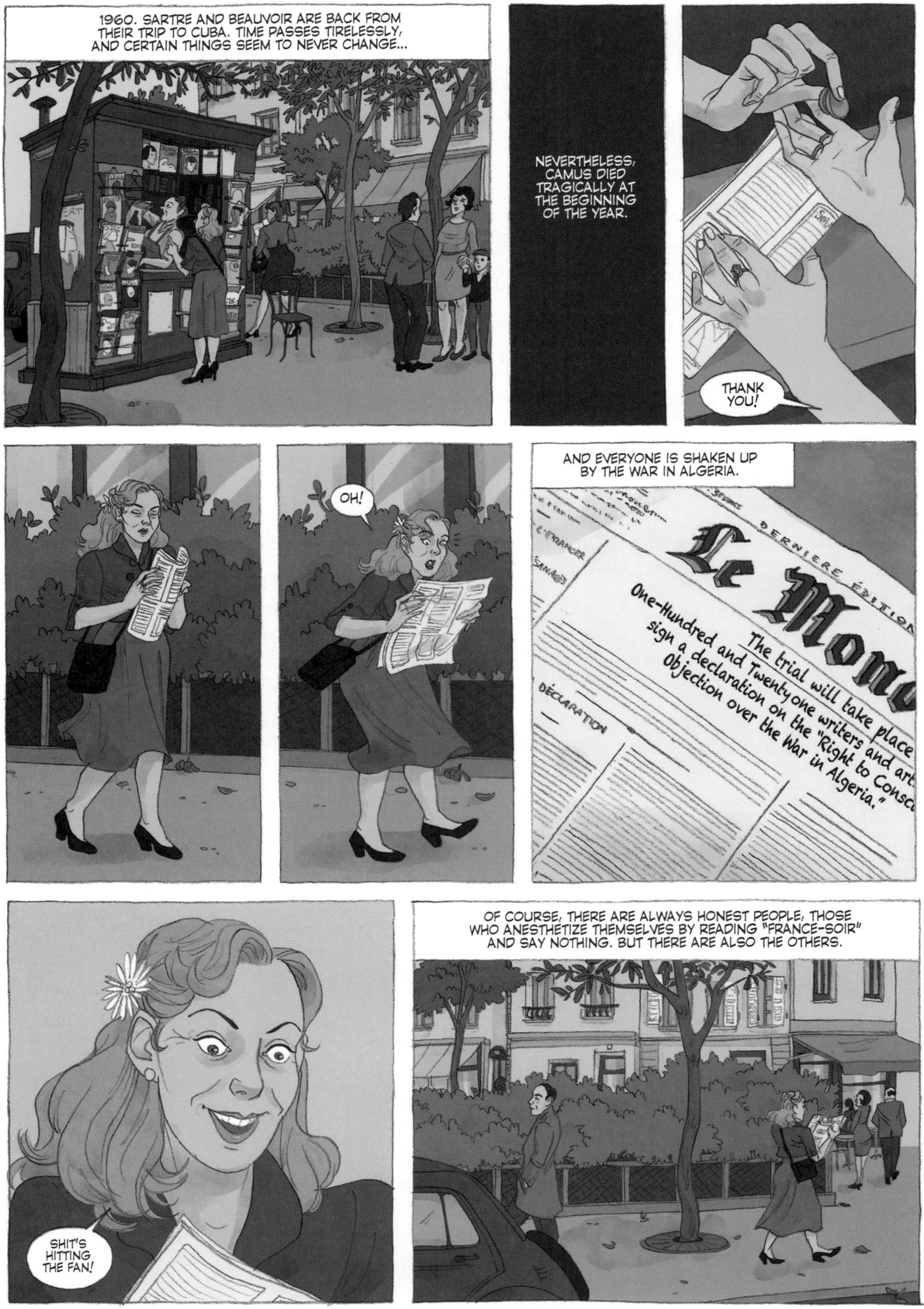
1960. SARTRE AND BEAUVOIR ARE BACK FROM THEIR TRIP TO CUBA. TIME PASSES TIRELESSLY, AND CERTAIN THINGS SEEM TO NEVER CHANGE...
NEVERTHELESS, CAMUS DIED TRAGICALLY AT THE BEGINNING OF THE YEAR.
THANK YOU!
OH!
AND EVERYONE IS SHAKEN UP BY THE WAR IN ALGERIA.
DERNIERE EDITION
The trial will take place
One-Hundred and Twentyone writers and art
sign a declaration on the "Right to Consc
Objection over the War in Algeria."
DÉCLARATION
SHIT'S HITTING THE FAN!
OF COURSE, THERE ARE ALWAYS HONEST PEOPLE, THOSE WHO ANESTHETIZE THEMSELVES BY READING "FRANCE-SOIR" AND SAY NOTHING. BUT THERE ARE ALSO THE OTHERS.

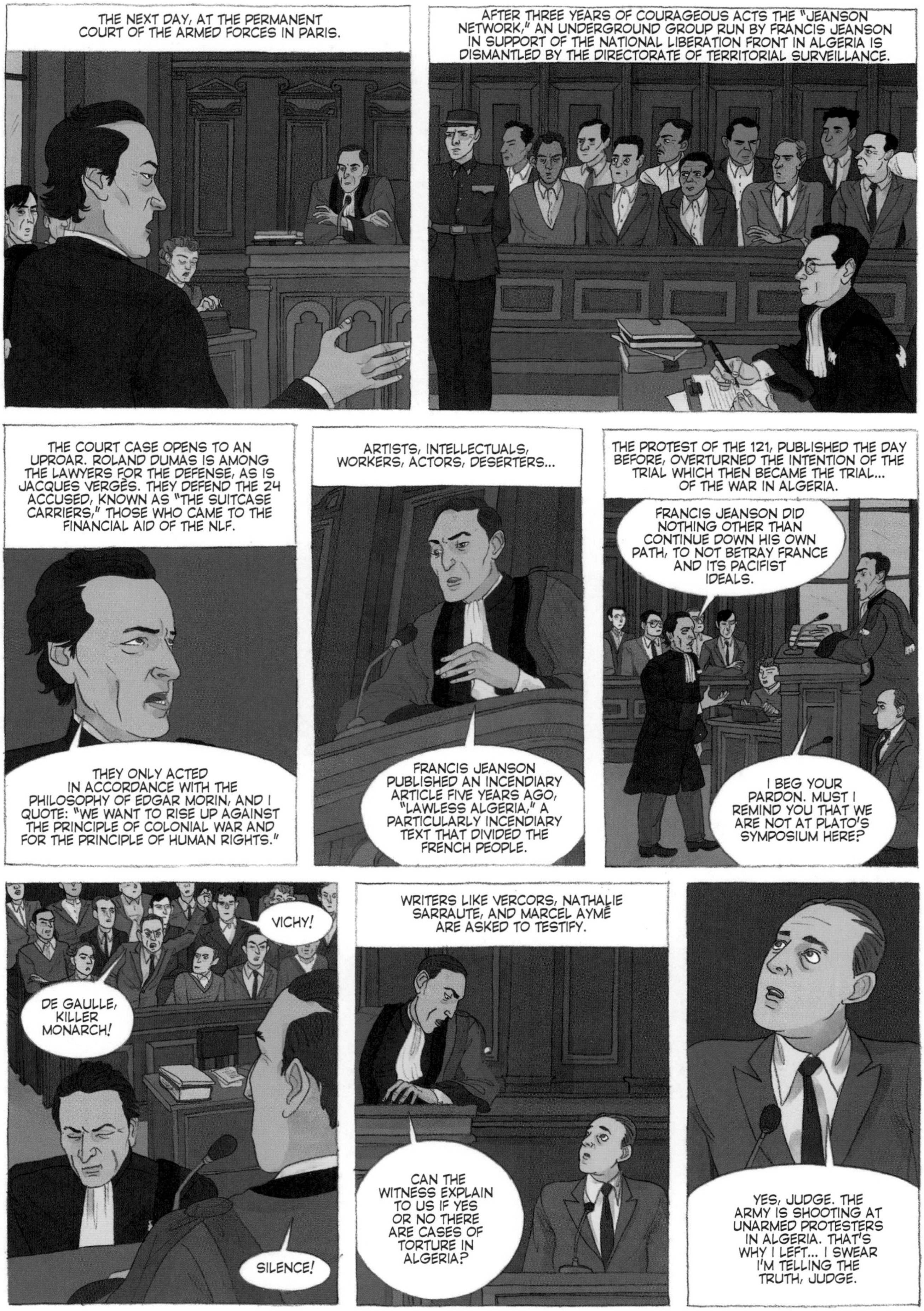
THE NEXT DAY, AT THE PERMANENT COURT OF THE ARMED FORCES IN PARIS.
AFTER THREE YEARS OF COURAGEOUS ACTS THE "JEANSON NETWORK," AN UNDERGROUND GROUP RUN BY FRANCIS JEANSON IN SUPPORT OF THE NATIONAL LIBERATION FRONT IN ALGERIA IS DISMANTLED BY THE DIRECTORATE OF TERRITORIAL SURVEILLANCE.
THE COURT CASE OPENS TO AN UPROAR. ROLAND DUMAS IS AMONG THE LAWYERS FOR THE DEFENSE, AS IS JACQUES VERGÈS. THEY DEFEND THE 24 ACCUSED, KNOWN AS "THE SUITCASE CARRIERS," THOSE WHO CAME TO THE FINANCIAL AID OF THE NLF.
THEY ONLY ACTED IN ACCORDANCE WITH THE PHILOSOPHY OF EDGAR MORIN, AND I QUOTE: "WE WANT TO RISE UP AGAINST THE PRINCIPLE OF COLONIAL WAR AND FOR THE PRINCIPLE OF HUMAN RIGHTS."
ARTISTS, INTELLECTUALS, WORKERS, ACTORS, DESERTERS...
FRANCIS JEANSON PUBLISHED AN INCENDIARY ARTICLE FIVE YEARS AGO, "LAWLESS ALGERIA," A PARTICULARLY INCENDIARY TEXT THAT DIVIDED THE FRENCH PEOPLE.
THE PROTEST OF THE 121, PUBLISHED THE DAY BEFORE, OVERTURNED THE INTENTION OF THE TRIAL WHICH THEN BECAME THE TRIAL... OF THE WAR IN ALGERIA.
FRANCIS JEANSON DID NOTHING OTHER THAN CONTINUE DOWN HIS OWN PATH, TO NOT BETRAY FRANCE AND ITS PACIFIST IDEALS.
I BEG YOUR PARDON. MUST I REMIND YOU THAT WE ARE NOT AT PLATO'S SYMPOSIUM HERE?
VICHY!
DE GAULLE, KILLER MONARCH!
SILENCE!
WRITERS LIKE VERCORS, NATHALIE SARRAUTE, AND MARCEL AYMÉ ARE ASKED TO TESTIFY.
CAN THE WITNESS EXPLAIN TO US IF YES OR NO THERE ARE CASES OF TORTURE IN ALGERIA?
YES, JUDGE. THE ARMY IS SHOOTING AT UNARMED PROTESTERS IN ALGERIA. THAT'S WHY I LEFT... I SWEAR I'M TELLING THE TRUTH, JUDGE.

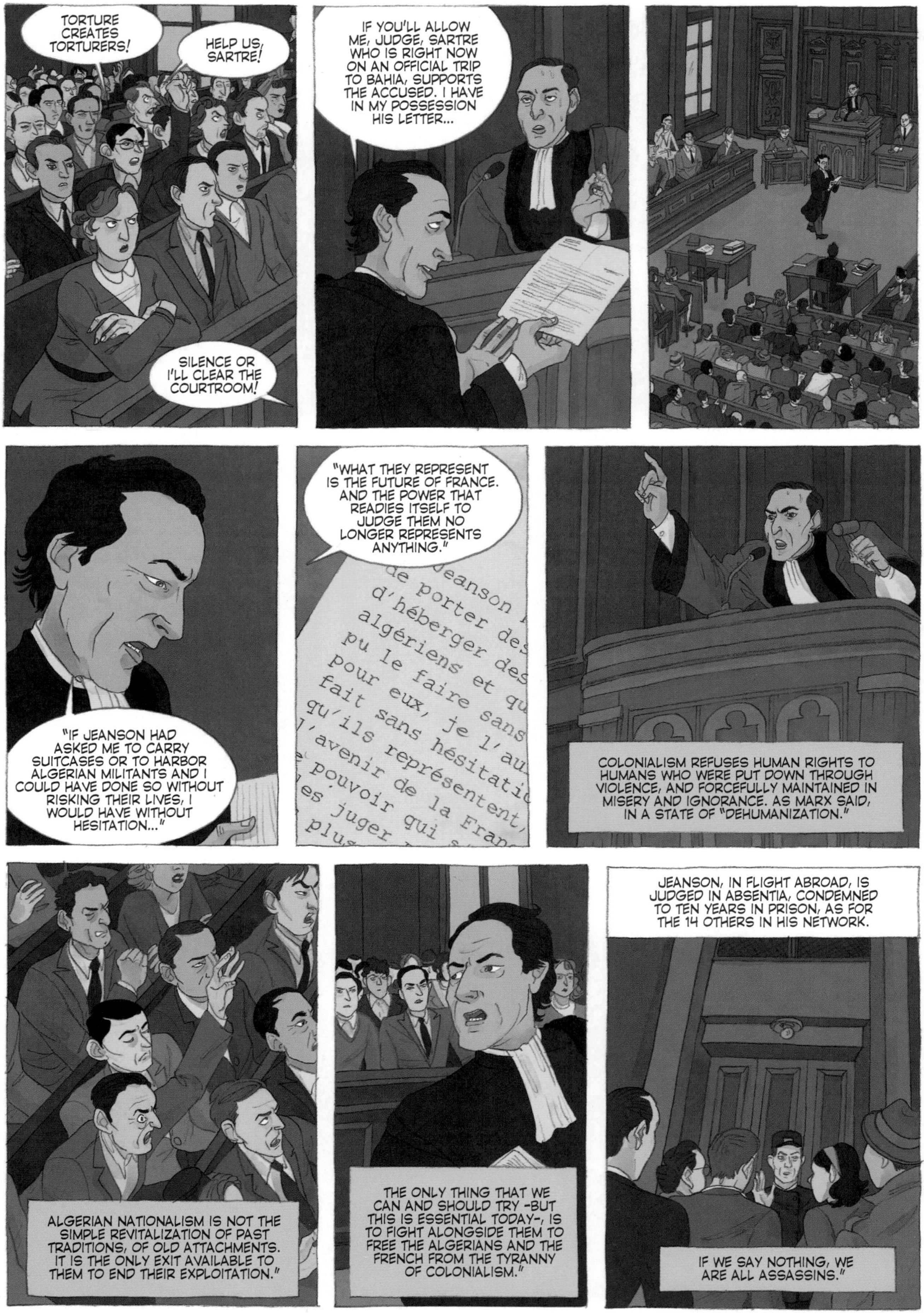
TORTURE CREATES TORTURERS!
HELP US, SARTRE!
SILENCE OR I'LL CLEAR THE COURTROOM!
IF YOU'LL ALLOW ME, JUDGE, SARTRE WHO IS RIGHT NOW ON AN OFFICIAL TRIP TO BAHIA, SUPPORTS THE ACCUSED. I HAVE IN MY POSSESSION HIS LETTER...
"IF JEANSON HAD ASKED ME TO CARRY SUITCASES OR TO HARBOR ALGERIAN MILITANTS AND I COULD HAVE DONE SO WITHOUT RISKING THEIR LIVES, I WOULD HAVE WITHOUT HESITATION..."
"WHAT THEY REPRESENT IS THE FUTURE OF FRANCE. AND THE POWER THAT READIES ITSELF TO JUDGE THEM NO LONGER REPRESENTS ANYTHING."
de porter des
d'héberger des
algériens et
pu le faire sans
pour eux, je l'au
fait sans hésitati
qu'ils représentent,
l'avenir de la Fran
pouvoir qui
es juger
COLONIALISM REFUSES HUMAN RIGHTS TO HUMANS WHO WERE PUT DOWN THROUGH VIOLENCE, AND FORCEFULLY MAINTAINED IN MISERY AND IGNORANCE. AS MARX SAID, IN A STATE OF "DEHUMANIZATION."
ALGERIAN NATIONALISM IS NOT THE SIMPLE REVITALIZATION OF PAST TRADITIONS, OF OLD ATTACHMENTS. IT IS THE ONLY EXIT AVAILABLE TO THEM TO END THEIR EXPLOITATION."
THE ONLY THING THAT WE CAN AND SHOULD TRY -BUT THIS IS ESSENTIAL TODAY-, IS TO FIGHT ALONGSIDE THEM TO FREE THE ALGERIANS AND THE FRENCH FROM THE TYRANNY OF COLONIALISM."
JEANSON, IN FLIGHT ABROAD, IS JUDGED IN ABSENTIA, CONDEMNED TO TEN YEARS IN PRISON, AS FOR THE 14 OTHERS IN HIS NETWORK.
IF WE SAY NOTHING, WE ARE ALL ASSASSINS."

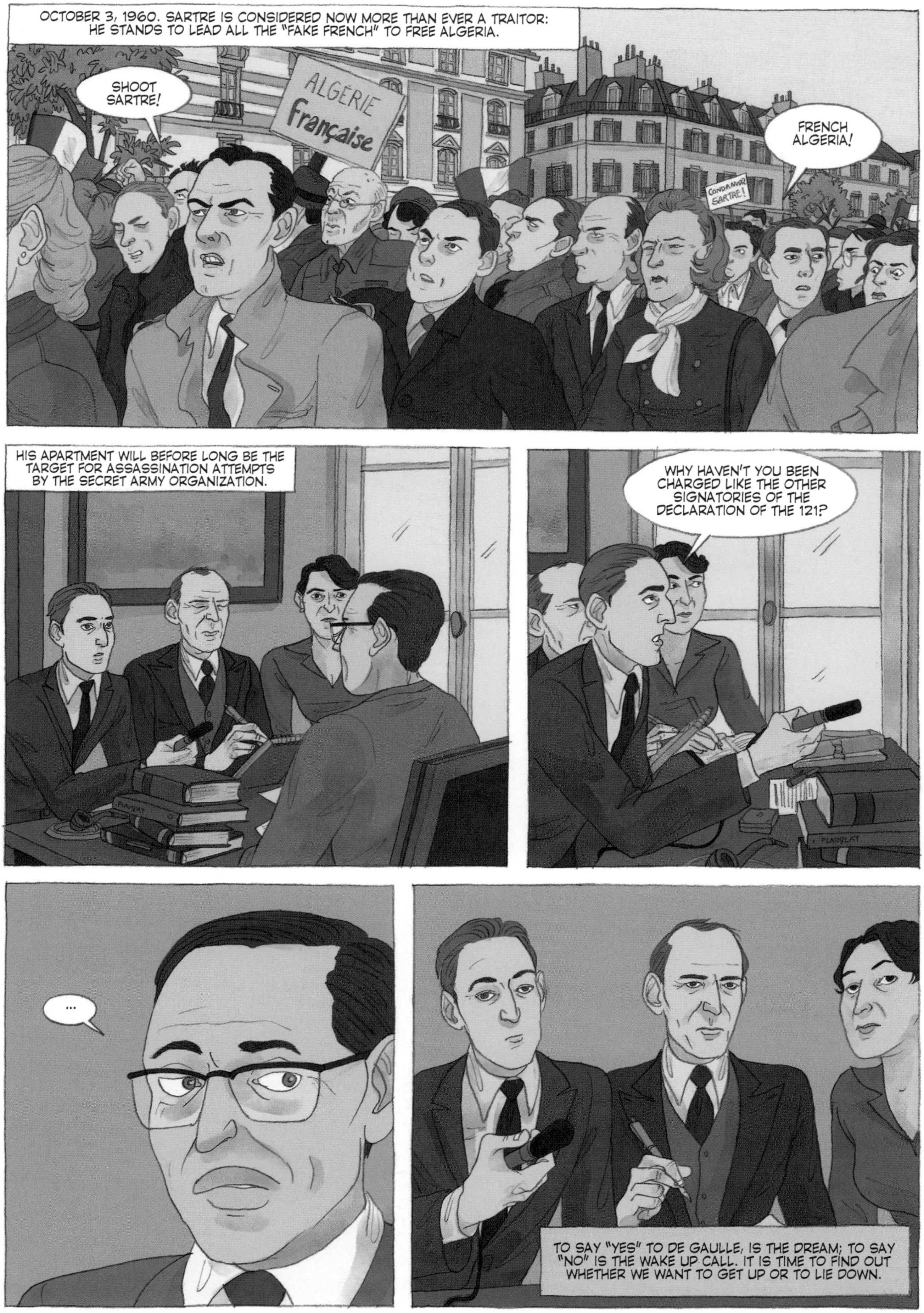
OCTOBER 3, 1960. SARTRE IS CONSIDERED NOW MORE THAN EVER A TRAITOR: HE STANDS TO LEAD ALL THE "FAKE FRENCH" TO FREE ALGERIA.
SHOOT SARTRE!
ALGÉRIE Française
FRENCH ALGERIA!
HIS APARTMENT WILL BEFORE LONG BE THE TARGET FOR ASSASSINATION ATTEMPTS BY THE SECRET ARMY ORGANIZATION.
WHY HAVEN'T YOU BEEN CHARGED LIKE THE OTHER SIGNATORIES OF THE DECLARATION OF THE 121?
...
TO SAY "YES" TO DE GAULLE, IS THE DREAM; TO SAY "NO" IS THE WAKE UP CALL. IT IS TIME TO FIND OUT WHETHER WE WANT TO GET UP OR TO LIE DOWN.

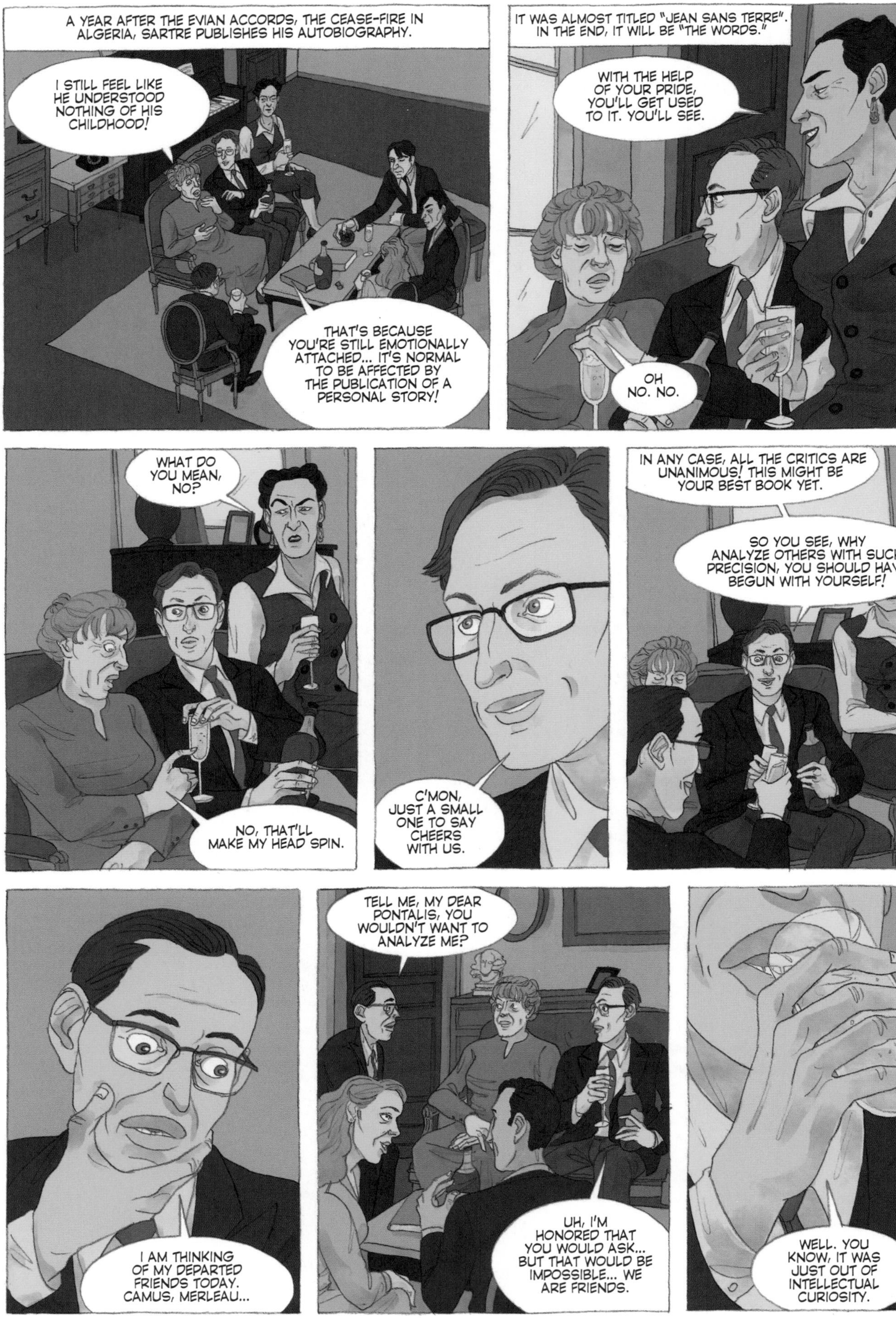
A YEAR AFTER THE EVIAN ACCORDS, THE CEASE-FIRE IN ALGERIA, SARTRE PUBLISHES HIS AUTOBIOGRAPHY.
I STILL FEEL LIKE HE UNDERSTOOD NOTHING OF HIS CHILDHOOD!
THAT'S BECAUSE YOU'RE STILL EMOTIONALLY ATTACHED... IT'S NORMAL TO BE AFFECTED BY THE PUBLICATION OF A PERSONAL STORY!
IT WAS ALMOST TITLED "JEAN SANS TERRE". IN THE END, IT WILL BE "THE WORDS."
WITH THE HELP OF YOUR PRIDE, YOU'LL GET USED TO IT. YOU'LL SEE.
OH NO. NO.
WHAT DO YOU MEAN, NO?
NO, THAT'LL MAKE MY HEAD SPIN.
C'MON, JUST A SMALL ONE TO SAY CHEERS WITH US.
IN ANY CASE, ALL THE CRITICS ARE UNANIMOUS! THIS MIGHT BE YOUR BEST BOOK YET.
SO YOU SEE, WHY ANALYZE OTHERS WITH SUCH PRECISION, YOU SHOULD HAVE BEGUN WITH YOURSELF!
I AM THINKING OF MY DEPARTED FRIENDS TODAY. CAMUS, MERLEAU...
TELL ME, MY DEAR PONTALIS, YOU WOULDN'T WANT TO ANALYZE ME?
UH, I'M HONORED THAT YOU WOULD ASK... BUT THAT WOULD BE IMPOSSIBLE... WE ARE FRIENDS.
WELL. YOU KNOW, IT WAS JUST OUT OF INTELLECTUAL CURIOSITY.

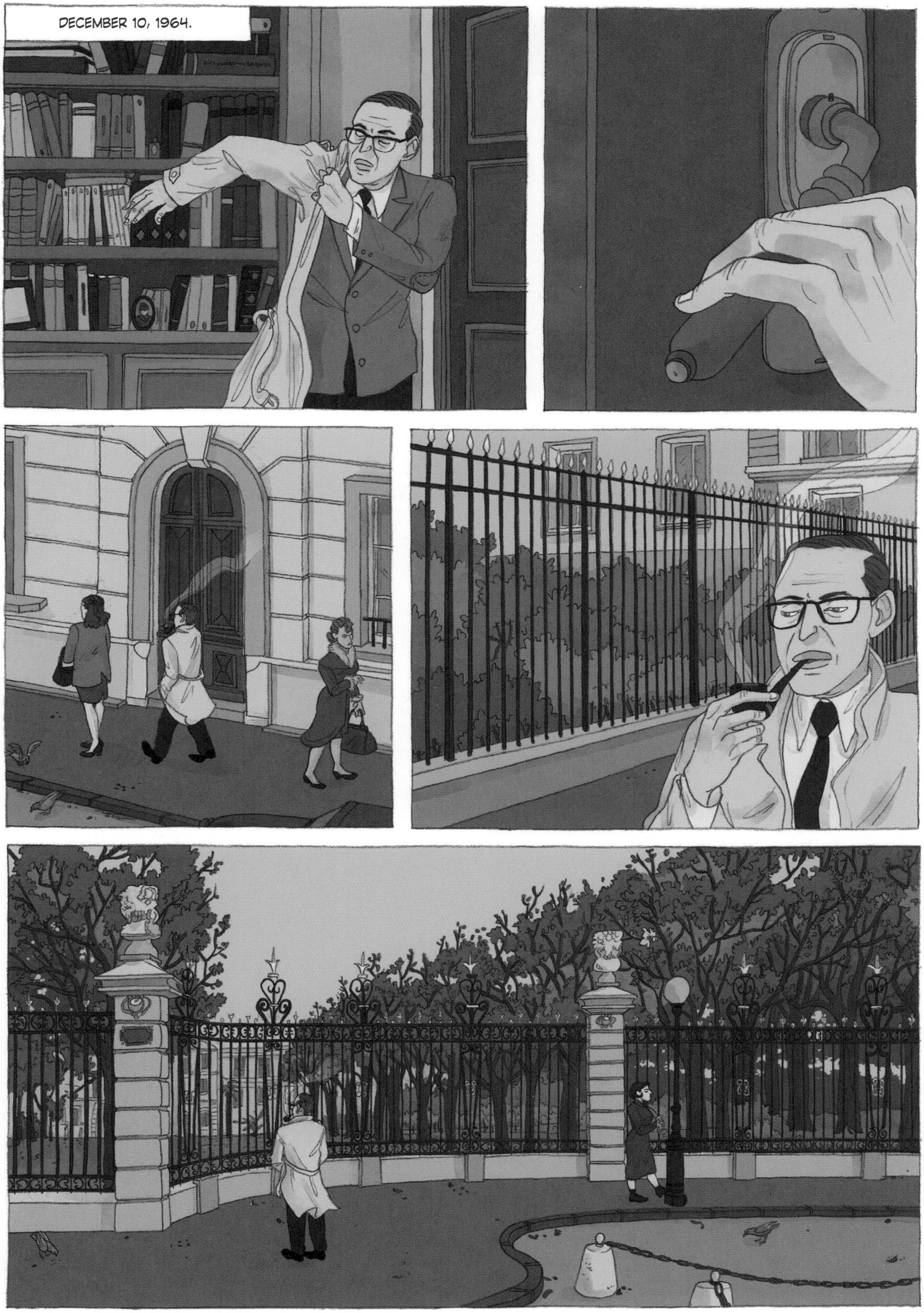
DECEMBER 10, 1964.

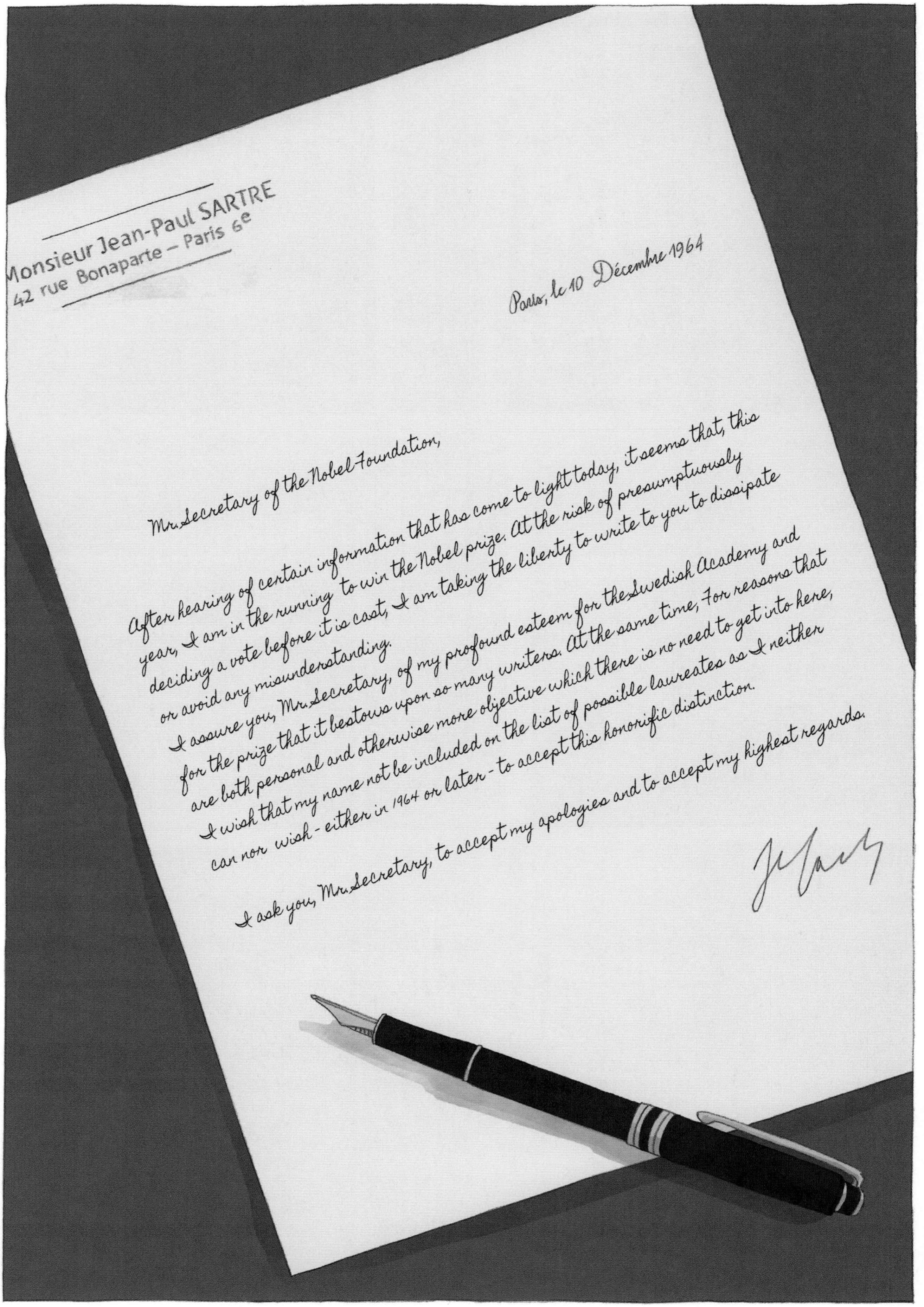
Monsieur Jean-Paul SARTRE
42 rue Bonaparte – Paris 6e
Paris, le 10 Décembre 1964
Mr. Secretary of the Nobel Foundation,
After hearing of certain information that has come to light today, it seems that, this year, I am in the running to win the Nobel prize. At the risk of presumptuously deciding a vote before it is cast, I am taking the liberty to write to you to dissipate or avoid any misunderstanding.
I assure you, Mr. Secretary, of my profound esteem for the Swedish Academy and for the prize that it bestows upon so many writers. At the same time, for reasons that are both personal and otherwise more objective which there is no need to get into here, I wish that my name not be included on the list of possible laureates as I neither can nor wish - either in 1964 or later - to accept this honorific distinction.
I ask you, Mr. Secretary, to accept my apologies and to accept my highest regards.

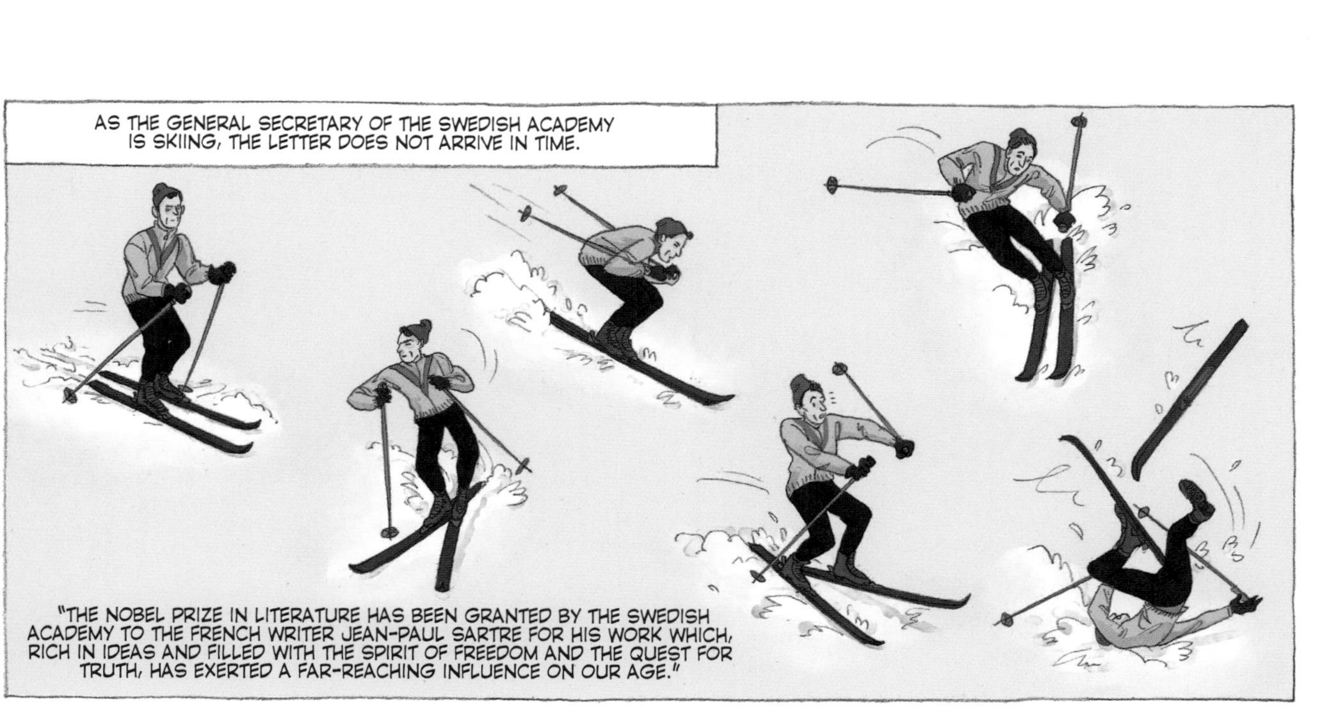
AS THE GENERAL SECRETARY OF THE SWEDISH ACADEMY IS SKIING, THE LETTER DOES NOT ARRIVE IN TIME.
"THE NOBEL PRIZE IN LITERATURE HAS BEEN GRANTED BY THE SWEDISH ACADEMY TO THE FRENCH WRITER JEAN-PAUL SARTRE FOR HIS WORK WHICH, RICH IN IDEAS AND FILLED WITH THE SPIRIT OF FREEDOM AND THE QUEST FOR TRUTH, HAS EXERTED A FAR-REACHING INFLUENCE ON OUR AGE."

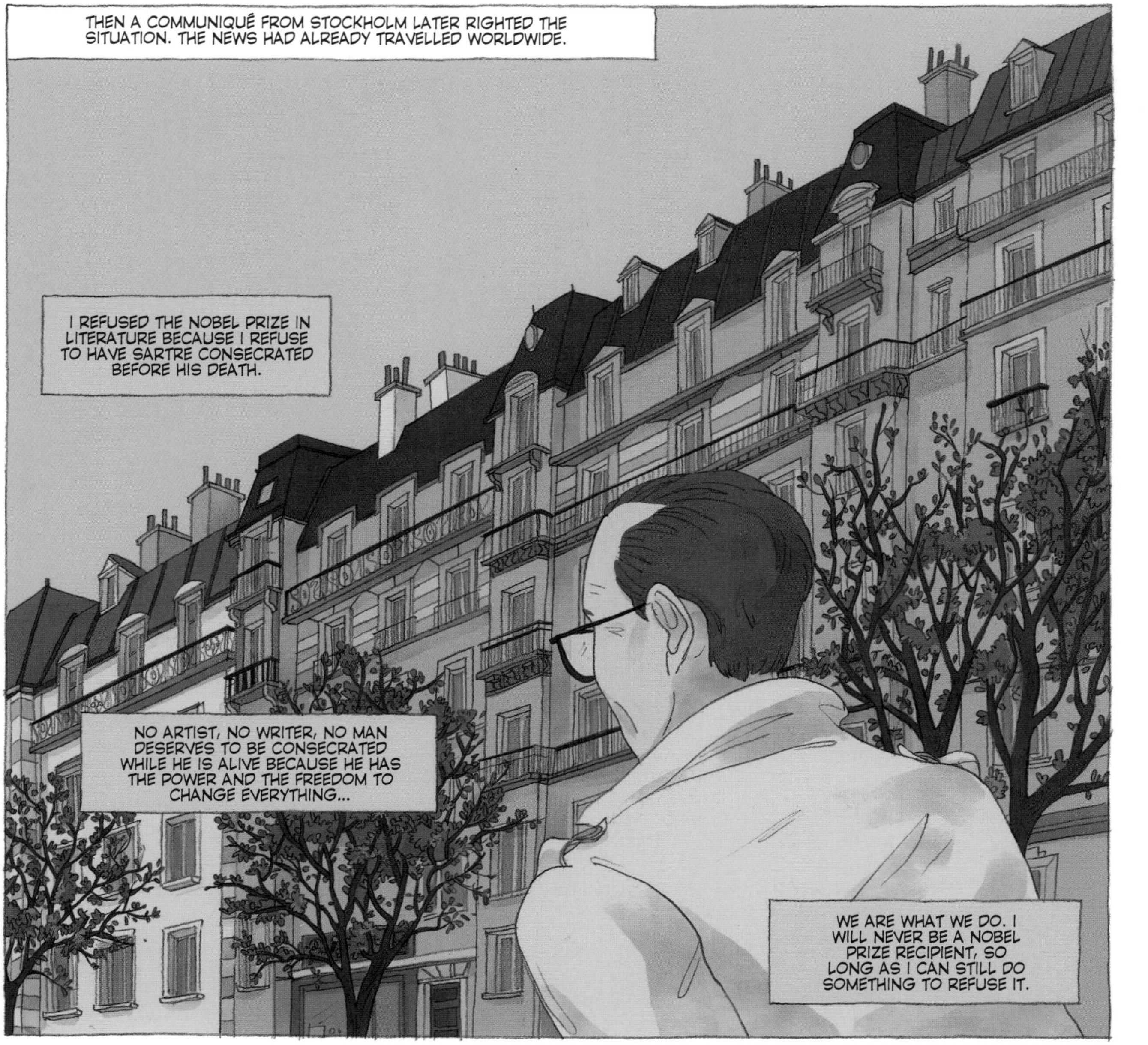
THEN A COMMUNIQUÉ FROM STOCKHOLM LATER RIGHTED THE SITUATION. THE NEWS HAD ALREADY TRAVELLED WORLDWIDE.
I REFUSED THE NOBEL PRIZE IN LITERATURE BECAUSE I REFUSE TO HAVE SARTRE CONSECRATED BEFORE HIS DEATH.
NO ARTIST, NO WRITER, NO MAN DESERVES TO BE CONSECRATED WHILE HE IS ALIVE BECAUSE HE HAS THE POWER AND THE FREEDOM TO CHANGE EVERYTHING...
WE ARE WHAT WE DO. I WILL NEVER BE A NOBEL PRIZE RECIPIENT, SO LONG AS I CAN STILL DO SOMETHING TO REFUSE IT.

EPILOGUE

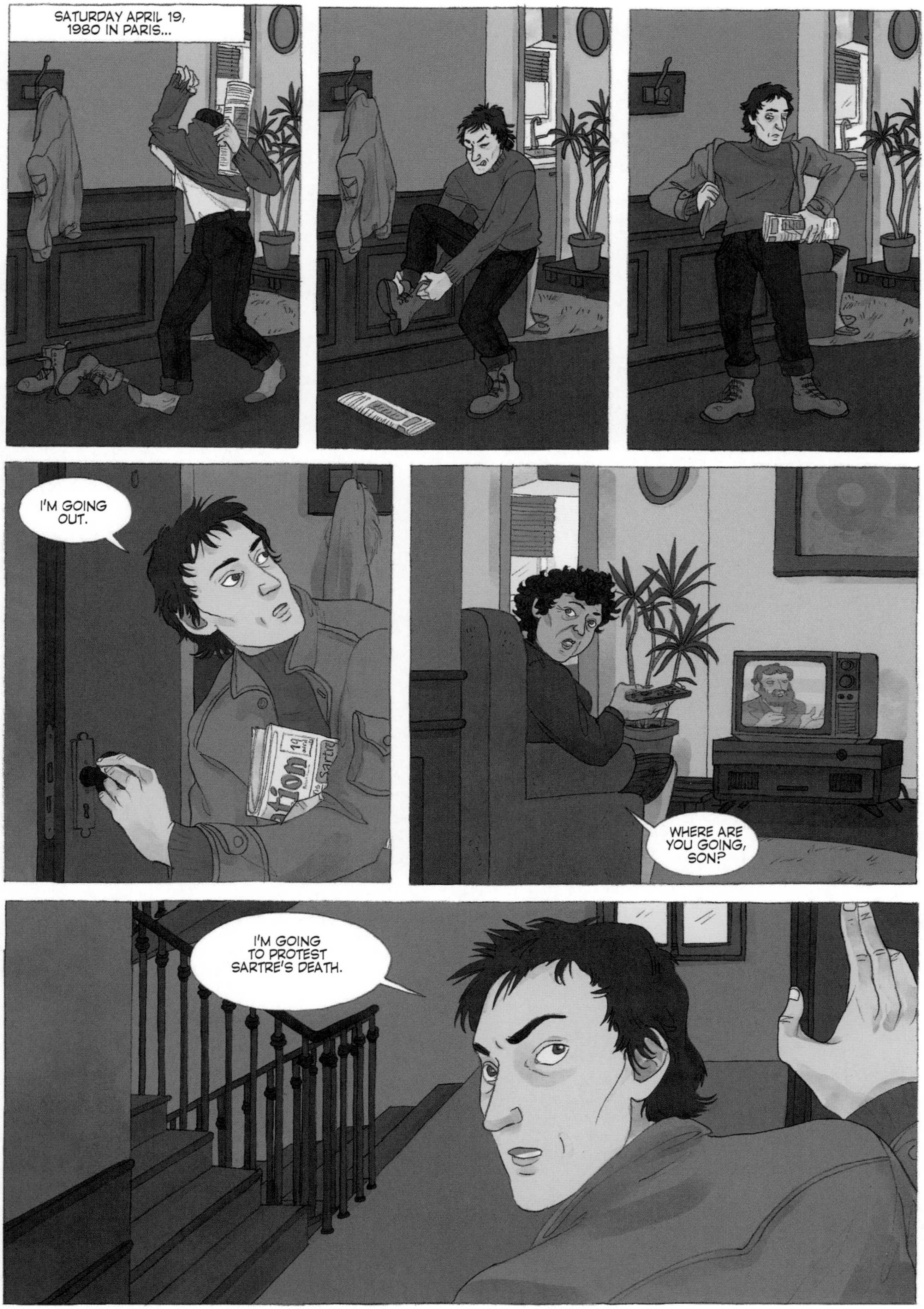
SATURDAY APRIL 19, 1980 IN PARIS...
I'M GOING OUT.
WHERE ARE YOU GOING, SON?
I'M GOING TO PROTEST SARTRE'S DEATH.

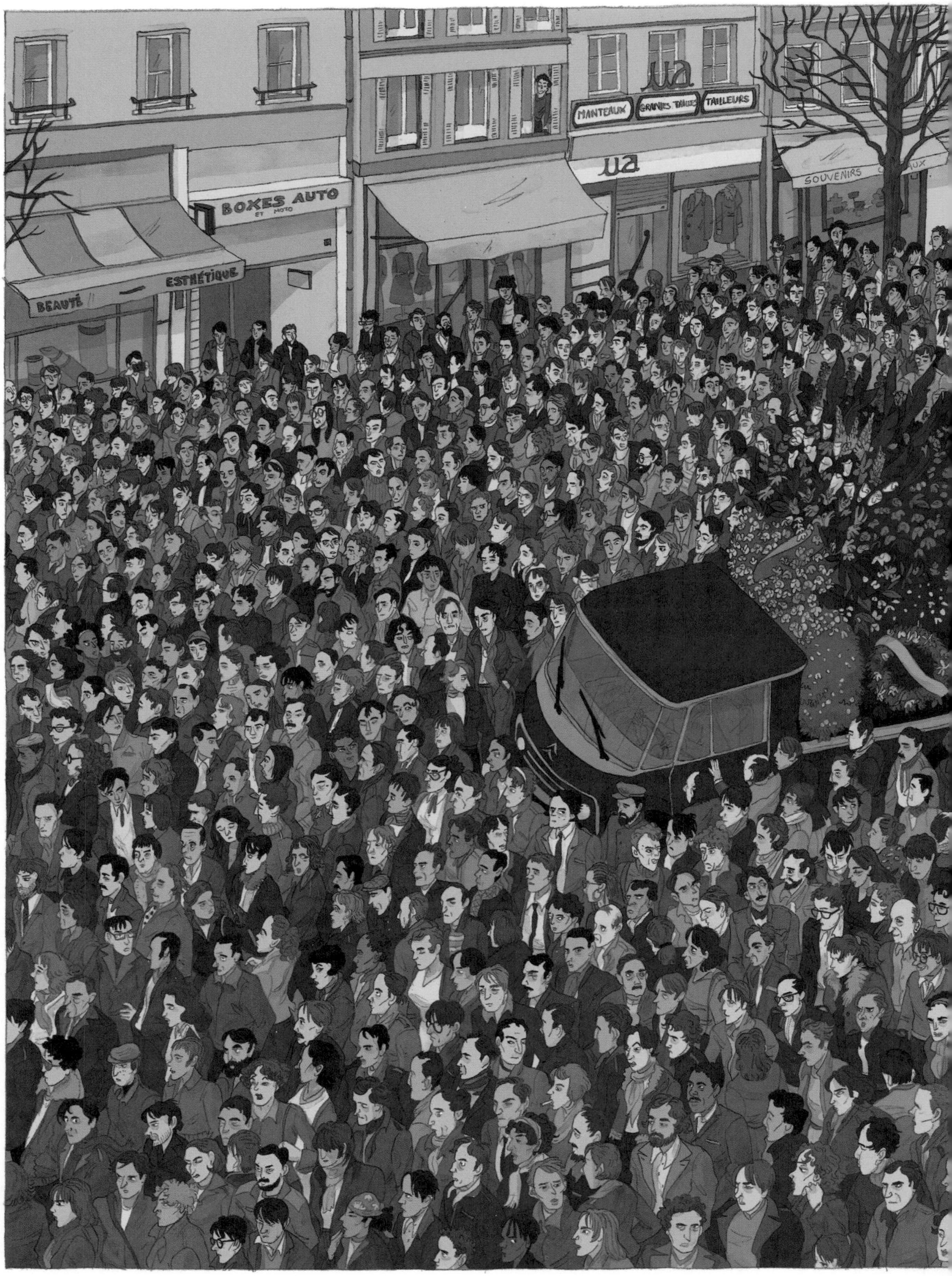

BOXES AUTO
ET MOTO
BEAUTÉ
ESTHÉTIQUE
MANTEAUX
GRANDES TAILLES
TAILLEURS
SOUVENIRS

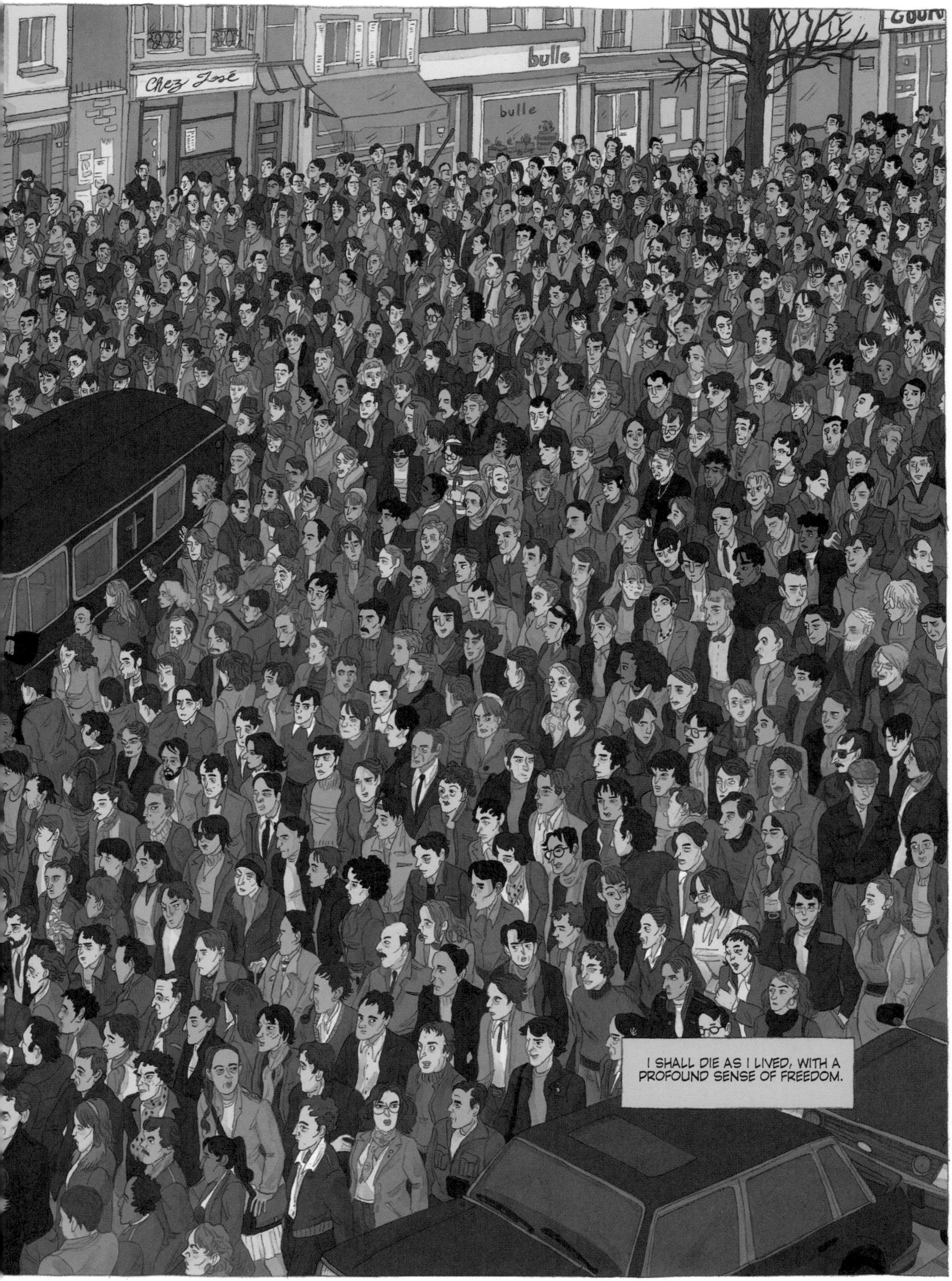
Chez José
bulle
bulle
I SHALL DIE AS I LIVED, WITH A PROFOUND SENSE OF FREEDOM.

Summary of events from 1964 to 1980

In 1965, Sartre adopts Arlette Elkaïm. Simone de Beauvoir adopts Sylvie Le Bon.

In 1968, he is concerned about the War in Vietnam, and about his role as president of the Russell Tribunal.

During the student protests of May '68, Sartre, rattled, reclaims his role as an isolated writer more than that of a public intellectual. He nevertheless meets with Daniel Cohn-Bendit, a leader of the movement; their interview is published in *Le Nouvel Observateur.*

January 30, 1969 Anne-Marie Mancy passes away at the age of 87.

February 10, 1969, a meeting is organized at La Mutualité. Sartre finds a note on his podium: "Sartre, be clear, be brief: we want to discuss guidelines to approve." It is a meeting organized by Michel Foucault to protest the expulsion of thirty-four students alongside reforms to the university system proposed by right-wing minister Edgar Faure.

In 1969, with *L'homme au magnétophone* (The Man with the Tape Recorder), Sartre underhandedly attacks psychoanalysis. "I am not a false friend, but I am a concerned follower of psychoanalysis."

March 22, 1970, Jean-Pierre Le Dantec, director of the communist proletarian revolutionary newspaper *La Cause du people*, and his successor, Michel Le Bris, are arrested. Sartre takes over the newspaper, as well as *Tout!* and *J'accuse*. In June, he participates avidly in a guerrilla distribution of the newspaper, alongside Claude Lanzmann, Simone de Beauvoir, Robert Gallimard... the police intervene. Once again, his cautious role as a spokesman allows others to more easily be freed and heard.

October 21st, 1970 brings the opening of the trial of Alain Geismar, one of the leaders of the May '68 protests. Sartre refuses to testify in court, knowing all too well that no one will listen to him. Rather, he decides to express himself publicly: In the Place Bir-Hakeim, he climbs onto an overturned trash can in front of factory workers at a Renault plant. Only a handful of Maoists come to listen to him, but this act will have an impact on the Geismar affair.
Sartre continues writing by working tirelessly on *The Family Idiot,* 2,802 pages of existential psychoanalysis on Gustave Flaubert. The first two volumes are released in 1971, then the third in 1972. Why Flaubert? "Because he is the opposite of what I am." He misses out on the structuralist movement, which is made up of the ethnologist Claude Lévi-Strauss and the psychoanalyst Jacques Lacan. Sartre gives unfortunately little credit to Foucault and only accepts one debate with Louis Althusser at the École Normale Supérieure. In December 1972, Benny Lévy, becomes Sartre's secretary under the name of Pierre Victor. ENS graduate and philosopher, he is one of the directors of the proletarian left.

In 1972, Michel Contat and Alexander Astruc along with Simone de Beauvoir create a moving series of filmed interviews notably: *Sartre by himself.*
Sartre protests with Foucault, Clavel and Mauriac against the racist attacks targeting immigrant workers in the Goutte-d'Or neighborhood of Paris. He takes part in creating the press agency Libération, which leads to the daily newspaper *Libération* on May 23rd 1973.

December 4th, 1974, after receiving permission from the German government, he visits Andreas Baader, leader of the Red Army Factor, who is leading a hunger strike to protest the terms of his arrest. With the help of Daniel Cohn-Bendit ("Dany the Red") in the translation, Sartre interviews Andreas for a half an hour. Sartre considers the political acts of Badder-Meinhof group interesting from a revolutionary point of view, but that the terrorist methods employed here were unacceptable and unjust. In spring of 1974, he travels to Portugal when the "Carnation Revolution" breaks out so he can march in support of the far left. Overcome by quickly worsening dizzy spells, Sartre ends up losing the use of his left eye. He manages to still distinguish some shadows and movements.

In March 1979, the "Peace Now?" colloquium is organized by *Les Temps modernes*, bringing together Palestinian and Israeli intellectuals.

June 26th, 1979, Sartre visits the Elysée Palace with, among others, Raymond Aron to ask Valéry Giscard d'Estaing, the President of the Republic, to act in aid of Vietnamese and Cambodian refugees.

Jean-Paul Sartre succumbs to a pulmonary edema on the night of April 15th, 1980 in l'Hôpital Broussais in the 14th arrondissement in Paris. He had been hospitalized there since March 20th.

About those who stood alongside Jean-Paul Sartre and Simone de Beauvoir...

CHARLES SCHWEITZER
(Pfaffenhoffen, 1844-1935)

Charles Schweitzer is Sartre's maternal grandfather and comes from a small town in Alsace, Pfaffenhoffen, the French name comprised of the most F's. Playing the role of spiritual father, even substitute father, he embodies a true intellectual model and brings the little Poulou into the passionate world of books at a very young age. Authoritarian and influential on his whole family, his wife Louise and his daughter Anne-Marie, this white-bearded German teacher preached the virtues of honor and loyalty. When Sartre steals a few pennies from his mother's purse hoping to spoil his friends at the local pastry shop, as a punishment, Charles Schweitzer ignores Sartre for months.

ANNE-MARIE SCHWEITZER
(Saint-Albain, 1882-1969)

Anne-Marie Schweitzer is Sartre's mother. She marries Jean-Baptiste in Paris in 1904. Sartre's father is a *polytechnicien* and Naval officer who dies of yellow fever fifteen months after the birth of Jean-Paul. Sweet and of a peaceful nature, no doubt a little too modest, she is a devoted mother and accomplice. Attentive to her son's talents, she never ceases to be amazed. She remarries Joseph Mancy in 1917, a Navy Admiral whom Sartre hates. She is known for her, porcelain-like air and her innocent smile, which betray her lack of confidence but make her shine when she is playing the piano.

PAUL NIZAN
(Tours, 1905-1940)

Paul Nizan is his first close friend. The two met in high school. His style, his elegance, his "air of mischievous absence" and his mastery of the art of repartee make him out to be an inimitable dandy always out to cause trouble. With their Breton nicknames, "R'hâ" (Nizan) and "Bor'hou" (Sartre) declare themselves superheroes as they undertake years of mentoring all across Paris. Nizan publishes *Aden Arabie* in 1931 before becoming a philosophy teacher. He joins the communist party, then leaves it a few years later, not without suffering stifling retaliation. He has two children with Rirette. He dies at the front in Dunkirk in 1940.

René Maheu

(Saint-Gaudens, 1905-1975)

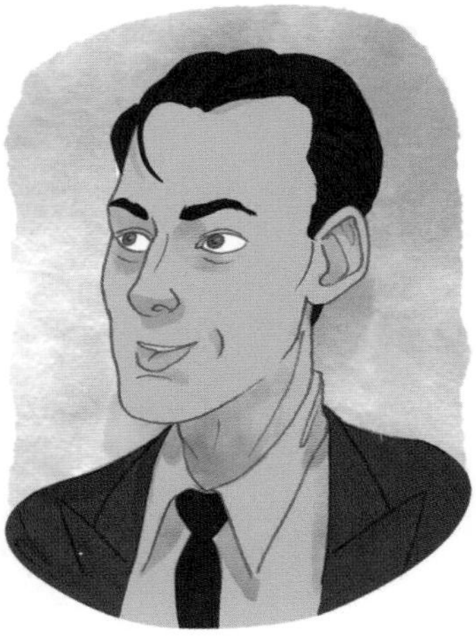

Already a friend of Simone de Beauvoir, Maheu meets Sartre while studying at l'École Normale Supérieure. It is he who gives Beauvoir the nickname Beaver partially because of the closeness between Beaver and Beauvoir, but also because she has the mind of a builder and gets around in groups. After having spent several years with the dynamic duo Sartre-Nizan, René Maheu becomes a philosophy teacher. He spends time, most notably, teaching in Morocco. First acting as cultural attaché in London, he moves later to become the director of the France-Afrique d'Alger agency. In 1946, he joins UNESCO, of which he will be the director from 1961 to 1974.

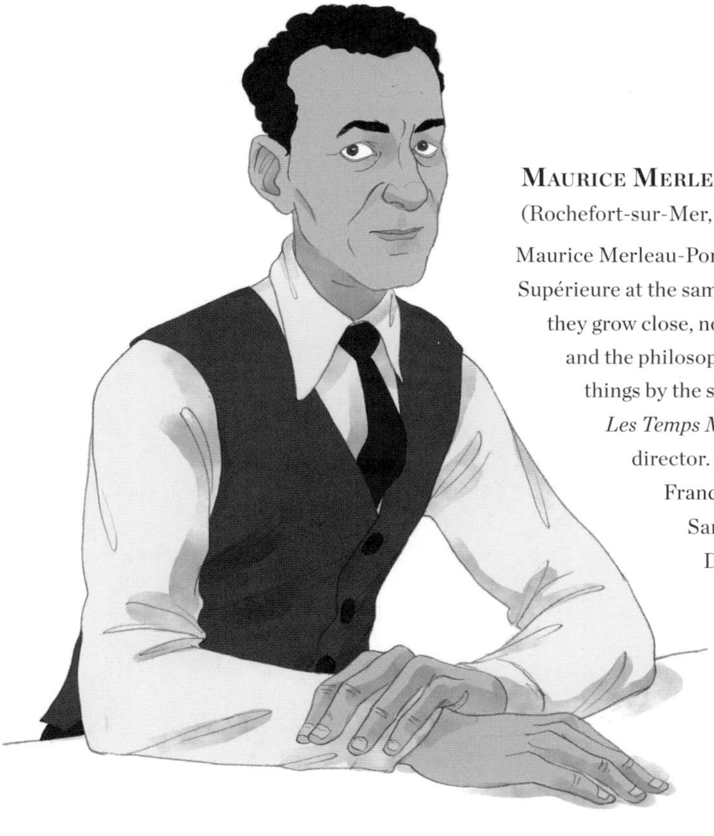

Maurice Merleau-Ponty

(Rochefort-sur-Mer, 1908-1961)

Maurice Merleau-Ponty, known as "Le Ponteaumerle," studied at l'École Normale Supérieure at the same time as Sartre. It isn't until the beginning of the war that they grow close, notably through the resistance group "Socialism and Liberty" and the philosophy of phenomenology, which searches for the essence of things by the study of phenomena. He is a founding member of the review *Les Temps Modernes* as an editorialist, but turns down becoming its co-director. In 1952 he becomes the Chair of Philosophy at the Collège de France. In the same year he leaves the review after a dispute with Sartre over an article. He died of a heart attack while reading Descartes's *La Dioptrique*.

Hélène de Beauvoir

(Paris, 1910-2001)

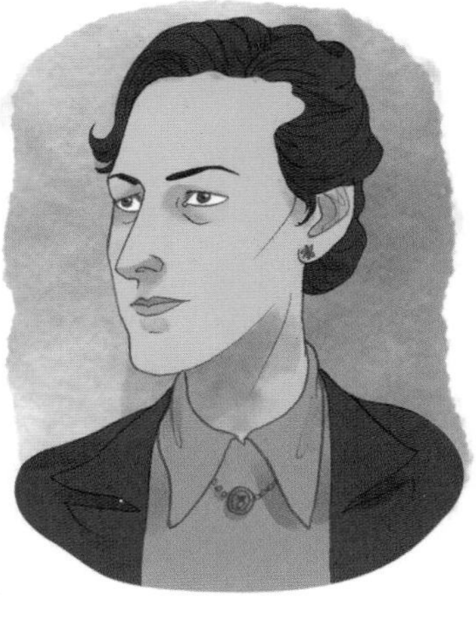

Hélène de Beauvoir, nicknamed "Poupette," is Simone's younger sister. Accomplices from childhood, they distinguish themselves by their chosen mode of expression: for Poupette, it's engraving and painting. Her first exhibition is noticed by Picasso when she is only 25 years old. With the help of her sister she moves and sets up her studio. Thanks to Sartre she meets her future lover, Lionel de Roulet, who will quickly erase the scars left by her former lover, Jean Giraudoux. Despite the couple's many moves around Europe and elsewhere, Poupette will never stop painting and always remains part of the small Sartrian family.

FERNANDO GERASSI

(Istanbul, 1899-1974)

Fernando Gerassi is a painter. He first studied the philosophy of Heidegger and the phenomenology of Husserl in Germany before meeting Simone de Beauvoir in Paris during the Roaring Twenties, frequenting the cafés *Le Dôme* and *La Rotonde* as she did. They form a close friendship based on trust and a similar sensibility. After declaring himself against the Spanish Civil War, like Picasso, he leaves Europe for America with his wife Stepha at the beginning of the Second World War. Sartre and Beauvoir remain in close contact with the couple and their son Tito. They spend time together during Sartre and Beauvoir's trips to New York.

JACQUES-LAURENT BOST

(Le Havre, 1916-1990)

Jacques-Laurent Bost, known as "Le Petit Bost," is a writer, screenwriter, and journalist. Bost falls under the spell of Sartre's classes while the philosopher is teaching in Le Havre. A pastor's son, he no doubt found the saving grace that his curious mind needed in philosophy class. After the Liberation, he is sent to Germany by Camus as a war correspondent for *Combat*. Next he publishes *Dernier des Métiers* in 1946 and becomes a famous reporter. Welcomed at a very young age in the little family of Sartre, not only would he never leave it but he would become a major pillar of the group. He also keeps several passionate relationships close to his heart, most notably with the Beaver: their correspondence will be published.

BIANCA BIENENFELD

(Lublin, 1921-2011)

Bianca Bienenfeld, affectionately nicknamed "La Petite Polack" or known under the pen-name Louise Védrine, is a student of the Beaver at the Lycée Molière in 1937. She becomes her teacher's lover, then Sartre's, all the while joining the group. None of this keeps her from meeting her future husband, Bernard Lamblin, while studying philosophy. Lifting the veil on a whole life of involvements with powerful friends, she publishes *Memories of a Disturbed Young Lady (Mémoires d'une Jeune Fille Dérangée)*, the title playing on Beauvoir's *Memories of a Dutiful Daughter (Mémoires d'une Jeune Fille Rangée)*. The book was released soon after the publication of Beauvoir's biography by Deirdre Bair (who revealed the true identity of Louise Védrine, which had up until that point remained a mystery).

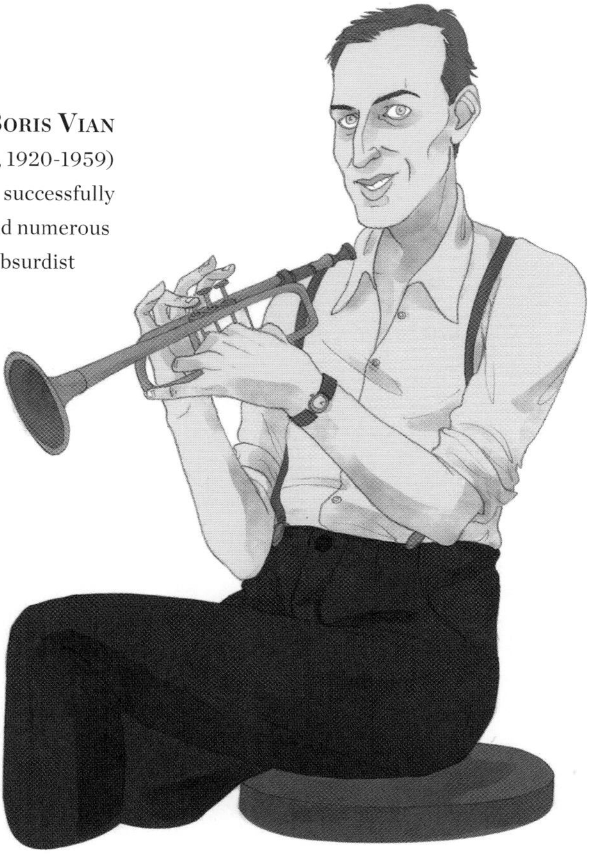

Boris Vian

(Ville-d'Avray, 1920-1959)

Boris Vian is a writer, poet, lyricist, and jazz trumpeter. He successfully delves into all literary genres, playing hide and seek behind numerous pseudonyms, plays on words, and other mind games. A true absurdist poet, he can be found among the *zazous* in the *caveaux de jazz* in Paris, from the famous *Tabou* to the *Caveau des Lorientais*. With Michelle, they are faithful friends to Jean-Sol Partre and Simone de Beauvoir. His pronounced taste for words and his fascination with the *comédie humaine* feed his creativity, his dark sense of humor, and his love for swing and partying... all of this despite a melancholic mood that only his closest friends know how to tame.

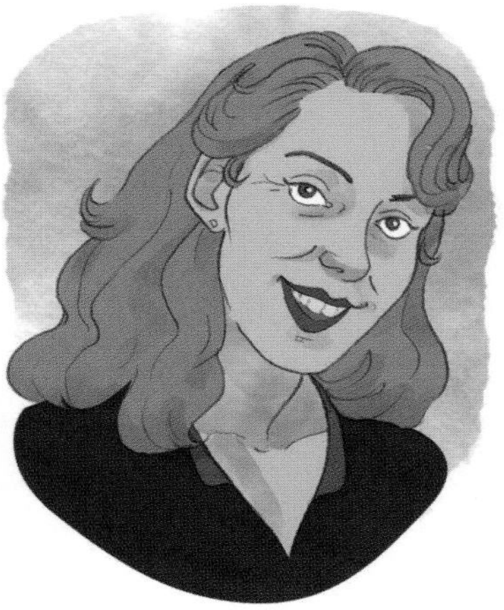

Michelle Vian

(1920)

Michelle Léglise is a woman of letters, a translator and one of the great muses of Saint-Germain-des-Prés. Her girlish ways, her lively mind, her faithful heart, and her eternal *joie de vivre* impacted everyone who crossed her path, whether they were her close friend or her partner for the night. First married to Boris Vian from 1941 to 1952, the jazz lover then was tied to Jean-Paul Sartre from 1949. She is part of the *Les Temps Modernes* team, translating texts, typing them on the typewriter. They travel together often and remain close until his death.

André Malraux

(Paris, 1901-1976)

André Malraux is a writer and French politician. In his youth, he writes in an anticolonialist newspaper, then leaves for Vietnam where he will have a run of bad luck, particularly due to the illegal sale of artwork. With his 1933 *La Condition Humaine*, a novel inspired by his revolutionary experience, he receives the Prix Goncourt. He takes a very active role in the Resistance and takes part in the battles of the Liberation. During the Occupation, he meets Sartre, but the two willful minds will never manage to agree on which strategies of resistance to adopt. When the war ended, he grows closer to De Gaulle until he is made Minister of Culture in 1959, which will eventually distance him from Sartre and Beauvoir.

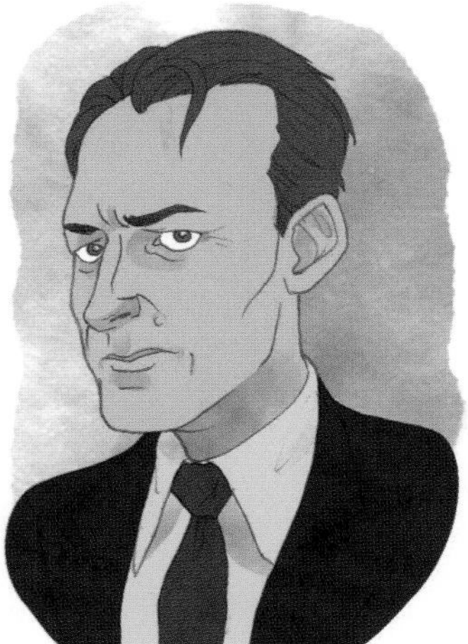

Olga and Wanda Kosakiewicz,
The "Kos" sisters
(Kiev 1915-1983) (Kiev 1917-1989)
Olga, alias Zazoulich or Iaroslaw, is a stage actress under the name Olga Dominique. Her personality and her beauty inspire certain characters in novels by Sartre and Beauvoir. She becomes their mistress, which does not come without complications. She marries Le Petit Bost.

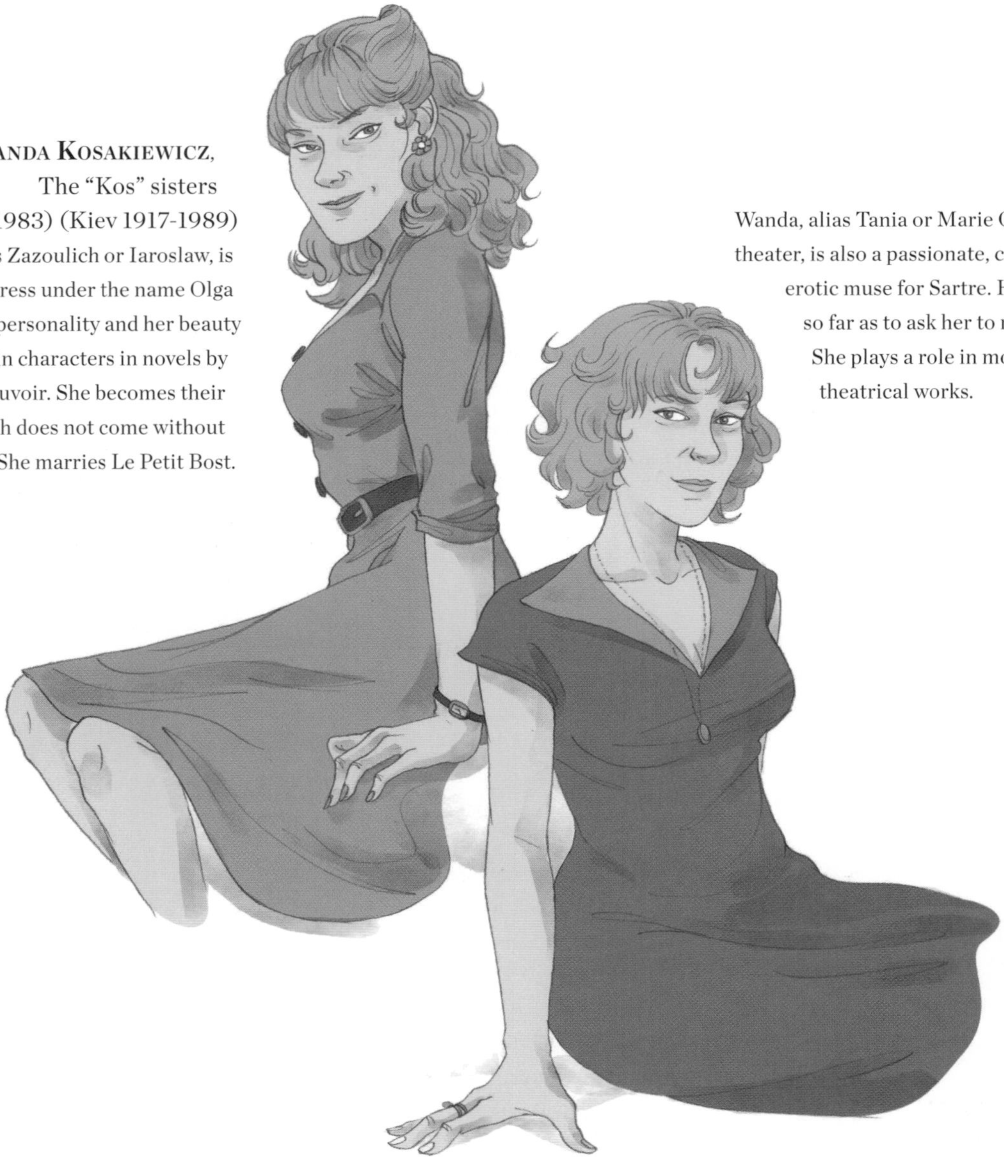

Wanda, alias Tania or Marie Olivier in the theater, is also a passionate, cerebral, and erotic muse for Sartre. He will go so far as to ask her to marry him. She plays a role in most of his theatrical works.

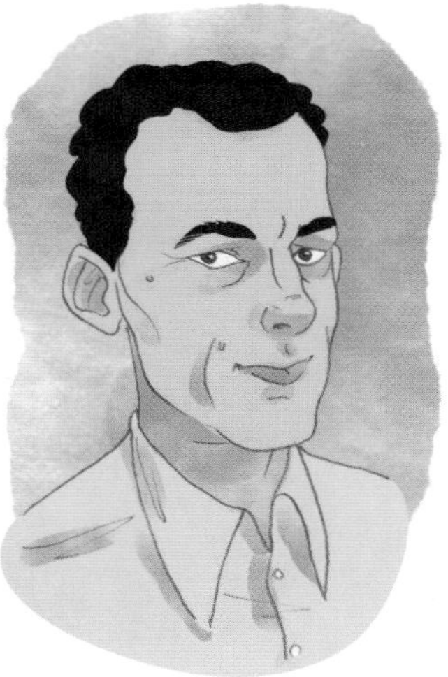

Albert Camus
(Mondovi, 1913-1960)
Albert Camus is a writer and philosopher. An activist, he resolutely joins the French Resistance, particularly by directing the newspaper Combat. As a great revolutionary humanist, far from the closed off philosophical mainstream, he is outraged by all forms of totalitarianism. Unfortunately, he breaks up as friends with Sartre, after a long, close but often stormy friendship. He receives the Nobel Prize in Literature in 1957. A good and upstanding man, faithful to his ideas without compromise, it is said that he gives off a particular aura, perhaps too strong for some. He will die tragically in a car accident with Michel Gallimard.

Dolorès Vanetti

(1912-2008)

Dolorès Vanetti is an actress and journalist. She acts in several theaters in Montparnasse before leaving for New York where she hosts a radio show in French for the Office of War Information. She is the one who "gave" America to Sartre, in his words. She has New York in her blood, even though she never completely lost her "petit accent français." For Sartre, it was love at first sight in the radio studio. For the Beaver, she was a threat. A very real threat as Dolorès often spends time in Paris, loving Sartre "frightfully"

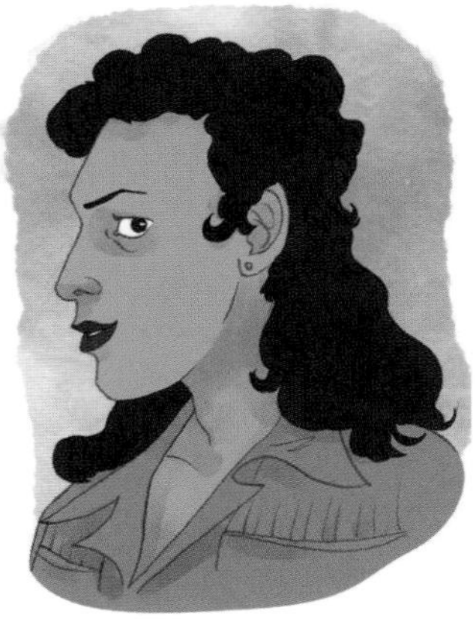

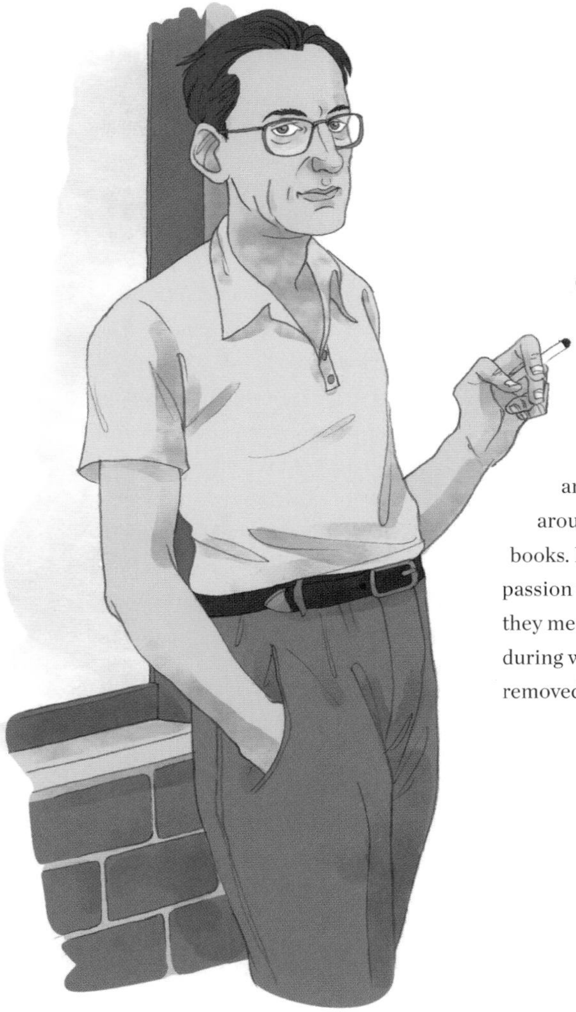

Nelson Algren

(Detroit, 1909-1981)

Nelson Algren is an American writer. He works odds jobs in his youth – one in particular in a hamburger factory – , boxes and frequents neighborhood bars, the charm of all of which is not lost on the Beaver. He moves to Chicago and becomes an editor. A keen observer of the world around him, he criticizes American society in his books. He takes an early interest in sociology, an academic passion which he will share with Simone de Beauvoir when they meet in 1947. Their bilingual love lasts fifteen months, during which the Atlantic is crossed often. Simone never removed Nelson's ring from her finger.

Jean Genet

(Paris, 1910-1986)

Jean Genet is a poet, writer, and playwright. He has a happy childhood with a host family in the country before stealing something at the age of 10. Sartre will later confirm the profound existentialist angle on this act, which is a choice but also a tiny fissure from Genet's original wound, being abandoned by his mother. Genet publishes his first collection of poems, *The Man Sentenced to Death*, in 1942, then becomes friends with Sartre and the Beaver to whom he dedicates his *The Thief's Journal*. Sartre later writes *Saint Genet, Actor and Martyr,* an existential psychoanalytical essay on his friend which has an explosive effect on Genet.

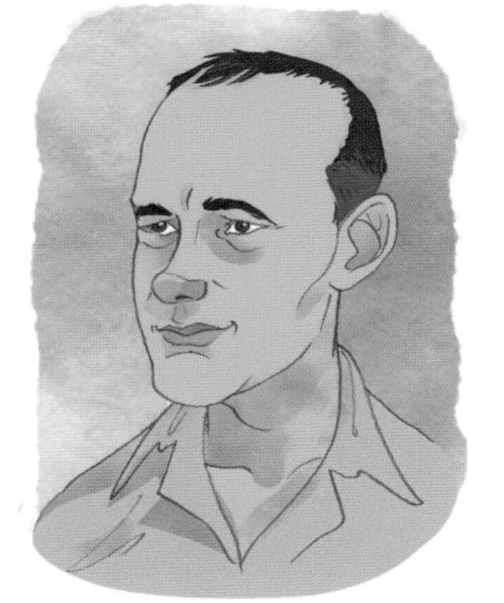

JEAN CAU
(Bram, 1925-1993)

Jean Cau is a writer. While first and foremost a journalist with *Combat* during the war, he still spends plenty of time with the *zazous* at the *caveaux de jazz*. After studying philosophy, he writes to Jean-Paul Sartre in 1946, asking him if he needs a secretary. Immediately seduced, and not simply by his accent from the South, he accepts. Until 1957, the two will be inseparable. In a small office set up at 42 rue Bonaparte, Jean Cau organizes conferences, the publication of articles, communication with Gallimard, the mail, and so much more. After publishing a few articles in *Les Temps Modernes*, his writing intensifies: he will go on to publish more than sixty works, novels, and collections of poetry.

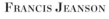

FRANCIS JEANSON
(Bordeaux, 1922-2009)

Francis Jeanson is a philosopher and journalist. A Resistant during the war, he later meets Sartre through Camus, who eventually bestows the direction of *Les Temps Modernes* on him in 1951. The ironic twist is that it is Jeanson who causes them to quarrel: he writes the critique of Camus's *L'Homme Révolté*, an essay which produces mixed opinions among the editors. Jeanson is mainly known for his anticolonial activism and for the underground network that bears his name which aids the members of the National Liberation Front during the Algerian War. He is harshly sentenced, then granted amnesty six years later.

JEAN-BERTRAND PONTALIS
(Paris, 1924-2013)

Jean-Bertrand Pontalis is a philosopher, writer, and psychoanalyst. He takes Sartre's courses, which is how they meet and form their friendship. He becomes a philosophy professor himself all while being analyzed by the famous psychoanalyst Jacques Lacan. He contributes to the first Dictionary of Psychoanalysis and later founds the Psychoanalytic Association of France, distancing himself from the Lacanians. He, of course, writes for *Les Temps Modernes*, but also in the *Nouvelle Revue de Psychanalyse;* which is not at all out of place. He shares a love of literature with Sartre, for want of a love of psychoanalysis.

SELECTIVE BIBLIOGRAPHY

Mauricette Berne (under the direction of)
Sartre, Paris, Bibliothèque National de France, Gallimard, 2005 *in French*

Philippe Cabestan
Dictionnaire Sartre, Paris, Ellipses, 2009 *in French*

Annie Cohen-Solal
Sartre: A life, New York, The New Press, 2005 *translated from the French by Anna Cancogni*

Jacques Colette
L'Existentialisme, Paris, PUF, coll. <<Que sais-je ?>>, 1994 *in French*

Albert Camus
The Outsider, London, Penguin, 2012 *translated from the French by Sandra Smith*
The Rebel: An Essay on Man in Revolt, New York, Vintage International, 2012 *translated into English by Anthony Bower*

Simone de Beauvoir
Adieux: A Farewell to Sartre, New York, Pantheon, 1984 *translated from the French by Patrick O'Brian.*
The Second Sex, New York, Alfred A. Knopf. 2010 *translated from the French by Constance Borde and Sheila Malovany-Chevallier*
The Blood of Others, New York, Pantheon Books, 1983 *translated from the French by Yvonne Moyse and Roger Senhouse*
The Mandarins, South Bend, Ind., Regnery/Gateway, 1979 *translated from the French by Leonard M. Friedman*
Letters to Sartre 1930-1939, New York, Arcade Publishing, 1992 *translated from the French by Quintin Hoare*
She Came to Stay, Cleveland, World Pub. Co., 1954 *in English*

Gustave Flaubert
Madame Bovary, New York, Viking, 2010 *translated from the French by Lydia Davis*

André Gide
The Fruits of the Earth, New York, A.A. Knopf, 1949 *translated from the French by Dorothy Bussy*

Martin Heidegger
Being and Time, Bloomington, Indiana Univ. Press, 2008 *translated from the German by William Large*

Edmund Husserl
Ideas Pertaining to a Pure Phenomenology and to a Phenomenological Philsophy – First Book: General Introduction to a Pure Phenomenology, The Hague, Nijhoff, 1982 *translated from the German by F. Kersten*
Ideas Pertaining to a Pure Phenomenology and to a Phenomenological Philosophy – Second Book: Studies in the Phenomenology of Constitution, Dordrecht, Kluwer, 1989 *translated from the German by R. Rojcewicz and A. Schuwer*
Ideas Pertaining to a Pure Phenomenology and to a Phenomenological Philosophy – Third Book: Phenomenology and the Foundations of the Sciences, Dordrecht, Kluwer, 1980 *translated from the German by T.E. Klein and W.E. Pohl*

Bianca Lamblin
A Disgraceful Affair: Simone de Beauvoir, Jean-Paul Sartre, and Bianca Lamblin, Boston, Mass., Northeastern University Press, 1996 *translated from the French by Julie Plovnick*

André Malraux
Man's Fate, New York, Random House, Modern Library Collection, 1933 *translated from the French by Haakon Chevalier*

Karl Marx and Friedrich Engels
The Communist Manifesto, Pluto Press, 1888/ 2008 *translated from the German by Samuel Moore*

Maurice Merleau-Ponty
Sense and Non-sense, Evanston, Ill., Northwestern University Press, 1964 *translated from the French by Hubert L. Dreyfus and Patricia Allen Dreyfus*

Jacques-Alain Miller

Interview with Jean-Paul Sartre in *Un début dans la vie*, Paris, Gallimard, 2002 *in French*

Paul Nizan

Aden, Arabie, New York, Columbia University Press, 1987 *translated from the French by Joan Pinkham*

François Noudelmann and Gilles Philippe (dir.)

Dictionnaire Sartre, Paris, Honoré Champion, 2004 *in French*

Michel Onfray

Appetites for Thought: Philosophers and Food, London, Reaktion Books, 2015 *translated from the French by Donald Barry and Stephen Muecke*

Jean-Paul Sartre

Life/ Situations: essays written and spoken, New York, Pantheon Books, 1977 *translated from the French by Paul Auster and Lydia Davis*

Baudelaire, London, Horizon, 1949 *translated from the French by Martin Turnell*

War Diaries: Notebooks from a Phony War, New York, Pantheon Books, 1984 *translated form the French by Quintin Hoare*

Nausea, New York, New Direction, 2007 *translated from the French by Lloyd Alexander*

The Transcendence of the Ego, New York, Noonday Press, 1957 *translated from the French by Forrest Williams and Robert Kirkpatrick*

The Freud Scenario, London, Verso, 1985 *translated from the French by Quintin Hoare*

The Roads to Freedom: I. The Age of Reason, New York, A.A. Knopf, 1947 *translated from the French by Eric Sutton*

The Roads to Freedom: II. The Reprieve, New York, A.A. Knopf, 1947 *translated from the French by Eric Sutton*

The Roads to Freedom: III. Troubled Sleep, New York, A.A. Knopf, 1951 *translated from the French by Gerard Hopkins*

The Words, New York, Vintage Books, 1981 *translated from the French by Bernard Frechtman*

A Phenomenological Essay on Ontology, New York, Pocket Books, 1966 *translated from the French by Hazel E. Barnes*

Witness to My Life, New York, Scribner's, 1992, *translated from the French by Lee Fahnestock and Norman McAfee*

Quiet Moments in a War, New York, Scribner's, 1993, *translated from the French by Lee Fahnestock and Norman MacAfee*

Existentialism and Humanism, New Haven, Yale University Press, 2007 *translated from the French by Carol Macomber*

The Family Idiot: Gustave Flaubert 1821-1857, Chicago, University of Chicago Press, 1981-1993 *translated from the French by Carol Cosman*

Cosman

L'imaginaire, Paris, Gallimard, 1940 *in French*

Saint Genet: Actor and Martyr, Minneapolis, University of Minnesota Press, 2012 *translated from the French by Bernard Frechtman*

Théâtre complet, Bibliothèque de la Pléiade, Paris, Gallimard, 2005 *in French*

Truth and Existence, Chicago, University of Chicago Press, 1992 *translated from the French by Ronald Aronson.*

Patrick Vauday

Sartre et la psychanalyse sans inconscient, in *Ornicar* (revue), march 1985 *in French*

Boris Vian

Écrits pornographiques, Paris, Le Livre de Poche, 1998 *in French*

Froth of the Daydream, London, Rapp & Carroll, 1967 *translated from the French by Stanley Chapman*

Films and Documentaries
Alexandre Astruc and Michel Contat

Sartre par lui-même. Le temps de la réflexion. Le temps de l'engagement, 1977, Paris, Éditions Montparnasse, 2007 *in French*

John Huston – *Freud: The Secret Passion*, 1962

Louise Wardle for the BBC - <<Sartre>>, third episode of *Human, All Too Human*, 1999

Radio
Raphaël Enthoven, Frédéric Worms, François George and Juliette Simont

<<Sartre, la liberté dans tous ses états>>, *Les Vendredis de la philosophie*, France Culture et Naïve, 2007 in French

Mathilde Ramadier and Anaïs Depommier

http://pommebleur.tumbler.com/

http://mathildramadier.wordpress.com

Other biographies available from NBM Graphic Novels:

GHETTO BROTHER- Warrior to Peacemaker
Julian Voloj, Claudia Ahlering
GIRL IN DIOR
Annie Goetzinger
THOREAU, A Sublime Life
A. Dan, Maximilien Le Roy
ELVIS
Philippe Chanoinat and Fabrice Le Henanff
GLENN GOULD: A Life Off Tempo
Sandrine Revel
BILLIE HOLIDAY
José Muñoz, Carlos Sampayo
To come:
MONET: Itinerant of Light (Oct. '17)
Efa, Salva Rubio
THE DEATH OF BILLY THE KID (Mar. '18)
Rick Geary
See more on these and order at:
NBMPUB.COM

We have over 200 graphic novels available.
Catalog available upon request.
NBM
160 Broadway, Suite 700, East Wing,
New York, NY 10038

Julian VOLOJ • Claudia AHLERING
GHETTO BROTHER
WARRIOR TO PEACEMAKER

Annie Goetzinger
Girl in
Dior

A. DAN · LE ROY
THOREAU
nbm

Elvis
nbm

SANDRINE REVEL
GLENN
GOULD
A LIFE OFF TEMPO
nbm

MUÑOZ & SAMPAYO
BILLIE HOLIDAY
nbm

EFA · RUBIO
MONET
nbm

The TRUE DEATH of Billy the Kid
RICK GEARY

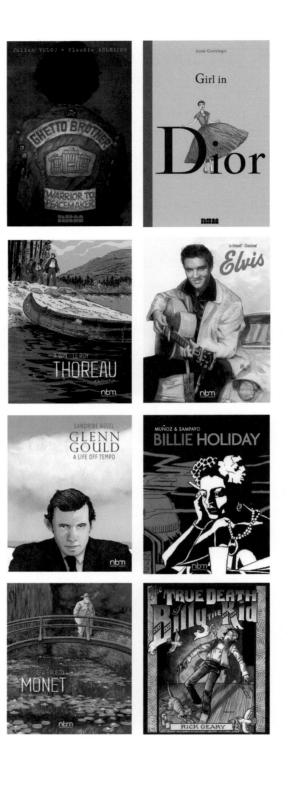